Government and Politics in Western Europe

Britain, France, Italy, West Germany

YVES MÉNY

Translated by
JANET LLOYD

OXFORD UNIVERSITY PRESS

Oxford University Press, Walton Street, Oxford OX2 6DP
Oxford New York Toronto
Delhi Bombay Calcutta Madras Karachi
Petaling Jaya Singapore Hong Kong Tokyo
Nairobi Dar es Salaam Cape Town
Melbourne Auckland
and associated companies in
Berlin Ibadan

Oxford is a trade mark of Oxford University Press

Published in the United States
by Oxford University Press, New York

This English edition has been translated from an adapted version of
the original French publication Politique comparée
© Éditions Montchrestien 1987
translation by Janet Lloyd © Oxford University Press 1990

First published 1990
Paperback reprinted 1991 (twice), 1992

British Library Cataloguing in Publication Data
Mény, Yves
Government and politics in Western Europe: Britain,
France, Italy, West Germany.—(Comparative European politics)
1. Western Europe. Politics I. Title II. Series III. Politique comparée. English
320.94
ISBN 0–19–827336–3 / ISBN 0–19–827337–1 (Pbk.)

Library of Congress Cataloging in Publication Data
Mény, Yves.
Government and politics in Western Europe: Britain, France,
Italy, West Germany/Yves Mény; translated by Janet Lloyd.
(Comparative European politics)
Adapted translation of: Politique comparée: Etats-Unis, France, Grande-Bretagne, Italie, R.F.A.
Includes bibliographical references (p. 1. Comparative government. 2. Europe—Politics and
government—1945– I. Title II. Series
JF52.M36 1990 320.3'094—dc20 89–71139
ISBN 0–19–827336–3 / ISBN 0–19–827337–1 (Pbk.)

Printed in Great Britain by Biddles Ltd, Guildford and King's Lynn

COMPARATIVE EUROPEAN POLITICS

General Editors: Hans Daalder and Ken Newton

Government and Politics in Western Europe

COMPARATIVE EUROPEAN POLITICS

Comparative European Politics is a series for students and teachers of political science and related disciplines, published in association with the European Consortium for Political Research. Each volume will provide an up-to-date survey of the current state of knowledge and research on an issue of major significance in European government and politics.

Preface

This book is an adapted version of the French volume published in 1988 under the title *Politique comparée: Les démocraties*. However, it is not simply an English translation of that work. The original version, which was addressed essentially to a French audience, has been radically rewritten and reorganized. For obvious reasons, related to the structure of different university courses and teaching programmes, the analyses devoted to the United States have been replaced by studies of the political scene in France which are fuller than those offered in the version prepared with French students in mind.

Furthermore, this book is aimed at a different intellectual market. In France, the comparative study of political systems is an underdeveloped field: the number of authors engaged in such research could be counted on the fingers of one hand. But in Britain and particularly in the United States, this area of research has been cultivated more intensively and more profoundly. I have frequently found both the information and the stimulating ideas contained in Anglo-American books extremely useful. However, I think that this book, unlike many other, excellent textbooks, has something new to offer in that it constitutes an attempt at a systematic comparison between four democracies whose systems it examines not one by one but all together. In this analysis of the institutions and political life of the great European democracies, I have tried to convey the spirit as well as the letter of the various systems, and to avoid the pitfalls of ethnocentrism and of drawing simplistic parallels. I have also tried to provide a number of concrete examples in order to help students, situated as they are in the midst of the cut and thrust of theory and debate of today's 'market-place', to pick out the empirical evidence that they need to stimulate their thoughts and lend weight to their ideas. Whether or not I have succeeded in combining these aims is up to the reader to decide. The path leading to an analysis that lies between a general textbook of political science and a series of 'country studies' is clearly a tricky one to tread!

I am very conscious of the many areas of interest that this book neglects. Little or nothing is said about armies and churches, defence policies, the Welfare State, etc. For obvious editorial reasons, it has been necessary to make choices—some of them as painful and controversial as the selection of the countries to include in this study. It is with a keen sense of all these limitations and constraints that I venture to submit the products of my researches and reflections to the critical appraisal of the reader.

This book would certainly not have been possible, in its present form at least, without the benefit of many exchanges and discussions with numerous colleagues and English and American friends. I am particularly grateful to those whose comments and advice made it possible to produce this adaptation of the French text. Finally, I should like to thank Janet Lloyd for her magnificent translation, and Andrew Knapp, whose help has been invaluable to me in the preparation of the final manuscript.

Y.M.

April 1990

Author's Note

In the light of recent events in Europe, it would be difficult to disagree with Oscar Wilde's observation that 'it is better not to prophesy, especially about the future'. The speed with which the communist system collapsed in East Germany, staunchest ally of the USSR and cornerstone of the Warsaw Pact, took even the most seasoned political observers by surprise. This year the electorate of a reunified Germany returned a democratically elected government for the first time in over fifty years.

When this volume first appeared in print, however, one could still speak of 'West' Germany. In deciding to reprint the volume in its original form, we have opted for prudence rather than prophecy, as our response to what is an unfinished process: political and legal union have been achieved, but the considerable problems of social, political, and economic integration will continue to exercise the energies of the new Germany in the coming decades. Our consideration of the role of West Germany in Europe, and its model of government, still offers much which is germane to any discussion of the new Germany.

Y.M.

November 1990

Contents

Abbreviations

BDA	Bundesvereinigung der Deutschen Arbeitgeberverbände (German Confederation of Employers' Associations)
BDI	Bundesverband der Deutschen Industrie (German Federation of Industrial Companies)
BHE	Block der Heimatvertriebenen und Entrechteten (Refugee Party)
CBI	Confederation of British Industry
CDU	Christlich-Demokratische Union
CFDT	Confédération Française Démocratique des Travailleurs
CFTC	Confédération Française des Travailleurs Chrétiens
CGC	Confédération Générale des Cadres
CGIL	Confederazione Generale Italiana del Lavoro
CGT	Confédération Générale du Travail
CGT-FO	Confédération Générale du Travail—Force Ouvrière
CGTU	Confédération Générale du Travail Unitaire
CID-UNATI	Confédération Interprofessionnelle de Défense et d'Union Nationale d'Action des Travailleurs Indépendants (shopkeepers' organization)
CISL	Confederazione Italiana dei Sindicati dei Lavoratori
CNPF	Conseil National du Patronat Français
CNSTP	Confédération Nationale des Syndicats des Travailleurs Paysans (farmers' union)
CODER	Comités de Développement Économique Régional
CONSOB	Commissione Nazionale per le Società e la Borsa
CP	Communist Party
CSU	Christlich-Soziale Union
DAG	Deutsche Angestellengewerkschaft
DATAR	Délégation à l'Aménagement du Territoire et à l'Action Régionale
DBB	Deutscher Beamten Bund
DBV	Deutscher Bauernverband (farmers' union)
DC	Democrazia Christiana
DGB	Deutsche Gewerkschaftsbund (German Confederation of Unions)
DIHT	Deutscher Industrie- und Handelstag (German Federation of Chambers of Commerce)

DKP	Deutsche Kommunistische Partei
DP	Democrazia Proletaria
EDF	Électricité de France
ENA	École Nationale d'Administration
FDP	Freie Demokratische Partei
FEN	Fédération de l'Éducation Nationale
FFA	Fédération Française de l'Agriculture (French Agricultural Workers' Union)
FLM	Federazione dei Lavoratori della Metallurgia (federation of metalworkers)
FNSEA	Fédération Nationale des Syndicats d'Exploitants Agricoles
FO	Force Ouvrière
IG Metall	Industrie Gewerkschaft Metall
IRA	Instituts Régionaux d'Administration
IRI	Istituto per la Reconstruzione Industriale
KPD	Kommunistische Partei Deutschlands
MODEF	Mouvement de Défense des Exploitations Familiales
MRP	Mouvement Républicain Populaire
MSI	Movimento Sociale Italiano
NFU	National Farmers' Union
NPD	Nationaldemokratische Partei Deutschlands
PAF	Christian Democrat Faction (Piccoli, Andreotti, Fanfani)
PDM	Progrès et Démocratie Moderne
PDUP	Partito Democratico di Unità Proletaria
PLI	Partito Liberale Italiano
PME	Petites et Moyennes Entreprises
PMI	Petites et Moyennes Industries
PRI	Partito Repubblicano Italiano
PSDI	Partito Socialista-Democratico Italiano
PSI	Partito Socialista Italiano
PSOE	Partido Socialista Obrero Español
PSU	Parti Socialiste Unifié
PSUP	Partito Socialista di Unità Proletaria
RAI	Radiotelevisione Italiana
RATP	Régie Autonome des Transports Parisiens
RI	Républicains Indépendants
RPF	Rassemblement du Peuple Français
RPR	Rassemblement pour la République
SDP	Social Democratic Party
SFIO	Section Française de l'Internationale Ouvrière
SNP	Scottish Nationalist Party
SPD	Sozialdemokratische Partei Deutschlands

SVP	Süd-Tyrol VolksPartei (party of the German-speaking minority in Alto-Adige)
UDF	Union pour la Démocratie Française
UIL	Unione Italiana del Lavoro
UNR	Union pour la Nouvelle République

Introduction

COMPARATIVE POLITICAL STUDIES

The goal of a study of comparative politics is to identify, analyse, and interpret the similarities and dissimilarities between different political systems, and its justification is that we may thereby arrive at an understanding of their fundamental processes that reaches beyond purely institutional formalism. Research of this kind proves particularly stimulating and rewarding when the political systems under consideration resemble one another sufficiently closely without being altogether similar. This is the case with the European democracies, for they share a number of characteristics but differ from one another in respect of their histories, myths, and values.[1]

A priori, each of the four great West European democracies studied here has a well-defined personality of its own, and this is bound to complicate an overall comparison. France and Britain both have a long democratic tradition developed over the course of two centuries, whereas the other two countries, West Germany and Italy, had experienced only brief interludes of democracy before the establishment of the current republican systems of government. But even between France and Britain there are many obvious differences: Britain is a model of stability and continuity, whereas since 1789 France has experimented with virtually every conceivable form of government; the French system is the product of a revolution, whereas Britain has been evolving with slow, progressive changes ever since the seventeenth century. In Britain it proved possible to establish democracy without breaking with the monarchy, whereas in most European countries setting up a democracy involved doing away with the monarchy.

The various political and constitutional paths that these different countries have followed have affected more than their respective systems of values and their political cultures. Each country's institutions, rules, procedures, and traditions are deeply marked by its past, even where that past has been forcibly repudiated. France, Italy, and West Germany all owe much to their earlier political systems, even the least democratic of them, in sectors such as political and social economy, administrative structures, civil and penal legislation, and so on. The different paths that these countries followed towards democracy and their good or bad experiences along the way have also helped to shape their institutions and the fashion in which these are run.

Variations in institutions and in the organization of different interests and parties do not result solely from the similar or different experiences of the countries involved. They are also the product of each country's political culture, as it has been forged by its history and by past or present dominant ideologies. We may thus seek a society's distinctive and dominant characteristics as Almond and Verba did in their well-known work *The Civic Culture*. It is true that the dangers of subjectivity and schematization that such a venture implies make it a risky one, as does the exaggerated importance ascribed to cultural phenomena at the expense of other factors, particularly economic ones. But in a comparative study, such an approach has the merit of underlining the importance of this particular variable (namely, the political culture) in the functioning of the political system. Furthermore, some of the problems raised by resorting to the notion of a political culture may be palliated by complementing it with the concept of 'subcultures'. Within the political culture of Italy, for example, we can distinguish between two subcultures, one Catholic, the other Communist, which are all the more important since they are strongly rooted and territorially distinct: some regions are 'white', others 'red'. The political cultures and subcultures of individual countries contribute in varying degrees to the similarities and dissimilarities between their political systems.

THE COMMON HERITAGE

Nevertheless, these differences should not stand in the way of a comparative study for, despite all that separates them, the European democracies possess in common ideals and institutions which are peculiar to them as a group and so unite them. These may be listed under four main headings: the affirmation of pluralism, the specific mechanisms that allow for the expression of choice, the organization of balanced institutions with limited powers, and the subordination of the public authorities to higher rules (constitutionalism).

The Affirmation of Pluralism

The affirmation of pluralism lies at the heart of liberal democracy and operates in several spheres: the economic, the social, and, finally, the political.

Economic pluralism. A liberal democratic State allows different agents to operate freely in the market as entrepreneurs and traders, and does not itself seek to appropriate the means of production. There can be no doubt that in the past, as now, liberal democracy and a free market went hand in hand and developed in conjunction. However, the association between them does not go unchallenged and is not without its problems. Just as there is no such thing as an ideal democracy, no market is perfect: the economic pluralism of theory is often replaced by oligopolistic or monopolistic situations in practice; 'natural' mechanisms for regulating the market are impeded by obstructions and economic crises. In both cases, intervention on the part of the State is necessary and/or legitimate.

Furthermore, the impact of socialist ideals has been considerable. Everywhere, the State has intervened at one level or another: at the level of production and trade (by introducing legislation such as Anti-Trust laws or through take-overs involving industrial share-holdings or nationalization) or else at the level of distribution and redistribution of the resources produced by economic activity (for example, in the Welfare State). In short, to differing degrees, all the Western democracies—even the United States—are today countries with *mixed economies*, where the public and private sectors both operate, either in partnership or in competition. But debate on the need, advisability, and extent of such intervention, which runs contrary to 'pure' liberalism, is a constant factor in public life, not only in countries with an interventionist tradition (such as France), but also in those where *laissez-faire* doctrines have predominated (such as the United States).

Social pluralism implies the acceptance of autonomous groups, which are considered as the normal, desirable means of organizing individuals. However, this form of the pluralist ideal has given rise to many dissenting views. In this domain, philosophers such as Montesquieu and Rousseau are in conflict, as are systems such as those of the United States and France: the notion of intermediary groups acting as the bases of democratic organization is opposed to that of the Jacobin view, according to which nothing at all should stand between a citizen and the State, between an individual's will and the general will. But despite these differences, it is generally accepted today that groups are a natural means of democratic expression.

Political pluralism does not, in principle, depend upon the two other forms of pluralism, but it is difficult to see how it could exist without at least a minimum of economic and/or social pluralism. Political pluralism is identified, both historically and practically, with the affirmation of certain liberties, liberties that are at once economic, political, and social: freedom of assembly, freedom to form associations, religious freedom, the right to property. The affirmation of these liberties entails at least one important consequence: recognition of the freedom of choice and the right to defend this in an appropriate manner.

The Expression of Choice

The acceptance and recognition of political pluralism necessarily implies organized competitiveness and an acceptance of its consequences—both political and institutional. The organization of electoral competition must in the first place be governed by rules sufficiently strict and neutral not to appear to be electorally favouring one or another group. Excluded groups will be inclined to bring complaints against not only particular rules as they are applied, but the whole political system which does not guarantee them an equal chance of acceding to power. The evolution of the Western democracies has been characterized, right from the start, by a long, slow progress towards processes favouring the expression of choices: lowering the voting age and the extension of suffrage to women, the control of constituency boundaries, the financing of elections, etc. But it should be emphasized that, despite all the improvements achieved, universal consensus is still a long way off.

The acceptance of competition means more than simply agreement over the modalities of electoral battle. It requires the defeated to abide by the electoral results and to respect the majority rule. But the majority must, in its turn, tolerate the opposition and not exercise power exclusively to its own benefit. The archetype of a country where such mutual limitations are accepted is Britain, where the winner's right to exercise power is limited by the recognized rights of 'His/Her

Majesty's Opposition'. France, in contrast, with its background of revolutionary struggle and strong ideological polarization, has found it very difficult to accept the idea that the defeat of the party in power leads naturally and ineluctably to the opposition's accession to government. The constitutional history of France has been punctuated by a series of attempts to manipulate the electoral system and by *coups d'état*. Uncertainties remained even under the Fifth Republic. Not until 1981 and 1986 did the practices of first alternation, then 'cohabitation' become confirmed, conferring upon the institutions involved their full legitimacy and political stability. It was this transformation of violent conflict into political competition which remained peaceful as a result of the recognition of the opposition's right to accede to power that prompted Robert Dahl to declare the institutionalization of the opposition to be 'one of the greatest and most surprising social discoveries of the human race'.[2]

The Limitation of Powers

At the centre of the liberal constitutional machinery lies the principle of the separation of powers, conceived as an instrument to check authoritarianism or absolute power.

People have often been amazed by how many different interpretations have been produced for the principle propounded by Montesquieu in the eighteenth century, and by all the different ways in which it has been implemented. The separation of powers is a fundamental principle upon which all the Western democracies rest but in none of them is it interpreted or, above all, 'lived' in the same way. That there are differences should not occasion surprise if one bears in mind that the principle itself promotes no logical or organizational advantages. It is dictated by a fundamental imperative: power must be checked by power. Adopting this as a central principle, it is perfectly possible to set up a whole range of different institutions which will vary according to the limitations deemed desirable and the balances—or imbalances —that one is seeking to promote. Checks and balances will play a more or less important role depending upon the political system, but they will always be central to the structure of liberal constitutions. From this point of view, France remains a system in which the imbalances strongly favour the executive in its relations with both the legislature and the judiciary. Furthermore, France—officially, at least—has so far implemented the principle of separation only partially, that is, as a separation between different functions. For many years it has continued to resist any territorial division of powers that would go beyond purely administrative decentralization. Although the situation is more complex in practice, in general in France the territorial distribution of powers has never gone as far as in, for example, West Germany.

The separation of powers, both horizontally/functionally and vertically/territorially, remains the corner-stone of democratic liberalism. It is the principle upon which the new democracies of Germany and Italy based themselves after the Second World War, and the basis upon which the Fifth Republic was built (particularly after the law of 3 June 1958), as were also the new democracies of Greece, Portugal, and Spain, following the demise of their dictatorships.

The Rule of Law and Constitutionalism

The limitation of powers was enacted by the obligation imposed upon governments—and especially the executive—to submit to a body of superior rules that guaranteed the citizen respect for his liberties and legal procedures. The rights gradually established by the British Parliament, the Amendments to the American Constitution, the *État de Droit* in France, and the German *Rechtsstaat* have together produced a whole panoply of more or less solemn laws (e.g. the Declaration of Human Rights, the General Principles of Law, Higher Law) that constitute a corpus of rules to which the Western democracies of today adhere and to which the countries of Europe have collectively given their approval, in particular through the European Convention on Human Rights.

But the *État de Droit* implies more than respect for individual liberties: it also involves the authority of a higher law that imposes its rules and constraints upon public powers as a whole. This policy of self-restraint accepted by the political power can be guaranteed by rigorous procedures and rules (such as those governing amendments to the Constitution) and, above all, by the conviction of citizens in general, and the élite in particular, that respect for higher law and the order that it establishes constitutes the essential basis of political consensus and stability. The virtues of the Constitution and the desire to preserve it as a means of welding together the social and political body—even if adjustments sometimes prove necessary—are particularly strong in countries such as Britain, where the Constitution has long been held in respect. The central importance of such a fundamental higher law was also manifested after the Second World War in Italy and West Germany where, following the experiences of Fascism and Nazism, it seemed more important than ever to provide the nation with a set of democratic rules that applied to everyone. Within this group, France has often appeared to play an isolated and idiosyncratic part: the Fourth Republic provoked radical opposition from both the right and the left from the start; and the Fifth Republic seemed destined for a similar fate. Only very gradually did the left come to accept the 1958 Constitution (the presidential election of 1965 was decisive in this respect) and it was not until later that it did so wholeheartedly. The cohabitation initiated in 1986 also had the merit of persuading politicians as a body to support the central importance of the Constitution despite the disagreements between their respective parties. 'The Constitution, the whole Constitution, and nothing but the Constitution' has become the new leitmotif. The new support for constitutionalism was safeguarded further by the establishment of the Constitutional Council, which now effectively guarantees respect for the fundamental law. The Council is not simply an adjudicatory instrument: despite fleeting disagreements over particular issues, it has also become the most effective instrument of the general consensus that now presides over respect for the Constitution. One reason why the constitutional weaknesses of France could so often be laid at the door of the deep political and social divisions in the country was that, in the absence of some body capable of controlling those conflicts, they could so easily be exacerbated and get out of hand.

CHALLENGES FACING CONTEMPORARY DEMOCRACIES

The Western democracies are based upon a variety of beliefs, myths, and values. However, this does not mean that a complete consensus exists among them or that these democracies are not subject to criticisms and even attacks that put them at risk. As the European democracies developed after the First World War, their fragility in the face of economic crises and upheavals of a social or political nature became apparent. Until the 'golden sixties', with some exceptions (France, in particular, weakened by her colonial wars), the Western democracies seemed fairly confident, on account of their economic prosperity and the American military umbrella which contributed so much to the political and military stability of Western Europe. But, from the mid-1960s on, there arose a series of problems that presented many challenges to democracies both old and new, and once again brought into question their very bases, namely: participation, representation, identity, State intervention, and legitimacy.

Participation

Conflict arose on two fronts. On the one hand criticism was aimed at the opportunities for electoral participation, which were declared to be limited, arbitrary, and reductionist. It was suggested that formal electoral participation should be complemented by participation that was 'real': concrete participation in the work place and the home. In both the United States and Europe, 1968 marked the climax of these utopian ideas which, on the whole, left behind no more than a few institutional residua and never managed to eclipse the dominant mode of participation. The second wave of criticism concerning participation was even more radical, since it rejected the very principle of elections as the democratic method of participation. The electoral scene was denounced as a theatre of illusions designed to render ineffective the collective or even revolutionary potential of the people. Although this leftist critique was often tempered by more moderate criticism of the inadequacies of electoral participation, many of its consequences were more serious, and sometimes even led to violence designed to create a 'more democratic' society. Some countries (e.g. Italy and Germany) were seriously shaken by this crisis, which was to affect them for over ten years and which was aggravated by economic difficulties. But virtually the only long-term consequences of these shock waves was a clearer understanding of the limitations of electoral participation (but also of its indispensability) and a new stimulus to thought on the subject of democracy and its machinery.

Representation

The problem of representation raises the eternal question of the relationship between the representatives and the represented. All the Western democracies have rejected the idea of a definite mandate binding on the representatives, but none has gone so far as to declare total autonomy for the representative. In practice, the theory of the representative's mandate is counterbalanced by the role played by the political parties, which devise programmes and adhere to them, even when the mandate that they receive is due to an electoral system in which a minority of the electorate can produce a majority in Parliament. The problem becomes particularly acute when party programmes are radicalized. This happened in Britain between the late 1960s and the early 1980s, following a period of greater consensus described as 'Butskellism' (from the names of Butler and Gaitskell, the one a Conservative and the other a Labour Chancellor of the Exchequer). Such electoral and political swings become a source of tension; once invested with power, governments tend all too quickly to forget that it is only by convention that they have been entrusted to represent the nation as a whole, even if, in reality, they do not represent an absolute majority of the electors (as has been the case in both Britain and France ever since the Second World War). The conventions connected with the principle of majority rule can only function correctly and maintain acceptance if they are reconciled with the principles of respect for the opposition and moderation in the exercise of power.

However, the problems of representation are not limited to the meaning and scope of the representative's mandate. They also concern the more or less tenuous links that are established between representatives and represented. Since the dawn of the age of democracy in Europe there has been no shortage of voices raised against the diversion of popular power into the hands of an oligarchy (Robert Michels) or a restricted élite (Pareto, Mosca). Those who denounce this corruption of the democratic principle stress the extent to which power is concentrated in a few hands (see Burnham's analyses of the power of 'organizers', and the denunciation of the 'Iron Triangle' by Wright Mills and the American left) and the insidious osmosis that operates between various élites—political, economic, military, and so on. Such criticisms are rebuffed by the defenders of liberal democracy (Robert Dahl and Raymond Aron, for example), who, while recognizing the existence of powerful ruling élites, accept its inevitability (whatever the regime) and emphasize that in a liberal democracy those élites are never monolithic. They constitute a 'polyarchy' composed of elements competing with one another within and between given political and economic sectors. This situation tends to preclude domination by a restricted group. All the same, even if we accept the realistic pessimism of that analysis (that perfect and total democracy does not and cannot exist), the conclusion to be drawn must vary from country to country: the structure of élite groups, their recruitment, and their circulation differ from one Western society to another. The rifts that can develop between the élites and the people, or within the élites themselves, can give rise to tensions which are sometimes resolved by violent confrontation when the élites do not manage to engineer agreements and procedures which, while recognizing the existence of these conflicts, make it possible to contain them peacefully. The American War of Independence, the tensions within the Weimar Republic and in Italy and Austria between the wars, and the 1871 Commune in France are all examples of the temporary incapacity of political systems to create a consensus on what the rules of the game should be. In contrast, some systems, sometimes described as examples of 'consociational democracy' (Austria, Holland, and Belgium), have, despite numerous and profound cleavages, devised sophisticated institutional arrangements and promoted agreement between the various élite groups in such a way as to guarantee stability and civic peace.

Identity

In Western democracies, the different identities that make up the nation are organized with varying flexibility. Building a State in many cases proved a long and arduous process but one that appeared to reach completion in the years following the Second World War and the great territorial upheavals that resulted from that conflict. Since then, however, economic, social, and territorial changes have provoked disputes, often of a radical nature, over the way in which power is organized and the balance established between the central power and the periphery. Throughout Europe, the 1960s and 1970s saw first the emergence, then the growing strength of regionalist movements that challenged the institutions of the State and advocated replacing them with a 'Europe of regions'.[3] The European democracies were obliged to respond to these challenges by introducing new forms of integration of a politico-institutional nature (regionalization). For although a discreet veil is often drawn over this, there can be no doubt that the Western States are no different from any others on this point: the right to secede can only be won by force, so integration has to be the only possible political solution.

The Crisis of the Welfare State

The 1970s and 1980s have seen the development of two types of diagnosis and criticism of the situation of contemporary States—

criticisms and diagnoses that also reflect the evolution of ideologies. At first, the Welfare State was criticized less for its excessive interventionism than for the bureaucratic and financial consequences of its policies. The governments of the Western democracies were turning into modern dinosaurs, rendered impotent by their interventionist excesses. Richard Rose's expression 'government overload' makes the point that it was the Welfare State's methods of intervention that were being brought into question rather than its ultimate aims. Along with the economic crisis of the 1970s, however, there developed a neo-liberal body of criticism, voiced initially by a handful of political experts and economists, then adopted by the governments of Margaret Thatcher and Ronald Reagan. The order of the day became 'deregulation' and 'rolling back the State', so as to restore to market forces the freedom of which they had been deprived by government intervention. It is too early for a full assessment of this liberal 'revolution', but there can be no doubt that in the Western democracies the persistent rise of economic and social intervention on the part of the State has been checked.

But over and above the vicissitudes of various policies and divergent views on whether State intervention in the economy is good or harmful, the fundamental question is that of the relation between the public and the private sectors. Given that liberal democracy in principle seeks a balance between the autonomy of the individual and government action, the difficulty is to determine where the dividing line should come. Many have considered excessive social interventionism to indicate an insidious transformation of liberal democracy. Valéry Giscard d'Estaing even settled, rather simplistically, on a level of public expenditure based on the gross national product in excess of which a system becomes socialistically inclined or even socialist, without imagining that even his own government would overstep that magic threshold. Since, in reality, no general agreement is possible between extreme 'libertarians', liberals, interventionists, and socialists, the dividing line is bound to be fluctuating and contingent, and to result from choices determined by democratic logic. It is probably this need to choose moderate policies that gives liberal democracy its value, but at the same time it creates certain difficulties; for it involves the permanent challenge of establishing a balance between the public and the private spheres, individual autonomy and State intervention, *laissez-faire* and economic or social interventionism. Practically speaking, the survival of liberal democracy can only be assured at the price of this kind of adaptation and compromise. These are the issues at the heart of political debate, and it is they that constitute the government's objectives and the *raison d'être* of the system. If the equilibrium necessary for the 'common weal' cannot be achieved, the legitimacy not only of the government but possibly of the system itself will be in danger of being called into question by those whom economic 'progress' and radical *laissez-faire* policies have abandoned.

Legitimacy and Violence

The legitimacy of the Western democracies rests upon their citizens' acceptance of the rules and procedures for selecting their representatives, choosing their governments, and determining public policies. That legitimacy can be assessed both positively and negatively: by the people's participation in the political process and by the absence of any violent, systematic, and general rejection of the rules of the game. The most remarkable consequences of this legitimacy are the consensus from which the institutions benefit, the acceptance of turn and turn about, together with a rejection of violence as an instrument of change. Nevertheless, the balance necessary to democracies is fragile, at the mercy of groups that have no hesitation in resorting to violence or that see revolution as the only true instrument of change. The collapse of the Weimar Republic and the Austrian Republic between the two wars demonstrates the fragility of democracies in the face of violence. During the 1970s and the early 1980s, the European democracies—particularly Italy and Germany—suffered attacks on their political systems from minority but determined groups, whose aim was to destablize the system and force it to adopt repressive policies that would justify a posteriori accusations of 'Fascist State'.

In other cases, violence, though less organized and less conceptualized, is regarded by certain groups or individuals as the ultimate (or simply the most effective) means of obtaining satisfaction for their demands: such cases are widely diverse, ranging from race riots in Britain to the violent action of small groups (regionalists, for example) or professions that resort to action in the streets when negotiation fails to bring them satisfaction (farmers and small shopkeepers in France). Sometimes political violence and straightforward criminality become intermingled and reinforce each other, helping to weaken or undermine the functioning of State institutions: this type of violence is common in Italy, where organizations such as the Mafia and its variants frequently graft themselves on to the margins of the political system. In this way, social and political violence sometimes become quasi-endemic, despite the consensus of the majority. During the 1970s these disturbances to the functioning of democracy gave rise to a current of pessimism that was fuelled further by international tensions and the economic crisis: in 1974, for example, Michel Crozier, Samuel Huntington, and Joji Watanuti prepared a report for the Trilateral Commission which underlined the fragility and ungovernability of Western societies and suggested limiting 'the excesses of democracy' in order to prevent the Western liberal political system from collapsing. Yet, despite their call for a much-tempered democracy, the years 1970 to 1980 were notable for the vigour displayed by the Western democracies and the appeal that they had in countries subjected to authoritarian regimes (not only Spain, Portugal, and Greece, but also Argentina, the Philippines, Chile, and even the Eastern bloc countries).

It would appear from this brief account of the major characteristics of liberal democracy that its internal problems stem, to a certain extent, from its virtues: the moderation of power, the limitations set upon State intervention, the right of free expression, the recognition of the opposition's right to criticize and to exercise power, and the affirmation of public liberties are so many sources of weakness that make it impossible to consider the establishment of democracy to be definitive. The sombre experiences of the inter-war years in Europe constitute the most obvious illustration of the fragility of the remarkable system that has flourished in the small peninsula of Europe, spread to America, and seeks, with varying success, to set itself up as a universal model. Of course, the value of liberal democracy stems not only from its own intrinsic merits (which are great, despite all the criticisms levelled at it) but also from the failure of alternative models (such as the socialist or popular 'democracies' of the Third World). Its value also stems from the fact that its founding principles are at once fundamental and capable of adaptation in both space and time: there are more ways than one of conceiving of the separation of powers, of organizing the protection of liberties and the manifestation of opinions, and of determining the desirable degree of economic and social intervention.

In the last analysis, what makes liberal democracy so valuable, despite all its inadequacies and shameful failings, is the fact that it is *perfectible* and offers people the possibility of struggling peaceably to establish alternatives. To be sure, most democracies protect themselves against the radical option—that is to say, the elimination of liberal democracy itself—but, as history has amply demonstrated, the barriers that they erect are not always insurmountable and, despite any number of constitutional safeguards, it has on occasion proved possible to kill democracy by turning its own weapons against it.

Because of the principles upon which they are founded and the procedures by which they are governed, the liberal democracies offer a wide range of options: a greater or lesser separation or collaboration between the powers (functional fragmentation), a greater or lesser geographical dispersion of authority (territorial fragmentation), and a greater or lesser degree of State intervention in the economic and social spheres. So, even within the democratic family, significant disparities do exist: between the Scandinavian social democracies and the economic liberalism of America; between the differing concepts of liberty and equality in France and in Britain; between German federalism and British and French centralization; etc. In short, the respective histories, cultures, economies, choices, and constraints of the various Western societies have made it possible for them to present many different ways of resolving the fundamental question of how to provide 'government of the people by the people and for the people', the quest for what was known in the ancient world as 'good government'. It is in the hope of reaching a better understanding of that quest, and its groping progress, that we shall now embark upon our comparative study of the political systems of four democracies which, because of their histories, their political and economic importance, and their contributions to the construction of a democratic ideal, have played and continue to play a primary role: the United Kingdom, the Federal Republic of Germany, Italy, and France. The complexities and pitfalls of such an undertaking prompted me to opt deliberately for as simple as possible a method of presentation so as not to make the student's first steps in comparative analysis any harder than necessary. First, I shall describe the origins and manifestations of pluralism —the parties, the interest groups, and the cleavages between them; next, I shall give an account of the mechanisms of representation and popular expression. This will lead on to a study of State institutions (parliaments, governments, and bureaucracies). Finally, we shall examine an important counterbalance that operates within some democratic systems: the constitutional courts.

Politics and Society: Cleavages

Every political society is split by cleavages whose origins, nature, and magnitude vary enormously.[1] They may be economic or social, sectorial or territorial, ideological or symbolic, long-standing or recent, deeply rooted or transient. It is important, at the outset, to assess their impact upon the formation of political attitudes and behaviour. For, while the whole range of cleavages that separate groups within societies and set them against each other is to be found virtually everywhere, the cleavages themselves vary greatly in intensity, distribution, and manner of combination. The ethno-linguistic division is crucial in Belgium, important in Spain, but no more than residual in Italy; economic divisions are deeper in Europe than in the United States; the religious divide, though still significant, has lost its importance. The intensity of any division varies from one country to another;[2] and it may also vary through time within a given society, for divisions may become less important as a result of changes in circumstances and in the ability of either masses or élites to mobilize their strength. Thus, in Belgium, the linguistic and regional issue was for a long time obscured, then played down by the agreement between the Flemish and Walloon élites to set up a centralized francophone system. Increasing opposition to that system brought the initial consensus into question again and eventually led to new modes of power-sharing and power division. Similarly, the urban–rural divide, which Sidney Tarrow has described as 'the fundamental division in French society', was particularly acute until the Second World War but after that became progressively less so, as urbanization increased and the rural population declined. Then again, the territorial divisions between the various fractions of a German Empire built up from a plethora of tiny kingdoms and states virtually disappeared in the maelstrom of the Second World War and the displacement of populations that followed it. Today, only Bavaria still preserves its own particular socio-political structure, whose major manifestation is the dominance of the CSU.

The distribution of cleavages and the ways in which they combine also exhibit great variety. Sometimes factors dividing off a group compound one another, reinforcing the group's specific individuality. When a minority linguistic group is concentrated in a particular, well-defined area where it practises its own religion, belongs to a particular social class (of peasants, for example), and identifies with a specific political party which represents it, all the makings of confrontation come together. To return to the case of Belgium, the Flemish community is concentrated in one half of the territory, and is Catholic and politically to the right, while the Walloons are francophone, more secular, and politically inclined to the left. Given, furthermore, that wealth and power were for a long time concentrated in the hands of a francophone élite, it is easy to see why the Belgian crisis has been—and remains—so difficult to resolve. The situation of Austria in the period between the two wars, where two opposed blocs, one Catholic, the other Socialist, adopted entrenched attitudes, presents an even more dramatic example in that it led to civil war (as did, even more tragically, the situations in Spain in the 1930s and in Lebanon today). It proves easier to mediate between the divisions that cut through a society when cleavages are 'cross-cutting' rather than 'overlapping'. Such is often the case in contemporary Western societies. Cross-cutting cleavages tend to off-set one another: for example, some Catholics are rich, others poor, some bourgeois, others workers, some rural, others urban, some more conservative politically, others less so. Cross-cutting cleavages of this kind help to create solidarities between different groups and reduce the likelihood of the conflict and violence that are so common where cleavages overlap.

Another important factor is the ability of the various political systems to overcome cleavages by *ad hoc* institutional means. Liberal democracies already by definition offer some kind of answer to this problem; their acceptance of different groups and of pluralism, and their legitimization of opposition and limitation of majority power provide so many means of converting social conflicts into political ones that may be peacefully resolved. In countries where cleavages are particularly acute and overlapping, however, the problem is harder to resolve.

A few democracies (Belgium, Austria, The Netherlands, and Israel) have attempted to overcome such divisions by setting up mechanisms or institutional arrangements that Arendt Lijphart[3] has labelled 'consociational democracy'. Lijphart stresses that the survival of such systems depends upon four preconditions: a capacity to recognize the dangers of this kind of fragmentation; a genuine will to preserve the system; the existence of élites capable of rising above the divisions; and the possibility of introducing appropriate solutions to satisfy the demands of subcultures.

But in the last analysis, whatever the intensity and structure of the cleavages, the capacity of political systems to overcome them will depend upon three factors: first, an ability to register the existence of new cleavages as they appear—socio-economic changes (e.g. the French Communist Party's inability to cope with changes in the French working class), international changes, whether military, political, or economic, and the emergence of new values; secondly, the ability of the social groups concerned to accept compromises and not regard certain of their own distinctive features as 'non-negotiable'; and thirdly, the ability of the political élite groups to prepare and organize political solutions rather than exacerbate conflicts and passions.

The solutions arrived at and the balances achieved will produce significant new political configurations, with far-reaching consequences. These will affect the structure of the political scene and the party system, the degree of conflict occasioned by the establishment of a political agenda, the organization of policy-making processes (e.g. the distribution of functions in Belgium, Holland, and Israel, 'transformism' in Italy, and so on), and the composition and functioning of the bureaucracy (i.e. the degree to which it is politicized, and whether appointments are proportionally divided between the parties). Shortage of space precludes our considering all the dimensions and implications of all the divisions that affect political systems. But let us concentrate upon three whose impact upon political behaviour has often been underlined: the class cleavage, the religious cleavage, and territorial and ethnic divisions.

CLASS AND POLITICS

In most Western countries it is still the socio-economic cleavages that constitute the surest indicators of political behaviour. The connection between class and politics is primarily—but not exclusively—

expressed by the political parties, each of which attracts and activates a section of the electorate upon that basis. Thus, in the relationship between class and politics, there is an objective element (membership of such-and-such a social group), and a subjective, psychological element (the *feeling* that one belongs or does not belong to such-and-such a class). That is why, although the socio-professional divisions generally used to classify social groups do make it possible to understand and predict political behaviour, we should remember that other parameters also intervene to confuse the correlation.

In France, for example, the opinion polls conducted by specialist institutes before and after elections show that there is a strong correlation between membership of a socio-professional group and political orientation.

In 1981, 65 per cent of French workers voted for Mitterrand, 35 per cent for Giscard. An inquiry carried out in 1978 showed that, on a left–right spectrum, 87 per cent of workers were on the left, 13 per cent on the right; 26 per cent of farmers were on the left, 74 per cent on the right;[4] and so on. Guy Michelat and Michel Simon[5] have attempted to improve the predictability of this correlation by constructing a more sophisticated social indicator: this is an 'indicator of the objective membership of the working class' and it is composed on the basis of the socio-professional groups not only of the subject questioned, but also of the father and (in the cases of married women who were not the heads of their households) the head of the household. The conclusions of Michelat and Simon were clear: leftist tendencies increased in proportion to the number of working-class attributes exhibited by the voter. Nevertheless, as the percentages mentioned above show, no hard-and-fast link can be established between class membership and political orientation, even in categories representing extreme cases and coming closest to being archetypes, that is, workers and peasants.

A correlation between class and political behaviour seems to be established more firmly in Britain than anywhere else. Most British observers have emphasized that social class constitutes the fundamentally explanatory variable—even if not the only one. Pulzer,[6] for example, writes that all other forms of explanation for electoral behaviour are simply 'embellishment and detail'. In 1938, Harold Laski noted that 'a party is essentially what is implied in the economic interest of its supporters';[7] and whereas, up to the beginning of the twentieth century in Britain, 'we have had, for all effective purposes, a single party in control of the State',[8] the birth of the Labour Party produced a fundamental break, introducing opposition based on class. The close correlation between class membership and political behaviour was explained by the homogeneous and urban nature of British society and also by the absence of other powerful cleavages that might have counterbalanced or weakened class oppositions. Samy Finer, for example, writes, 'Class is important—indeed central—in British politics only because nothing else is.'[9]

If there is thus basic agreement on the class-determined nature of the vote in Britain, it is also generally agreed that that determining relationship is becoming weaker. In his classic *Modern British Politics*, first published in 1965, Samuel Beer emphasizes that, compared with the period between the wars, British politics in the 1950s were characterized by a decline in class antagonisms.[10]

During the same period, Butler and Stokes's study[11] revealed 'an aging of the class alignment', although a strong correlation between political orientation and class persisted, particularly among socially stable electors. (Among socially mobile electors, on the other hand, the correlation was much weaker.) The weakening of the class factor was particularly noticeable during the 1970s, when the electorate was being drawn into new divisions (Scottish and Welsh nationalism, the Common Market) and the traditional working-class basis of the Labour party was affected by profound economic changes.[12] Paradoxically enough, those changes pushed ideological polarization to the limit: under the aegis of Mrs Thatcher, the Conservative Party leaned radically to the right while the Labour Party was undermined by internal clashes between its left and right wings. This resulted in the birth and development of the Social Democratic Party and the formation of a coalition with the Liberal party, producing the 'Alliance'.

Even in States such as Italy and West Germany, where left-wing parties claim to represent a class vote, identifying with the working class, the situation is in reality more complicated. Several factors have combined to undermine the connection between class and political behaviour. The first has to do with the evolution of classes and socio-professional categories. Poorly educated manual workers living in the large cities are gradually giving way to new categories of people who are more highly qualified, better educated, and more attuned to the values of post-industrial society (the quality of life, leisure activities, and so on) than to the traditional problems of the working class.

In the West, furthermore, what remains of the working class, in the classic sense of the expression, is in part composed of immigrant workers without the right to vote.

The new industrial demography has spelled decline for the French Communist Party, unwilling or unable to adapt to these changes. The new electorate identifies far less firmly with a set of values expressed by a single political party. Its more complex behaviour is affected by a host of new and changing factors and this explains both the fluidity of the voting pattern and the differences to be found between one voter and another in what are objectively similar situations.

There is a second possible explanation for the fact that most parties, particularly social democratic ones, cross class boundaries. It is of a strategic nature. In the democracies of today, no party that aspires to power can afford to limit its appeal to a single class (particularly the working class), for to do so would be to condemn itself to perpetual opposition. The formation of the new French Socialist Party at the Épinay Congress was entirely due to a desire to build a government party made up of various sectors of an electorate drawn from both the right and the left. The modernization of the party undertaken at the Toulouse Congress in November 1985 was part of the same process.

However, the French Socialist party was not willing to commit itself to as lacerating and spectacular a revision as that undertaken by the German Social Democratic Party in 1959. Up until then, the SPD had pursued the line of the Social Democrats of the Weimar Republic: it continued to proclaim itself the party of the working class and, with its Marxist-tinged ideology, its share of the West German vote remained around 30 per cent. It did not break through the one-third barrier until after the Bad Godesberg Conference held in 1959, when a new programme and strategy were declared. The SPD now dropped its claim to be the party of the working class and instead became 'the party of the people', proclaiming its acceptance of the fundamental principles of the market economy and putting them at the service of justice and democracy. This volte-face paid off: the SPD thereafter consistently gained ground, becoming the leading party of West Germany in 1972.

Although the Italian Communist Party has remained faithful up to 1989 to its original self-definition, the party of the working class, its organization, concepts, and strategy have undergone many adjustments. By playing down democratic centralism, it was able to distance itself from the Leninist concept of the party. As Pasquino has pointed out, the arrival on the scene of new strata of non-manual workers and the lowering of the voting age to 18 in 1975 helped to change the 'party culture': 'Sheltered by the broad shield of Gramsci, the Italian CP had, over the years, been diluting the impact of cultures that were alien to it; but in the mid-seventies, this phenomenon made itself felt even at the heart of the party.'[13]

Finally, in the mid-1970s, it adopted its historic strategy of compromise. This was prompted by the realization that not only was it difficult for the left as a whole to win a majority but even with a majority of 51 per cent, it would not be possible for it to govern, given the national and international conditions in which communist parties come to power. (The Italian CP had been traumatized by the unfortunate experiences of Chile.) The party justified its new strategy by denouncing the illusion that 'in the event of the parties and groups of the left succeeding in winning 51% of the votes and of the parliamentary representation, that fact alone would guarantee the survival and action of any government representing that majority'.[14]

In truth, the prudence of the Italian CP was not new-found. Its flirtation with the Christian Democrats was not solely justified by the place that the DC held in the Italian State as a whole. The Italian CP had always been aware that the party of De Gasperi and Aldo Moro was draining off a significant fraction of the working class, particularly in the south and in the 'white' fiefdoms of the north, such as the Veneto. Despite the fact that the number of working-class supporters of the DC continued to fall, in 1982 workers still represented 11.8 per cent of the 1,300,000 members of the party (as opposed to 15.2 per cent in 1959). The Christian democratic movement is certainly one of the best illustrations of the limits of the socio-professional variable and the importance of subcultures and other non-economic divisions.

RELIGION AND POLITICS

As Alain Lancelot points out, 'in nearly all countries, religion and class are the most discriminatory of variables'.[15] It may seem a paradoxical observation to make at a time when religious practice is on the wane everywhere in the Western world, whatever the religion —whether Catholic, Anglican, Lutheran, or Calvinist. Yet the influence of religion endures, as if the values connected with it persisted and were directing political behaviour despite the decline of religious practice and the weakening of institutional allegiances. A comparison between the various European democracies and the place held within each by one or several religions will help us to grasp the variations that may exist in the relations between religion and politics. In a study of these relations, there are three major elements to consider:

- the relations of Churches to the State,
- the relations of Churches to society,
- the relations of religious values to political values.

Church and State

The relations between Churches and the State cover a wide spectrum that ranges from the principle of total separation to quasi-identification between a dominant Church and the State apparatus. However, examples of these two extremes, which were still to be found in an almost pure form during the nineteenth and even the early twentieth centuries, have today given way to much more fluid situations which vary relatively little from one State to another. Two countries are marked by the tradition of a dominant religion: Italy and Britain. In Italy, that domination has been at once sociological, institutional, and political, whereas, in Britain, the Church of England's official status gave it a pre-eminence that has slowly been eroded in practice by the relative progress made by Catholicism. The privileged position and national character of the Church of England explain how it was that, in the nineteenth century and even the early years of the twentieth, it looked as if it was one of the pillars of the political and constitutional system. (The abdication of Edward VIII in 1936 was the last and most spectacular manifestation of its influence.) The Church of England was so closely identified with the values of the ruling class that it has been described as 'the Tory Party at prayer'. Today, that is no longer the case, even if the monarch is still the head of the Church of England and even if the ecclesiastical peers continue to sit in the House of Lords. Nowadays, its constitutional pre-eminence has virtually no significance, and other Churches have managed to hold on to their autonomy (the Church of Scotland), or have acquired it since the nineteenth century (the Catholic Church). In Britain today, the juridical pre-eminence of the national Church accommodates a full acceptance of religious pluralism (accompanied by a collapse of religious practice).

Although religious influence is declining in Italy too, the history of the Catholic Church, its geographical placing, and its monopoly (95 per cent of Italians belong to the Catholic Church) all contribute to its predominant position. Its relations with the modern Italian State were initially fraught with conflict, however. From 1870, when Garibaldi's men took Rome, the centre of Christianity, and proceeded to make it the capital of the Kingdom of Italy, thereby completing the unification of the peninsula, until the Lateran Pact of 1929, the Church and the Catholics deliberately organized themselves outside, and even in opposition to, the liberal State. The Catholic world set itself up as a self-sufficient alternative power and was more concerned to bend the State to its will than to become an integral part of its structures. When the Fascist regime offered the Church a privileged status and considerable financial assistance, it neutralized a potential adversary, allowing it to develop within its own autonomous sphere. In 1947, when the Italian Constitution was drawn up, its creators sought to reconcile, on the one hand, the tradition of separation between the Church and the State desired by the fathers of Italian unity (Cavour: 'a free Church within a free State') and, on the other, the situation inherited from the Concordat established by Mussolini.

Hence the formulation of Article 7 of the Constitution, which declares that 'the State and the Catholic Church, each within its own order, are both independent and sovereign' but which goes on to make it clear that 'their relations are governed by the Lateran Pact'. The fact that many moves made by the Church were badly out of step with the evolution of Italian society gave rise to many tensions during the 1970s and 1980s until 1984 when the Vatican and the Italian government came to an agreement. The *aggiornamento* (bringing-up-to-date) of the Concordat was particularly concerned with religious teaching in schools (which now became optional), the financing of the Church by the State (which was now replaced by voluntary funding paid for by the people, as in Germany), and religious works (which now fell more or less under common law). In short, despite certain historical and geographical links, relations between the Italian State and the Catholic Church have weakened. The crucifix continues to be displayed in all public places (schools, administrative offices, law courts, etc.), but the State has secularized itself in recognition of the increasingly marked transformation of Italian society.

In West Germany, relations between Church and State are characterized both by religious pluralism and by the change in the balance of faiths that took place after the Second World War. Before the war, the majority of the population were Protestant, but they were particularly affected by the partition of Germany, for most of the Catholics were concentrated in the south and west of the country. The Catholics moved from the position of a defensive minority to one of parity with the Protestants. A sense of oppression, or at least of being pushed aside has, nevertheless, helped to shape the behaviour of the Catholic Church: under the Empire and during the Weimar Republic, the Catholic Party was concerned to protect Catholics, as was the Vatican, particularly during the period of the Third Reich. The Concordat that the Church signed with Hitler in 1933 and its attitude towards the Nazis were both expressions of the particular kind of relationship that obtained, obscuring the need to defend more universal values and individuals who fell outside its authority. Alfred Grosser puts the point emphatically:

One cannot fail to be struck by the persistence of one particular theme in [Church] documents: it is first and foremost the Catholics who must be defended . . . And while, in Germany, the Church defended the Catholics first and foremost, one of the Pope's major preoccupations certainly also appears to have been the protection of the German Catholics.[16]

The Catholics were not alone in compromising themselves with Hitler. One section of Protestants supported him and tried to set up a Reich Church that would unite the twenty-nine German Protestant Churches. They were opposed by the members of the Confessional Church, born in 1934, which was hostile to Nazism. It was the activists in this movement who in 1945 reorganized the German Evangelical Church (EKD), which was no longer to stand for 'a specifically German type of Protestantism, but would be a German branch of world Protestantism'.[17] The painful Nazi experience had shown that the Christians had committed 'sins of omission' even if not 'sins of commission'. The better balance that now obtained between the religious forces was to make it possible to bring Catholics and Protestants closer together and to form an organization that included both groups, the CDU.

An important juridical and financial connection still exists between the State and the members of the Churches. As laid down by the Concordat, the government levies an ecclesiastical tax (the *Kirchensteuer*) amounting to between 8 and 10 per cent (depending on the region) of the taxes paid by citizens who have not explicitly declared their intention to leave the Church to which they have been attached. Despite the fact that church attendance is extremely low among Catholics and virtually non-existent among Protestants, almost 90 per cent of West German citizens continue to pay the Church Tax, thereby assuring the Churches in Germany of substantial funds, more substantial than those received by the Churches of any other country apart from America.

In France, relations between Church and State have been difficult, for, until the nineteenth century, the political power had always sought to free itself from the influence of Rome and between 1902 and 1905 it even broke the juridical links (the Concordat) between France and the Vatican. Twentieth-century French history has thus been marked even more than previously by pro-clerical and anti-clerical tensions, particularly since the religious divide coincided almost exactly with the right–left one. The First World War and the great movement of national unity prompted by the conflict with Germany made it possible for tensions to diminish and for less antagonistic relations to be established both with the Church of France and with Rome. However, the period between 1930 and 1960 was poisoned by a number of episodes: the fears that the Popular Front inspired among Catholics; reinforcement of the Left's mistrust by the support that most of the French bishops and clergy gave to the Pétain regime between 1940 and 1944; and recurrent clashes over the question of private schools (90 per cent of which were Catholic) up until the late 1950s.

Church and Society

Political behaviour is also affected by the relations between Churches and society. Sometimes the Churches deliberately limit themselves to a strictly religious role, avoiding any competition with the State; sometimes, on the other hand, they establish an outright counter-society, reacting against the interventions of a State whose legitimacy or policies they challenge. Although countersocieties of this kind tend to be growing weaker today, they still manage to create subcultures whose impact on the vote may be crucial.

In Britain, where the Church of England is, so to speak, part of the State and was, for a long time, part of the official Establishment, the influence of religion has made itself felt more through a transfer of values into the political world than through the construction of any network of ecclesiastical institutions. The only part of the United Kingdom where the religious divide determines political behaviour is Northern Ireland, where Catholics and Protestants stand in opposition. Even here, it is legitimate to wonder whether it is really a case of religion determining political divisions or whether the latter stem from other distinctive (but not necessarily exclusive) factors of differentiation. In other words, the religious divide might in part express economic and social cleavages that are no less important but are somehow absorbed and concealed by the division that carries a greater historical and emotional charge. In contrast, the fact that the Scots for the most part adhere to the Presbyterian Church has had no real impact upon their political behaviour. The most that can be said is that their distinctive religion may have contributed to the recently manifested feeling of a specifically Scottish identity, just as have the separate Scottish judicial system and specifically Scottish legislation in the area of Scottish mores and culture. In other words, in Britain, the Churches have developed no networks of the kind that the Catholic Church has created on the Continent.

France, Italy, and Germany, in contrast, do possess a tight network of institutions (mostly created by the Catholic Church), which provide a framework for the faithful and a basis for the party that represents their views, whatever their class. Membership of the same faith becomes an element which overrides all social differences, ignores economic disparities, and cements the organization of the entire group. This phenomenon is more highly organized within the Catholic Church on account of its desire to convey and put to work an influential message that relates to every aspect of both private and social life: education and sexual life obviously enough, but economic and social doctrines too. Furthermore, the existence of a hierarchy determined to maintain respect for the faith and its dogma leads to inflexibility and conflicts within the State. The anti-clericalism provoked by this kind of interventionism, both doctrinal and material, reinforces the embattled mentality of the Church and isolates Catholics from the rest of society. Such was the situation of Catholics in Germany in particular at the time of Bismarck's *Kulturkampf* policies, of French Catholics in the 1905 to 1920 period, and of Italian Catholics from 1870 to 1929 (throughout which period the Roman nobility even went so far as to wear mourning). The subculture produced by this isolation manifested itself in the proliferation of educational, social, and mutual-help institutions, and it is no accident that they are most numerous in the countries that have a strong Catholic tradition, such as France, Italy, Germany, Spain, and Belgium. The hold that these secular institutions controlled by the Churches maintained over all sectors of economic and social life fostered the tendency to consider every question in clerical or anti-clerical terms and to bypass class distinctions in the name of common membership of the same religion. The most striking example of the influence of this Catholic subculture on political behaviour is presented by the divisions relating to educational matters. For a long time, the problem of private schooling provided the cement that bonded the Catholics together—regardless of class—and it was this that constituted the most acute source of division between the political parties. Up until the late 1960s, this situation turned the Christian parties into conglomerations of Church members whose principal point in common was the faith that they shared. The Christian parties were expected to protect the doctrine and interests of the Churches and Christians were expected to vote for *their* party.

In France, the networks established by the Catholic Church were every bit as dense and active as those in Italy and Germany. Not only did the Church set up Catholic Action movements particularly among the young (young Catholic farmers, students, and workers) but up until the 1950s it managed to maintain its influence in many of its traditional sectors of intervention (for instance, the health and social sectors and, even more, in education); furthermore, it penetrated a number of sectors that were neglected by the State (agricultural training, for example). In the 1950s, the influence of the social framework provided by Catholicism was at its peak: everywhere, the Church controlled schools, hospitals, youth hostels, sporting and cultural associations, and even cinemas, quite apart from engaging in its more specifically ecclesiastical works. With the decline of the influence of Christianity and of religious vocational work, the importance of this network has diminished considerably. Nevertheless, the French Church has made a significant impact through its influence on the training of the ruling élites in many sectors of society, particularly among employers and in the trade unions.

However, instances of Catholic activism in support of a party have been becoming more circumspect and less common. In the first place, the Church found itself bound to recognize that Catholics no longer, as in the past, identified themselves as belonging to one *particular* party, even if it was that of the Christian Democrats. Their party loyalties were now spread more widely. Secondly, it was noticed throughout the dioceses, in the course of legislative campaigns (in 1972 in Germany) and referendums (on divorce and abortion, in Italy), that Catholic voters no longer accepted the precepts of the Church so unquestioningly or, at least, had no desire to impose upon society as a whole the beliefs and convictions of a small fraction of it, even if they happened to belong to that fraction. In the third place, it is always risky for the Church to declare undivided support for one particular political movement. Defeat for that party turns into defeat for the Church itself, as indeed proved the case for the Italian Catholic Church, which had totally committed itself to the campaign to repeal the law on divorce. Under the influence of currents of opinion extremely close to the Church and of the traditionalist Catholic movements (Communione e Liberazione, for example), the Christian Democratic Party took a risk in venturing into this campaign and was deeply traumatized by its defeat. The referendum showed that the Catholics were no longer in a position to impose their own choices and that some of the Christian Democrat electors were voting for the party more through conservatism than through their religious faith. This set-back led, on the rebound, to a crisis in the relationship between the Church and the Christian Democrats that undermined relations that had remained stable for thirty years, despite all the changes in Italian society.

Religious Values—Social Values

Despite the often close relations maintained between the Churches and their respective States, and despite the close-knit framework organized by the Catholic Church, the most striking phenomenon of the past twenty years has been the decline of religion in Western countries. The resurgence of fundamentalist movements should not be allowed to mask the essential facts: the influence of the Churches, as institutions, has weakened, regular church attendance oscillates between 10 and 20 per cent of the population from one country to another. In these circumstances, it seems fair to ask, with Alain Lancelot: 'Can we speak of a decline in the *"religious vote"* as we speak of the decline in the "class vote"?'[18] Inglehart bases his reply to that question on the example provided by The Netherlands, where a general weakening of religious practice preceded the dramatic decline of the religious vote in the 1970s.[19] According to Inglehart, there is a more or less long delay between the decline of religious practice and any electoral expression of this detachment. It is a plausible interpretation, but it prompts one to ponder the significance of that delay. The evolution noted by Inglehart may simply result from accidental circumstances. For many other analyses on the contrary emphasize that modes of behaviour persist in the long term, whatever the changes undergone by the electorate. It would appear that people's perceptions of real circumstances are often shaped by applying a virtually unchanging interpretative grid determined by a system of values or a cultural tradition so remote that it leaves hardly a trace and is barely remembered in any explicit terms.

Consequently, we may well wonder whether, despite the declining impact of Church institutions and personal Christian allegiances, Christian values have not become such an integral part of certain societies that they persist quite independently of the religious services and practices that expressed them in the past. The fact that the values preached by the Churches are recognized and accepted even by non-believers ensures that society remains affected by them even though religious practice has waned. Some social groups and regions maintain stable political modes of behaviour structured by Christian or conservative political parties despite the decline of the Churches. Or, to put it another way, as Gordon Smith does, if religion used to be a means of identifying with the dominant values of society, even now it still plays an important role as a constituent element in a wider social order: 'but the direction of influence is reversed: religion no longer determined political loyalties, the political loyalty was still supported by a religious value'.[20] The regions and social classes that were in the past the most influenced by religious values—in particular by the Catholic Church—continue to show a marked preference for right-wing parties: the Bavaria of the CSU, the White Veneto, Southern Italy, Alsace, and Paris continue to be dominated by Christian democrat or Conservative parties, while anti-clerical areas continue to vote for the left. Helmut Kohl was certainly correct, in 1973, when he declared the '"C" of the CDU to be just as modern as in 1946', but now the political parties can no longer count on the automatic, inter-class support of all Christians. Only truly political tactics can win back those supporters, as Alfred Grosser pointed out in the late 1970s: Kohl's CDU and Andreotti's Christian Democrats are now, following the experiences of the past decade, learning that lesson and striving to put it into practice.

TERRITORY AND POLITICS

In a study on the evolution of the concept of territory, Gottman[21] notes that territory in itself is a neutral concept but that it acquires political significance through the interpretation and values that people ascribe to it (for a variety of reasons—ethnic, historical, linguistic, etc.). A territory may become the foundation of a society whose modes of organization and whose language, religion, and types of behaviour define its identity both positively and negatively (in contrast to neighbouring societies). It may thus become the symbol or indeed the very expression of an identity that is reinforced by all the mechanisms of political representation and also of symbolic representation. The importance of a territory for its people has always been great, for to organize a territory implies organizing power, given concrete form by structures, equipment, and frontiers. The myth of the 'New Frontier' in the United States, and all the squabbles and wars in Continental Europe testify to the power of the notion of territory, as do the survival of parishes and the resurgence of regionalism.

In Europe, the nation state has emerged out of conglomerations of various societies, all heterogeneous by reason of race, language, or religion. The nation state *par excellence* is represented by France, the model of a successful empire that turned 'Peasants into Frenchmen', to borrow the title of a study by Eugen Weber. In contrast, Britain and Austria have gone through terrible upheavals that resulted, on the one hand, in Irish independence, on the other in the fragmentation of the Hapsburg Empire. Germany and Italy were constructed in the nineteenth century from a plethora of states, kingdoms, and principalities, whose respective cultural and, in some cases, political imprint is sometimes detectable even today. Furthermore, in Europe, both the late nineteenth century and the period between the wars were poisoned by the problem of nationalities. Today, the map of Europe essentially corresponds to a map of nationalities, but the problems have not all disappeared yet: the principle of nationality as the basis for the construction of a nation state contains the seeds of its own destruction. Within every nationality, it is always possible for a minority, however small, to claim its own autonomy or even independence, in the name of its specifically individual characteristics: the 250,000 inhabitants of Greenland, the 200,000 Corsicans, and the francophone inhabitants of the Jura region can claim to deserve the same rights as the Danes, the island of Malta, and the canton of Berne.

Such claims are usually asserted on a territorial basis, as is borne out by the creation of Israel, by the conquests of Hitler, or, alternatively, by the failure of claims put forward by the Gypsies.

When a minority organized on a territorial basis sets out to win recognition for its rights or, more modestly, its individuality, several possible strategies are open to it: the inhabitants of a given territory can make sure that it is represented by an autonomous political party; alternatively, it can see to it that the national party is divided along regionalist lines; or else, finally, it can manifest its specific individuality through political behaviour that diverges from that of the nation as a whole, behaviour that some observers have suggested calling 'sectionalism'.

The Minority Parties

The most radical non-violent means for a minority to express its own identity lie in organizing specific representation for itself and rejecting integration into the national party systems. (I do not propose to take into consideration forms of 'exit' such as campaigns of violence, assassination, etc.). That identity, manifested by a language, a culture, or customs peculiar to the minority (or, at the very least, a sense of the need to defend its own particular characteristics by opposing the dominant culture) may be expressed politically through a party whose aspirations and ambitions are organized on an infranational territorial basis. The emergence and survival of such parties are connected on the one hand with the existence of homogeneous, territorially concentrated groups and, on the other, with the forms of 'access' that are allowed by the institutional system. Thus, in West Germany, the destruction of local solidarities and the dispersion of local populations as a result of the Second World War, and the absence of non-German-speaking groups have made it possible for a homogeneous German society to emerge, a society in which nationalist parties seem pointless. (There is, it is true, a small Danish minority located along the Danish–German frontier, but its protection is assured by a treaty between the two bordering States.) In contrast, the 'peripheral' regions of France, Italy, and Britain, at least those with the most marked identities, have sometimes organized themselves politically around regional parties. Situations where the political parties are organized on a purely nationalist basis are potentially destructive to a State, as can be seen from the example of the Austrian Empire from the end of the nineteenth century onward, or that of Britain faced with the secession of Ireland. To a lesser degree, the very existence of political parties organized territorially constitutes a challenge to the Western representative systems. For in these systems—ideally—the parties are not supposed to represent specific interests of territories: such parties constitute dangerous competition for the political parties that are usually organized in relation to non-territorial cleavages.

Nationalist parties may of course position themselves either to the left or to the right on the political spectrum. For a long time, regionalist parties stood for conservatism and tradition and provided a means of expression for classes on the wane or other groups denied central power. The climax of that identification with right-wing values was reached in the Second World War, when many regionalist parties were willing to strike a pact with the devil, that is, the Nazis.

But during the 1970s, the balance shifted to the left or even the extreme left, as regionalism rediscovered the voice of utopian social- ism (as purveyed by Proudhon, for example) and teamed up with the ecologists and the advocates of self-management who emerged after 1968. Whether they incline to the right or the left, regionalist parties often tend to behave as if they held a hegemony, rallying—or attempting to rally—the entire local population to their banner. Two cases in point are the SVP (the German-speaking party of the Alto- Adige), which obtains over 60 per cent of the votes in its region, and the Unione Valdotana in the Valley of Aosta; and, in the period between the wars, to achieve a similar status was the ambition of Breton regionalists, who proclaimed that they were 'neither Red nor White, but Breton'. But not many regionalist parties succeed in seizing a dominant position in their 'own' territories. That is partly because non-territorial divisions (such as class and religion) usually tend to win out; and also because the regionalist parties have difficulty in reconciling their hegemonic pretensions with the persistent internal quarrels that tend to divide them.

A good illustration of these erratic movements is provided by the Scottish Nationalist Party (SNP), which in 1934 emerged from the fusion of two regionalist parties but in 1942 once more split, this time into the moderate devolutionists on the one hand, and those who favoured independence on the other; the latter took over the SNP. During the 1950s the SNP made little progress, but in the late 1960s it made a leap forwards, becoming (in terms of votes obtained) the second largest party in Scotland, in the 1974 elections. The size of the nationalist vote and the weakness of the Labour Party both encouraged the interests of the two organizations to converge, but that very strategy then helped to divide the SNP, which now oscillated between socialist options and a more moderate attitude. The failure of the referendum of March 1979 and Labour's fall from power marked the beginning of a new period of decline: in the 1979 General Election the SNP won only 17.3 per cent of the vote, which produced two elected members of Parliament, and it slipped back into third place. This defeat was followed by an expulsion of 'leftists' from the party and a further setback in the 1983 and 1987 elections. If, as Derek Urwin holds, citizens must be recognized to have to choose between a 'right to roots' and a 'right to options', more and more of them seem to be opting for integration into national organizations in preference to the charms of their nationalist roots.

The Federalization of National Parties

The influence of territorial cleavages in politics may manifest itself in ways less radical than those offered by the nationalist parties but more effective than simply forming pressure groups within the parties. In between those two extremes, one comes across flexible solutions of a 'federal' nature in which minimal centralization is combined with a large measure of freedom of action for the various constituents of the group as a whole. Such is the case, for example, of the Liberal Party of the United Kingdom, which is organized as a federation of four separate and quasi-autonomous parties that correspond to the four territorial divisions of the UK (England, Wales, Scotland, and Northern Ireland). This structure explains, in particular, how it was that the Liberal Party proved particularly sympathetic to the claims of the nationalists in the 1960s and 1970s.

But the most telling and important case is that of the CSU, the Bavarian Christian democratic party. Although we should remember that victory or defeat for the Christian Democrats depends upon the accumulated votes of the CDU and the CSU, the fact remains that the CSU is, for all that, a separate, autonomous party. Although the deputies of the CDU and the CSU admittedly sit together as a single parliamentary group, each party has its own organization. The autonomy of the CSU is reinforced by the fact that it truly does constitute a 'State party', being solidly anchored in Bavaria. The CSU has made one or two attempts to implant itself outside Bavaria (in 1957, for instance, it obtained two members of the Bundestag in Saarland); but these should be regarded more as manœuvres designed to intimidate the CDU than as a true nationwide strategy of expansion for the party. For, in principle, the CDU and the CSU each refrain from poaching in their partner's preserve. The arrangement is part of the two parties' agreements on co-operation—agreements according to which, furthermore, the two parties combine to form one parliamentary group (or *fraktion*) and between themselves settle upon a common candidate for the post of Chancellor (an arrangement which in practice favours the CDU, but also gives the CSU a chance to negotiate and to apply pressure).

All the same, the CSU has had to pay a price for its identification with one particular region together with its right-wing ideology: it would be virtually impossible for a leader of the CSU ever to become Chancellor, at least so long as the party remains as it is at present. The situation naturally plays into the hands of the Liberal Party, which is seen as an indispensable counterweight to the CSU.

Specificities of Political Behaviour

The connection between territory and politics may also manifest itself in forms which, though less institutionalized, still have an important impact upon the way that institutions function. The determining character of one or another variable upon a particular territory sometimes imparts a homogeneous and stable political orientation to that territory. The influence of religion, the class vote, or a particular cultural tradition sometimes dictates the political and electoral configuration of a territory—and also of particular electoral constituencies. As Alain Lancelot points out, 'Behind all the statistics hides a society, with its network of interrelations, its currents of influence and its dominant ideas.'[22] When the political behaviour of a territory is particularly stable and homogeneous, the parties sometimes control veritable strongholds, whose survival may have nothing to do with the causes that created them. According to Klaus Von Beyme,[23] the electoral strongholds of the various parties tend to perpetuate themselves in two types of situation: '(1) in countries where the class conflict is more dominant than religious, language or regional differences (Great Britain); (2) in areas where traditional conflicts (the centre v. the periphery, or clericalism v. anti-clericalism) have been submerged in a subsequent class conflict in such a way as to survive in certain areas and provide party strongholds'.

Territorialized political behaviour and the persistence of its manifestations are to be found in all Western systems. In Britain, the Liberals are particularly strong in the 'Celtic fringe' of the kingdom, but the polling system makes it almost impossible to convert this relative strength into electoral success. The situation is such that Wales is sometimes called the 'rotten borough' of the Liberal Party. It is the Labour Party that has benefited most from the situation, becoming the principal party both in Scotland and in Wales. It is easier to understand the devolutionist policies of Labour in 1978–9 if one bears in mind that the nationalists, in Scotland in particular, were threatening its position even in its most solid strongholds. In Italy, the regional nature of political behaviour is even more striking: the south and the Veneto are dominated by the Christian Democrats (in the Veneto, the Christian Democrat Party comes close to polling an absolute majority of votes), whereas the Italian Communist Party is unquestionably the dominant party in central Italy, in the former states of the Holy See.

These 'sectionalist' phenomena (to borrow Jean Blondel's expression)[24] have certainly been persistent, but now, particularly under the impact of accelerating social change, they are beginning to be less so. For example, the strongholds of the French Communist Party around Paris and those of the Radicals in the south-west have shown many signs of weakness over the last two decades. The Christian Democrats have lost ground all over Italy, proving most resistant in their strongholds of the south and the north-east—up until the late 1970s, at least, for at that point the effects of the collapse of the 'White subculture' began to be felt.

There is thus an aspect to socio-political divisions that is both functional and territorial. On a territorial level, the centre–periphery division between on the one hand the élites and groups in power, on the other marginal territorial groups, must always be taken into account in the building of a nation state, but even in the oldest and most solidly constituted of States, the traces of that division have by no means disappeared. The functional dimension is apparent in the struggles involved in the share-out of economic resources and in clashes of values, ideologies, and religions. On the basis of this schema, Lipset and Rokkan[25] have suggested an analysis of European political development that takes as its starting-point the great historical fractures that are the sources of the major divisions in European national societies and that, even today, still structure political life. Rokkan[26] emphasizes that those fractures were brought about by three different types of great revolution: the national revolution, the industrial revolution, and the international revolution.

The national revolution gave rise to the State–Church division and also to the division between the centre and the periphery (exemplified by conflicts between Rome and national Churches; and conflicts between central élites and ethno-linguistic peripheries). The Industrial Revolution of the nineteenth century constitutes the second critical phase in which industrial and urban interests on the one hand, and agricultural and rural ones on the other, came into opposition. The urban–rural divide was to dominate the political life of the nineteenth and early twentieth centuries. It was expressed chiefly through economic policies and conflicts between the partisans of Free Trade policies and those who supported protectionism through Customs and Duty tariffs. But the Industrial Revolution was also, and above all, to produce the division which set the holders of capital in opposition to the work-force, the division that even today determines one of the most fundamental and deeply anchored oppositions in political societies: namely, the right–left opposition.

Finally, Rokkan shows how the international revolution was to produce a division that essentially affected the workers, setting in opposition the partisans of an international revolutionary movement and those who opted for national integration, in other words, the communists and the socialists. Not all these splits have been sufficiently marked or enduring to constitute the basis of political formations which could be seen as embodying the effects of the divisions that had appeared in the course of these three major revolutions; for, as Lipset and Rokkan point out, while the political parties of the West may well express obvious or latent oppositions and divisions, their virtue is that they also make it possible to surmount some of them. In other words, the political parties that express and reinforce pre-existing cleavages are at the same time instruments through which negotiations may be held over conflicting demands, and compromise and agreement may be reached. Historical processes take different forms in different countries, depending on the capacity of élites to accept compromise and the persistence or eradication of ancient divisions. Each society is thus progressively structured by political parties which, even as they express certain divisions, repair others. The particularly paradoxical feature of political parties is that on the one hand they express oppositions and divisions (as the etymology of the word 'party' suggests), yet, on the other, they serve as an instrument of cohesion and co-operation, and also make it possible to bypass a certain number of antagonisms and divisions.

In order to understand how structural divides can be turned into party systems in this fashion, Lipset and Rokkan suggest that we should ponder upon the way in which protest movements and the representation of interests are expressed within each society, and they put forward the following hypothesis: the process of creating a party system depends upon crossing a number of 'thresholds', namely, legitimization (recognition—or not, as the case may be—of the right to criticism and opposition); incorporation (the inclusion or exclusion of individuals and groups in the choosing of representatives); representation (can new movements hope to win a place of their own or must they join pre-existing movements?); and the nature and extent of the power of the majority (are the powers of the majority that emerges from the poll limited, or can it implement major structural decisions that affect the system?)

The interest of Rokkan's 'genetic' analysis lies in the emphasis that it lays upon the interconnection between structural divides and political parties and the way in which it shows how, in the course of the historical process, the parties have helped to reinforce certain divisions and to attenuate others. In this way, it explains the persistence of political divisions[27] that are anchored in oppositions that seem to be out of date and no longer of any relevance. The key factor is thus not so much the creation or transformation of political parties, but rather the permanence of the divisions for which they stand.

Political Parties

The existence of political parties competing for power within a framework of rules that guarantee equal chances for all is one of the fundamental characteristics of pluralist Western democracy. With hindsight, it seems that this key element in the democracies of today is interconnected with the process that has shaped liberal democracy, even if the development of the political organizations known as the parties and that of the institutions of pluralist democracy have not always been in harmony.

To be sure, history provides many examples of political groups taking up arms in their struggle for power: the conflict between the Guelphs and the Ghibellines in Renaissance Florence, clashes between organized clubs during the French Revolution, the opposition between the Montagne and the Marais or the Jacobins and the Girondins all foreshadow party political forms involved in the political game. But at the end of the eighteenth century in Britain, political parties in the modern form began to emerge, in circumstances that were—admittedly—fraught with conflict. Men such as Burke defended the principle of organized parties: 'Party is a body of men united, for promoting by their joint endeavours the national interest, upon some particular principle in which they are all agreed,'[1] but the idea was generally criticized on the grounds that these 'factions' would introduce divisions in relation to the monarchy and the exercise of power. The debate was resumed in France, under the Restoration, in virtually the same terms, for the Ultras of 1815–16 (Chateaubriand) appealed to the English model as they attempted to impose their views on a monarch who was too moderate for their taste. But, despite the Anglomania felt on this score by a section of the political élite, it was relatively late in the day that France eventually came to accept a true party system. The contrasting evolutions of these two countries show that the birth of political parties is not always a natural concomitant of the extension of universal suffrage; and contemporary history demonstrates *ad nauseam* that party structures may be created and may develop and improve even when the practices of so-called universal suffrage amount to no more than a sham of democracy. The political party, as an instrument for winning and administering power, is essentially linked with a historical turning-point in Western democracy, as it developed in Britain.[2] But the determining factor was that, as the democratic system more or less modelled on Britain spread, there developed a conviction that *political parties are the instruments best adapted to political struggle*. That assumption was to find startling confirmation in Marxist analyses and in the 1917 Revolution, which made the Communist Party the instrument through which the working class could first win and then administer power. At this point, the debate shifted: the question was no longer, as in the nineteenth century, whether there should be political parties, but whether the party system should be pluralist or monolithic. Thenceforward the whole debate was to concentrate upon the respective merits or flaws of multi-party and single-party systems; but the existence of party organizations was by now to some extent accepted as a constitutive element of the political system itself: thus the proliferation of States that followed the Second World War was accompanied by a corresponding proliferation of political parties. Institutional and political mimesis extends also to the creation of parties, although the imitations in some cases remain somewhat artificial. In developing countries, in particular, the parties created and organized often bear no more than a formal resemblance to the models claimed to inspire them, whether the framework be that of a single-party system or of a pluralist one.[3] This makes it much more difficult to establish comparisons, although some interesting attempts to do so, such as those that Kenneth Janda[4] undertook in the 1970s, have made a fundamental contribution to our understanding in this area.

Limiting ourselves to the parties of the European democracies, we must remember that party systems stem from the combination and relative significance of a number of factors. They may not all be present in all the countries in question and they vary in importance from one to another. Among these factors we should include the structure and intensity of divisions, the importance of historical divisions (in revolutions, and civil or religious wars), the impact of international events (such as the French Revolution of 1789 and the Russian Revolution of 1917), the nature of the system (presidential or parliamentary), the type of electoral system, and the ability of existing parties to adapt and thus discourage the emergence and development of new competitors. All these factors interact, determining the structure and evolution of the parties. Let us now study these interactions and their results from two different angles: first, from that of ideology, then from the point of view of the institutionalization and organization of the parties. The chapter concludes with an analysis of the party system.

The term 'ideology', as used here, applies generally to the whole extensive system of ideas and values to which political groups claim to relate. These ideas and values may vary greatly in intensity within a single political system, from one political system to another, and from one period to another. In a system such as that of the United States, for example, the values to which each of the parties subscribe are so little differentiated that ideology appears to be of secondary importance in comparison to defending the interests championed by the respective groups. The role of ideology may also vary in importance from one political system to another: the ideological spectrum is more open-ended in France and Italy than in West Germany or Britain. Finally, the intensity of ideology may vary from one period to another. In the 1960s, many observers were hailing 'the end of ideologies', but subsequent events have proved that in reality it was a matter not so much of a collapse of ideology as of a realignment.

Some political observers have rejected the term 'ideology' in favour of concepts more indeterminate but, it is claimed, more appropriate to the diversity of the situations analysed: 'political temperament' (Siegfried), for example, or 'intellectual family' (Thibaudet). It is true that such expressions give a better idea of the orientation of parties such as the French Radicals or the various national versions of Christian democratic parties. Their disadvantage, however, is either to distinguish only in the broadest fashion between different groups (a left-wing temperament or a right-wing temperament), each of which may encompass several competing groups, or to lay so much emphasis upon the 'intellectual' element as to obscure the 'mixed' nature not only of the values but also of the interests promoted by the ideology.[5] Conscious though I am of the arbitrary nature of any classification of political parties, each of which possesses its own very individual history, I shall nevertheless now distinguish five major sets of parties: those representing liberalism, the conservatives, the wide spectrum of socialist parties, the Christian Democrats, and finally the 'land' parties (agrarians, regionalists, ecologists).

Liberalism

Liberalism in Europe can pride itself on a fine past and justly claim that Western democracy, in both its philosophy and its institutions, owes much to it. But precisely because the liberals have evolved the essentials of their original creed without managing to broaden the social bases of their support, their organized electoral power is now much reduced, even though their philosophy has by now penetrated the institutions and even the programmes of many of their rivals. It is difficult to determine the profile of a political group that is now much reduced despite its widespread influence.

The term 'liberal' first made its appearance in Spain at the beginning of the nineteenth century, when it was used to denote the promoters of the Cadiz Constitution of 1812. It then spread to Britain (through the writing of Bentham) and France, where men as diverse as Benjamin Constant and Chateaubriand flourished the torch of human liberties. But it was not until the mid-nineteenth century that the Whigs turned themselves into the Liberal Party, which remained powerful up until the First World War. In France, the liberals became influential under the July Monarchy[6] and during the Third Republic. In Italy, the liberals played a crucial role in the construction of the unified Italian State.

In the nineteenth century what all liberals shared was their hostility to the notion of absolute monarchy, their defence of individual liberties, and the stand that they took on broadening the basis of suffrage. In other words, the liberals favoured a constitutional system of government that would guarantee both individual liberties and property within the framework of a political system that was both moderate and balanced. However, beyond this consensus on general principles, liberals were divided over the methods, scope, and pace of reform. There were 'conservative' liberals, whose aims went no further than to protect the interests of the bourgeoisie for which they spoke (the Orleanists in France, for example); 'radical' liberals, hostile to all forms of monarchy, who had emerged from the republican movements of France and Italy in particular; and anti-clerical liberals, wherever the Church had become identified with the most reactionary forces, as in France and Italy. Whether gathered into a single political formation or divided into several parties with different names, the liberal movement has always been weakened by the internal tension between change (liberties, suffrage) and conservatism (property). Herriot's description, 'heart on the left, wallet on the right', sums up the dilemma of liberals of all kinds, and also the contradictions within the bourgeois classes from which their members are mostly drawn. Today, having failed to reconstitute their social bases and win over new social strata, the liberal parties of Europe are everywhere divided or weakened. But that does not mean that their influence is by any means negligible.

In West Germany, the small liberal party (FDP) certainly plays an essential role, as is shown by the fact that it has shared power continuously except from 1957 to 1961 (when the CDU–CSU had an absolute majority) and from 1966 to 1969 (when there was a grand SPD–CDU–CSU coalition). The FDP emerged from the reconciliation of its two branches, the left and the right (into which it had split during the Weimar Republic). The source of its influence and of its weakness too lies in what has been called its 'original sin in the face of power'. The constant temptation to share power multiplies the rifts and dissidences that undermine it, but at the same time gives it a strength and an influence quite disproportionate to its size. Due to the peculiar mechanisms of the German polling system, the FDP tends to hold the balance of power in German politics. Although its committed supporters are believed to constitute barely 3 per cent of the electorate (below the fateful 5 per cent barrier), it sometimes polls over 10 per cent (as in January 1987), due to deserters from other parties, who are anxious to check the influence of their radical wings (the SPD left or the CSU). Despite the many phases of its evolution and the undeniable changes that have taken place within it, the FDP is still characterized by a number of fundamental features: a policy of openness towards the East; marked reservations over too close an association between Church and State (particularly in the area of education); a hostility towards interventionist or 'socialist' economic policies (such as mixed management); and an unwavering support for personal liberties and State constitutionality. In short, over and above its incidental ups and downs and its sporadic adaptations to passing fashions and fleeting alliances, the FDP is doing its best as a custodian of liberal patrimony.

In Italy, the liberal position is less rosy.[7] There, in the aftermath of Fascism and the Second World War, liberals failed to find themselves a satisfactory position between the left (Socialists and Communists) and the Christian Democrats. The conditions in which the political parties came into being in Italy, particularly the Pope's interdiction against Catholics accepting political responsibilities (more or less effective up until 1919), thwarted the emergence of a great liberal or conservative party that could represent the interests of the bourgeoisie. Furthermore, the liberals in Italy are split into two parties, neither of which carries much weight: the so-called Liberal Party itself (PLI) and the Republican Party. Given that within the socialist family the PSDI is, despite its title, more democrat than socialist, Italian liberalism certainly appears very divided. After the war, the PLI became the heir to Giolittian liberalism rooted, particularly in the south, upon its control over clienteles. However, having failed to seize the reins of central power, the PLI was soon forced to give way to the Christian Democrats in the south and attempt to recapture votes in northern and central Italy by approaching economic circles and reinforcing its links with businessmen. Its relations with the Christian Democrats were thus uneasy despite the fact that, from 1948 on, it frequently shared power with them in coalition governments. Such relations were against both the economic interventionism of the left-wing Christian Democrats (the nationalization of electricity, for example) and also the special relations with the Church. Meanwhile, the Republican Party, for its part, stood for republicanism and an attachment to the secular values of an enlightened bourgeoisie which rejected the philosophies of both the Socialists and the Christian Democrats, even if the necessity for coalitions meant that it sometimes shared power with one or other of those parties. The Republicans, who maintain close links with business circles but at the same time are firm defenders of a liberal and secular Republic, attract no more than 3 to 4 per cent of the vote. But it is significant that their stronghold should be Lombardy, especially Milan, where the impact of history tends to combine with economic interests.

The British Liberals were initially the most influential, then—up until quite recently—the most disadvantaged of all the European liberals. Not that their electoral strength is by any means derisory: after a long period out in the cold from 1931 to the 1970s (when their highest poll was 11.2 per cent in 1964), the Liberals won back a share of the electorate: 19.3 and 18.3 per cent in the two elections of 1974, 13.8 per cent in 1979, 25.4 per cent in conjunction with their Social Democrat allies in 1983. But the electoral system of 'first past the post' on a single ballot reduced these fine results to a handful of seats in Parliament (14 and 13 in 1974, 11 in 1979, and 17 in 1983). The Liberal Party, active up until the First World War, was far harder hit by the extension of the suffrage in 1918 and the emergence of class division as the determining variable than by internal conflicts within the party and the clashes between Lloyd George and Asquith. But at an electoral level its decline—which was, however, by no means continuous—seemed impossible to arrest. However, the tensions in British society that have surfaced since the 1970s, producing reper-cussions inside both the major parties, have imbued the Liberal ideology with a new impetus expressed in three directions.[8] In the first place, British Liberals, faithful to their tradition of individualism, have tried to dilute the concentration of power at all levels. They propose shared management in industry and a federal structure for Britain. Secondly, they have rejected 'confrontation politics', that is to say the mechanisms and procedures that have set up and that perpetuate the two-party system: they therefore advocate electoral reform. Thirdly, they are campaigning for more openness towards the rest of the world on the part of the United Kingdom (greater support for the UN, encouragement for the Common Market, and freer trade).

Despite the diversity of their interests and their political fortunes, the European liberal parties clearly share a number of preoccupations: commitment to personal liberties and property, distrust of the State and its interventionism, and an inclination for open relations with the rest of the world, especially their European partners. And although they have not managed to set themselves up as majority parties, their political influence, whether in government or in opposition, is con-siderably stronger than might be supposed from their hold over the electorate. Although they have not been successful in renewing their social base, the parties that share liberal tendencies have managed to retain an important place in Western political systems, both through power-sharing and through their defence of an ideological inheritance that other political parties have to a large extent made their own.

The Conservative Parties

To delineate the conservative ideology, as defended by the conservative parties, is difficult for a number of reasons. In the first place, there are many conservative variants, all constantly evolving. Secondly, it is quite exceptional—and the important exception is Britain—for the conservative ideology to be purveyed by a single political party within a given political system.

The term 'conservative' appeared at the beginning of the nineteenth century, in reaction to the French Revolution. In 1817, Chateaubriand published a newspaper called *Le Conservateur*; and in 1835, Sir Robert Peel made his declaration of the 'Conservative Principles'. After that, the Tories became the Conservative Party. But Britain is virtually the only country where the Conservatives use that word to proclaim their identity. Everywhere else, particularly in France, the conservative tendency adopts a variety of other names. This is not—as might be imagined from the post-1945 ideological climate—because of a reluctance to identify with a discredited and unattractive banner. On the contrary, in the nineteenth century, some conservatives proudly proclaimed their support of counter-revolutionary values and were not afraid to attack liberals and radicals of every kind. The principal reason for the eclipse of the term 'conservative', particularly in France, lies in the split that developed among those faithful to the traditional values. The conservatives became divided in the first place over the extent of their commitment to the counter-revolutionary struggle, and secondly over the monarchist question. Alongside the Ultras, who followed the line of Bonald and De Maistre,[9] and the Ultramontanes, such as Lammenais,[10] the conservative tendency included many more moderate men (starting with Louis XVIII himself), who preferred compromise to the politics of confrontation, and conservative French gallicans, who were hostile to the sway of Rome. After 1830, the conservatives split into Legitimists and Orleanists, and the Second Empire further confused the situation, as it drew into the conservative camp some of the latter-day supporters and beneficiaries of Napoleon and the Revolution.

If the nineteenth-century conservatives in France and Spain were divided by the question of the monarchy, another rift was caused by the subject of relations between Church and State. In Italy, the Pope's interdiction forbidding Catholics to engage in political life (up to 1919) blocked the formation of a major conservative party. The right, in power from 1860 to 1876, was advantaged by the strict census rules that applied to suffrage and that made it possible for it to govern despite the fact that it was very much a minority group. The practice of 'transformism', adopted by Depretis, constituted a new metamorphosis of conservatism. Gramsci, in his study of the *Risorgimento*, analyses the phenomenon as follows:

> It is even fair to say that the whole of Italian political life from 1848 on . . . is characterized by transformism, that is to say by the formation of an increasingly broad ruling class within the framework that the moderates established after 1848 . . . through a progressive yet continuous absorption . . . of the more active individuals who had come either from allied groups or from opposed ones, that had previously appeared to be violent enemies.[11]

The creation of Don Sturzo's Popular Party and of the Christian Democratic Party after the war had the effect of confusing the situation still further, as this prevented the formation of a true conservative party. Today, for example, the Christian Democrats still constitute a composite group that it would be wrong to define as a purely Catholic party. Notwithstanding this ambiguity, Mario Caciagli feels justified in declaring that 'despite its own protestations and those from a few other quarters, the Christian Democrats have always constituted the Conservative party of modern Italy. In the past, that was by virtue of its history and the place it held. Today, it is as a result of its social basis and the interests that it represents and defends.'[12] Similar phenomena can be observed at the end of the German Empire and during the Weimar Republic, when the Centre Party served as a refuge for many Catholics; and also under the Fourth French Republic, when the MRP, the Independents, and the Gaullists shared the conservative vote between them.

Attitudes towards the question of the nation, and nationalism in all its successive forms, constitute another component of the conservative tendency and also a cause of its internal divisions. Some conservatives are naturally drawn towards the idea of a State that respects the intermediary groups that revolutionaries tend to destroy and that are threatened by those who favour centralization at all costs. This group has included not only the Ultras of 1815 but also the conservatives of the German states hostile to Prussian domination (for example, the German Hanover Party, which opposed Prussia's annexation of Hanover in 1866, and obtained nearly 40 per cent of the vote there in 1881), the activists of Action Française and the Vichy regime, and the

Italian Monarchists and Christian Democrats of 1945–6. On the other hand, circumstances can sometimes turn the vociferous partisans of a decentralized State into ardent nationalists: the right wing of the Italian Unità was Jacobin and nationalist in the same way that Bismarck was nationalist and Lincoln's Republicans were federalist. The British Conservatives were hostile to the independence of Ireland in the same spirit as that of the Bonapartists, who opposed provincial autonomy. Wars and defeats, colonial expeditions, and the subsequent disintegration of empires are all factors that upset usual classifications and usual allegiances. When the circumstances are sufficiently dramatic, the conservative nationalist tendency can transcend traditional political divisions. In 1870 and 1914, virtually, the whole of France became nationalist, supporting the tricolour, even at the risk of allowing itself to be seduced by the partisans of the *coup d'état* (Boulanger). Similarly, defeat (as in Germany), or the frustrations of victory combined with an economic crisis (as in Italy) sometimes exacerbate conservatism to the point where it favours dictatorship. The shock produced by decolonization in France produced other reclassifications: the most extreme wing of conservatism opposed de Gaulle by every means possible, not excluding the most violent.

Conservatism has also long been characterized by its attachment to private property and to the principle of authority and by its reservations regarding universal suffrage, whose development it blocked or slowed down until the beginning of the twentieth century. But here again, the conservative group may at certain times and in certain of its sections be divided by considerably more than mere questions of emphasis. In principle, conservatives are certainly hostile to State intervention and fiercely defend the right to property. But in none of the Western countries has that prevented them from adapting to the needs of the Welfare State. All the Western democracies devote between 35 and 50 per cent of GNP to public spending; nor has this situation been brought about solely by socialist or social democratic policies. De Gaulle was responsible for the post-war nationalizations and he practised interventionist policies in the 1960s; and in 1979 it was Valéry Giscard d'Estaing who completed the gradual nationalization of the steel industry.[13] In Italy, the Christian Democrats inherited Mussolini's legacy of State industry and continued to expand it considerably until the end of the 1960s. The same ambiguity pervades conservative attitudes towards authority at every level of society. In this respect, too, the conservative group is profoundly heterogeneous, for while it is natural for it to welcome the paternal but firm authority of moderates, some tendencies (monarchists) dream of an absolute form of authority, unshared or even dictatorial.

In the last analysis, conservatism is primarily characterized not so much by a fixed and homogeneous body of doctrine, but rather by a *state of mind*:[14] pessimism as regards the individual, hence the need for authority; distrust of the idea of progress, although conservatives have themselves often been the instruments of economic and social change (de Gaulle, Margaret Thatcher); pragmatism, which makes them willing to make adjustments to their principles; and the defence of interests that are judged to be fundamental, such as the rights of private enterprise and property. In countries where conservatism is organized as a single force, the ambiguities and contradictions of this way of thinking can be reconciled within the party itself (as in Britain and, to a lesser degree, Italy and West Germany, if one regards their respective Christian Democrat Parties as conservative parties). However, in countries where historical circumstances did not permit unification, conservatism finds expression in many factions that are sometimes deeply hostile to one another and that can only be brought to co-operate in exceptional circumstances: the Gaullists and the extreme right in France, for instance; and the Christian Democrats and the MSI (the neo-Fascist Italian Social Movement) in Italy.

Since the Second World War, however, ideological conflict within conservative parties has been largely on the wane, for a number of reasons. In the first place, the conservative parties are generally 'parties in office' which, if they are to act, are forced constantly to accept compromises and the 'legacy' of their opponents. Secondly, conservative parties are obliged by the relentless law of universal suffrage to go 'hunting' beyond the confines of their preferred preserves, namely the middle and lower bourgeoisie. Their electorate is—must be—popular too. There are workers who are conservative in France, as there are in West Germany, Italy, the United States, and Britain (the 'Tory' worker) and the party must win or keep their votes if it is to avoid defeat. Finally, in the absence of any fixed doctrine, conservatism tends to be opportunistic, taking in whoever or whatever may be useful to it in the prevailing circumstances and the spirit of the moment. What would have been unthinkable in the nineteenth century—an alliance between liberals and conservatives, for instance—is commonplace today and the frequent practice of coalition government renders the ideological doctrines of political parties in general and the conservatives in particular more fragile and more fluid. During the 1950s, in Britain, this pragmatism was dubbed 'Butskellism'. In the 1970s and 1980s it was, however, replaced by a return to ideology, chiefly under the influence of the New Right. The neo-conservatives, whose torch-bearers have been or are Ronald Reagan and Margaret Thatcher, have been emulated more or less everywhere, including France, where Jacques Chirac, as late as 1976, was claiming to speak for 'French-style Labour'. The common denominator is criticism of the all-pervading tentacles of the State. But the battle is only waged against one particular section of the State, the part which initiates intervention in the economic sphere and social matters. In contrast, the policing part of the State is more than ever called upon in the name of security, both internal and external. This return to the principles of the old conservatives is often more a matter of words than of deeds, but it nevertheless reflects the ideological evolution of Western societies concerning the role and place of the Welfare State.

The Christian Democrats

The Christian democratic parties are not exclusively Catholic (the CDU is a mixture of Protestants and Catholics and the Scandinavian Christian democratic parties are essentially Protestant in inspiration). Nevertheless, it is undeniably in predominantly Catholic countries (Belgium, Italy, West Germany, and France) that the Christian democrats are most firmly anchored.[15] But the birth and development of Christian democratic parties are themselves conditioned by other elements in the political picture, in particular by the existence of liberal or radical parties that constitute a direct threat to the Church and the Catholics. In this respect, the total failure of the Christian democrats in post-Franco Spain is remarkable, as is the fact that they are completely absent from Ireland, where all the parties proclaim their allegiance to the Church. As we have noted in our discussion of conservative ideology, since the 1960s particularly many overlaps have developed between conservative and Christian democratic doctrines. Christian democrats and conservatives may find themselves in agreement in a number of respects: pessimism as to human nature, attachment to the right of property, to non-extremist groups, and to the authority of those legitimately invested with it (heads of families, etc.). There is nothing surprising about this doctrinal agreement. Quite apart from the fact that the Catholic Church itself took up position in the die-hard conservative camp throughout the nineteenth century, the conservatives in part found their inspiration in the precepts of religion, whose natural defenders they considered themselves to be. 'The compact between throne and altar' was no mere figure of rhetoric. Nevertheless, the European Christian democratic movement was born from a twofold 'dissidence': first, towards the most hardened conservatives, who were totally unresponsive to the 'social question'; secondly, towards the Church itself, which was initially hostile to the formation of Catholic political parties which would collaborate in the establishment of a democracy. For democracy was itself condemned as one of the 'errors of our times' by a whole succession of popes up until Leo XIII. In 1832, Gregory XVI, naming no names, condemned Lammenais together with all those who 'under the cover of religion are everywhere attempting to ignite the flames of innovation and revolution'. It is true that, in 1892, Leo XIII, in his encyclical 'In the Midst of Solicitudes', recommended that French Catholics should accept the Republic, but papal support for socially involved Catholics continued to be extremely measured, as is attested by Pius XI's condemnation of both Action Française and the movement of Marc Sangnier, who founded the Popular Democratic Party. The papacy continued for a long time to attempt to dissuade Catholics from taking an active part in politics, trying to persuade them, instead, to concern themselves solely with charitable works. It was only out of necessity (for the Church was losing influence) and because the experience of the German Zentrum had not proved altogether negative (the Centre Party had, after all, made it possible to put up some resistance to the *Kulturkampf* and the persecutions of Bismarck) that the Pope made a few concessions: in the elections held before 1914, a few Catholic candidates came forward (winning 4 per cent of the vote in 1909 and 6 per cent in 1913), but it was not until after the First World War that Don Sturzo was allowed to launch himself fully into politics, provided he agreed to a division of tasks: Catholic Action, placed under the authority of the Pope, would be responsible for providing a social and religious framework for Catholics; meanwhile, the party would organize them, more autonomously, on the political level.

The conditions in which the Christian democratic parties made their appearance and the strong influence of Church doctrine certainly explain some features of Christian democratic ideology and policies. But it cannot be denied that, as they have evolved, these parties have considerably modified their original exclusive orientation.

One characteristic feature of Christian democratic ideology is a forthright rejection of the extreme doctrines put forward by capitalism on the one hand and Marxism on the other. Both represent forms of materialism that run counter to the unswerving teaching of the Church. It was characteristic of their desire to establish a distance from both types of materialism that the title given to the programme that the CDU elaborated in 1947 should be 'CDU überwindet Kapitalismus und Marxismus' (the CDU outdoes capitalism and Marxism). The 1945–6 programmes of the Italian Christian Democrats and the French MRP were inspired by a similar distrust. The position that they adopted reflected the hierarchy of Christian democratic values inspired by Church doctrines: the spiritual comes before the material and economics should be put to the service of mankind. It is on this basis that the Christian democrats dissociate themselves from the conservatives, for whom social interests take second place to the dictates of the economy. This Christian democratic order of priority had a number of concrete political consequences, particularly after the Second World War: policies favouring families and economic planning in France; support for craftsmen, shopkeepers, and small-scale farmers in Italy; and a policy of shared management in the mining sector and the steel industry in West Germany were all products of that humanist and social conviction. But the Christian democrats could not maintain their position of equidistance from capitalism and communism for long. The post-war success of the Christian democrats stemmed as much from the collapse of the traditional right-wing parties, ostracized after the fall of the authoritarian regimes of Italy, France, and Germany, as it did from the intrinsic appeal of the new political groups themselves. No doubt they did constitute the party for Christians, but they also spoke for the moderate right. The Christian democratic parties were, from the start, torn between, on the one hand, those doctrines that distanced them from the right and, on the other, their electorate, which was more conservative than the party leaders. Those that remained more faithful to their ideals than to the tendencies of their voters, such as the MRP in France, paid the price for doing so. First they were weakened, then they collapsed. In contrast, with the Cold War playing into their hands, the CDU–CSU and the Christian Democrats in Italy succeeded in playing down their initial anti-capitalism and became converted to the market economy (now conveniently renamed 'the social market economy' in West Germany, where it was represented by Ludwig Erhard, an enthusiastic proponent of economic liberalism).

The second characteristic of the Christian democratic movement is the importance that it attaches to the values of education and morality. For a long time, Christian democratic parties were expected to adopt the Catholic Church's position on such matters (the Protestant Churches meanwhile took a more liberal line), and this no doubt delayed their secularization. In West Germany, Italy, and France, the pressure for denominational teaching remained considerable and the ways in which it was organized and financed and the manner in which it functioned often provoked violent conflict. Compromise solutions on the issue of relations between Church and State were not found until relatively late in the day and were frequently a source of acrimony in political life. The Fourth French Republic was in a constant state of agitation over the schools controversy, which was not resolved until 1958. But between 1981 and 1984, the country was shaken by new upheavals on this issue, a clear enough indication that the battle over schools was now a clash no longer between Catholics and the State, but between the right and the left. In West Germany, up until the late 1960s and despite the Concordat of 1933, there were many clashes in the *Länder* on account of their responsibility for educational policies, and not until 1983 did religious instruction become optional in Italian schools.

Family and moral questions were also for many years central to Christian democratic doctrine: marriage, divorce, contraception, and abortion were so many areas where Church law became Christian democratic programme. Only gradually did some Christian democrats come round to the idea that personal religious convictions should be kept separate from the party programme. As in the sphere of economic matters, the change was a product of necessity, that is to say it was brought about by constraints that stemmed from the changing nature of the electorate. Despite its massive official religious affiliations (about 90 per cent of Italians, Germans, and French Christian democrats belonged to either the Catholic or the Protestant religions), regular church-goers constituted only a small minority (10–15 per cent). The rest were less and less receptive to papal teaching and the Christian democratic parties were obliged to adapt to their voters.

Legislation on contraception and abortion and less stringent divorce procedures were introduced in France by governments that included 'centre' politicians from Christian democratic parties; and in Italy, the same reforms were brought about, willy-nilly, by governments that were dominated by the Christian Democrats. It is true that in Italy the reforms were carried out somewhat reluctantly and many Christian Democrat Deputies first opposed them in Parliament and subsequently insisted upon a referendum in the hope of repealing them. However, the result was disastrous for the Christian Democrats. When the referendum on divorce was held in 1974, those in favour of repealing the law (the Christian Democrats and the MSI) obtained no more than 40.7 per cent of the vote although the Christian Democrats, on their own, had ever since 1963, been oscillating around the 39 per cent mark. The collapse of Christian Democratic support showed that a proportion of the 'secularized' bourgeois electorate now preferred to vote for a small secular party rather than for a conservative 'Catholic' party. The Christian Democrat Party was faced with a crucial choice: should it be a Catholic party, a party of and for Catholics, or a moderate conservative one? In this respect, as in the economic domain, the Christian democratic parties moved closer to the conservatives. Indeed, it could be said that in the countries where they dominate a large section of the political spectrum, that is, Italy and Germany in particular, they have, under the pressure of circumstances, become *the* conservative party.

Finally, the post-Second World War Christian democratic parties have been resolutely European. Perhaps the fact that their leaders belonged to a supranational Church and their common faith made them readier than others to overstep nation state boundaries. At all events, it was undeniably men such as De Gasperi, Adenauer, and Schumann who were the builders of Europe, 'Vatican Europe' as the Communists stigmatized it in the 1950s. This is probably also the domain in which the Christian Democrats have been the most tenacious. For example, the MRP and its various centre-party emulators have tolerated a great deal and accepted many compromises, but they have always remained adamantly in favour of European unity.

The Divided Left

The birth of socialism in Europe in the nineteenth century marked a new departure in the relationship of political parties to voters and institutions and also in their relations between one another. Socialist parties claimed to work for one particular class, the working class, and they took up the struggle against bourgeois institutions, organized themselves into an 'International', and consigned both the liberals and the radicals, considered until then the 'revolutionaries', to the camp of the supporters of the established order. For many liberal parties, the advance of the socialist parties was to spell decline, even obliteration. Yet, initially, the main strength of the socialist parties came not from their militancy or their parliamentary representation—which until the turn of the century remained quite derisory; rather, it lay in their programmes' destabilizing effects upon the bourgeois monarchies and republics of the late nineteenth century. Nevertheless, the socialists, the 'reds', the 'sharers' (*partageurs*), and the other 'communards' were, from the start, divided by their own internal quarrels and their constant clashes over ideology and policies at both international and national level.

This was principally because of the large number both of key doctrines and of founding fathers of different *kinds* of socialism: the 'utopian communism' of men such as Proudhon and Fourier and the reformism of Louis Blanc and Pierre Leroux in France were opposed by the vigorous critical analyses of Marx and Engels, who were propounding a scientific socialism. The 1848 *Manifesto* was not simply a revolutionary proclamation; it was also a condemnation of all the forms of socialism that Marx and Engels deemed worthy of rejection. For they also condemned Lasalle's state socialism (see *The Critique of the Gotha Programme* (1875)) on the grounds that it compromised with nationalism and with the bourgeois State (particularly in the creation of production companies controlled by the proletariat but dependent on State aid). Their condemnation of Bakunin and the anarchists was even stronger: they were guilty of attacking the State without first tackling the causes which brought it into being and which continued to justify its existence (capitalist accumulation). Over and above these early clashes and the excommunications that tore socialism apart, we should take into account the many individual modes in which social-ism took hold in the various countries and the manner in which Marxist theories became known there. Germany and France present two strongly contrasting examples of the reception that Marxism received from local socialists. In Germany, the thought of Marx and Engels was widely diffused and discussed, due to the unified Social Democrat Party created in 1875, and also through Karl Kautsky and

Rosa Luxemburg. In France, on the other hand, it became known much later and even then only in a limited fashion (very few editions and translations into French were published before the end of the century). In the hands of the Guesdistes, it was, furthermore, transformed into an often simplistic and doctrinaire vulgate. The situation was compounded by the many factions into which socialism had split in France, for it was not until 1905 that they were belatedly drawn together in the SFIO. Jaurès had to pay the price for this unification, and claimed that he too derived his inspiration from Marxism, but this was more a matter of convenience than of true conviction. Far from easing these tensions, the 1917 Revolution exacerbated them throughout Europe. When the Third International was formed under the aegis of Lenin, it produced a deep and lasting split among socialists, dividing them into reformist socialists on the one hand, and communists hostile to the bourgeois order and committed to Moscow on the other.

At the level of organizations designed to rally the working-class masses, the contrasts are equally striking. As early as 1890, the powerful German SPD won 1,400,000 votes and 35 seats in the Reichstag and could muster 120,000 trade unionists (by 1905, it had 40,000 party activists). In France and Italy, on the other hand, socialist movements were unco-ordinated at both the political and the trade union levels. The Italian Socialist Party did not take shape until 1891, the SFIO not until 1905, and the trade unions did not organize themselves into a confederation until 1906 in France (the CGT), and 1907 in Italy (the Confederazione Generale Italiana del Lavoro: the CGIL). Furthermore, political structures and party organization remained separated by a wide gulf. In France, the Amiens Charter officially rejected setting up links between the trade unions and the party (in contrast to the situation of British trade unionism).

In Britain, a workers' party was formed as a direct result of action taken by trade unionists. In 1899, the Trades Union Congress decided to set up a 'Labour Representation Committee'. It came into being in 1900 with the purpose of ensuring parliamentary representation for the workers by co-ordinating the various political groups: to wit, the Independent Labour Party (with 13,000 members), the Marxist Social Democratic Federation (with 9,000 members), and the Fabian Society which, despite its small membership (861 in 1900), had a huge intellectual impact on the constitution and doctrine of the party.

The socialist parties born at the beginning of the century, together with the Western communist parties, are certainly those that most strongly proclaim their commitment to an ideology, a doctrine, and a programme. But precisely because their ideological positions were the most uncompromising, their conflicts, crises, and histories have been the most dramatic. It would not be possible to describe the history and processes of evolution of socialist ideology in the limited space at our disposal. The most we can hope to do is sketch in the broad outlines of development in a few key areas such as the economy, access to power and the exercise of it, and internationalism.

In the domain of the economy developments have often been radical but they have varied from one country to another. In Britain, Clause 4 of the Labour Party's Constitution commits itself to seeking public ownership of the means of production and the 1945 party manifesto, 'Let us Face the Future', advocated the nationalization of all basic industries. Gaitskell, who regarded Labour's policy of nationalization as the cause of its string of defeats in 1951, 1955, and 1959, tried hard to 'modernize' the party Charter on this point.[16] But he was not successful. Despite the fact that the Labour Party was far less deeply penetrated by Marxist ideology than the German SPD, it did not manage to produce its own variant of the 'Bad Godesberg' SPD U-turn. Indeed, in that same year, 1959, the SPD accepted the lesson of its own successive failures, particularly that of 1957, and played down its nationalization policy, declaring open competition and enterprise to be essential elements in the economic policy of the Social Democrats.

The behaviour of the French Socialist Party that rose from the ashes of the SFIO and the clubs of the left in the 1960s was more hesitant. There can be no doubt that nationalization was only desired by the left wing of the party and many voters, activists, and leaders did not really consider that aspect of Socialist Party doctrine to be of fundamental importance. But two other considerations pushed the Socialist Party into the policy of large-scale nationalization that it eventually carried out in 1981–2. One was the tactical necessity to come to an agreement with the French Communist Party, which was determined to make nationalization the corner-stone and goal of any government of a united left. The second was the relative disregard—not to say lack of understanding—shown by most socialists towards the economy and the market. Not until 1983 did François Mitterrand voice praise for the mixed economy, not until 1984 did the process of gradual and partial denationalization begin, and it was 1985 before the Socialists, at the Toulouse Congress, qualified their choice of a State-administered economy. In Italy, both Socialists and Communists had moved towards a realistic acceptance of the mixed economy in a more pragmatic fashion and without making any radical changes to their programmes. In truth, the Christian Democrats' move into the public sector had made the advantages of a nationalized or State-controlled economy seem much more relative in the eyes of the left.

The question of access to power and the exercise of power is unquestionably one of the crucial points that for many years divided socialists from communists. For the socialists, winning power was a matter of legality and elections; for the communists, right up until the Second World War, participation in electoral competition to gain access to Parliament was motivated above all by a desire to subvert bourgeois institutions. Their ideal remained the revolution, as achieved by the model brother party of the Soviet Union.

The threat of Nazism and Fascism, and the Spanish Civil War changed the attitudes of Western communist parties, for they now learned a lesson from the socialists of Germany and Italy, who refused to collaborate with the bourgeois parties to oppose Hitler and Mussolini. The strategy of the Popular Front in France and Spain was adopted with the blessing of Stalin, who was becoming worried by the rising power of Nazi Germany. In 1936, Maurice Thorez proclaimed:

Perhaps History will declare that one of the great merits of the Communist Party in France is, to borrow Nietzsche's words, to have given all values a new value. We have readopted the Marseillaise and the banner of our forefathers, the soldiers of Year Two. We have readopted those verses on liberty . . . We have behaved as Marxists, rejecting dead slogans but retaining the living content that certain things, even legacies of the past, express.[17]

The Second World War and the Resistance made it possible for the Italian and French Communist parties to become integrated into new institutions by taking an active part in their creation and establishment. The French and the Italian parties both played active roles in government up until the 1947 crisis and the outbreak of the Cold War. At this point, the French Communists, despite having been the leading party under the Fourth Republic, and the Italian Communists, who constituted the country's second largest party, were kept out of central government as a result of what is known in Italy as the

conventio ad excludendum. Not until 1981 did French Communists
obtain a slight measure of representation in a government dominated
by Socialists. In Italy, the reintegration of the Communists came
about more indirectly and covertly, due to the Government of
National Unity of 1976 to 1979. The political crisis, by which the
Christian Democrats were particularly affected, and the conviction of
Berlinguer, the leader of the Italian Communist Party, that even with
a 51 per cent majority a government of the left would be unable to
survive and operate made it possible to initiate a system of 'non-
distrust'. The minority Christian Democrat Government was supported by the Italian Communist Party, which was consequently
informally involved in all government decisions. The strategy of
'historic compromise', the modern version of Italian-style 'transformism', set the seal on the Italian Communist Party's integration into the
system. Paradoxically enough, although officially excluded from
central power, the Italian Communist Party constitutes an essential
element in the Italian political panorama. With as much support as the
Christian Democrats and despite the crisis produced by the death of
its leader in 1984 and its persistent failure to win power, the Italian
Communist Party has managed to make itself and remain the first
party of the left, attracting almost 30 per cent of the vote.[18] Recently,
however, the Italian Socialist Party has been gaining ground under the
leadership of Craxi (winning nearly 15 per cent of the poll in 1987).
The two rival parties are now competing more fiercely than ever for
the leadership of the left. At its eighteenth Party Congress, held
in March 1989, the Italian Communist Party was forced, by the
crisis now affecting it, to adopt a programme of Social Democrat
inspiration.

The fact is that socialist parties of the social democratic type have
themselves by now evolved so far as to become viable government
parties. Not only have they been obliged to accept the rules of the
bourgeois constitutional game, they have also had to make their
doctrinal rhetoric and their political programmes credible in the eyes
of the public. The SPD was the first to engage in this kind of
ideological spring-cleaning, in 1959, declaring: 'From being the party
of the working class, the social democrat Party has become the party of
the people.' Although the SFIO in effect made a similar move in 1947,
when it rejected an alliance with the Communists, the French Socialists had much more difficulty in divesting themselves of language
inspired by Marxist jargon and a programme founded upon a break

with capitalism. During the 1960s, the Socialist Party in Italy similarly adopted strategies closer to those of the political centre, an approach which at times earned it the nickname of the 'neither–nor' party, although its decision to seek the middle way also won it the prestigious intellectual approval of the philosopher Noberto Bobbio, who wrote as follows: 'The Socialist Party is a median party, that is, a classic party of coalition, be it with the right, the left or the centre, either in government or in opposition. Like it or not, a median party is a coalition party, that is, it can only make its influence felt by entering into a coalition.'[19] The SPD, which in 1987 was hoping to acquire an absolute majority on its own but failed, and which refused then to ally itself with the Greens, might do well to apply that analysis to itself, as might the French S.F.I.O. which, after its split with the French Communist Party, cannot for long put off the prospect of alternative alliances. As we have seen, the logic of institutions has effected one change in the ideology of socialist—and even communist—parties; the logic that must apply to 'government parties' prompts further evolution, no doubt fraught with difficulties. This is shown by the case of the Italian Communist Party which, having abandoned the principle of dictatorship by the proletariat together with most of its Leninist doctrine, has by now even reached the point of turning into a social democratic party.

One distinctive feature of the socialist movements was the way in which, from the outset, they banded together to form a workers' International. The First International was created in London, in 1864, when the International Association of Workers was set up. But constant clashes with the supporters of Proudhon, Mazzini, and above all Bakunin caused Marx to transfer the association's headquarters to New York in 1872. The disintegration of the First International made it possible to set up the Second International in 1889, marking the centenary of the French Revolution. But although these associations were based upon the idea that 'proletarians do not have a country' and that nationalism was a product of bourgeois culture, they foundered utterly when the First World War broke out. Numerous pacifist moves were initiated but they were a total failure as the French, British, and Belgian socialists refused to sit down at the same table as the German ones. The informal conference held at Zimmerwald in Switzerland in 1915 was also a failure, although its delegates did agree to refuse to follow the radical line defended by Lenin (namely, that of 'turning this war into a civil war'). The Second International managed to survive despite the divisions that appeared between socialists, along lines defined by the belligerent States, and also the internal rifts caused by some of the individual choices made by its members. (For example, Mussolini was excluded from the Socialist Party on the grounds of his ardent support for Italy's entry into the war, after having earlier been an equally determined pacifist.)

However, all this dissension certainly heralded future rifts. In 1920 and 1921, Blum with his followers in France and Turati with his in Italy were excluded by the party's left wing, which remained faithful to Lenin and the Soviet Communist Party. Relations between the socialist and the communist parties in Europe were appalling up until the Second World War: the German Communists fought mercilessly against their former SPD comrades, sometimes even going so far as to join forces with Nazi groups. Up until 1934, the French Socialists were similarly dragged through the mud, being denounced as 'social Fascists'; and the post-war period of reconciliation that followed was also short-lived. The outbreak of the Cold War revived the atmosphere of hatred, mutual insults, and dirty tricks. The CGTU split into the CGT, of Communist allegiance, and the reformist CGT-FO, which was close to the Socialists. Nenni's refusal to burn the bridges between the Socialist Party and the Italian Communist Party in 1947 resulted in Saragat's departure to form a dissident Social Democrat Party, the PSDI.

The Second International had been powerless to prevent nationalistic rifts. The Third International then proceeded to split the socialist movement definitively into social democrats on the one hand and communist parties on the other. A true International, which would certainly override national divisions, did exist, but not so much for the benefit of the world-wide working class as for that of a pitiless and unprincipled dictatorship.

Not until the 1970s did the links of Western Communist parties with Moscow begin to loosen. It took no less than the repression in Berlin and Budapest, the Khrushchev report, the invasions of Czechoslovakia and Afghanistan, and further repression both in Poland and elsewhere to undermine that mechanical alignment of all brother communist parties. The attempt that the Italian, Spanish, and French Communists made to create a 'Euro-communism' hung fire, faced with Moscow's hostility and as a result of the unequal determination of the three parties involved in this strategy for autonomy. By the late 1970s and the 1980s the scene varied greatly from one country to another. In Spain and France, the Communist parties have collapsed, but the Italian Communist Party remains powerful due to developments of both an internal and an external nature which have brought it closer and closer to being a social democratic party.

Meanwhile, the socialist parties have managed, by dint of adapting their ideology, to quit their role of eternal opposition and to become government parties (in Italy, Spain, Austria, and Greece). The socialist and social democratic parties of Western Europe are also loosely bound together in a Socialist International (which, apart from its name, has very little in common with the early Internationals). They have become the defenders and engineers of the kind of democracy that their fathers used to deride. As for the heirs to the original socialism, now as then they are divided and weak: the limited number of activist troops of the extreme left throughout Europe has not deterred them from indulging in esoteric and sectarian squabbles. Their intellectual influence has been by no means negligible for all that, particularly in the late 1960s and the 1970s. But hardly anywhere, neither in West Germany, nor in France, nor in Britain, has the extreme left been able to overcome the obstacles of electoral legislation and win parliamentary representation. Italy is the only country where, because of an extremely proportionalist electoral system, it has been possible for representatives of this kind of socialism, which is supported more by intellectuals than by the working class, to find a place at Montecitorio (the seat of the Chamber of Deputies).

The 'Land' Parties: Regionalists and Ecologists

Regionalist parties and ecologists differ on many counts, by reason of their ideologies, how they are organized, where they are based, and their political and electoral influence, but they have one essential point in common: their interest is centred almost exclusively upon a *single* problem (they are single-issue parties) and all other questions are perceived from that angle and treated in relation to it. Furthermore, both regionalists and ecologists are interested in defending not so much individuals but rather the land, with a view to protecting either its cultural or its natural attributes. In both cases it is a matter of salvaging an identity threatened either by other more powerful cultures and élites or by economic development that is regarded as destructive.

The European regionalist parties are concerned with the survival of minorities within the nation states, particularly where the State in question has already been established for several centuries and the nationalities that it has absorbed have been so thoroughly integrated that only a few subsidiary pockets of resistance survive. It is true that the great empires were dismantled initially in the nineteenth century and then again following the First World War, in the name of the principle of nationality, but the new map of Europe created at least as many problems concerning minorities as it resolved ones concerning 'nationality'. The Second World War introduced a new batch of territorial tensions, and the manner of their resolution was in many cases brutal: consider the massive displacement of peoples and the rigid domination of the Soviet Union in Eastern Europe. The political problem of regionalism was thus an essentially Western one; and it was a particularly marked feature of the 1960s and 1970s. The phenomenon took all observers by surprise and many analyses and explanations have been produced to account for it. The first point to note is that the regionalist phenomenon affected almost all the countries of Western Europe, especially Spain, Belgium, Britain, Italy, and France, but the ways in which it found political expression varied considerably. In some places, regionalist parties are non-existent or insignificant yet electoral behaviour is or has been parochial (e.g. the Christian Democrat vote in Alsace and Brittany); in others, in contrast, political parties are organized on a specifically regional rather than national basis (as in Belgium). Between these two extremes, many intermediate situations are possible, such as those where regionalist parties have either acquired a dominant position (as in the Alto-Adige, the Valley of Aosta, and the Basque region) or else are at least competitive (Scotland, Corsica).

Thus, regionalist ideology may be expressed by political parties but, given their electoral weakness in most cases, is not expressed solely by them. Virtually everywhere, the regionalist parties are minority parties: invariably so at a national level, and frequently also at a regional or even local level. However, the electoral impact of these minority parties does not provide a fair reflection of the influence of the regionalist ideology in most European countries. This ideology has varied considerably from one period to another and often differs profoundly from one country to another. In France, regionalism remained, up until the 1950s, a right-wing movement, frequently reactionary in character, and certainly nostalgic for past forms of culture, economy, and administration. But, with the passing of time, the regionalist movement has become more radical, sometimes adopting the language and methods of action of the left or the extreme left, identifying with more or less Marxist doctrines, so that it has eventually convinced the parliamentary left that regionalism amounts to more than just a struggle on the part of reactionary country yokels. The themes of 'internal colonialism' and 'dependence' were taken up in both France and Britain, where part of the Scottish and Welsh nationalist movements adopted a radical position as they began to express the views of certain intellectual strata and sections of the urban middle classes. In Italy, regionalism stands for something rather different. In 1946–7, the Christian Democrats regarded it as a democratic 'guarantee' that would stand in the way of the extreme kind of centralization that tends to foster dictatorships; but when they gained power, their attitude soon changed. Now it was the left, in particular the Italian Communist Party, that laid claim to pockets of regional power, in order to oppose the Christian Democrat hegemony. Furthermore, regionalism took on a quite distinctive character in the three frontier regions (the Valley of Aosta, the Alto-Adige, and the Friuli–Veneto–Julian Alps region) and the two islands (Sardinia and Sicily) that still possess marked linguistic, cultural, and economic identities.

During the 1970s, observers pondered upon the roots of regionalist ideology and also the reasons for its success. Many factors were suggested but none provided a general explanation: neither language, nor religion, nor culture, nor economic underdevelopment can on their own account for the birth of the regionalist ideology. To do so, any analysis of these factors needs to be complemented by a number of observations. First, through the emphasis that it lays on defending a particular territory, a regionalist ideology has a 'catch-all' character. Secondly, generally speaking, regionalist ideology has developed from the conjunction of two factors: on the one hand the existence of a particular identity (in some instances cultural, in others religious, in others economic), on the other an upheaval that affects the economic and social structures. These social changes, whether negative (an economic crisis) or positive (change and growth), often constitute the stimulus that triggers a series of regional claims and the development of a more or less widely diffused regional ideology. Regionalism may, in this way, become one of the best ways of promoting a number of different interests on a territorial basis. Regionalist ideology often smacks to some extent of indiscrimination, but despite—or perhaps because of—that eclecticism, the considerable success that it has enjoyed in Europe is quite remarkable. Today, most of the countries of Western Europe[20]—with the exception of Britain—are to some extent regionalized, even though (except in Belgium) their national parliaments incorporate no more than a handful of regionalists.

A similar mixture of conservative and radical ideologies is to be found among the ecologists. In this group, both voters and activists are drawn from a diverse ideological spectrum that includes attitudes ranging from disillusioned Marxism to a nostalgia for right-wing ruralism.[21] Furthermore, an element of protest is undeniably important to the ecology movement. Ecologism involves first and foremost the rejection of all modes of development that destroy the natural environment, and all technological decisions that are considered to endanger both the planet and the human race, such as the adoption of nuclear power. Only more latterly and in a secondary fashion have ecologist groups ventured into domains that were not initially theirs. Both the logic of political struggle and the character of various militant groups that have joined the movement have tended to render it more radical and both have, at the same time, given rise to many internal quarrels. The ecologists have broadened the base of their aims and have adopted many proposals emanating from minority groups and post-materialistic tendencies. Anti-militarism, respect for minorities, human rights, the fight against racism, and feminism are all causes that ecology movements have taken up or supported. It is particularly interesting to note that in Italy it is the Radical Party that adopts all these causes (although it did not initially show any particular interest in ecology), whereas in Germany it is the Greens who champion the values of the 'post-industrial society'.[22] These are the two countries where the ecologists' protest movement has acquired considerable importance, in West Germany under their own banner, in Italy in conjunction with the active Radical Party. On the other hand, up until the local and European elections in 1989, the ecology movement had not managed to take hold either in France[23] or in Britain, despite the fact that these are the two most 'nuclearized' States in Europe, at both the civil and the military levels. In both countries, the ecologists' share of the poll has been minimal and their parliamentary representation non-existent. However, as in the case of the regionalists, their impact has been by no means negligible. In Europe, as in the United States, ecology is now an item on the political agenda[24] and the ecologists have succeeded in more than just defending their own ideology. They have managed to diffuse it widely, albeit in a watered-down form, and to ensure that all party organizations and governments take it seriously.

THE INSTITUTIONALIZATION AND ORGANIZATION OF THE PARTIES

Political parties are now part of the Western 'political scene', indeed one of its essential elements. A democratic system without political parties or with a single party is impossible—or at any rate hard—to imagine. But this was not always the case, for initially political parties were considered to undermine democracy and were suspected of being either divisive (where parties = factions) or hardly in keeping with the democratic ideal (where parties = oligarchies). A dominant phenomenon of today, however, is the *institutionalization* of the political parties as powerful *organizations* that seek to monopolize mediation between the governed and those who govern.

The Institutionalization of the Parties

There are several aspects of the concept of party institutionalization. From a sociological point of view, it involves transforming associations that are structured to a greater or lesser degree into genuine organizations that are managed with a view to winning and exercising political power. This kind of institutionalization implies a combination of 'objective' elements (the parties being firmly established as institutions) and 'subjective' ones (acceptance of the parties, recognition of their legitimacy). From a more juridical point of view (inspired mainly by the ideas of Kelsen), institutionalization involves recognition for the political parties and their constitutional integration within the political system.

In his study of political parties, Janda establishes the degree of a party's institutionalization on the basis of three parameters: its age, the depersonalization of its organization, and its organizational differentiation. He investigates fifty or so countries and 158 parties considered to be representative of all the different parties noted throughout the world. It emerges from his study that the degree of a party's institutionalization depends firstly upon its age, which, in its turn, is connected with the development and age of the State in which it exists and that State's institutions. It is, then, not surprising that two of the most fully institutionalized parties turn out to be the American Democratic Party (founded in 1828) and the British Conservative Party (founded in 1832). In contrast, the French parties became institutionalized relatively late in the day (more or less at the dawn of the twentieth century), as if the instability of France's political institutions had delayed or prevented the organization of the various groups even though they had been clearly identifiable throughout the nineteenth century. The relatively long-standing institutionalization of some of the political parties of the Western democracies has another, negative consequence for party organizations of more recent date: it makes it difficult for new party organizations, not so much to emerge, but to develop, as they strive to find a place for themselves in the political spectrum. Only rarely do new parties manage to win places in parliament and even more rarely do they survive there. In the United States, third parties are excluded from the political game, and the European States have been almost as unwelcoming toward them. Few of the new parties that have attempted to take hold have been successful: the National Front in France, the Greens in West Germany, and the Radical Party in Italy are rare examples of parties that have succeeded in overcoming the institutional and political barriers. But even they have not been able to end the domination of the older political formations (the European parties are often products of two great revolutionary periods: 1787–9 in the United States and France and 1917 in the Soviet Union).

In truth, the only 'new' parties to be found on the political map have resulted either from transformations of earlier declining political formations or from the reunification of groups split asunder in the past by some political crisis or other. In this respect, it is in France that the party system has undergone the most fundamental recomposition, by very reason of the low level of institutionalization there in the past. Up to the 1980s the various manifestations of Gaullism facilitated the formation of a vast movement incorporating all the components of the authoritarian right. In contrast, the UDF has so far produced no more than an undisciplined federation of various liberal and centre-right sects. As for the Socialist Party, it has become the leading French political party by dint of building upon the ruins of the 'old firm', the SFIO, and by federating the many organizations of the nebulous 'New Left' (ranging from the PSU to the clubs of the Convention of Republican Institutions).

There is a second criterion for assessing the institutionalization of a political party: depersonalization. It is a point that Monica and Jean Charlot have emphasized:

This indubitably constitutes an essential condition for the continuity of an organization, to the extent that it allows it to outlive the lifespan of its founder, however prestigious he may be. Until a party (or any association) has surmounted the crisis of finding a successor to its founder, until it has drawn up rules of succession that are legitimate in the eyes of its members, its "institutionalization" will remain precarious'.[25]

In this respect, the Gaullist party provides a rare example of recent institutionalization for a major political party in the West. Its survival and force are the more remarkable in view of the fact that, at the outset, the 'party' consisted of no more than a vast 'gathering' cemented together by the personality of General de Gaulle. Once over the periods of uncertainty occasioned first by the political retirement, than by the death of the founder of the Fifth Republic, the Gaullist party, under the leadership of Jacques Chirac, managed to turn itself into a powerful party machine.[26]

Thirdly, the institutionalization of a political party depends upon how successfully it is organized as an instrument for mobilizing political support and winning power. In most Western countries there exists no *ad hoc* structure specially designed for political parties, so these tend to take shape within the legal frameworks that cater for other organizations, that is, associations generally. But the particular category of the political parties does possess specific organizational characteristics, both as regards means (the recruitment of activists, party organization, the selection of candidates at election time) and as regards methods. A political party is different from a simple association, a group with common interests or a club, although it may borrow or preserve some of the features of those types of organization. Generally speaking, parties only survive if they can depend upon rigorous organization whose structures are defined in relation to particular ends and needs. The so-called parties that fail to set up such organizational systems are bound to vanish. The party of l'Uomo Qualunque in Italy (the Man-in-the-Street's party) after the Second

World War, the Refugee Party in West Germany, the Poujadiste party in France, were in reality no more than sectional protest organizations and all disappeared through want of being able or knowing how to turn themselves into true party organizations. This organizational element is developed to a greater or lesser degree in all the various Western States, but it is undoubtedly in the United States and France that it took the longest to evolve.

Although political parties have become an essential element of Western democracy, their existence is not always 'constitutionally recognized'. This was generally true of pre-war constitutions and remains so in countries such as the United States and Britain. However, many post-war democratic constitutions sought to give the political parties a constitutional status. The Constitutions of Germany and Italy and the Constitution of the Fifth French Republic (and equally the Spanish Constitution of 1978, the Portugese Constitution of 1976, and the Greek Constitution of 1975) all give political parties a status, a status that may be defined—albeit in imprecise terms—both negatively and positively. Furthermore, in these States, and also in those which do not explicitly recognize a constitutional status for political parties, ordinary laws and Supreme Court decisions have delineated the political parties' role and place within the political system.

The Italian Constitution was the first to move towards constitutional recognition for the political parties when it declared in Article 49: 'All citizens have the right to associate freely in parties so as to contribute, in accordance with the democratic method, towards the determining of national policies.' This somewhat elliptical formulation was the result of a laborious compromise between the various forces that had emerged together from the Resistance but did not share, for instance, a common vision of democracy. It was for this reason that the National Constituent Assembly rejected all amendments designed to impose 'the democratic method' in the *internal* as well as the external dealings of the parties. It was, of course, chiefly against the Communist Party, with its own particular set of rules, that such amendments were aimed. In 1958, the French Communist Party was the object of a similar amendment (also rejected) which attempted to ensure that 'the parties be obliged to respect the democratic principles contained in the Constitution'.

The German Constitution, on the other hand, was more insistent, but such differences can be explained by the political contexts peculiar to each system: whereas France and Italy had to take into consideration powerful Communist Parties, which respectively represented close on one-quarter and one-third of the electorate, West Germany sought to guard against the Communist Party, which was dominant in the Soviet zone, and also against the rebirth of a neo-Nazi party. Article 21 of the constitutional law of West Germany stipulates that the political parties' 'internal organization must correspond to democratic principles'.

The objectives attributed to the political parties also vary from one system to another. The most restrictive concept of these was that adopted by the Fifth French Republic—which is hardly surprising in a Constitution stamped with the seal of General de Gaulle. It declares that 'the parties aim to express the suffrage of the people'. In West Germany, their role is defined in a more ambitious manner: they 'co-operate to form the political will of the people'. Finally, the Italian parties are declared to help 'to determine national policies'—a formula which attributes to them an essential function close to that which Article 20 of the French Constitution allots to the government ('the government determines the policies of the nation'). As Pierre Avril points out, 'Herein lie the beginnings of a basis for a partitocratic state.'[27]

Another consequence of such constitutional stipulations is that, while parties may be freely created, they do not hold a monopoly over representation. The text of Article 49 of the Italian Constitution does not refer to parties *per se* ('All citizens have the right to associate . . .') and the text of the French Constitution mentions 'parties and political groups'. The text of the German Constitution might have given rise to a restrictive interpretation, but the Constitutional Court has always ensured that the parties of the Bundestag do not claim any monopoly and, in the law of 24 July 1967 on the political parties, 'party' is given a relatively wide definition. But while the law dispelled the shadowy zones of misunderstanding that might have been engendered by Article 21, at the same time it turned the parties into true public organizations (the Constitutional Court described them as *Staatsorgane* (organs of the State), whose structures, rules of functioning, and finance are all strictly controlled by the State.

Although the creation of political parties is, in principle, free in the European States, there are many restrictions and prohibitions. In some cases the restrictions are more or less symbolic (as, for example, in Article 4 of the 1958 French Constitution, which declares that parties 'must respect the principles of sovereignty and democracy'), but it may be that the more insidious they are, the more effective.

Over and above such more or less visible restrictions built into the political system, measures of a more severe nature may restrain the activities of the parties, even to the point of banning them. In France, the Republic has a long-standing 'Republican tradition' of banning parties hostile to the 'Republican form of government', a regime that a series of constitutions since the Third Republic have declared it to be impossible to revise. These prohibitions affect all associations that 'strike at the integrity of the [national] territory' and 'the Republican form of government' and they are sanctioned not only by the 1901 law but also by a new law adopted on 10 January 1936, at the time of a struggle against extreme right-wing groups. These vague formulas have effectively been used to dissolve many political groups— associations, movements, and parties of every kind. Successive governments have struck in turn or simultaneously at the extreme right, the extreme left, overseas nationalist movements, many regionalist movements within France itself, and so on. The imprecise phrasing even made it possible for the Vichy Government to order many dissolutions in the name of the 'Republican form of government'. There are no statistics on the total number of associations dissolved; but it would seem from a few soundings taken in connection with protests against administrative decisions of dissolution that, since the Second World War, several dozen groups have been banned from official activity. One is bound to regard the procedure as shocking both because of its scope and because of the inadequacy of the guarantees provided: decisions of the government can take effect with very little warning and are subject to very limited controls. Furthermore, the question of whether it is effective remains in doubt.

As for West Germany, in Article 21.2 of its Constitution, it tackles unambiguously the very principle involved in the banning of extremist parties: 'Those parties which, according to their goals and the attitudes of their membership, seek to strike at the fundamental free and democratic order, to topple it or to compromise the existence of the Federal Republic of Germany, are unconstitutional. The Federal Constitutional Court is empowered to rule on the question of unconstitutionality.' The federal government has sought to ban extremist parties on two occasions: first, the neo-Nazi Sozialistische Reichspartei, on 19 November 1951; then the Communist party

(KPD), on 22 November of that same year. In the case of the party of the extreme right, sentence was quickly passed, on 23 October 1952, but in that of the KPD it was much delayed both by procedural battles and also by indecision on the part of the court. Sentence was eventually pronounced on 17 August 1956, in a document of over 300 pages. With the passing of time, and as the State of West Germany became more confident, the existence of a Communist party was no longer considered a threat. In October 1967, the *Länder* Home Secretaries decided to tolerate the creation of a new communist party. However, to get round the earlier decision of the Constitutional Court, the party's name was changed and it became the Deutsche Kommunistische Partei (DKP); also, the statutes were adapted in such a way as to take account of the motivation behind the 1956 sentence. Similarly, the extreme right resurfaced in the late 1960s, taking care to steer clear of doctrines and language that were too reminiscent of Nazism. The electoral impact of both parties was limited, however, although it is true that the NPD made noticeable progress in many regional elections in the late 1960s. But, in 1969, the NPD, notwithstanding that progress, failed to break through the 5 per cent barrier, nor has it done any better in national elections since that time.

European political systems all, to a greater or lesser degree, favour the integration of parties recognized to be compatible with the values of democracy as defined by their constitutions, and the rejection of parties that do not fit into the system. It is unquestionably in West Germany and Italy that the political parties are the most fully integrated into the State, constitutional recognition there being but one—albeit the most solemn—of the forms taken by that integration. *Parteienstaat* and *partitocrazia* may not be completely realized concepts yet, but the two expressions testify to what Gerhard Liebholz calls the tendency of parties to identify with the people.

Although the forms of integration are less fully developed—and are, indeed, much criticized—in countries such as France and Britain the fact remains that the parties in the system are the necessary avenues of communication between the governed and the government, and that their roles have tended to grow in importance. Concurrently, 'outsider parties' have been confined to the touch-line by electoral legislation. Italy is probably the most open country in this respect, adopting an extremely liberal attitude towards access to Parliament, but the price it has had to pay for this has been high: small groups within the party system have proliferated; there have been constant operations of political 'transformism' designed to integrate parties outside the system and, as a matter of principle, the Italian Communist Party has been excluded from a central governing role (the famous *conventio ad excludendum*).

Party Organization

Party organization is a problem that has given rise to a series of monographs and reflections that must be accounted some of the most stimulating works in political science. They range from Robert Michel's study *Political Parties: a Sociological Study of the Oligarchic Tendencies of Modern Democracy* (1914) to Maurice Duverger's classic work *Les Partis politiques* (1951) and include many analyses on party organization and the explanatory force of organization as a variable.

Maurice Duverger, in particular, considers organization to be a key element for the understanding of not only the parties themselves but also the Western political systems in general. In the preface to the 1981 edition of his book, he acknowledges that his model is 'centred on [party] organization'.[28] In other words, each type of party has its own particular method of organization, and this constitutes its essential characteristic. Since Duverger set up that paradigm, many critical studies of it and variants to it have been put forward. Let us take a brief look at them before analysing how the tension between democracy and oligarchy that persists within the parties may be resolved.

By way of a summary, let us note that Duverger draws a contrast between two major types of political party, élite parties and parties of the masses, and he stresses that the distinction has nothing to do with whether the parties are large or small; it is not a matter of the size of their membership. It is not size but structure that is important. He explains that élite parties cannot be defined by reference either to their statutes or to the official statements of their leaders. On the other hand, he is inclined to believe that the absence of any register of members and of any regular levying of subscriptions and a vagueness in quoted statistics may well constitute significant characteristics. A party of the masses, on the other hand, is characterized by the register of its members, its levying of subscriptions, and its autonomous funding during elections. The first of these two groups is composed of the 'bourgeois' parties, the second of the socialist, communist, and Fascist ones although, quite apart from their ideology, the latter differ from one another on a number of counts. But Duverger recognizes that

> several types of party do not fit into this general schema: namely, the Catholic and christian democrat parties, which occupy a position more or less midway between the old parties and the socialist ones; the 'Labour' parties based on unions and co-operatives, with an indirect kind of structure . . . ; agrarian parties that display a wide diversity of types of organization and are only operative in a limited number of countries; and parties of an archaic or prehistoric type . . .[29]

Duverger's typology provoked a stimulating debate still not exhausted and of such wide scope as sometimes to obscure the essential question. One of his most acid critics was Aaron Wildavsky, who produced a methodological critique and attacked Duverger on the basis of his falling victim to four 'illusions': the illusion of one-dimensional history (belief in the existence of forces that lead to identical historical experiences despite the diversity of cultures); a mystical illusion (belief in the natural, binary nature of certain phenomena); the illusion of formal demonstration (Duverger's presentation of an abstract schema impossible either to attack or to verify); and the illusion of a representation that is divorced from reality (all exceptions that contradict the model are ignored).[30] However, most of Duverger's critics have taken up their positions on his own terrain, pointing out the inadequacy and incompleteness of his typology and suggesting possible additions or modifications to it. Duverger's typology has thus been expanded for example to include the catch-all party defined by Kirchheimer, the voters' party (Jean Charlot), and Eldersveld's stratarchic party (inspired by the American model, where power is held at every level of organization).

To escape from the impasse reached in this debate on the typology of party organization, William Wright[31] has suggested considering the two opposed types of party as the two extreme poles of a continuum, the one being described as the 'rational-efficient model', the other the 'party democracy model'. The attraction of this new version of the typology lies partly in its undisguised neutrality (neither of these ideal types is said to be more modern or better than the other) and above all in that it makes it possible to accommodate other, intermediate types in between the two theoretical poles.

One undeniable advantage is that the various parties can all be contained within this theoretical continuum instead of being forced into a binary typology often ill-suited to account for the wide spectrum of different parties and all the different ways in which they have evolved. For in the context of electoral competition, all parties are obliged to borrow characteristics and practices which are in principle alien to them. Traditional élite parties have to adopt strategies and structures borrowed from the parties of the masses (they must produce programmes and recruit supporters). Equally, the parties of the masses are tending to behave more like the élite parties (devising more pragmatic programmes, for example, and recognizing the autonomy of their parliamentary representatives).

No parties, whatever their nature, are monolithic organizations, even in cases where their methods of organization tend to turn them into docile and disciplined instruments (communist parties, for example). Party organizations comprise a number of facets, in principle all complementary but in practice often antagonistic or at least differentiated. Most parties consist of three separate essential components: the party apparatus, *stricto sensu*, which organizes the party at every level; the 'party in office', that is, the group which holds or shares power or has done so in the past (members of parliament, ministers, and even those elected by subsidiary bodies); and the party-in-the-electorate.[32] Each of these three has its own interests and strategies which sometimes coincide with those of the other two but sometimes do not. As Pierre Avril puts it, the party

cannot be reduced to a structure built up in the form of a pyramid, nor to a juxtaposition of concentric circles. Rather, it is defined by the interaction between the electoral, the social, and the State domains: operating three-dimensionally, it can never quite be reduced to any of these three planes. Rather, you could say, it occupies the whole of their geometric space.[33]

Both the business of engineering agreements and that of resolving disagreements raise the fundamental problem of democracy within the party. The problem was posed remarkably acutely at the beginning of the century by Robert Michels,[34] who based his observations on the example provided by the political parties in Germany, in particular the Socialist Party. Noting that democracy cannot exist without organization (for he harboured no illusions about direct democracy), Michels nevertheless recognized that democratic practices tend to become deflected in organizations such as trade unions and political parties, to the benefit of the leading party members who control the apparatus. He wrote as follows: 'The party, as an external formation, a mechanism or machine, is not necessarily identified with the register of members as a whole, even less with a particular class. As it becomes an end in itself, developing goals and interests of its own, it gradually moves away from the class that it represents.'[35]

The tensions between the various components of a party and those within its apparatus determine a series of complex interrelations which we may try to classify under three main headings: relations between the apparatus and the electorate, relations between the apparatus and the 'party in office', and relations within the apparatus itself (i.e. internal democracy).

Relations between the party apparatus and the party electorate are marked firstly by the various kinds of distance that tend generally to separate the masses from élites. On the one hand there are the professionals who control communications, monopolize statements, and formulate political promises—professionals who, through their cultural, social, and professional attributes are clearly distinguishable from the mass of citizens in general and from their own electorate in particular (although communist parties are careful to try to prevent such a gap developing). Then there is an electorate whose only means, in many cases, of making itself heard is through an infrequent poll, while its means of control are limited and its demands often distorted if not ignored. The few studies that have been devoted to 'electoral promises and demands' point out clearly the lack of correspondence that often occurs in electoral campaigns between the latent demands of the citizens and the parties' electoral promises. This mismatch frequently occasions considerable embarrassment for the party apparatus, especially in electoral competitions in which every party seeking power has to try to win over members of the electorate quite alien to its own particular ideologies and programmes yet possibly open to persuasion. Once the beguilements of the election are over, party apparatuses are often extremely hard put to it to hang on their electoral base, as the German Social Democrats learned to their cost in 1983 and the French Socialists in 1986. The parties' basic task is to maintain the support of their voters and to avoid disputes and desertion, or, as Hirschman put it in his tripartite scheme, to maintain *loyalty* and avoid *voice* and *exit*.

For not only in organizations where the ideology is all-important, but in 'catch-all' parties too, voters are easily lost once they become aware of the disparity between their expectations and the reality. In circumstances such as these the French Communist Party has been called a 'sieve' and Malraux's definition of Gaullism realistically reflected similar fluctuations: 'Everybody is, has been, or will be Gaullist'! Hence the constant, more or less successful attempts either to adapt the apparatus to the voters or, on the contrary, to maintain it unchanged at any cost, even it means changing its electorate or losing it altogether. Social democratic and bourgeois parties have generally favoured the former option, extreme parties the latter, in the name of the ideological purity that the apparatus defends and embodies.

But as well as being marked by certain ideological and social disagreements, the relationship between the party apparatus and the electorate also depends upon *quid pro quo* arrangements that sometimes afford the latter a measure of control. The *quid pro quo* mechanisms (patronage as opposed to ideology) that Max Weber[36] regarded as an essential element in the typology of political parties, amount to more than simply offering the voters certain material advantages in return for their votes, although such practices, frequently used by the Democratic Party in the United States, were also common in Europe so long as suffrage remained limited. However, with the advent of universal suffrage, patronage shifted from the individual to the collective level. While the practice of offering advantages to individuals may not have disappeared, those advantages were 'dematerialized'. They now tended to take the form of small services such as bringing influence to bear or exerting pressure to obtain certain favours. The fact is though that, short of cutting themselves off from their bases, political parties cannot unilaterally decide what their political offers will be. Even if the political programmes that they elaborate 'activate vigorous and clear-cut solutions that in many cases have not been called upon earlier', they are not in a position to ignore the demands of society in general, for, if they do, they are in danger of severing the links between the party apparatus and the citizens and of provoking negative reactions on the part of the electorate.

Where there are few or no institutional possibilities for channelling that pressure, there is a danger that it will be brought to bear upon the parties through the development of violent means (terrorism, extreme right-wing or left-wing movements), anti-system parties (such as the Poujade movement and the RPF in France, the Uomo Qualunque party in Italy), or new parties which take up some of the electorate's unsatisfied demands (the nationalist and the Social Democrat parties in Britain, the National Front in France, the Greens in West Germany).

The 'party in office' is constituted by the group of party members who hold (or have held) office within the State institutions. They may include members of parliament, ministers, and even, to varying degrees, those elected to local office. The relations between this fraction of the party that exercises (or has exercised) power and the party apparatus (where the influence of activists makes itself felt more strongly given that many of their leaders are distracted by the administration of power) are often marked by tensions and conflicts that stem from the different nature of their respective roles. The intensity of these conflicts is itself determined by a whole series of complex factors. Chief among them are: the degree of flexibility or inflexibility of the party ideology and apparatus; the relative importance of elected representatives and activists, and the *practical* possibilities of acceding to power. Clearly, the danger of friction is greater in cases where the party has a firmly rooted ideology, a powerful apparatus, and a large number of elected representatives with responsibilities to exercise than it is in flexible organizations, in élite parties whose programmes and ideologies amount to little more than a few vague general declarations of intent, or in small doctrinaire parties where there can be no clash with the elected representatives since none exist. The fact is that tensions are likely to arise in the debate between those with responsibilities to exercise and those who remain outside the decision-making circles of the State. The French Communist Party, for example, is so keen to ward off 'municipal cretinism', that is to say, a managerial dilution of its elected representatives, that as far as possible it avoids putting up Communist mayors of large cities to stand in national elections. The governments of Mauroy and Fabius, for their part, found it very difficult to explain to the Socialist Party why they favoured a 'pause' in essential reforms and policies to gain acceptance for these ideas. Under the aegis of Chancellor Schmidt, the SPD–FDP coalition also frequently clashed with the left wing of the Social Democratic Party, which was deeply hostile to the installation of missiles in Germany. But the classic case of tension between a party apparatus and a party in office is that of the British Labour Party. In particular, clashes occur constantly between the National Executive Committee, where local party members and trade unionists are dominant, and the 'Parliamentary Labour Party', which includes

Labour members from both Houses. In 1981, the clashes were such as to prompt a splinter group to secede and form the new Social Democratic Party. The conflict began when the left wing which wanted to introduce the reselection of candidates at the next General Election and to deprive Members of Parliament of any influence in the choice of a leader, clashed with the moderates, who demanded autonomy for the parliamentary group. In 1981, when it was decided that the trade unions should control 40 per cent of the votes, and the local constituency parties and parliamentary group 30 per cent each, those who opposed putting the parliamentary group in a minority decided to leave the party.

It might be supposed that in élite parties, whose ideology and apparatus are both more flexible than in the 'parties of the masses' (the socialists in particular), conflicts would be unlikely to break out. Yet even here they are not absent. For example, in 1956, the tensions within the German Liberal Party brought into collision those who supported Adenauer's policies (in particular, the FDP Government ministers) and those who opposed them. This led to a split. In 1962, a similar situation arose in France where, on the occasion of the referendum some ministers of the Independent party rallied to General de Gaulle and, led by Valéry Giscard d'Estaing, formed a party of Independent Republicans.

All the same, it would be exaggerated to suppose that these conflicts are invariably expressed in clashes between the group of elected representatives on the one hand, and the party apparatus on the other. In truth, the dividing lines are far more complex and, just as the party in office finds support and co-operation in the party apparatus, the latter is not without its own champions within the parliamentary group or amongst the elected representatives in general.

Depending upon the circumstances and the problems involved, conflicts sometimes take place between the government and a section of the parliamentary group which may be drawn from a number of elements in the party: back-benchers, rank-and-file representatives, and *franchi tiratori* (the Italian deputies of the majority who vote against the government when the ballot is secret) are sometimes recalcitrant or even, in extreme cases, rebellious when the policies followed by the government that they support seem to them too far removed from the programme that they themselves have promised to adopt and fight for.

In these complex and shifting relations, the most one can do is recognize the existence of a wide spectrum of possibilities that range from the strictest discipline to the widest autonomy. The communist parties are at one of these extremes, adamantly proclaiming their allegiance to the party apparatus (consider the case of the French Communist ministers who in 1947 voted against the proposals of the government of which they were themselves members). During the 1970s and 1980s, however, such tensions have become more intense and less discreet, for the most part ending with either the departure or the exclusion of those in dispute. Next in line after the communist parties come the extremist parties of both the right and the left, whose discipline tends to be more inflexible the more limited their chances of exercising power. Next come the socialist parties and the bourgeois or Christian democratic ones. In these, the problem is frequently complicated by the existence of many well-organized factions. Finally, the American parties are positioned at the opposite extreme. Here, the party apparatus is so incapable of imposing any line of conduct that there is virtually no conflict to speak of. Whereas the free vote is becoming the exception in European parliaments (where it is tolerated more or less only on questions such as the abolition of the death penalty or abortion), it is the rule in the United States.

All parties seek to appear to the outside world as organizations united around a programme, with a team or a leader to guide them. Unity is claimed all the more emphatically when the party concerned declares itself to be the sole spokesman for a particular group or social class: divisions must be unacceptable when a party regards itself as, for example, *the* party of the working class (just as certain trade unions profess to be *the* workers' or *the* farmers' trade union). The logic behind this monopolistic and unitarian attitude is quite simple: unity must be guaranteed by iron discipline, even at the cost of exclusions and expulsions. Admittedly, the objective is seldom achieved. Only communist parties, through their use and abuse of the principle of democratic centralism, have succeeded here. Small parties of the extreme left and occasionally of the extreme right and a few regionalist parties have also endeavoured to guarantee their unitarian purity, but at the cost of periodic 'purges' and splits that have in many cases drained them of all life.

Other political parties have been obliged, willy-nilly, to accept their internal divisions in the name of the democracy that they claim to represent, but that process is not an easy one. The reluctance to accept divisions within a party is certainly understandable. How far can pluralism go without producing centrifugal and potentially destructive tendencies? The political vocabulary reflects the ambivalence of attitudes towards the phenomenon of fragmentation. Up until the nineteenth century the word 'party' denoted a 'faction', but the latter term then took over from 'party' with derogatory connotations, while 'party' came to be accepted and used to denote the various political groups. In English, the word 'faction' continues to be used (although Sartori suggested replacing it by 'fraction'). The French use the terms *courants* (currents) (particularly to refer to the Socialist Party) and *tendances* (tendencies) more or less indiscriminately. The Italians speak of a *corrente*, or sometimes an *area*.

The causes and the scope of factionalism within the parties vary greatly and a general interpretation of the phenomenon would be hard to find. It clearly occurs in widely diverse parties: élite parties and voter parties, parties of the masses and mini-parties, pragmatic parties and ideological ones. The formation of factions is encouraged by factors of various kinds: some are of an ideological, others of a 'charismatic' nature, while yet others are related to clientship or electoral problems. They combine in forms that vary from one party to another, but in most parties they are all at work to some degree.

Ideological factors. Parties which are endowed with strong ideologies but still accept debate and diversity are likely to contain factions which clash over the more or less dogmatic interpretation of the party creed. They frequently represent the whole range of divisions that arise in the political world in general between the left wing, the right wing, the centre, radicals, and so on. For example, in Britain, before the creation of the SDP, the Labour party included a right wing, to wit the Social Democratic Alliance (which broke away in 1981), the revisionists of the Manifesto Group (set up in 1974), and the moderates led by William Rodgers under the banner 'Campaign for a Labour Victory'. The German SPD[37] was also divided into groups representing the centre right (Vogel Kreis) and the centre left (Frankfurter Kreis), but leftist elements have exerted an increasing influence on party decisions, particularly in the area of nuclear policy, both civil and military. In France, the Socialist Party in 1978 revised its regulations to admit the legitimacy of different tendencies although it imposed some limits (most importantly on the autonomy of funds). The party then proceeded to organize itself around the various 'currents', each of which set out its own political strategy and the programme promoted by its own leader (Mitterrand, Mauroy, Rocard, and Chevènement).

In the interests of unity and synthesis, these have, since 1981, desisted from drawing attention to their individual differences at their Party Congress. Nevertheless, the principal factions continue to be very much alive and sometimes display as much energy in opposing one another as they do in fighting their common adversaries.

The 'charismatic' factor. This factor is equally important. It naturally plays a part in right-wing parties, where quarrels over personalities or 'leadership battles' are more common than ideological conflicts. But it would be simplistic to suppose that factionalism is inspired on the left purely by ideology and policies, on the right by personality clashes. The truth is that there are no factions without leaders, whatever the party, and even within the most ideological factions that leadership is always an essential cause of internal divisions.

Of course, personality clashes are more marked in élite parties where the different tendencies are not strongly organized and may amount to no more than vague allegiances (seldom formalized by voting) to the principal personalities of the party. For instance, in the case of the Radical Party under the Third and Fourth French Republics, one can hardly speak of factions or tendencies, for the internal divisions were essentially determined by clashes between the leading personalities in the party.

On the other hand, the Italian Christian Democrat Party provides a good illustration of a party where there is a mixture of strategic, or even ideological, divisions together with others established by the various faction leaders. In 1976, for example, six different factions could be distinguished: Area Zac (named after the former party secretary, Zaccagnini), which brought together men such as Marcora, Rognoni, De Mita, and Andreatta; the Dorotheans (Piccoli, Bisaglia, and Gaspari); the Fanfanians; the supporters of Andreotti; those of Donat-Cattin, Rumor, and Colombo; and, finally, the little group known as *Proposta* or *Amici di Prandini*.

In 1982, these factions, while continuing to exist, came together in coalitions reacting, in different ways, to the new Secretary-General, De Mita, and the political line that he was adopting. Area Zac joined up with the PAF group (Piccoli, Andreotti, and Fanfani), which included the Dorotheans and the Fanfanians. Together, these two factions accounted for 65 per cent of the votes at the Christian Democrat Congress and it was they that set up the new De Mita leadership. Then there was the 'opposition' group (known as 'Pre-amble', as it was insisting on an explicit declaration to the effect that the Italian Socialist Party would be the Christian Democrats' preferred choice for a partner).[38] Both these factions were dominated by strong personalities, but they certainly reflected many aspects of the Christian Democrat Party: its divisions over strategy and alliances, its different sensibilities, and its general internal pluralism.

Factors connected with clientship. The strength of a faction or tendency does not depend solely on the originality of its political line and the magnetism of its leader. Also to be taken into account is the support that the faction and its principal personalities can attract through practices of patronage or clientship both inside and outside the party. Inside the party, a particular faction and its leader will win over considerably more supporters if they are in a position to offer rewards—whether or not of a symbolic nature—to their faithful followers. Factions must also be able to guarantee their supporters candidacies in the national and local elections (e.g. the battle over candidacies in the French Socialist Party, in 1985–6), posts in the administrations and town halls that they control, and in the public, semi-public, or even private sectors (e.g. associations), and also rewards within the party apparatus itself (posts as party officials, advisers, experts, and so on). The existence of factions certainly has the effect of inflating the number of posts and titles, as new ones are created to keep pace with 'demand'. (It should be pointed out, however, that the phenomenon also exists in parties which do not tolerate fractional organizations, such as the French Communist Party, in which one in every four members is a 'cadre'). Needless to say, it is a phenomenon that is accentuated in cases where a party has a real chance of acceding to power. In Italy, many a place for a party activist has been found in the regional bureaucracies, as also in West Germany, where the *Länder* have been so accommodating that the close intermingling of bureaucrats and politicians is sometimes referred to as *Verfilzung* (interweaving).[39]

Of course, these practices of patronage are just one facet of a wider policy of clientship that reaches beyond the party itself and enables a leader and his faction to establish their own local and regional strongholds. Fanfani is solidly established in Tuscany, Donat-Cattin in Liguria, De Mita in Apulia, and Colombo in Basilicata. Similarly, in West Germany, where Johannes Rau is the SPD's strong man in the Rhineland, his challenger, Oskar Lafontaine, is solidly established in Saarland. In France, the two federations of the Nord-Pas-de-Calais (under Mauroy) and the Bouches du Rhône (under Defferre) were for many years the dominant factions in the SFIO and are still extremely powerful in the Socialist Party.

Electoral factors. The polling system is not the major element in determining configurations of power within a party. But in the context of political parties, as in the overall political system, it does affect the line-up of factions and helps to establish a particular set of rules for the political game. The evidence of all the different political parties of Europe shows well enough that the polling system is not an essential factor: for factions exist everywhere, whatever the country's polling system may be, and a party's modes of internal organization and voting are no sure indication of whether or not it is divided into factions. Nevertheless, the introduction of proportional representation does help to develop and reinforce factions, particularly when combined with other divisive elements, such as those connected with policies, personalities, or clientship. It then becomes a means of stabilizing the respective strengths of the various schools of thought and the more or less regionalized groups that are in conflict inside the party.

Thus, the percentage of votes obtained by the various factions in the Italian Christian Democrat Party are essential when it comes to determining the extent to which they should be represented on electoral lists, the formation of the government, and the distribution of public posts and functions. Allocations are worked out strictly in proportion to the results obtained, in accordance with the 'Cencelli' rules (so-called after the name of the Christian Democrat official responsible for devising the rules of this 'division of spoils'). For example, Area Zac, which won 30.2 per cent of the vote in the Party Congress of 1982 obtained 30 per cent of the government posts reserved for the Christian Democrats in the Craxi Government, in 1983. The PAF faction, which had won 34.6 per cent of the vote, received as its share 35 per cent of the Christian Democrat ministries, and the opposition (Preamble) group was also allocated a percentage of portfolios that tallied with its results at the Congress (35 per cent). As a journalist noted in the *Corriere della Sera*, the 'Cencelli handbook' had been 'respected'.[40]

THE PARTY SYSTEM

By party system, we mean 'the whole collection of parties as they interact in a given political system'. In Western countries, the fundamental characteristic of this structure of interrelationships is party pluralism. There are two reasons for this. One is the belief that democracy cannot be achieved through a single organization holding a monopoly; the other, the *de facto* circumstances (all the Western democracies do include several parties). But the number of parties varies greatly from one country to another and for a long time political analysts tended to regard that as an essential factor in the understanding of a party system. They would contrast two-party systems, for which Britain constituted the model, with multi-party systems, for which France provided a good illustration. Meanwhile, single-party systems could be observed in the socialist countries or in those where totalitarian regimes insisted upon unquestioning obedience.

The Two-Party or the Duopolistic System?

A purely two-party system is more of an ideal concept than a reality. Even in the few countries which are considered as prototypes of the two-party system (Britain, the United States), the situation is often more complex either because of the existence of small minority parties or because the system goes through phases of being a three-party system.

It would therefore be more accurate to borrow an expression from the realm of economics and speak of 'duopolies', to underline the essential point, for this is not so much the number of parties (which, in reality, is *never* limited to two), rather the fact that one of those two duopolistic parties holds power for periods of varying length, alternating with the other major party and without help or support from any third party. The polling system does not completely rule out the formation of third parties but, all the same, in general its effect is to ensure the supremacy of the two established ones. However, it did not prevent the rise of the Labour Party in Britain between the two World Wars or its crushing victory in 1945. As Monica Charlot observed in 1976, 'Britain has not entered into a multi-party system, but the two-party system is nevertheless under serious threat, as is shown by the fact that, for the first time since 1910, two consecutive elections less than a year apart have been unable to produce a decisive majority government.'[41]

Multi-Party Systems

What distinguishes pluralist party systems from duopolistic ones is, as we have seen, not so much the number of parties involved as the dominant position of two of them. The dividing line between the two types of party system is thus a flexible one, for the balance between the various parties depends upon the changes that affect ideologies, polling systems, prevailing circumstances, and so on. A number of variants to Duverger's typology have accordingly been suggested, to take account of such swings of the pendulum and intermediate situations (e.g. party realignment). To reflect hybrid situations, Jean Blondel suggests a typology with four components: two-party systems, systems with two-and-a-half parties, multi-party systems in which one party is dominant, and pure multi-party systems.[42] This has the advantage of conveying a better idea of the real situation. The drawback to it, however, is that it was worked out chiefly on the basis of the West German movement towards a two-party system during the 1960s and 1970s and it has been somewhat invalidated by the developments of the early 1980s. A few years later (in 1976), Sartori made a useful contribution to the analysis of party systems by making a distinction between *categories* (defined by fragmentation) and *types* of systems (determined by the *ideological distance* between the parties and the degree of their polarization).[43] By taking this new variable into account, Sartori is able to distinguish, within multi-party systems, between moderate pluralistic systems and polarized systems in which the parties are separated by a wide ideological gap (given that some of them are anti-system parties, as is the case in France and Italy). Of course, any new typology attracts criticism, debate, and suggestions for readjustments of various kinds. We shall not, for example, go into the clash between Sartori, who defines the Italian party system as a 'polarized pluralist system', and Giorgio Galli, who regards it as an 'imperfect two-party system'.[44] We shall limit ourselves to describing first the pluralist systems in which the political 'market place' is divided between parties that are relatively evenly balanced, and then those in which one political group holds a dominant position.

According to Sartori's typology, centripetal pluralist systems are defined principally by three features:

- a small ideological gap between the principal parties;
- a propensity to form coalitions between different parties, even when they favour different programmes;
- essentially centripetal competition.

In contrast, the polarized pluralist model is characterized by:

- a wide ideological gap between the parties;
- the existence of anti-system parties;
- competition of a centrifugal nature.

At first sight, the democracies that correspond most closely to the centripetal model would appear to be the countries sometimes described as 'consociational' (Switzerland, Holland, and Belgium— until, that is, regionalist and federalist parties made their appearance there). However, it would be exaggerated to assimilate consociationalism and centripetal pluralism, for the latter model lacks some of the characteristics of consociational systems, namely, the religious and linguistic divisions that underlie the political culture of those States. Rather, centripetal pluralism can be said to be embodied in States where, by reason of the contradictions and heterogeneity of both the right and the left, the competition is played out at the centre. The role of the centre is crucial, not because of its own intrinsic strength, but on account of the weakness of both the right and the left.

Paolo Farneti has pointed out that the dynamics of this system result from the competition between parties all of which aim to forge an alliance at the centre, since the price to pay for being permanently in opposition is greater than that involved in participating in a mixed coalition.[45] On the basis of these characteristics, France under the Fifth Republic may be considered as an example of centripetal pluralism. On the other hand, Sartori, who is deeply suspicious of the Italian Communist Party, balks at classifying Italy in this category, presenting it instead as an example of polarized pluralism comprising centrifugal and anti-system parties in the form of the MSI and, above all, the Italian Communist Party. On this point, Paolo Farneti's view is less extreme and—to my mind—more realistic. For him, Italy constituted a polarized pluralist system from 1944 to 1961, but as from 1965 fell into the centripetal pluralist category. And Farneti interprets the historic compromise as a refusal on the part of the Communist Party to destroy the existing centripetal tendencies at work. It preferred this course to the option of radically changing the system by bringing in a left-wing coalition—which would, anyway, have been of a heterogeneous nature. All the same, the price to be paid for such centripetal tendencies may be a heavy one, involving a widening gap between the general electorate and élite groups, a simultaneous isolation of right-wing or left-wing minorities that are tempted to embrace radicalism, and a depoliticization of public opinion.[46]

Farneti's application of Sartori's model seems to me more in line with the ideological and political evolution of Italy than Sartori's own interpretation. Many studies have shown that in the course of the 1970s, ideological polarization[47] became less acute, and all observers of Italian political life agree on the Italian Communist Party's integration into the political system, at the same time recognizing that its chances of acceding to power are slighter than ever: it may no longer be an anti-system party, but it is certainly still confined to the periphery of that system.

Party pluralism may be inegalitarian when the political scene is dominated by a party that is not only powerful but also central to most alliances. A dominant party cannot be defined simply in terms of size: the French Communist Party under the Fourth Republic and the Italian Communist Party were respectively the strongest and second strongest forces in their own political systems; but neither was in a dominant position. To be so, a party must also be the key element in the constitution of any political coalition: this has been and still is true of the Italian Christian Democrats, who hold a central position. No government can be formed without them since there is no leftist alternative.

Being in a dominant position is not necessarily a lasting situation, despite what the Italian example might suggest, for in the first place the word 'dominant' may be applied to a whole collection of different situations varying from hegemony (as in the case of the Christian Democrats during the 1950s) to far more competitive situations such as those that have been a feature of the relations between the secular Italian parties and the Christian Democrats during the 1980s. Secondly, multi-party systems with one dominant party sometimes evolve into duopolistic or even quasi two-party systems. In West Germany, the CDU–CSU undeniably held a dominant position up until the early 1960s. Then, what developed at first appeared to observers to constitute a genuine two-party system or at least a 'two-and-a-half party system', to borrow Jean Blondel's expression. But the 1980s have produced a trend in the opposite direction, with the FDP in decline, the Greens reinforcing their presence in the Bundestag in 1987, and the Republicans (the new right-wing party) winning seats at the *Land* level and in the European elections of June 1989.

Under the Fifth Republic, France also went through periods when one party predominated (1962–73) but, since the early 1970s, Gaullist supremacy has been called into question both by the progress of the UDF and by the Socialist Party, which has been winning back left-wing voters temporarily seduced by General de Gaulle. Today, pluralist systems with one dominant party are the exception rather than the rule in the Western democracies: the Italian Christian Democrats and the Spanish Socialists are more or less alone in dominating party systems of that kind.

Concentration, Fragmentation, Coalitions

This study has repeatedly drawn attention to the necessarily fluctuating nature of any classification of parties in particular political systems, given that those parties are bound to be affected by new developments. Concentration or, conversely, fragmentation are constantly recurring features in the life, development, and demise of political parties. Such developments tend to fall into three main patterns: in the first the number of parties decreases, in the second it increases, while in the third it remains more or less stable but the parties' relative strengths change.

West Germany exemplifies the first of those patterns. Between 1953 and 1983, the multi-party system turned into a three-party system[48] or even a virtually duopolistic one, as a result of the decline of the FDP in the late 1970s. When the Federal Republic held its first elections, the CDU–CSU and the SPD together accumulated only 60.2 per cent of the vote. But in 1953, they won 74 per cent (totalling 83.5 per cent together with the FDP), and between 1957 and 1987 they scored over 80 per cent. The Communist Party (15 seats in 1949), the extreme right (2 seats), and the Bavarian Party (17 seats) had all been eliminated by 1953. The only survivors from this political massacre were the Deutsche Partei and the Refugee Party, but the latter also fell victim to the 1957 elections. Only the Deutsche Partei went on to win 17 seats in 1957, but that was because it had allied itself to the CDU, which had refrained from opposing its candidates in its strongholds of Lower Saxony and north-eastern Germany. When it tried to become autonomous in 1961, however, the German Party bought its own one-way ticket out of the electoral scene. The supremacy of the two major parties has remained strong, due in part to a polling system that is most unfavourable to small political groups, but since 1980 the position of the two major parties has weakened. Between them, they shared 90.7 per cent of the vote in 1972 and 91.2 per cent in 1976, but this fell to 87.4 per cent in 1980 and to 87 per cent in 1983. By January 1987 they polled a 'mere' 81.3 per cent. After a period of strong concentration, the German system has again started to fragment and it is impossible to predict whether the phenomenon is due to temporary circumstances or whether the much-quoted values of post-industrialism will become lastingly embodied in the new party organization of the Greens.

The most interesting example of a fragmentation of the party system is that of Britain, the homeland of the 'two-party system'. From the end of the Second World War up until the 1974 elections, the two parties between them attracted 90 per cent of votes, but this then fell to 75 per cent, dropping even further in 1983 to 70 per cent. The beneficiaries of this disaffection from the two major parties were sometimes the centrifugal parties (in October 1974, Plaid Cymru and, especially, the Scottish National Party, which won 11 seats), and sometimes parties of the centre, whether old (the Liberal Party, which won 13 seats in 1974 and 11 in 1979) or new (the SDP which, in alliance with the Liberals, won 23 seats in 1983). But the relatively modest score of seats conveys only a weak reflection of the shock undergone by the party system: the Labour Party had polled no more than 27.6 per cent of the vote (although that gave it 209 seats), while the Alliance pressed hard on its heels with 25.4 per cent.

The third pattern is one where the number of parties remains stable, but the balance of their relative strengths shifts in a quite striking fashion. Italy provides a good example. After an exceptional result in 1948 (48.5 per cent of the vote), the Christian Democrats stabilized at about 40 per cent in the 1960s, then entered upon a slow, twenty-year-long decline (up until 1979 it polled 38–9 per cent of the vote). In the national elections of 1983 its score fell to 32.9 per cent. It reached its nadir in the 1984 European elections, when the absence of any major issues and the death of the Communist Party's much-admired leader, Berlinguer, had the effect of turning the Communists into the country's leading party. Immediately after the war, they had been weaker than the Socialists (obtaining 18.9 per cent of the poll as against the Socialists' 20.7 per cent in 1946). However, in 1953 it became the leading party of the left, a position which it regularly improved up to 1984. But the Italian Socialist Party obtained almost 15 per cent in 1987 and the Italian Communist Party is now facing a troubled and uncertain future.

A similar phenomenon has taken place in France, but in reverse. Here, the Socialist Party, which currently represents close on one-third of the electorate, first overtook, then far outstripped the French Communist Party, which in 1986 found itself back at the same level as in the 1930s. But the French Socialist Party's success was the culmination of a long fight to win back socialist or centre-left voters after the collapse of 'the old firm', the SFIO. On the right, similar realignments have taken place, a fact which makes it fair to say that France, of all the post-war Western democracies, has undergone the most radical transformations: the RPF gradually collapsed under the self-defensive onslaught of the parties that it was seeking to hold up to public obloquy, but the Gaullist movement took its revenge in the early 1960s, smashing the MRP and the moderate parties of the right (Independents) and appropriating the spoils. On the other hand, the centre's attempts to restructure itself, under the aegis of Valéry Giscard d'Estaing, were less impressive. The UDF umbrella takes in supporters of the centre, liberals, and radicals, who are allies by necessity but who oppose one another to the extent of refusing to commit themselves to any more than a flexible confederation of

Fragmentation and realignment almost always make it necessary to set up coalitions in order to form governments. With the exception of Britain, no country has eluded that constraint. Government of a country by a single party (normally with a majority but sometimes with only a minority) is the exception rather than the rule.[49] In France it has happened only twice between 1945 and 1988, with the short-lived Fabius Government, which lasted from July 1984 to March 1986[50] and the Rocard Government installed in June 1988. The same goes for West Germany and Italy. The CDU–CSU governed alone for only four years, from 1957 to 1961, and the only periods when the Italian Christian Democrats headed an undivided minority government (a government of a single shade) were from August 1953 to January 1954 (the Pella Government), from May 1957 to June 1958 (the Zoli Government), from February 1959 to February 1961 (the second Segni Government, the Tambroni Government, and the third Fanfani Government), from June to November 1963 (the Leone Government), from June to November 1968 (the second Leone Government), from August 1969 to February 1970 (the second

Rumor Government), and from March 1974 to August 1979 (the Moro Government and Andreotti's government of national unity): this adds up to about eight years over the 1945 to 1989 period. In truth, of all the countries studied, Britain is alone in having escaped the arithmetical or political need to resort to coalition governments since the Second World War.

In 1962, William Riker tried to establish a theory of coalitions,[51] which was followed by Dodd[52] and Budge and Farlie.[53] These formal theories, founded for the most part upon criteria of size but also upon ideological disparities and the types of policy adopted, fall a long way short of providing a completely satisfactory explanation for the variety of existing coalitions, no doubt because they postulate rational behaviour (by no means a safe assumption to make), and their record as a basis for prediction is not particularly impressive. For example, Riker's concept of a 'minimal winning coalition', which assumes that coalitions are formed in such a way as to exclude all members not essential to the constitution of an absolute majority, is only partially substantiated by the facts and does not account for either minority governments or coalitions that are far wider than is arithmetically essential, such as, for example, the big CDU–CSU–SPD coalition in West Germany that governed from 1966 to 1969.

It is clear, in the first place, that some coalitions are deliberately constructed to include more groups than are strictly necessary from the point of view of the parliamentary balance of power, and even that parties which, on their own, already hold a majority sometimes enter into coalitions with small parties. One instance in point was the big coalition in West Germany mentioned above, but plenty of other examples are provided by the many centre–left coalitions in Italy during the 1960s, and the *Pentapartito* coalition of 1983 to 1989. For instance, in 1983 the majority necessary was 316 votes but the actual majority amounted to 366, while the three small secular parties controlled respectively 29 (PRI), 23 (PSDI), and 16 (PLI) seats. Theoretically, it would have been possible to do without one, or even two, of those parties and still obtain the 'minimal winning coalition' of Riker's theory. In France, under the Fifth Republic, the Gaullists always sought to extend their majority in the direction of the centre, even when the support of the Independent Republicans already gave them an absolute majority.

Even more paradoxically, a party with an absolute majority sometimes chooses to form a coalition with a small allied political group.

Such was the situation in West Germany in 1957, when Adenauer included representatives of the small Deutsche Partei in his government despite the fact that the CDU–CSU had obtained an absolute majority. De Gasperi proceeded in similar fashion between May 1948 and June 1953, even though the Christian Democrats had won more than 50 per cent of the seats. In France too, finally, both the Gaullists, from 1968 to 1973, and the Socialists, from 1981 to 1986, decided to include their electoral 'allies' in the government, even though there was no parliamentary necessity to do so. How should we interpret these situations? We must fall back upon explanations of a political nature to discover the logic of behaviour that appears irrational from a purely formal point of view.

One possibility is that periods of serious crisis are likely to produce large coalitions. They constitute a form of government of national unity. Such an interpretation might explain, in particular, the big coalition formed in West Germany at a time of serious economic crisis (even if, looking back, it looks relatively minor in comparison to the crisis of the 1970s).

A second explanation might be that an arithmetically weak majority that is theoretically adequate for the purposes of government may be threatened by the insufficiency of legitimacy that results from the narrowness of that majority and the 'quasi-victory' of the opposition. This was Berlinguer's justification for the historic compromise: he pointed out that a left-wing majority needs more than 51 per cent of the poll in order to govern. The gap between an arithmetical majority and true legitimacy is often accentuated, in continental Europe at least, by the obvious discrepancy that exists between a parliamentary majority and an electoral minority. The CDU–CSU obtained no more than 50.2 per cent of the poll in 1957, the Christian Democrats only 48.5 per cent in 1948, the Gaullists only 43.65 per cent on the first ballot in the 1968 election, and the Socialists only 37.51 per cent in 1981 (also on the first ballot). Increasing the parliamentary majority is a way of calling for wider support from the electorate and public opinion.

A third explanation may lie in the relations that obtain between parties that might conceivably form a coalition, given their ideological proximity and electoral alliances. For parties allied out of necessity but hostile and competitive by nature, sharing power in a coalition may be mutually advantageous: the dominant party draws in those that are less dangerous to it when included in a coalition than when left out (e.g. the French Communist Party from 1981 to 1984); meanwhile, it is in the interest of small minority parties to band together so as to be integrated all together into the coalition, even when they are not all strictly needed in order to create an absolute majority (as in the case of the Italian *Pentapartito*). In these types of situation, it is essential to distinguish between two kinds of party whose individual character-istics might be conveyed by the labels 'support parties' and 'pivot parties'. Support parties are the parties that are necessary to convert a relative majority into an absolute one (the Independent Republicans in France between 1962 and 1968, for instance, or the FDP in West Germany). Pivot parties are parties around which coalitions cluster (the UNR in 1962, or the Christian Democrats). In France and Italy, the pivot party is also a dominant party, but this is a situation that has only evolved over the past ten years. The role of the Gaullists and the Christian Democrats as pivot parties has been stabilized by the rising power of their respective allies, the UDF and the Italian Socialist Party.

The opposite situation is created—in flagrant contradiction to the theory of democracy—by minority governments, whether formed by a single party or by a coalition. Unknown in Britain (except from February to October 1974, when the Labour Government could count on only 301 votes out of 635) and West Germany, minority govern-ments can only survive with the support of a parliamentary majority (not included in the government). Such situations have frequently arisen in France under the Fourth Republic, and in Italy. In these circumstances it seems as though the implicit coalition agreed within parliament can only be set up on condition that it is not reflected in the composition of the government. In polarized systems, such para-doxical situations are more likely to occur in the presence of a party or parties which, it is felt, cannot at any cost be allowed to accede to power (the Communist Party and the National Front in France, the Italian Communist Party and the MSI in Italy).

Since they do not operate actively and visibly within the govern-ment, parties which simply support a government in parliament carry no formal responsibility for its decisions. Sometimes an even more complicated situation is created by the establishment of parliamentary coalitions which are not reflected in the composition of the govern-ment, as is demonstrated in the case of the Government of National Unity in Italy from 1976 to 1979: as always since the Cold War, the Communist Party was excluded from the ministerial team, but this time it was fully associated with government policies at a parliamentary level. Although the participation of the Italian Communist Party was not official, the effect of it was reflected in the quasi-unanimous support—at parliamentary level, at least—that was given to the policies adopted during this period. The Italian Communist Party subsequently paid a heavy price for that 'support without participation': its percentage of the vote fell from 34 per cent in 1976 to 30.4 per cent in 1979 (whereas the Christian Democrats forfeited only 0.4 per cent, dropping from 38.7 to 38.3 per cent).

THE FUNCTIONS OF THE POLITICAL PARTIES

Political parties are one of the fundamental elements in contemporary liberal democracies. The place that they occupy is itself a consequence of the very concept of democracy, founded upon the pluralism of interests, the unanimous rejection of a single-party system, and political competition in the choosing of leaders and policies. But over and above that fundamental and crucial choice, Western political parties appear to be playing an increasingly important role as a consequence of the functions that they assume in the life of liberal political societies. It is fair to say, without exaggeration, that the political parties 'control' the entire political process from the raising of political consciousness to the elaboration of policies and their implementation. Admittedly, the political parties are by no means the only agents involved (not only is the party system pluralistic, but the parties themselves hold no monopoly over the exercise of some of their functions), and their role, furthermore, varies from one country to another. But they are usually the essential agents in political life. Let us review the major functions that the political parties discharge, for this will make it possible to gauge their impact within Western political systems.

Integration and Mobilization

The evolution through which the liberal democracies progressed from a concept of individualistic and unco-ordinated political participation to a more realistic acceptance of communal action within the framework of *ad hoc* organizations had, by the nineteenth century, made it possible for parties to emerge, parties capable of organizing and expressing the choices of citizens who shared common ideals and interests. But the decisive phase in this evolution came with the creation and development of workers' parties that specifically proclaimed themselves to speak for a particular class and possessed a powerful, unifying ideology together with an apparatus comprising militants and grass-roots organizations set up to mobilize electoral support. To defend themselves against this kind of apparatus and these potentially destabilizing modes of mobilizing support, the bourgeois parties were obliged to improve their own powers of integration and mobilization. It is significant that it should be the American parties (which have never been confronted by the 'challenge' of workers' parties) that are the least efficient in this respect and face the most vigorous competition from the *ad hoc* organization of interest groups. But even where the parties constitute the major means of mobilizing and integrating support, they may at any time face competition and need to revise their methods. In Italy and West Germany, for example, the parties that together make up the 'constitutional spectrum' (to borrow the Italian expression designating the parties that originally formulated the Constitution) have found themselves under threat from both non-violent challenges (the Radical Party in Italy, the Greens in West Germany) and violent ones (both right-wing and left-wing terrorism) and have seen traditional methods of mobilizing support supplanted by new ones.

Even the two dominant parties of Britain, which, combined, claim several million members are undergoing a crisis of activism and were recently losing voters to third parties. Finally, it is worth noting that in France, where the parties were long characterized by their weak performance in the area of mobilizing and integrating support, they have been expanding their role over the last two decades, in response to external challenges: the Gaullist movement was attracting and mobilizing support for a charismatic leader, who claimed to be anti-party; and on the left, the collapse of the SFIO in the late 1950s and the 1960s encouraged the emergence of a large number of political clubs which were seen as substitutes for the left-wing parties that seemed incapable of winning over many of their potential voters. However, in both these cases, the developments in the end turned out to be to the benefit of the more powerful parties (the RPR and the Socialist Party) and to strengthen them further. The French example is particularly interesting, for it shows that in Western countries the political parties are seen, even in unfavourable circumstances, as the principal and natural instruments of political mobilization.

Passing crises may shake them but, so far, nothing has succeeded in calling their supremacy in question. Only the American parties find themselves in a seriously competitive situation, being confronted by powerful interest groups, whose legitimacy as a rule goes unchallenged.

Influencing Voting Patterns

In the area of mobilizing and integrating supporters, the political parties do face a measure of competition from other groups. But when it comes to electoral promises, their monopoly is virtually absolute. In the nineteenth century and at the beginning of the twentieth, candidates for election were frequently 'Independents' and their chances of success were by no means negligible. Today, a wide range of Independents still stand as candidates but their chances of election are virtually nil. Even when a candidate's links with his party are weak (as they tend to be in the United States and in France, in the case of élite parties such as the Radicals and the Republicans), to stand a chance of being elected it is important to be recognized by some party, to carry a party 'label'. As we have seen, in connection with the party identification of voters and the typology suggested by Parisi and Pasquino (who speak of 'a supporter's vote', 'an opinion vote', and a 'bargaining vote'), to degrees that vary depending on the country, the time, and the parties, electoral behaviour is dictated by the voters' support for particular parties and by a preference for one candidate rather than another that has nothing to do with individual personalities.

Of course, the parties' hold over the way that people vote is disputed and by no means unwavering. The party monopoly may be challenged both politically and ideologically. A political challenge arises when, from time to time, groups or individuals seek to break the monopoly by organizing anti-party movements. But this usually amounts to no more than a flash in the pan or a total flop (the Poujade movement, l'Uomo Qualunque). 'Ideological' challenges are rooted in the liberal constitutional tradition, which started out by rejecting political parties as the instruments of political structuring and subsequently refused to recognize their monopoly: in West Germany, the Federal Court rejected a proposal that the 5 per cent elimination clause should be applied in the financing of electoral campaigns; in Italy, the mode of polling in principle makes it possible for an extremely wide range of groups and individuals to win seats; in France in the past, the rules that applied to the presentation of candidates for presidential election were designed to prevent the parties from controlling all candidacies (although that is no longer the case).

Yet if the parties' hold over voting patterns is undeniable, it should also be remembered that it is not altogether unwavering. Voters sometimes change their minds and the volatility of the electorate can become a major problem for the political parties. They have to try to maintain the loyalty of their voters by means of the ideology that they purvey (and are obliged to adapt as circumstances and voters change: something that the French Communist Party failed to do), the programmes that they put forward, and the advantages that they promise (and deliver if ever they accede to power).

Recruitment of Political Personnel

This is another area where the parties' monopoly is virtually total, at least in so far as central institutions are concerned. At a local level, the parties' sway is usually less general, particularly in France. But the most fundamental aspect of the situation lies not so much in these differences but in developments which here, too, at the local level, have tended to give the parties a quasi-monopoly over the recruitment of political personnel. In truth, what is implied by the 'nationalization of political life', or 'politicization', is the growing influence that the political parties are acquiring even at an infranational level.

As regards the executive personnel, the situation differs from one system to another, depending on whether it is presidential, semi-presidential, or parliamentary. In parliamentary systems, the political parties certainly do hold an almost absolute monopoly, for parliamentary tradition dictates that ministers be members of parliament. However, under the Fifth Republic, in France, more than a quarter of the ministers, on average, were picked from outside Parliament. In such a case, the influence of the parties at first sight seems more limited, but it could well be that, on the contrary, by penetrating the upper administration they considerably extend their political monopoly. It should be added that the parties, either directly or indirectly, control many appointments in a number of areas: these include the judiciary (the Constitutional Courts), public administration (the German and French 'spoils' systems), the non-departmental government agencies (the *sotto-governo* in Italy), the economic sector (public or partly State-owned businesses), culture (public or subsidized theatres, museums, foundations, etc.), and health (particularly in Italy). State expansion to a large extent entails expansion of the political parties, although it is sometimes difficult to judge exactly which comes first.

Elaboration of Policies

It is probably in this area that the parties' position is weakest, however loud and emphatic their claims. With very few exceptions, political parties generally present themselves as potential 'parties in office', that is to say, parties which either aspire to the exercise of power, or currently exercise it, or have done so in the past. In the West, the communist parties are virtually alone in rejecting, or claiming to reject, the constraints that the function of government in Western capitalist countries would impose (although the emphasis of such claims vary considerably from one communist party to another). To exercise power or seek to do so, political parties must put forward programmes and policies to the voters and undertake to implement them if they accede to government. But the business of devising a programme and putting it into operation is affected by many conditions and subject to many pressures. In the first place, it is conditioned by the international situation as well as the political, economic, and social structures of the country concerned. The space for manœuvre available to political parties is much more restricted than their ideology may suggest. The evolution of the European socialist parties testifies to their recognition of that fact and also to the limitations that may be imposed upon political aspirations. But above all, even though the political parties may to a large extent control the electoral game, in the economic, social, and administrative spheres they come up against many other agents whose power in their own particular sectors is frequently much greater. Even where political parties are capable of putting forward more or less ambitious programmes, they face strong competition from interest groups of all kinds and from bureaucracies that play an essential part in drawing up and implementing public policies.

Even so, despite these limitations, the parties play a significant role. Their contribution to the construction of a political programme is decisive, for only they can turn latent, diffuse, and hitherto rejected claims into government programmes: for example, the issue of abortion was bound to remain an ethical, social, and judicial problem until such time as the political parties identified themselves with the more or less clearly expressed desires of society. The parties, whether they are in the majority or in opposition, play an equally important part in channelling and satisfying demands. However, this can be a risky business for a political party, particularly if it is more concerned to represent particular interest groups than to mediate and synthesize conflicting public demands. Finally, the parties also help to fulfil a 'feedback' function, establishing channels of communication between the citizens and the government and thereby helping to temper and modify government policies.

Of course, we cannot overlook the fact that these functions are fulfilled by parties of many different kinds, operating within political systems that offer them a variety of opportunities. But, on the whole, the European democracies all provide relatively similar frameworks for the operations of their political parties: the parties hold a virtual monopoly as regards the organization of the electoral game and political life generally (although it is a monopoly that is occasionally disputed); but they operate in a far more pluralist and competitive context when it comes to carrying out their mandate, that is, in the whole process of policy-making. Here their claim to legitimacy is not nearly so strong, and this leaves room for other modes of organization, influence, and action to operate: the role and functions of interest groups are defined by the context of this pluralist competition.

3

Interest Groups

The formation of groups is a phenomenon common to all societies, for the individual relation between the voter and power, as elaborated in theory by certain schools of political thought, does not in reality find full expression anywhere. The countless different groups in which individuals gather together and interact range from more or less extended families to tribes or ethnic groups and from informal groups to powerfully structured organizations.

All these groups are formed in the name of common interests of one kind or another: affective, family-based, ideological, corporative, professional, or convivial, etc. In the widest possible sense of the expression, all are in some way interest groups. But as used in political science, the expression has acquired a narrower and more precise meaning. It refers to those groups which, in a wide variety of forms, seek to promote their own particular interests *vis-à-vis* the political authorities. Conversely, the political authorities enter into relations with these groups, occasionally to ban them, sometimes to control them, frequently to associate them with their own actions. An interest group is thus distinguished from other groups by the fact that it interacts in some way or other with the State institutions and the parties engaged in the struggle to win and exercise power.

The modes of interaction vary, being more or less structured (the unemployed, pensioners, women, and consumers all constitute vast heterogeneous groups, which even today are often hardly organized at all); moreover, they are affected by the attitudes and ideology of those who hold political power. A group's access to those in power is facilitated or impeded depending upon its relative proximity to them: for example, it is easier for employers than for unions to obtain the ear of the Thatcher Government or the Bush administration. But a government's attitude is often ambivalent: as President, General de Gaulle professed a loathing for the world of finance ('the policies of France are not created in the inner enclosures of the Bourse'). Yet his Governments maintained close relations with economic groups, mainly in the context of planning. Finally, though groups mainly seek to exert pressure on particular territorial or functional segments of the State, their influence does not stop there: a consumer group may boycott a particular product or brand; pensioners, as a group, influence political decisions through the sheer weight of their numbers, and so on. Groups do thus have the power to exert pressure on the State, to influence market economies, and to use the market to exert pressure on the State. (Consider the pressure exerted upon investors by anti-apartheid groups in the United States, in an effort to influence the policies of the American Government.)

From this point of view it is possible to establish a kind of spectrum within the category of interest groups, in which they can be classified according to the intensity of their modalities of action and organization. But in any such attempt at classification we should exclude on the one hand groups that—as such—have no relations at all with politics and, on the other, those whose declared purpose is to win political power, in other words the political parties; for both categories are different in kind from interest groups that are set up to influence those in power. As we make those exclusions, however, we should not underestimate how tenuous the dividing lines sometimes turn out to be: any group, however unconcerned to influence the politico-administrative power, may from time to time or in particular circumstances be prompted to take action to obtain advantages or to oppose decisions contrary to its particular interests: even the most anodyne of friendly societies can become an interest group if it mobilizes its forces under the influence of a leader and/or in reaction to some event that affects it. And equally, an interest group may try to organize itself in such a way as not simply to influence those in power but to try to win power for itself and exercise it. Such a group tries to turn itself into a party by stepping squarely into the politico-electoral arena: one example is provided by the Refugee Party in West Germany, another by groups of ecologists in many parts of Europe. But it is a difficult change to make, as is shown by the failure of the Poujade movement in France and the abortive attempts of Italian employers to set up a political group to represent their interests directly. The principal exception to the rule is constituted by the Labour Party, created to give political expression to the interests of the English working class and its trade unions. As is shown by these examples of unorganized groups turning to activism and interest groups turning into parties, in the context of political science the definition of an interest group rests upon both *organizational factors* and *modalities of action* designed to influence (but not to win) political power. The action that interest groups aiming to influence the political authorities take is likely to be criticized by some and applauded by others, but it is central to the definition of democracy whatever its form: pluralist, oligarchic, or neo-corporatist.

ORGANIZATIONAL FACTORS

In the name of their attachment to pluralism, liberal democracies today recognize both the existence and the legitimacy of these groups in society. However, that has not always been the case. France, by reason of its hostility to *ancien-régime* corporations and in the name of a popular sovereignty that tolerated nothing that stood between the State and the individual, was the country which most virulently declared its aversion to such groups with so-called common interests. It was only by virtue of the irresistible pressure of circumstances (in particular, the organization of trade unions to defend the working class) and a struggle on the part of those who favoured intermediary bodies (often recruited in circles hostile to the Revolution) that the existence of groups became first tolerated, then accepted and recognized. In this respect, France was relatively late in coming to accept all the implications of political liberalism, in particular the pluralism of interests, for it did not do so until the end of the nineteenth century. But even when the other Western democracies accepted the legitimacy of groups in principle, they still excluded organizations considered suspect or a hazard to social order: everywhere trade unions had to fight for a legal and official existence and, in this respect, Britain, the United States, and France differed hardly at all from the more authoritarian regimes of Germany and Italy at the end of the nineteenth century. But the distrust of groups that States manifest does not always take its most radical form, namely, banning. It may be expressed in a wide variety of rules and restrictions to limit the groups' field of action or to control their activities. As a result, the organization of interest groups is subject to twofold constraints: first, those inherent in any form of action, which make it necessary to adapt the organization of the group to the achievement of its objectives; secondly, those imposed by the political authorities, which sometimes force groups to adopt institutional forms and predefined structures.

Constraints on Action

Almond and Powell, in their *Comparative Politics*,[1] suggested distinguishing four types of interest group, according to their modes of organization: those without rules, those that do not take the form of associations, those that are institutional, and those that are associations. Only the last two categories are sufficiently highly organized to be considered as interest groups that aim to exert some influence on political authorities. Institutional groups such as public administrations, the Churches, and the Armed Forces possess structures not originally designed for the purpose of promoting their own particular interests but, when necessary, they can make use of their strong organization to bring influence to bear upon political and administrative decisions. Groups that take the form of associations, on the other hand, are specifically constituted to organize the interests that they represent (trade unions, professional groups, associations, etc.).

The primary function of bureaucracies is not the promotion and defence of their own particular interests. All the same, quite apart from or even to the detriment of their primary functions, these organizations can become powerful interest groups capable of influencing or determining policies to the advantage of their own sectional or personal interests. If that happens, a kind of symbiosis develops between the interest groups and certain segments of the State apparatus which, together, use their privileged means of access to the public authorities for their own ends. In these circumstances, the administrative service concerned, instead of working for all and sundry, gradually becomes primarily preoccupied by its own interests and those of its members, blocking or completely undermining any government reforms that affect it. The Ministry of Education in France has often been cited as the prototype of the kind of bureaucracy that is concerned more with the interests of the teachers of whom it is composed than with the educational policies that are its *raison d'être*. More generally, the *Grands Corps de l'État* in France, the Civil Service in Britain, the *Dirigenza* in Italy, and the senior civil servants of Germany often manage to impose their own views on matters that affect their personal or sectional interests. In many cases, the institutions that they direct have their own internal associations or friendly societies and these constitute the official organs for the expression of their own particular interests, but we should not be misled by this. The group's real influence stems from its internal control of the bureaucracy.

But institutional interest groups are not formed solely to defend the personal interests of their members or to block reforms that would affect them adversely. They are also there to influence the decisions of other institutions and other segments of the bureaucracy: it is, for example, worth noting that in all Western countries, locally or regionally elected representatives have organized themselves into powerful federations or associations on the basis of a 'united front' in which all distinctions of size, political affiliation, and ideology are wiped out.

The Association of the Mayors of France provides a good illustration of this kind of local institutional group, set up to exert pressure on the central government. Associations of a similar type are to be found in Britain (although they are less influential than in France): the Association of Metropolitan Authorities, for example, and the County Councils' Association. In West Germany these are powerful associations by very reason of the development of co-operative federalism (for example, the Association of German Towns, the Deutsche Städtetag, is extremely influential). In Italy, the Association of Regions, although formed recently, has acquired considerable political influence, together with a permanent representative body in Rome whose task is to do the rounds of the ministerial offices, the corridors of Montecitorio (the Chamber of Deputies), and the Palazzo Madama (the Senate).

Equally, alliances are sometimes set up between institutional interest groups and others that take the form of associations, when their respective interests converge. These may constitute veritable 'policy clusters' in which administrations and specific groups find themselves in a position of mutual dependence as they attempt to influence policy-making. An example is provided by the relations between farmers' associations and Ministries of Agriculture.

This confusion may come about all the more easily when, as in France, the bureaucracy tends to present itself as embodying the public's general interest. Its decisions acquire a high juridical and political status the effect of which is to obscure the private interests that are involved at a second level. The shift that then takes place away from the general interest that the administration is supposed, in principle, to represent to the selfish interests of the civil servants involved comes about all the more easily given that the definition of the general interest does not emerge from public debate but is itself proclaimed unilaterally by the administration.

Organization is crucially important if interests are to be co-ordinated, expressed, and defended. Interests that are diffuse and unorganized are usually ill-protected. Such was for a long time the plight of consumers and equally of the unemployed, for until the unemployment crisis prompted greater awareness, with the result that various measures were taken on their behalf, the unemployed, for whom no trade union really assumed responsibility, were without protection. The need to organize is both social and juridical: only with at least a modicum of organization will an interest group acquire cohesion and make its voice heard. It is that requirement that, in France, for instance, explains the success of the 1901 Law on Associations.[2]

A major reason for the proliferation of groups must be the expansion of State interventionism, whether in the form of rules and regulations or of financial interference. These days, few sectors remain unaffected by State action and this encourages the crystallization of interests hitherto diffuse and unorganized. The area in which the creation of such groups has been the most spectacular is that of the environment, where nowadays any development plan, however local, gives rise to defence movements. Sometimes these groups prove to be extremely powerful, not so much as groups capable of determining what is ultimately decided, but rather as 'veto groups' strong enough to block and prevent public action (e.g. halting the construction of nuclear plants in Italy, West Germany, and the United States).

A second reason for the proliferation of *ad hoc* groups is that the central, federal organizations find it difficult or even impossible to preserve their monopoly of the representation of interests. In France, for example, the CNPF has often been reproached by small and medium-sized firms for ignoring *their* specific problems in its negotiations with the State. Nicoud's CID-UNATI was set up as a reaction against the Chambers of Commerce, which were accused of neglecting the needs of small businessmen. In Italy, the famous Bresciani steel producers dissociated themselves from the dominant steel-industry group controlled by the IRI, reckoning that they were being sacrificed in Brussels on the altar of the State-owned steel industry. As Suzanne Berger points out:

The first of the conclusions that emerge from the apparent political opportunism and organizational volatility of the interest groups representing the traditional middle classes is that the economic and social demands of these strata can be expressed in a variety of different types of organizations. Because the range of organizational variation extends from groups that push their claims in violent and illegal opposition to the state to groups that collaborate in essentially corporatist arrangements, the issue of which organizational groups predominates at any time is a highly consequential one for other actors in the system and for the prospects of stability or transformation.[3]

A number of mammoth groups stand out from the heterogeneous collection of associations: the confederations of employers, the trade unions, and the agricultural organizations. In all the Western countries, these groups have special access to the public authorities, if only by reason of their size and powerful organization.

Employers' organizations. In every country, business interests are represented by at least one if not several national organizations. In Germany, the Confederation of Employers' Associations, known as the BDA, the diversity of whose members prevents it from concluding pay agreements and imposing its own directives, sometimes comes into conflict with the powerful Confederation of German Industry, the BDI, which is comprised solely of industrialists. In 1977, these two organizations, without merging, sought to co-ordinate their respective policies by appointing a common Chairman, Hans-Martin Schleyer (kidnapped and assassinated in the autumn of 1977 by the Red Army Faction). Finally, the strong Federation of Chambers of Commerce (DIHT) lends its support to both these groups, which are divided more along professional lines than by any fundamental divergences. In Italy (although for different reasons), a similar division along professional lines separates the Chambers of Commerce, Confindustria, which represents private employers, and Intersind, which co-ordinates the public sector.

In Britain, the Confederation of British Industry (CBI) resulted in 1965 from a merger between the Federation of British Industry and other smaller organizations,[4] with the notable backing of George Brown, then Minister for Economic Affairs and keen to introduce overall planning. In France too, the CNPF[5] and the Chambers of Commerce are very influential, although in the 1970s their authority met a stiff challenge from the Petites et Moyennes Entreprises (PME) and the Petites et Moyennes Industries (PMI) and the Nicoud movement. Nevertheless, it is important to note that following the nationalizations of 1982, firms in the public sector continued to belong to the CNPF, possibly in the secret hope of counterbalancing the groups within that organization that were deeply hostile to socialist policies.

No government can afford to ignore groups that are not only powerful but also indispensable to the elaboration and implementation of its economic, fiscal, and social policies, etc. But the traditions and nature of the relations between public authorities and major employers' groups vary from one system to another. In France, the interventionist tradition and overall planning policies have turned the employers' spokesmen into special partners in State policy-making. In Germany, similarly, the influence of the employers' federations is strong, and they are frequently quite naturally consulted by the State, for Germany has a long tradition of co-operation between the political authorities and the economic powers in the country. As in France, the expression 'social partner' (*Sozial Partner*), which conveys an image of solidarity (virtually unknown in the value systems of English or American businesses), and the institution, since 1951, of co-management (*Mitbestimmung*) in the coal and steel sectors testify to the 'corporatist' style of the relations that exist between representatives of the economic sector on the one hand and the public authorities on the other. Traditions such as these account for the preference that some States show for negotiation with a limited number of responsible partners.

However, State partners such as these often have to face competition from businesses or groups big enough to operate outside centrally co-ordinated associations. This is or frequently has been the case with the most powerful of industrial federations (such as the Chambre syndicale de l'automobile in France, and, in the past, the Chambre syndicale de la sidérurgie) or companies such as ICI in Great Britain. In Italy, relations between Cofindustria and the giant Fiat company have not always been good on account of the strong Christian Democrat influence among the employers, and it was only in the early 1970s that they began to improve, when Agnelli was elected Chairman of the Confederation. But whatever the relations between Fiat and Confindustria, there remains the basic fact of the influence and impact of a single firm that holds virtually a national monopoly in its own sector. Similarly, German banks (which are privately owned) and

Italian ones (which are nationalized) and, even more, the banking and financial circles of the City of London constitute veritable States within States.

The employers usually seek to present a united front to the outside world, particularly in their dealings with the public authorities. However, they are themselves heterogeneous and divided. Clashes often occur between small and big businesses, between the sectors that are protected and those that are competitive, between the industry and the service sectors, between liberals and corporatists, and between socially minded employers and authoritarian ones. The strength of the larger organizations stems in part from the fact that their own interests *as organizations* frequently coincide with those of the public authorities, who are often happy negotiating with a limited number of partners, all in a position to guarantee that agreements will be respected and that the anticipated co-operation will be forthcoming.

Trade unions. Apart from the employers' organizations, the trade unions constitute the other most powerful collection of interest groups. But the trade unions differ from the employers in that they are far more divided, if only because their organization often depends upon an ideological or political programme: they are divided between reformist, social democratic, and revolutionary tendencies; they are to varying degrees linked with particular political parties; and they are out to promote either purely professional objectives or, alternatively, vast social projects. Furthermore, as interest groups, the trade unions are obliged to fight on two fronts at once: the world of business and employers, and the public authorities responsible for social regulations and frequently also for wage policies and the arbitration of disputes.

A preliminary evaluation of trade union power may be made on the basis of the degree of the unions' unity or fragmentation. It is in France that the unions appear to be the most divided, both because they are widely dispersed and because of their lack of collaboration. The Confédération Générale du Travail (CGT, close to the Communist Party), the Confédération Française Démocratique des Travailleurs (CFDT, close to the Socialists), the Force Ouvrière (FO, moderate), the Confédération Française des Travailleurs Chrétiens (CFTC), the Fédération de l'Education Nationale (FEN), and the Confédération Générale des Cadres (CGC) compete with one another and also with the many autonomous unions in each sector to attract members for whom there is no particular advantage in joining anyway (except in a few closed shops such as publishing or the docks). Furthermore, except in rare periods of trade union unity, inter-union relations have at every level been marked by distrust or even open hostility. A similar situation obtains in Italy, except that the 1970s there were marked by strong co-operation, particularly within the inter-union Federation of Metalworkers (FLM), which even operated under a single leadership. But since 1984–5 tensions have reappeared, although the situation has not deteriorated to the competitive and acrimonious level of the 1950s and early 1960s. The Confederazione Generale Italiana del Lavoro (CGIL), which is close to the Communist Party, comprises a minority of Socialists and Christian Democrats (a reflection of the initial consensus established in June 1944 between the three principal parties in the 'Rome Pact') and is the most powerful of the confederations. As in France, the Cold War led to a split in the trade union movement: in 1948, the Christian Democrats left the CGIL to form a 'free' CGIL, which two years later became the Confederazione Italiana dei Sindacati dei Lavatori (CISL). In 1950, the trade unionists close to the Social Democratic Party (which had separated from the Italian Socialist Party (PSI) in 1947) also formed their own trade union, the Unione Italiana del Lavoro (UIL). These three unions, which frequently took common action between 1968 and 1985 (when, in the spring, divisions between them became apparent in the referendum on the indexing of wages) are unquestionably the most powerful trade union organizations and the ones that can count on the ear of the Italian public authorities. But they are frequently outnumbered —particularly in the public sector—by the collection of small, autonomous unions whose strength lies, not so much in the overall size of their membership, but rather in the virtual monopoly that they hold over a number of key professions or sectors (civil aviation pilots, train drivers, etc.).

The German unions are in a less divided situation as competition between the three major organizations is essentially confined to the sector of the public services and employees. The Deutsche Angestelltengewerkschaft (DAG), whose creation in 1945 was prompted by hostility towards the principle of unions formed on the basis of professions, is essentially composed of employees from both the public and the private sectors, but is somewhat in decline. The Deutscher Beamten Bund (DBB) is a federation of civil servants; this union includes rather more public employees than its rivals and enjoys a dominant position in the highest echelons of the Bund civil service. Finally, the Deutscher Gewerkschaftsbund (DGB) is a powerful confederation of seventeen unions, one-third of whose members belong to the metalworkers' union (IG Metall). However, despite its great power and the monopoly that it holds over the representation of many sectors of industry, even this confederation is not proof against many internal rifts between the various individual federations that compose it. As regards the public authorities, the DGB is an interlocutor that cannot be ignored. But its authority is limited by the strength of the seventeen individual unions, all of which energetically defend their own autonomy.

On the face of it, the British unions present an image of strength in that nearly all gather together under the banner of the Trades Union Congress. In reality, however, divisions abound. These result, in the first place, from the considerable disparity between the size of different unions. Another divisive factor is the disparity between the various unions' organizational structures: some are fragmented, allowing a large measure of autonomy to local sections, while others are very centralized, granting their general secretaries powers that are extremely wide—virtually dictatorial, some critics would claim. A third source of conflict lies in the unions' relations with the Labour Party: some belong to the Party *en bloc*, while others allow their members to make their own individual decisions. Then there are classical oppositions between unions of public employees and those from the private sector and, more recently, between blue-collar unions (in decline) and white-collar ones. These tensions sometimes run very high indeed and may be exploited either by the government (as in the miners' strike, which did not gain the support of the rest of industry) or by employers. The most recent illustration is provided by the Employment Act of 26 July 1988, which limits the powers of the trade unions and strengthens guarantees for non-strikers.

The strength of trade unions may also be gauged from the size of their memberships and, above all, the percentage of the total numbers of wage-earners that they represent. The trade unions of France are unquestionably among the weakest in Europe, for here the meagre trade union membership (about 2 million in all) is also reflected in the inadequacy of their funds and resources. In Italy, trade unionists are more numerous although numbers are tending to fall as a result of the economic crisis and changes taking place amongst wage-earners. In West Germany the level of trade union membership is high: about 12 million in 1980, that is, 40 per cent of the wage-earning population. In Britain there were 9 million trade unionists in 1988, but that was 3 million less than when Margaret Thatcher came to power. However, as well as these impressive figures and the disparities between the levels of trade union membership from one country to another, there are a number of other considerations to be taken into account. In Britain, union membership is in many cases compulsory. Many sectors where trade unions have long been established maintain a 'closed shop' system. Furthermore, in both Britain and Germany, union subscriptions are often deducted from wages at source and paid over directly to the union. The union is thereby guaranteed resources which enable it to provide its members with services and strike pay far in excess of anything that their French or Italian counterparts can expect. Finally, in Britain, West Germany, and Italy—but not in France—the practice of collective bargaining within the various industries is far more common; and the effect of this is to strengthen the unions, which alone are empowered to negotiate with employers and so are in a position to obtain tangible benefits for their members. In contrast, negotiation procedures in France tend to minimize the role of the unions at plant level, promoting instead that of the individuals who make up the confederal leadership. It is the latter who negotiate at top level with their opposite numbers from management or from the Government (or so it was until the Mauroy Government introduced reforms encouraging negotiations within the plant itself).

Agricultural organizations. These present a particularly interesting example of interest groups. In the first place, they display features that are reminiscent of both employers' associations and trade unions. Secondly, they continue to wield great influence, despite the un-checked demographic decline of agricultural areas as if, in politics, the land and its primary occupants, the farmers, were deemed to deserve special treatment.

At this point an observation of a general nature seems in order. Like Balzac's ass's skin (*La Peau de chagrin*), the agricultural world is shrinking fast. In Britain, farmers and farm labourers have for some time represented no more than a tiny proportion of the working population (3 per cent). In the United States, their number dropped from 30 million in the 1920s to 10 million by the 1970s, and in 1984 they represented no more than 2.3 per cent of the working population. A similar decline has taken place in West Germany so that, despite all the political declarations about maintaining the numbers of the agricultural population, today they total barely 1 million workers. In France, where the agricultural workers represent no more than 7 per cent of the working population, and in Italy, where they have been reduced from 17.2 per cent of the working population in 1971 to 11 per cent in 1981, the decline has been even more rapid than in the rest of the Western States.

However, this demographic decline has certainly not been reflected in a parallel loss of influence. On the contrary. In Italy in particular, the small landowners (the *coldiretti*) have been defended assiduously by the Christian Democrats, for whom they constitute a privileged group of clients. In France, too, relations between the farmers and the Gaullist Governments have always been marked by intense collaboration, notwithstanding outbreaks of violence from time to time: the notoriously unpopular 'drought tax' of 1976 was regarded by public opinion as typifying the preferential treatment meted out to the farmers. Similar analyses have been produced by observers of the situation in West Germany. For example, Grosser and Menudier describe the German farmers as constituting 'one of the most powerful pressure groups in West Germany, despite the fact that the importance of the agricultural sector in the context of economic life as a whole continues to diminish'.[6]

There are many reasons for the disproportionate degree of influence that farmers wield over politicians. The following points are worth noting: (1) many constituencies are predominantly rural and here the farmers constitute the most homogeneous and influential group because of the economic impact of their activities; (2) in the collective national consciousness, the issue of the countryside and nature tends to be a highly emotive one; (3) the farmers hold an important position at a local political level as a consequence of the policy of division into separate communes adopted in France and Italy, for example, and until the 1960s also in Germany.

But the crucial factor seems to be the particular structure of this social group and the way in which it is organized. In general, farmers band together under umbrella organizations that include agricultural producers of every kind: small-scale and large-scale, tenant farmers and landowners—organizations that look essentially to the State for support. Whereas industrial employers and trade unions must defend their interests in the face of their partners-cum-adversaries as well as the State, farmers, whatever their legal status, seldom need to fight on two fronts at once. Furthermore, because of the specific nature of their activities which, until quite recently, were not subject to the mechanisms of the market economy (or were only partially so), farmers, more than other social groups, have tended to be taken under the State's wing. Agricultural interests are frequently represented by a single, powerful organization, and the usual procedures adopted in their defence include negotiation, consultation, and institutional integration. This is certainly the case in Britain, where the National Farmers' Union (the NFU) represents 90 per cent of all British farmers,[7] in France, where the FNSEA, despite challenges from both the left and the right, can still justifiably claim to represent the whole of the agricultural sector, and in West Germany, where the Deutscher Bauernverband (DBV) represents virtually all the country's farmers. Here, furthermore, as in France and Italy, Chambers of Agriculture constitute a further essential source of support as well as an institutionalized instrument of communication between the economic and the political spheres.

The power of the agricultural organizations is such that, as Grosser notes, 'Liberalism is discounted in all countries that lay claim to a market economy.'[8] But that power seems to have peaked in the late 1970s. Since then, the economic crisis and the demographic decline of the agricultural sector have combined to check the effectiveness of agricultural interest groups. It is significant in this respect that, since 1980, government measures at both European and national levels have been designed to stem the flood of excess produce and the aid that gave rise to it, by reforming the mechanisms for supporting the market.

The Influence of Public Authorities

Interest groups must be organized if they wish to make themselves heard. But the public authorities that are their primary target are themselves by no means passive. Sometimes they ban groups (as did the Le Chapelier law of 1791 in France) but more often they seek to contain or control them by regulations, or even to limit the pressure that they bring to bear by integrating and institutionalizing them. Most solutions involving control through regulations are essentially liberal, while those involving integration are of a more corporatist inspiration.

Even in systems that are the most favourable to group action and that are prepared to accept groups as a constitutive element of liberal democracy, it sometimes proves necessary to intervene to limit jungle law and shady deals.

One example of this kind of control is provided in West Germany, where the law of 21 September 1972 establishes the procedure for groups seeking to enter into relations with Parliament and the government. All such groups must register with the President of the Bundestag, indicating their social purpose and their structure and stating the names of their leaders and representatives. Through this formality (which nearly 1,000 organizations observe), the group representatives gain admittance to the Bundestag, where they can make the necessary contacts and exchange information and, in some cases, may be invited to take part in hearings organized by parliamentary commissions. As can be seen, the obligation to register is hardly a stiff requirement, and it has had very little effect except in so far as group organizations have become more public. The German registration system was inspired by American legislation, but it is less complex and detailed, though it is true that in Germany lobbies are not as omnipresent as they are in Congress.

Public authorities sometimes adopt a more interventionist attitude towards interest groups, seeking to integrate them, either by formally associating them in the decision-making process, or by turning the groups into quasi-public institutions.

These days, public authorities everywhere consult interest groups, for it is no longer possible to administrate and impose regulations unilaterally. The European countries have frequently sought to set up a system of official consultation with the government's major 'social partners'. No doubt such attempts may be seen as stemming from the streak of corporatism and anti-liberalism by which the systems of Germany, Italy, and France are all to varying degrees affected. But they could also be interpreted as a quest for social and political consensus.

In Italy, consultation often takes place through public bodies which incorporate a selection of private interests. As Marco Cammelli writes: 'There is quite a marked tendency to integrate these interests into the politico-administrative circuit rather than have them apply autonomous and specific pressure from outside.'[9] In West Germany, consultation with social partners from the economic sector was given official status by the 1967 Economic Stabilization Law, under the label of 'concerted action', (*Konzierte Aktion*)—a move that was facilitated by the 'Grand Coalition' between the CDU–CSU and the

SPD at that time. However, its achievements were limited and, during the 1970s, interest in formal consultation of this kind waned. The lack of success of such consultations was particularly striking in Britain where the Labour Government of the mid-1960s (and in particular the Minister for Economic Affairs, George Brown) set up the National Economic Development Council composed of six trade unionists and six representatives from the employers' confederation, the CBI. In the event, the institutionalization of consultation (inspired by the French model of overall planning at this time, credited with responsibility for the economic boom) failed to supplant the system of 'government by committee' through which the public authorities took concerted action with their partners.[10]

Despite the somewhat disappointing results produced by integrating groups into consultative organs on more or less equal terms, France has remained faithful to 'administrative polysynody' and continues to set up countless committees and commissions of all kinds both within the State apparatus (personnel commissions) and in its dealings with groups. There is no systematic record of them all, but they are generally reckoned to run into many thousands. The policy of the French administration is to impose upon its partners a number of obligations and constraints that the groups must accept if they wish to be considered as legitimate consultants. In the first place, the public authorities rule out obstructive and violent groups and those that present too great a challenge to their preferred existing partners. Thus, up until 1981, the government refused to enter into dialogue with the minority trade unions of agricultural workers (MODEF, FFA, CNSTP) and in 1983 FNSEA returned in force to the corridors of power even though the minority unions had obtained one-third of the votes in the elections to the Chambers of Agriculture on 28 January 1983. By bestowing the label of 'representativity' (together with the financial aid that goes with these favoured relationships), the State sets up a fruitful deal: using this seal of approval,[11] it is able to select the partners that it prefers, albeit not without occasional mishaps. When marginal groups cannot make themselves heard in the corridors of power, they sometimes take to the streets and turn to violence. The French administration also employs the technique of 'official recognition', another way of selecting groups that was adopted, for example, in the cases of the committees for economic expansion in the 1950s and the associations for the protection of the environment that were recognized in the context of the law of 1976. As

Miriam Golden notes in connection with Italy, where these practices are also common,

the innumerable committees of experts established to back up central and local administrations are part of a proliferation of representative bodies, all with a common purpose: namely to increase the number of institutionalized interpreters of social interests; and also to profit from their implicit political legitimacy which provides them with new ways to express themselves.[12]

Institutional integration takes many different forms and is produced by a whole spectrum of juridical and organizational instruments ranging from groups that are only minimally integrated to others that assume the form of public organizations.

The first level of institutionalization is to arrange for the representatives of particular interests to operate as such within political bodies. It is a form of institutionalization that is not highly regarded either in Britain or in the United States, while in continental Europe it constitutes an unfortunate reminder of the corporatism of the Fascist regimes. All the same, a few systems modelled on this way of organizing interests still operate in Italy, West Germany, and especially France. In West Germany, it is worth noting the handful of 'Chambers of Workers' in the *Länder* of Saarland and in Bremen, but these are exceptional examples and the system is unlikely to be extended to the rest of the country. The post-war constitutions of Italy and France set up Economic Councils (in France, the Conseil économique et social, in Italy, the Consiglio nazionale dell'economica e del lavoro). Their function is to advise the government on economic and social matters, but in both countries the influence of these assemblies has remained marginal. France carried the experiment a little further, setting up the Comités de Développement Économique Régional (CODER) in 1964 and the Comités Économiques et Sociaux Régionaux, which took over from them in 1972. But de Gaulle's 1969 proposal to introduce changes in the Senate and to set up regional councils, in the form of assemblies where politicians could come into contact with the representatives of various interests, met with strong resistance and was rejected at the referedum of 27 April 1969.

The next level of institutionalization is reached when a private organization is granted public prerogatives or is made responsible for the management of public bodies. This often happens in France, where many associations are entrusted with public duties together with the prerogatives that go with them (the power to raise taxes and impose special regulations). But it also happened in Italy where, until the health reforms of the 1970s were introduced, the agricultural union, Coldiretti, a body that came under the law pertaining to the private sector, was empowered to manage the bodies that dealt with the social security of agricultural workers. Finally, in countries with civil law, certain groups are integrated by being brought under public-sector regulations. Here, Chambers of Commerce represent the best example. In Britain and the United States, the function of these is simply to co-ordinate and express the interests of their members. But the Chambers of Commerce of Italy, Germany, and France all have the status of public institutions. Another example of the curious osmosis that takes place between the private and the public sectors is provided by professional groups such as doctors and lawyers in France, or by the German body responsible for ensuring that the regulations are observed in the recruitment of labour and with respect to working conditions, Ordnung des Berufsstandes. The situation is similar in Italy, where, amid the veritable jungle of some 41,000 *enti pubblici*, the function of about 2,000 of them is to supervise the ordering and management of various sectors of economic and social life.

While the regulating and controlling function of some of these bodies is similar to that of the independent agencies and commissions of the United States, the structures of the two types of organization differ substantially. The orders or *enti* invested with the prerogatives that pertain to public services provide public organization for private interests; whereas in the case of the American agencies, the boards of directors are appointed by the public authorities according to the criteria of expertise, independence[13] (tenure of office is, as a rule, not renewable), and pluralism (the board members are, in principle, drawn from diverse walks of life).

INTEREST GROUPS AND THE POLITICAL SYSTEM

One reason why it is particularly difficult to apprehend the phenomenon of interest groups is that they are organized in so many different ways. Another is that they operate in so many different sectors—wherever power is held by the State—and that they do so in so many different forms. Let us try to sort out this confused picture by examining how interest groups operate in relation to two main parameters: the structure of the State and the politico-administrative characteristics of the system, all of which help to shape and direct the interest groups' modes of action. In conclusion, we shall examine the ways in which interest groups affect the functioning and nature of the political system.

Where Interest Groups Apply Pressure

In Western democracies, power is divided both functionally and territorially. The division of responsibilities between the executive and the legislative, and between central and local authorities is dictated by a country's constitutional patterns and historical heritage and by the relative power of various institutions at any given moment. Since the purpose of interest groups is to influence the public authorities and to prevent decisions that would be unfavourable to them, it is hardly surprising that they adopt modes of action that are closely related to the structure of public power, adapting these when shifts of power take place either within the central State apparatus or in the institutional balance between the centre and the periphery.

The legislature. For a long time parliaments provided the best places for interest groups to operate, because of their prestige and symbolic value. The decision to treat parliament as the major target was natural enough: this was where power both seemed to, and often did, lie; besides, members of parliament were the most accessible elements in the system. Take, for example the Third and Fourth French Republics. Alongside the political parties and parliamentary groups, many *ad hoc* groups were created to defend some specific interest or other. Despite the fact that, under the Fourth Republic, the rules of the National Assembly forbade 'the constitution, in the Assembly, of groups purporting to defend particular local or professional interests', such groups continued to operate in the guise of friendly societies or committees of inquiry: the interests of home distillers, private schools, forestry workers, and farmers were among those most vigorously championed in the French Parliament.

Although the British Parliament no longer has the power it once had ('short of changing a man into a woman', as the French say), interest groups still subject it to intense lobbying. But, as Max Beloff and Gillian Peele point out, this is chiefly in order to attract publicity and media coverage, for the groups are generally perfectly well aware that Parliament is unlikely to adopt a different line from that laid down by the executive. In the Italian Parliament, groups exert pressure mainly upon the commissions which, under certain conditions, are empowered to pass laws (known as *leggine*, or 'little laws'). The specialized nature of these commissions and their members and their relatively unpublicized activities make for an ideal situation for the defence of specific interests.

The pressure exerted by groups within parliaments is thus conditioned by the degree of autonomy that the parliaments concerned have retained in relation to the executive, the strategies that the groups adopt (discreet action or maximum publicity), and the greater or lesser degree of public access to the committees in which most negotiations take place. Finally, the influence wielded by pressure groups is also determined by the socio-professional origins of members of parliament. Without taking a sociologically deterministic view, it must be said that a parliament's composition is bound to affect the degree of ease with which particular groups gain a hearing. In the parliaments of the French Third and Fourth Republics, the liberal professions were over-represented; now it is the turn of the civil servants, in particular teachers from the public sector.

The executive. The primary targets of interest groups everywhere are the executive and its administration, as these have become the essential organs of decision at every level, from preparing the ground for a policy through to implementing and monitoring it. In France under the Fifth Republic, the central focus of pressure groups has shifted from the legislature to the executive and the administration. Civil servants have an ambivalent attitude: they hold considerable reservations where 'pressure groups' are concerned, considering them to be illegitimate, but are better disposed towards the recognized institutional spokesmen, who are indispensable when it comes to gathering information and ensuring that policies are correctly implemented.[14] Contacts between the administration and these recognized groups are constant, sustained, and frequently intimate, the more so as such dialogue is encouraged by the common education, recruitment, and careers of the élites involved. The attitudes that élites, both public and private, share, because of the training that they have all received in prestigious establishments of further education and in the *grandes écoles*, are reinforced by the 'old-boy network' that operates within those same sectors. A public administrator becomes a private one and finds it easy to enter into dialogue with his colleagues, who have risen along with him in their careers. It would no doubt be mistaken to leap to conclusions of corruption, connivance, and collusion, but the visible facts in France emphasize the high degree of interpenetration between the political, administrative, and economic sectors. This transformation of the role played by the administration in relation to the sectors under its control is not solely attributable to causes external to it, such as the intensity and efficacy of the action of interest groups. To a large extent it also results from the desire of each administrative section to defend its own preserve against other sections that threaten its power and influence. By protecting the groups that depend upon it, each section of the administration is to some extent protecting its own patrimony against encroachments from adjacent sections. Clearly, the relations between the administration and interest groups are far from one-sided. The groups certainly exert pressure but they are also treated as 'instruments' by the administrative sections involved, which use them to defend their own policies and interests. It is, after all, not uncommon to see a French or German Minister of Agriculture jubilating over farmers' demonstrations which, they say, are bound to strengthen their own position in negotiations with Brussels. Furthermore, it would be mistaken to regard the relations that obtain between administrations and interest groups as relations between two homogeneous worlds. In reality, administrations are every bit as fragmented, competitive, and divided as interest groups themselves are.

Politico-Administrative Cultures and Modes of Action

The concept of a politico-administrative culture relates to the body of rules and values that particular societies produce—rules and values that do not necessarily tally perfectly with those to which the system overtly subscribes. A good illustration is provided in France by the contrast between general, impersonal regulations and individual practice—all the 'arrangements' that make it possible for the system to function and that are consequently accommodated and accepted not only by society but also by the administration. The modes of action that interest groups adopt are determined by a number of specific factors: the nature of the group, its strategies, the means at its disposal, and the openings that the system affords it; and either they fit into the framework of the national politico-administrative culture or they are at odds with it. In other words, a group's modes of action are essentially determined by the means available to it and the extent to which the influence exerted by interest groups is tolerated by the political system and by society in general.

There are many possible modes of action for interest groups but they are unevenly distributed and vary with place and time. One essential and fundamental factor is *access* to the politico-administrative authorities that the group seeks to influence. Greater ease of access is enjoyed by strategically located groups, institutional groups, and those that the authorities have already recognized as 'legitimate interlocutors'. That applies in particular to powerful groups such as employers' associations, trade unions, and groups that are closely involved with the authorities. Access that is carefully controlled and limited discriminates powerfully in favour of particular groups ('representative' unions, officially 'recognized' groups, etc.). This means that some groups may be described as 'outside the system', just as certain political parties are. Two strategies are open to these marginal or rejected groups: they may either try to win acceptance by bowing to the regulations and convincing the authorities of their legitimacy; or they may violate the usual norms, adopting methods that are condemned but sometimes effective: destroying public buildings, violent demonstrations, refusing to pay taxes, kidnapping civil servants, blackmail, and so on. Such tactics, initially the weapons of the weak in many cases, are becoming more general as a consequence of the attitude of public authorities which, having declared their refusal to be blackmailed or to give in to violence, eventually agree to negotiate with the trouble-makers. This lesson has been learned even by those who favour action that respects the social norms. It should be pointed out that the public authorities are not always solely responsible for denying access to certain groups; sometimes it is a consequence of forceful pressure exerted by dominant groups which adopt a policy of boycott in order to preserve their own monopolies (e.g. the FNSEA, the farmers' union, in France).

A second factor is money. Here again, situations vary widely: American interest groups sometimes spend colossal sums in their endeavours to influence Congress, much more than is spent in Europe. Some groups are self-financing (businesses, and the English and American unions), others are financed by the public authorities themselves (unions and associations in France and Italy). In some countries, the use of money, in particular to influence political parties, is controlled. But in any event, misappropriation of public funds, corruption, and illegal funding are by no means exceptional. Groups that possess financial resources are often tempted to misuse them. This has been repeatedly illustrated by instances of corruption, whose full extent is not always discovered but which may involve figures as eminent as US Vice-President Spiro Agnew, President Leone in Italy (the Lockheed scandal), West German Finance Minister, Count Lambsdorff, and a number of others (the Flick scandal), and so on. Groups lacking money are obliged to resort to other means such as mass movements or demonstrations of a spectacular nature (hunger strikes, for example).

The third important factor is expertise, technical skill. There are at least two ways for groups to use the technical skills at their disposal: either they can get the public authorities to recognize them, as such, and thus win legitimacy and the right to dialogue as equals with the administration; or they can use their skills or influence in a particular area to operate in another field, that of politics, for example. In the first case, the interest group's impact upon the political power and the administration is plain to see, for the public authorities are dependent upon or even prisoners of the groups that possess the necessary information and knowledge. Dramatic examples of such situations are provided by the United States, where the oil and gas companies withheld from President Carter the information that he needed to implement his energy policies, and by France, where the government found itself in a position of dependence upon the steelworkers' association.[15] Other examples are provided by the numerous cases of over-investment provoked by optimistic forecasts made by groups with a vested interest in doing so (for example, the nuclear lobby in France, the 'cathedrals in the desert' in southern Italy). It is also possible for groups to intervene at the parliamentary level simply by drawing up a bill that some member of parliament is willing to introduce. This is common practice in the United States but it occurs to some extent in all parliamentary systems. Finally, there is now another way for groups to make use of their skills or status outside their normal and legitimate field. It is a practice that is becoming increasingly frequent as political life is more and more affected by the media: artists, scientists, and university professors are mobilized for causes of the most heterogeneous nature, causes which in many cases have very little to do with their own specialist fields. Nowadays any group that wants its voice to be widely heard is bound to engage in such tactics.

Pluralism, Oligarchy, or Neo-corporatism?

As was emphasized at the beginning of this chapter, attitudes towards interest groups and their role have varied greatly between different countries. On the one hand, France and Italy tend to regard such groups with considerable reservations. In United States, by contrast, the organization of interest groups is considered both to demonstrate and to guarantee the country's social and political pluralism. In the one case, the general interest is held to be served by the people's representatives (in effect, the government and its administration); in the other, it is conceived as stemming from the confrontation and reconciliation of numerous conflicting private interests.

Interest groups, those associations of citizens so admired by Tocqueville, are accordingly considered by a whole current of liberal thought—particularly in America—as a fundamental element of pluralist democracy. It was A. F. Bentley who proclaimed that credo the most forcefully:

The great task in the study of any form of social life is the analysis of these groups. It is much more than classification, as that term is ordinarily used. When groups are adequately stated, everything is stated. When I say everything, I mean everything.[16]

The thesis is important because of the emphasis that it lays upon processes rather than structures, but it goes much too far when it reduces all political activity (including that of the State) to the interaction of groups all considered to be more or less equal. The 'group' theory of political life was taken up half a century later by David Truman, who also tended to set all groups on the same footing, thereby to some extent recasting the classical democratic theory according to which all individuals, as citizens, are free and equal: Truman replaces 'individuals' by 'interest groups'. Not until the 1960s did attention shift to the differentiation and inequality between groups. But over and above these different assessments of the status of groups, it was generally agreed that the action of groups was good for democracy. This positive view was founded upon a notion of the healthiness of competition between groups, and also upon the realization that individuals may belong to a number of different groups that partially overlap (with cross-cutting divisions). This means that both affinities and differences exist between group members and these make for stability and consensus (because of the practical need for compromise). Of course, this optimistic but by no means groundless view is reinforced by the assumption that the capacities and statuses of the various groups are all comparable. This pluralist model was subsequently disputed, particularly in the United States, on the grounds, not so much of the group theory *per se*, but rather of the question of the concentration or pluralism of élites (for example, the disagreement, in the 1950s and 1960s, between those who regarded the United States as being controlled by an oligarchic élite (Floyd Hunter, Wright Mills) and those who maintained that it was a polyarchic pluralism (Robert Dahl, in particular)).

Although the optimistic view of groups has predominated in the United States, it has never been a universal one, as is shown by the attempts during the 1930s to bring the lobbies of Congress under control, and the trenchant criticisms voiced by many politicians and political theorists such as Ted Lowi.

But one of the most vigorous critiques of the 'group theory' was put forward by Mancur Olson[17] in his work *The Logic of Collective Action*. Olson challenged the central assumption in the theory, namely, that economic groups take action to defend the interests of the group and the individuals who compose it, to the personal benefit of the latter. Olson reckons that in *large* groups individuals are not usually prepared to make sacrifices in order that the group as a whole should attain its objectives, even if the result obtained by collective action would in the long run prove to be to the advantage of each individual. He shows that large economic groups (consumers, for instance) are much less powerful than small groups of industrialists that are organized and strongly structured. In other words, the existence of a common interest is not enough to set up a group that comprises all or virtually all those who are its potential members and that is capable of taking collective action. The case of the trade unions is typical of this paradoxical situation. Although their actions help to win advantages for all wage-earners, most of them attract the membership of only a small percentage of their potential supporters. And this discrepancy is even more striking in the case of consumer groups.

In France and in the rest of Europe, criticism of the relations between public authorities and interest groups take a number of different forms. One line taken is Jacobin and revolutionary in spirit: in the name of the State, it rejects all intervention on the part of groups, and even goes so far as to condemn their existence. It cannot be denied that this analysis contains the seeds of anti-democratic and totalitarian developments in the name of a State with a tendency to absorb everything into itself.

Another critical approach is not directed against groups in general, only against those of them that can control political power through a tight-knit oligarchy or plutocracy. This kind of criticism, from traditionalist and anti-republican circles, does not reject groups as such—on the contrary, for these constitute the intermediary bodies of which they so much approve. What it condemns is the control that a small handful of individuals hold over the reviled democratic system. In the eyes of these critics, the way to make society healthier is to bring back groups and to organize them—to the detriment of the individual —under the aegis of the State, the summit of this edifice of collective bodies. The corporative experiments of Germany, Italy, France (the Vichy regime), Spain, and Portugal testified to the collapse of the liberal democracies that had been founded upon the idea of 'free individuals, all equal before the law' and signalled the establishment of a new order in which groups, far from constituting an expression of pluralism, became no more than so many cogs in the State machinery. In a corporatist concept of society, groups are expected to play a determining part in the exercise of power, for the representation of organized interests takes the place of traditional political representation based on universal suffrage. Although all the European political systems that embraced this concept have disappeared, there can be no doubt that vestiges of that recent past still survive (the professional orders in France, the obligation to renegotiate collective contracts every three years in Italy).

However, the expression 'neo-corporatism', which has acquired considerable popularity, does not refer to those survivals so much as to new forms of co-operation between the State and various groups. During the 1970s, neo-corporatism gave rise to a school of thought that produced a series of extremely important studies.

What is neo-corporatism? We should do well to refer to the original definitions given by the leaders of this school, for although the theory has enjoyed considerable success, the concepts involved have not been expressed at all clearly and, furthermore, its field of application has been greatly expanded (meso-corporatism, micro-corporatism, etc.). For Philip Schmitter, one of the chief promoters of the theory, neo-corporatism may be defined as follows:

Corporatism can be defined as a system of interest representation in which the constituent units are organized into a limited number of singular, compulsory, noncompetitive, hierarchically ordered and functionally differentiated categories, recognized or licensed (if not created) by the state and granted a deliberate representational monopoly within their respective categories.[18]

The same author contrasts this neo-corporatist model with the pluralist model, which he defines as:

A system of interest representation in which the constituent units are organized into an unspecified number of multiple, voluntary, competitive, nonhierarchically ordered and self-determined (as to type or scope of interest) categories which are not specifically licensed, recognized, subsidized, created or otherwise controlled in leadership selection or interest articulation by the state and which do not exercise a monopoly of representational activity within their respective categories.[19]

As abstract models, the pluralist and the neo-corporatist options are clearly distinct and stand in contrast to one another. In truth, it is hard to see in what respect the definition of neo-corporatism distinguishes it from the classic corporatism tried out by the Fascist regimes, except in so far as it suggests it to be possible for the classic system of representation (parliaments) to coexist with a system designed for the representation of interests. Two questions then arise: first, can the neo-corporatist model be empirically verified? and secondly, is neo-corporatism compatible with the maintenance of classic liberal democracy?

The first question has prompted a spate of empirical research, particularly in the countries of northern and central Europe (Scandinavia, West Germany, Austria, and Switzerland), but also in Italy, Britain, and France. But, despite the abundance of literature on the matter, the answers are far from clear, for the degrees of corporatism may vary greatly from one country to another and even within a single State. It is generally recognized that the neo-corporatist model is inapplicable to the USA, Britain,[20] Italy, and France. Nevertheless, in France, for example, there are certain sectors, such as agriculture[21] and education, where in its essential components the model may be applicable.

On the other hand, Austria, West Germany, and especially Sweden do appear to fit the neo-corporatist model, for it is one that tends to find favour when power is held by social democratic parties that are close to the unions and prepared to support them as the primary negotiators with their partners, the employers, and to sanction the agreements that are reached. The essence of the neo-corporatist system seems to lie in the public status conferred upon these organizations and the agreements that they reach. The various agents involved in the negotiations confer legitimacy upon one another and guarantee to fulfil their mutual commitments. Problems nevertheless remain. In France, for instance, many features of the neo-corporatist model are detectable (where the structure and status of 'peak organizations' are concerned, for example). Yet these institutional elements do not lead to neo-corporatist policies even under the most favourable conditions (as between 1981 and 1986, when the Socialist Party was in power). Furthermore, since consultation and the conclusion of agreements are, in principle, indicative of neo-corporatist practices, it has sometimes been assumed, on the strength of such indicators, that a neo-corporatist model applies. That may be an altogether false assumption (particularly when it is suggested that the model applies not at the topmost levels, as in the original definition of neo-corporatism, but at intermediate levels (meso-corporatism) or local levels (micro-corporatism). The real situation thus appears to be extremely diverse, combining elements of both pluralist and neo-corporatist representation. But at this point it seems reasonable to ask: what is so 'new' about all this? In liberal democracies, interests have always been represented and, to varying degrees, organized and protected, for it is not as if liberal democracy ever existed in a pure state in some golden age before the appearance of corporatism. We know what pluralist democracies, with all their imperfections, are; and we are also familiar with the particular characteristics and vices of authoritarian corporatism. The question is, is there any place for a neo-corporatism that might combine traditional political representation with a new system for the representation of interests?

Lehmbruch believes there is. He has pointed out that neo-corporatism was not an alternative to pluralist democracy, but could interact with it in various forms.[22] Such a view seems open to only two interpretations: either it is unrealistic, or else it strips the neo-corporatist theory of most of its interest. It is fair to say that the idea of a compromise between, on the one hand, pluralist democracy and, on the other, forms of organization and intervention by interest groups that are fundamentally constricting, authoritarian, and oligarchic is unrealistic. If the neo-corporatist model is fully applied in practice, we should not beat about the bush but speak quite simply of corporatism.

That way, there is no danger of conferring legitimacy upon an authoritarian way of exercising power. On the other hand, if no more than dispersed and unsystematized corporatist elements are present, there is no need to construct a theoretical model which no longer explains what the liberal democracies of today really are: namely, confirmed pluralist systems within which it is possible for many heterogeneous elements bequeathed by each country's own particular history and traditions to coexist. In the democracies of the West, the aftermath of recent corporatist experiments lives on here and there, as do certain corporative practices of the *ancien régime*; but these 'foreign bodies' exist alongside other elements that are equally 'impure' from the point of view of classic democratic theory. For example, the representation of specific territories in upper chambers, the maintenance of traditional practices (such as inherited parliamentary membership in the House of Lords), and the persistence of community solidarities that win out over the political individualism of liberal constitutions. The wave of neo-corporatism may have stimulated interesting speculation, but it is fair to wonder whether it really helps to interpret or explain the evolution of Western democracies, either individually or collectively. The most interesting aspect of the neo-corporatist theory is that it has revealed and demonstrated that, contrary to American theories of the group-based nature of political life, groups certainly are not all equal and their functions are exceedingly diverse, ranging from the expression of particular interests to the formulation, determination, and implementation of public policies. But even in the cases where corporatism has made the deepest inroads, it is inconceivable that any of the Western democracies should forsake the classical form of parliamentary representation. Despite all its limitations, this remains the fundamental creed of liberal democracy.

4

Voters, Elections, and the Elected

The Western democracies are all founded upon election, for it is this that confers legitimacy upon power. But, as political and constitutional history teaches us, a declaration of intent may be a far cry from its realization, just as a constitution may be an imperfect guide to political practice. Sartori[1] has wittily remarked that 'election means selection', and it is quite true that for a long time the Western democracies retained devices designed to eliminate certain potential electors even in countries where suffrage was claimed to be universal. The trouble is that, as with any other idealistic principle, if power is to be attributed to the people or nation, certain juridical and political mechanisms are necessary and these may distort or even destroy the initial objective.

ELECTORAL SYSTEMS

Political democracy expresses itself partly by giving most of the population the right to vote. But the conditions in which that right is exercised, in particular the procedures of electoral competition, mould and determine the conditions in which democracy is played out. Even if the purpose of the 'rules of the game' observed by Western democracies is to transform the violence and conflicts inherent in social relations into a symbolic battle, the partners and parties concerned must also accept that transformation: the object is to settle peacefully upon a winner who will govern but do so under the best possible conditions for freedom and fairness. The balance achieved between these values varies from one system to another, depending upon their respective traditions, political and social cleavages, and ideologies. But all democracies strive to live up to the three principles of liberty, justice, and efficiency.

The Principle of Liberty

Between the ideal of men legally 'free and equal' and the reality, there is, as everyone knows, a vast gulf that electoral rules can only partly make good. Guaranteeing the formal conditions for the exercise of liberty is certainly the first step. Establishing measures that offer the voter the maximum degree of freedom of judgement, freedom from pressures, and freedom to express his preferences is quite another matter.

In most Western democracies, formal guarantees to safeguard the right to vote such as the secret ballot were established only in the late nineteenth or early twentieth century. In the United States, secret balloting was achieved only gradually, state by state, from 1888 onwards; in Italy, after the First World War; in Britain, in 1872; and in France, in 1913–14. In Italy, voters may choose whether to vote in a private polling booth, whereas in France they are required to do so. In Germany, where the secret ballot was established in 1919, electors are obliged by law to enclose in the envelope containing their ballot-paper a sworn statement to the effect that they have voted freely. So as to avoid abuses and pressures, ballot-papers are standardized and bear only the names of official candidates.

But freedom also means the right not to take sides, the right to abstain, to leave the ballot-paper blank or to spoil it. In Italy, West Germany, Britain, and France, voting is not obligatory, as it is in Belgium. But the assumption that one has a 'duty' to vote is stronger in some countries than in others. In Italy and West Germany there is usually a 85–90 per cent electoral turn-out and if that percentage falls by even a few points, much anxiety is voiced by the media and politicians. In Britain and France the percengage of abstentions is comparable (around 15 to 30 per cent), but the level varies from one kind of election to another (in local elections, for example, turn-out seldom exceeds 30–40 per cent in Britain). Abstention and blank or spoilt ballot-papers thus manifest the freedom of the electorate and are a necessary—if not sufficient—condition for democratic expression to function satisfactorily. Elections where 99 per cent participation is claimed are not invariably totally corrupt, but strong doubts are raised by the massive polls of Eastern socialist countries and the Third World. Significantly enough, it is only in Poland, of all the Eastern bloc socialist countries, that in recent elections participation has, despite all pressures, dropped to a level comparable with those in the West.

It would, however, be hasty to conclude that abstentions and blank or spoilt ballot-papers necessarily indicate the existence of a satisfactory freedom of choice. On the contrary, such manifestations of the voters' discontent or indifference often reflect their frustration in the face of the choices that are forced upon them and that they prefer to reject. This was the point that Khrushchev was making—although he was certainly in no position to preach—in his quip to American journalists as they pressed him with questions about the one-party system: 'I have never seen the difference between a donkey (Democrat) and an elephant (Republican).' It is true that in Britain Liberal or 'Green' voters have virtually no way of casting a useful vote, that French Socialists may feel some reluctance to vote for a Communist on a second ballot and that within the framework of proportional representation by list the French voters in 1986 had no way of influencing the choice of candidates listed. To mitigate such constraints mechanisms are sometimes introduced into list systems whereby the voters themselves select the candidates. This is the traditional procedure followed in small French communes, but only for municipal elections (and, since 1982, only in communes of less than 3,500 inhabitants). The voter is allowed to strike off certain names and to 'mix in' names from rival lists. In small, local communities, this is all greatly facilitated by the voters' personal and direct knowledge of the candidates. All the same, it is not a common procedure and the French electoral reforms of 1985 made no provision for any personalized mechanisms of the type that operate in West Germany and Italy.

In West Germany, seats are allotted on a proportional basis but still partly according to the principles of a one-vote ballot producing a relative majority. Effectively though, the voter has two votes to cast. With the first, he helps to choose a candidate at local constituency level; with the second, he expresses his preferences on a party list at *Land* level.

The voter thus uses his first vote to choose a candidate, then either confirms or corrects that choice by casting his second vote either for the same party or a different one. This type of election makes it possible to introduce local and personal considerations into a ballot on the basis of a proportional list which, without that opportunity for correction, would leave the political parties with a free hand. The most recent elections to the Bundestag, in 1980, 1983, and 1987, showed that German voters are fully aware of all the possibilities that the system offers them.

The FDP, with few local roots or charismatic leaders, was nevertheless regarded as an indispensable counterbalance to the dominant party of the moment: the SPD in 1980, the CDU–CSU in 1983 and 1987. The FDP was able to weigh in against the left wing of the Social Democratic Party in 1980 and Franz-Josef Strauss's right-wing CSU in 1983 and 1987. It thus helped to push the positions of first Chancellor Schmidt, then Chancellor Kohl towards the centre. Voters used the 'split ticket' to reflect both their personal and their political preferences, showing that they knew perfectly well how to make the most of the system. Rudolf Hrbek writes:

In 1980, the liberal constituency candidates only won 48.5 per cent of the second votes for their party, while 35.5 per cent of the FDP voters cast their first vote for the SPD candidate. In 1983, only 29.1 per cent of FDP voters also cast their first vote for the FDP candidate, while 58.3 per cent chose the CDU candidate. In both cases voters wanted their votes to influence the composition of the coalition.[2]

Italy, for its part, has a system of preference voting which, in theory at least, ought to correct the predominance of the political parties. The voter can choose whether to vote for the list as it stands or for a list that he can 'reconstruct' by changing the order of the candidates' names, provided they all appear on the same list. In constituencies of sixteen or more seats, each voter can express four choices (in smaller constituencies, only three). With his preference vote, he helps to elect the candidates of his own choice, disregarding the order of names fixed by the party. In the south, more voters (40 per cent) take advantage of the possibility of expressing a personal preference than in central and northern Italy (less than 20 per cent on average) and more voters from the Christian Democrats and the Italian Socialist Party do so than from the Italian Communist Party. The preference vote chiefly reflects local interests and internal struggles between different party factions and has come in for virulent criticism on that account. But, as is pointed out by Giuliano Amato (Professor of Constitutional Law and Bettino Craxi's *éminence grise*),

the fear of increasing the strength of the parties at a moment when their stock is low stands in the way of reform for the time being. Yet there can be no doubt that the preference vote produces two negative effects. In the first place, it very often makes Deputies dependent upon local or corporatist support, as when, in order to amass enough preference votes, they put themselves at the service of organized groups that are in a position to guarantee these to them: hospital employees, railway workers, Post Office employees. Secondly, it encourages the most powerful élite figures to rope themselves together with an entourage of unknown and weak candidates who, thanks to this 'double bet', achieve a success that they could never have won on their own.[3]

The secret ballot, formal guarantees, the right to abstain or to spoil the ballot-paper or leave it blank, and the possibilities for expressing a choice rather than simply voting for what is proposed are all examples of the kinds of liberty that the European democracies guarantee to their electorates. But it is worth pointing out that even the whole collection of them hardly does more than ensure a 'formal' liberty —though in itself no mean achievement—and does not guarantee any concrete exercise of it. If it did, the situation would be utopian and probably tyrannical. Concrete liberty would presuppose such specific and precise intervention on the part of the public authorities that their good intentions would soon be cancelled out by the conditions necessary for their realization. The most an observer can do is point out any overt or insidious infractions of the freedom of voters, recognizing that whatever remedies or palliatives may be introduced, they can never eliminate *all* the many pressures that are inseparable from the exercise of power and the constraints of social life.

The Principle of Justice

How should the Western democratic ideal summed up by the slogan 'one person, one vote' be translated into the representational system? In the contemporary period, Western democracies have sought to draw closer to the ideal of justice in two specific ways: either by adopting proportional representation or, within a framework of 'first past the post' voting systems, essentially by redefining constituency boundaries in a more equitable fashion.

More and more countries (Spain, Greece, and Portugal being the latest) are nowadays adapting proportional representation. (Virtually the only countries to retain the system of 'first past the post' on a single ballot are the United States and Britain and its former dominions.) As a result, democratic representational systems have tended to evolve towards their ideal, that is, towards a system in which it is possible for representatives faithfully to express and mirror the social body that chose them. The switch to proportional representation stems from a methodological and ideological assumption: namely, the idea that 'good government' more or less explicitly reflects not only a society's current opinions but also the particular characteristics of its social structure. Studies in political or administrative sociology frequently betray a yearning for a complete parallel between representatives and represented, pointing out, for example, that there are too many peasant mayors, not enough worker deputies, too many sons of the bourgeoisie in power, and so on. Some seem inclined to overlook the dangers inherent in such total parallelism. The quest for justice generally has spread beyond electoral systems themselves to many other sectors of political life—the administration, party organization, and so on. It has prompted the introduction of 'proportionalization' across the board: racial quotas; 'affirmative action'; systematic *proporz* for Flemish and French speakers in Belgium; quotas designed to protect the German-speaking minority in Italy's Alto-Adige region; quotas of women in the higher echelons of the political parties; and so on. The proportional voting systems of West Germany and Italy abide by the unwritten rule whereby all parties must present lists of candidates that are 'balanced' from the regional, professional, social, etc. points of view. Few countries, however, have gone so far as to institute overall proportional representation, as has Israel, where the entire country constitutes a single constituency.

German proportional representation. Because of the way it works, the German electoral system has often—wrongly—been described as a mixed system, that is, one that combines a majority voting system with proportional representation. This is not correct: the German system is strictly proportional,[4] but the distribution of seats is determined partly on the basis of a single-vote ballot. The German voter actually has two votes. With the first he can vote for a candidate in one of the 248 electoral constituencies of the country. With the other he can vote, at *Land* level, from a list of names (*landeslist*). Some of the listed candidates are also constituency candidates, but the voter is free to divide his vote favouring, for example, an SPD candidate and a FDP list. The list votes that are cast determine the number of seats allocated to each party. When all the votes won by the various parties at the federal level are added up, they are allocated according to the d'Hondt system and the seats are distributed amongst the *Länder*. Now each seat can be allotted to an individual. The first to be named are the 248 who came first in the constituencies. Then, in the case of each party, the number of seats thus obtained is deducted from the total due to it according to proportional distribution. The 248 seats reserved for candidates from the lists are therefore distributed in such a way that each political group receives a number of seats proportional to the number of votes cast for its list. If a group suffers in the first allocation because hardly any of its candidates came top, the second allocation makes it possible to redress the injustice.

As can be seen, the German system clearly manifests a desire for fairness but retains a personalized ballot that is characteristic of majority systems. However, the principle of fairness is to some extent affected by an exclusion clause: the only parties included in the allocation of seats are those which either obtained at least 5 per cent of the second votes (for the *Länder* lists) at the federal level, or which managed to win a seat in at least three constituencies. (Up until 1957, the requirement was 5 per cent of the vote at *Land* level or one constituency seat.)

The effect of this clause upon German political life and the constitution of coalitions is considerable, despite its seemingly modest character (particularly in comparison with the exclusion clause of 12.5 per cent that used to affect candidates in the second ballot in France). In Germany, the Refugee Party, which only won 4.6 per cent of the vote in 1957, despite its 27 seats in the preceding Bundestag, was thus eliminated. The extreme right-wing NPD, which won only 4.3 per cent of the vote in 1969, suffered the same fate. On the other hand, in 1983 the Greens, with 5.6 per cent of the vote, won 27 seats. A few decimal points less would have eliminated them altogether, leaving Helmut Kohl with an uncomfortable absolute majority in harness with his rival/ally, Franz-Josef Strauss. The 5 per cent clause thus constitutes a slight abuse of the principle of justice, but compared with most other Western electoral systems that of West Germany is one of the most equitable. The 1985 French electoral reform appeared on the face of it to be following the German example in insisting that parties should reach a 5 per cent threshold in order to be included in the distribution of seats. In reality, however, its effects were far more severe. The German threshold, applied on a national scale, was a *real* threshold, whereas the French threshold, when applied in small constituencies (50 departments elected no more than 2 to 5 Deputies), was, in practice, much higher.[5]

Italian proportional representation. The peculiarity of the Italian system is that it is based upon two chambers of equal standing. They are endowed with the same powers and are elected according to similar but not identical systems. The Chamber is composed of 630 Deputies. Up until 1963, the Constitution ruled as follows: 'The Chamber of Deputies is elected by direct universal suffrage, with one Deputy for every 80,000 inhabitants or for any fraction of over 40,000.' This ruling has since been revised. Seats are now distributed among the constituencies by dividing the number of inhabitants of the Republic according to the latest census by 630, and allocating seats in proportion to the population of each constituency on the basis of full quotas and the greatest remainders. The boundaries of constituencies within the separate regions respect regional boundaries but may incorporate two or more provinces. Except for the Aosta Valley, which gets only one seat, all the constituencies are allotted at least three seats. There are striking disparities: 5 constituencies have fewer than 10 seats each, 15 have between 10 and 19, 7 have between 20 and 29, and 4 large, densely populated constituencies have from 37 to 57 seats. As can be seen from this list, the Italian electoral constituencies are much larger than the French ones were in 1986, when only Paris and the Nord had 21 and 24 seats respectively, while most departments elected no more than 2 to 5 deputies. The system for the Italian Senate is similar to the one for the Chamber: Senators are elected in each region on the basis of a quota obtained by dividing the total electoral population by 315. With the exception of the Molisa region, which has only 2 Senators, and the Aosta Valley, which has only 1, the constitution allocates at least 7 senators per region.

As for the division of seats between the parties, Italian law settles for the method of the corrected quota, known as the *Imperiali* formula:

Quota = total number of votes cast in the constituency/number of
            seats + 2

This '$n + 2$' formula limits remainders to a minimum and these are then transferred to a single national college. This arrangement is particularly advantageous to small political groups that would be incapable of obtaining the minimal quota in any constituency. All the same, to be included in this national redistribution, they have to have obtained at least one seat in a constituency and a minimum of 300,000 votes nationwide. It is worth pointing out that this is by no means an exorbitant requirement since it corresponds to less than 1 per cent of the whole electorate (which numbers nearly 40 million).

The allocation of seats in the constituencies is determined by dividing the number of votes obtained by each party by the electoral quota. Remainders are transferred to the national college. Given the extremely low threshold, which eliminates only the very smallest groups, some tiny ones obtain representation through having won one seat in one constituency. For example, in 1976, the Proletarian Democracy Party, the Liberals, and the Radical Party with, respectively, 1.5, 1.3, and 1.17 per cent of the vote, managed to win parliamentary representation by obtaining one whole quota in a single constituency. In contrast, in 1972, the Italian Socialist Party of Proletarian Union (the PSUP), with a better score (1.9 per cent of the votes), was unable to obtain a full quota because its votes were more widely dispersed throughout the country.[6]

A different system operates for the Senate. Candidates present themselves to single-nomination colleges, where they must win at least 65 per cent of the vote in order to be elected. As no more than one or two candidates score highly enough, the operation then moves on to a second, more complicated stage. Within each region, the total number of votes obtained by each party is added up and seats are allocated according to the d'Hondt formula of greatest remainders. Once this distribution between the parties is completed, seats are allotted to individual candidates on the basis of the fraction of the quota that he or she has won. The paradox of the situation is that it allows several candidates to be elected in the same constituency despite the fact that in principle there should be only one. This happens when two or three parties happen to achieve their highest scores within one and the same constituency.

As we have seen, these two systems of proportional representation allow the various parties involved to be represented as accurately as possible.[7] Some Italian observers nevertheless point to the anomalies that remain: small parties with strong local bases are advantaged, while those with wider, national, and hence more diffused, support suffer.[8] All the same, these are relatively minor failures to match up to the principle of justice. No electoral system is perfect and the major defects of the Italian one lie elsewhere: the absolute guarantee that it provides for the strongest parties to get the men of their choice elected fosters 'professionalism' among those elected, produces internal party factions, and encourages a general *lottizzazione* of political and economic life.

Redefining constituency boundaries. Although majority voting systems do not precisely represent society's expressed opinions, they do try to correct inequalities by improving the demographic balance between constituencies. The combination of a majority ballot and unequal constituencies is likely to produce the greatest injustice. Quite apart from nineteenth-century Britain where, in 1831, the electors of Cornwall returned forty-two Members of Parliament, while large cities such as Manchester and Birmingham elected none at all, it is worth remembering that, under the Fifth Republic in France and since 1945 in Britain, no parliamentary majority has been backed by an absolute majority of votes. In 1981, the French Socialist Party obtained an absolute majority in the National Assembly on the strength of no more than 36 per cent of the vote at the first ballot, yet that did not prevent it from governing alone from July 1984 to March 1986. The growing discrepancy between votes and results indicates a need for corrective measures that could take only one of two forms: the adoption of proportional representation, which was the course taken by France in 1985–6; or a redefining of constituency boundaries.[9] The latter is the course periodically taken by the British and the Americans: it was also taken by France in 1986.

In Britain, the quest for more balanced constituencies began in 1944 with a law that created four Boundary Commissions, one for each nation in the United Kingdom, with the purpose of avoiding population variations of over 25 per cent. It was severely criticized, for if discrepancies of such magnitude were tolerated the reform was meaningless. A new law passed in 1958 accordingly referred to no specific percentage, leaving it up to the commissions to find the best kind of balance possible. In theory, the Speaker of the House of Commons presides over these commissions, but they are in fact placed under the authority of a High Court judge. The other two members of each commission are not supposed to be members of the House of Commons. Every fifteen years at least, the commissions are required to put forward proposals or suggest revisions in a report accompanied by a projected Order in Council to be put before Parliament. Parliament is free to accept or reject the proposals. As a result, no changes were made from 1954 to 1970, since the Labour Party was reluctant to make changes that might affect its level of representation. Even after the reforms effected in 1970, serious discrepancies remained. The largest constituency numbered 96,380 electors, the smallest only 25,000. Before the 1983 elections, the Thatcher Government embarked upon sweeping reforms, which left only 66 constituencies unaffected and increased their number from 635 to 650. In vain the Labour Party opposed a redefinition of boundaries that took account of the decline of inner cities and, as a result, threatened Labour strongholds. Furthermore, the reform reduced the representation of Scotland and Wales, hitherto over-represented and dominated by the Labour Party. Although the number of seats allocated to them was retrospectively increased from 71 to 72 in the case of Scotland and 35 to 36 in that of Wales, this was more than offset by the creation of 15 extra seats. The ratio of electors to Members of Parliament was certainly considerably improved in 1983, but disparities were not eliminated altogether. An average constituency now comprises 65,000 voters, but nine out of the eleven constituencies of Glasgow have fewer than 55,000, and in some of the smaller islands figures are even lower. Here the picture is one of sharp contrasts: close on 95,000 voters in the Isle of Wight but barely 23,000 in the Western Isles. Despite the progress made, the British system guarantees neither perfect equality nor a process of adaptation altogether independent of the parties. The majority party is neither obliged to take action nor to accept the commissions' conclusions. 'Self-restraint' and the pressure of public opinion are virtually all that can be relied upon to limit possible excesses on the part of the parties.

In the course of its chequered politico-constitutional history, France has experienced so many electoral reforms that, in order to avoid further polemics, it was decided under the Fourth Republic to base electoral constituencies upon the administrative unit of the department. But when a majority electoral system with two ballots was re-established in 1958, it became necessary to redefine the constituency boundaries. This was carried out by the executive, to which the moribund Fourth Republic had assigned full powers. The task was accomplished without any checks by Parliament or control through the courts at all, and a certain amount of gerrymandering took place as a result. By 1981, the shortcomings of the 1958 boundaries had become even more acute as a result of rapid urbanization, but nobody seemed inclined to tackle the explosive issue of reform. Changes were eventually introduced in two stages. In 1985, the Socialists returned to the earlier pattern, adopting the departments as electoral constituencies within a framework of proportional representation. This definition was certainly far from perfect, but there was one considerable political advantage to it: it was a pattern that had already existed and was therefore less open to criticism. After the right regained power in 1986, having promised to reintroduce the two-ballot majority voting system, it was impossible to return to the status quo. The delicate question of redefining the electoral boundaries had to be tackled. To avoid unrest and backsliding, Chirac requested his parliamentary majority to authorize him to issue an ordinance. The twofold advantage of this procedure was that it not only avoided clashes in Parliament but also eluded the control of the Constitutional Council. The only monitoring agent left was the Council of State (the Conseil d'État), which could only act in a consultative capacity. However, when this process was completed, Mitterrand refused to sign the ordinance, and Chirac was forced to readdress himself to the problem, this time using legislative means. Following all these processes, the Constitutional Council found itself empowered to exercise a measure of control which, although limited, nevertheless marked a profound change in French political mores.[10] The Constitutional Council has twice been called upon to demonstrate its methods of control. On the first occasion, faced with the law that authorized the government to alter electoral boundaries by ordinance,[11] the Council produced a whole list of conditions to be observed in the redetermination of constituency boundaries. Subsequently, in response to the law that adopted the boundaries[12] (after President Mitterrand had refused to sign the ordinance), the Council declined to claim 'general powers of assessment and decision identical to those of Parliament', and went on to declare 'that, in view of the variety and complexity of local situations that may call for different solutions even in respect of the same demographic regulation, it did not consider that the decisions of the legislature fell noticeably short of constitutional requirements'. The control that a constitutional judge can exercise is thus clearly imperfect and incomplete; nevertheless, substantial progress *has* been made in imposing some check upon arbitrary government action.

The Majority Principle

There are two aspects to the majority principle. First, the candidate who is elected is the one with either a relative majority (the 'first past the post') or an absolute one; secondly, it means that the government of the country is entrusted to those who hold a majority in parliament. The second factor is one that is common to all systems, but in systems of proportional representation it is undeniably considered less crucial than in majority voting systems. In the former, fair representation is a higher priority than efficiency—even if it means that no party can hold a majority. In the latter, the simplicity of an opposition between a majority and a minority is deemed preferable to the political advantages of electoral equity.

Adherence to the majority principle makes for efficiency but does not do away with ambiguities. In Britain, for example, the parliamentary majority more often than not masks an electoral minority. Since 1918, the only governments to win a majority of votes have been the 1931 National Government and the Conservative Government of 1935. Neither the Labour Party in 1945 and 1966 nor the Conservatives in 1959 and 1983 could claim to have obtained an absolute majority of votes, despite their overwhelming parliamentary majorities. But that is not the only artificial aspect to the system. It sometimes—but fortunately, seldom—happens that the party with the majority of votes holds a minority of seats (usually as a result of winning with over-large majorities in some constituencies while the rival party won with tiny majorities in a larger number of marginal constituencies). In 1951, for instance, the Labour Party obtained only 294 seats with its 13,948,605 votes, while the Conservatives won 321 with only 13,717,580 votes. In 1974, it was the Labour Party's turn to benefit from this anomaly, when it won 4 seats more than the Conservatives despite the fact that the latter obtained 240,000 more votes than Labour.

As Max Beloff and Gillian Peele have pointed out, the drawbacks of such a situation cannot be fully appreciated simply in terms of the comparative electoral strengths of the parties involved. The anomalies are heightened by the 'mandate' doctrine according to which 'a political party which secures the right to form a government thanks to the electoral system also claims the right when in power to put through any legislation it thinks fit so long as it is based on some policy statement contained in the party's election manifesto'.[13] Beloff and Peele point out that this 'mandate' theory is used as a justification even when the ruling party has only just managed to scrape a victory: 'The Labour governments of 1974–9 took office with the support of 37.1 per cent and 39.2 per cent of the voters at each election; but the rhetoric of the mandate persisted when the government's legislative proposals were discussed in Parliament and the country.'[14]

The persistence of such an unjust system can only be explained by the fact that it favours the interests of the two dominant parties, notwithstanding prevailing public opinion. It produces clear results and is a means of choosing governments, selecting representatives, and so on. Nevertheless, the English majority voting system gives rise to many protests, particularly from those whom it eliminates or marginalizes: the Welsh and Scottish Nationalist parties and, especially, third parties such as the Liberals and the Social Democrats, the Alliance in 1983 and 1987 (formed following an agreement between these two), or the Greens are all whittled away by the system. The British two-party system is not so much the result of a dual division in society, but rather a product of the constraints of the electoral system. In 1974, the Liberals obtained only 14 seats out of 635, despite winning 19.8 per cent of the votes. In 1983, the Conservatives walked off with 397 seats out 650 with no more than 42.4 per cent of the vote; Labour obtained 209 seats with 27.6 per cent of the vote; but the Alliance, despite a very good score of 25.4 per cent—almost as high as Labour's—had to settle for 23 seats. Despite the protests occasioned by the injustice of these results, the dominant parties still cling to the system. Resistance to change is such that Britain even rejected the introduction of proportional representation for the European elections, despite considerable pressure both nationally and from the European Community.

France is the only European country that uses a majority voting system with two ballots. Its choice of this system was largely a consequence of its rejection of both the other available options: the single-ballot majority system had always been considered as a 'guillotine' that eliminated third parties and was consequently unacceptable to a country in which the consensus is too fragile to allow only the two principal parties to emerge from the election. As for proportional representation, used often under the Third Republic and constantly under the Fourth, it became so closely equated with ministerial instability that most French voters became disenchanted with it. The compromise constituted by a single-name two-ballot voting system functions as follows. For the first ballot, all parties can put up candidates, in the hope of obtaining over 50 per cent of the vote or at any rate the best possible result. Candidates who win an absolute majority are elected. Where none manages this, there is a second ballot in which the winner is the candidate who obtains either an absolute or a relative majority. But the chances of winning are best for candidates from the left or the right who have managed to persuade the candidates closest to them who have done badly in the first ballot to stand down. If, for example, two left-wing candidates, one Socialist, the other Communist, both stand against a single right-wing candidate, they are both likely to be beaten by their opponent, who will attract all the votes from the right, while they are obliged to share the votes from the left. The incentive to regroup between the first and the second ballots is, accordingly, strong. In the first ballot, the competition is frequently between as many as five or six candidates, but the second becomes a battle between the left and the right in virtually all constituencies. In principle, the candidate with the best chance of winning benefits from the withdrawal of allies who originally stood as rivals in the first ballot. Furthermore, French electoral law increases the pressure to withdraw since it stipulates that candidates who at the first ballot fail to win the votes of 12.5 per cent of all persons on the electoral roll must stand down. As a result of this regulation, it can even happen that a *single* candidate remains since all his rivals have been eliminated, as happened, for example, in several constituencies in 1988. It is a system which allows for both the identification of two opposed blocks as the majority and the opposition, and at the same time the retention of a pluralist party system. Between 1958 and 1988, it always proved possible to establish a majority and to govern despite the existence of six or seven parties that are at once autonomous (from the point of view of their respective programmes and strategies) and at the same time dependent (from the point of view of elections and the formation of a Government). However, with better-balanced electoral constituencies and public opinion split more or less evenly between the two blocks, it sometimes happens that no party or coalition can put together a majority. Such was the situation of the Socialist Party in 1988, when it was obliged to govern with no more than a relative majority. However, although such a situation may be difficult in principle, it is less precarious than might be supposed, since the Constitution of the Fifth Republic provides the government with a number of trump cards (see Chapters 5 and 6).

CANDIDATES AND ELECTED REPRESENTATIVES: FROM
SELECTION TO ELECTION

Election is a technique whereby citizens choose their representatives in accordance with mechanisms fixed by the constitution or the established government. Like many other institutional and political mechanisms, election is a 'modern' procedure to the extent that, formally at least, it has taken the place of other, older modes of selection (co-option or heredity, for example) and is to be found in all the political systems of the West, the Eastern bloc, and the Third World. However, the democratic element in this by now virtually universal procedure varies enormously. Even in Western countries, where elections come closest to the ideal of free and open competition, much could be said about the inadequacies and imperfections of the system. A clearer idea of the strengths and weaknesses may be gained by examining the modes of selecting candidates and the sociological characteristics of those who are elected.

The Selection of Candidates

How does one become a candidate? It is tempting to reply: 'First, by wanting to be one,' if only to undermine the French myth of politicians who are 'urged to come forward by their friends', 'pressed to do so by public opinion', or who 'respond to the call of duty'. But wanting is not enough. Whatever the system, it is also necessary to surmount a number of barriers and undergo certain rites of passage. The forms taken by the selection of candidates vary from one country to another, but we may synthesize them around two contrasting possibilities. Selection may be, to varying degrees, national or local; and, to varying degrees, open or closed.

There are very few countries in which selection is effected on a purely local level or a purely national one. But it is rare to find an even admixture of the two. Most countries evolve in such a way that the national level comes to assume more importance than the local. This is certainly true of Britain, Italy, and West Germany. In the case of the United States, the opposite is true. In France, despite progressive centralization in the recruitment of candidates, local influences remain important.

On a spectrum of modes of selection ranging from local to national, France holds an intermediate position. For a long time, the selection of candidates for general elections remained in the hands of local élites, particularly those from the right wing. Only the Communist Party eschewed this localism, taking care to avoid what Maurice Thorez called 'municipal cretinism' by preventing most Communist mayors from presenting themselves as candidates in national

elections. Even the SFIO included local leaders and faithful supporters who were impervious to the influence of the party's national
organization. For centre and right-wing parties (particularly the
Radicals and Independents) individual personalities and local standing regularly constituted determining criteria in the selection of
candidates.

With the advent of the Fifth Republic, accompanied by a progressive bipolarization of political life and a restructuring of the
political parties, national considerations gradually superseded local
ones in the selection of candidates. Deputies who were recalcitrant or
too independent-minded were hauled back into line and forced to
knuckle under or else to face the challenge of candidates 'parachuted'
in from above. The Gaullist party (UNR) led the way in the adoption
of a centralized and disciplined strategy, favoured as it was by the two
trump cards that it held: the fact that it was already in power, and the
authority of its charismatic leader. Thanks to the support forthcoming
from an electorate fed up with unstable governments and parliamentary indiscipline, Deputies were soon forced to recognize that the
impact of personality was declining in elections, as the national
aspects of political life became more important. Nevertheless, it
would be mistaken to conclude that the 'local factors in national
political life' (to borrow Albert Mabileau's expression) disappeared
completely. Political parties generally ratify local choices. It is only
where there are local conflicts, dissent, or ambitious 'young Turks'
that the central party officials take it upon themselves to intervene and
impose their own views, often successfully.

Britain, West Germany, and Italy employ a combination of selection mechanisms at both the national and the local levels, but the
national level is the more important, essentially for two reasons: in the
first place, it is the political parties that dominate and control political
life; secondly, the effect of the existing electoral rules and situations is
to increase their influence still more. Shortage of space here precludes
any detailed account of the various ways in which the parties in these
three States operate, but it is significant that the three systems are
often described in terms that underline their fundamental nature:
'the two-party system', *Parteienstaat*, *Partitocrazia*. In all three
countries, political life is still built around large national organizations
which seek to gain control of the whole political field, attempting to do
so primarily by monopolizing the means of access to it. In Britain, this
is made much easier for them by the existence of safe constituencies

where, come what may, they can be sure that their official candidate will be elected (in South-East England for the Conservatives, in Scotland and Wales for Labour). In West Germany and Italy, these national organizations are advantaged by the very nature of the voting systems. Proportional representation and official lists of candidates make it easier to impose party discipline nationwide. In circumstances such as these, rebel lists are almost always doomed to failure while official candidates, if well positioned, may be sure of election. All the Italian parties are thus in a position to offer themselves the luxury of *fiori all'ochiello* (flowers in their buttonholes), that is to say candidates with prestigious names from the worlds of literature, the cinema, or business.

Butler and King, writing about Britain, made a startling comment that could also well be applied to Italy: 'Most MPs are selected, not elected,' and Monica Charlot makes an equally valid point when she notes:

When voters go to the polls, they are more concerned with political labels than with the personality of the candidates. For an aspiring candidate, the most difficult task is to secure selection as the Conservative or the Labour candidate for a seat that is not impregnable. In the electoral race in Britain, it is far harder to qualify as a candidate than to win in the grand finale.[15]

The same is true of Germany. Von Beyme clearly demonstrates that election to the Bundestag is a matter for professionals.[16] Since 1953, not a single independent candidate has won a seat in Parliament, despite the fact that the German Constitutional Court has pronounced favourably on the subject of political pluralism (declaring that the parties should not monopolize the public finances available for elections and that all candidates who have obtained at least 1.1 per cent of the vote should also receive State subsidies).[17]

However, despite the predominance of national organizations, selection is not totally centralized. In Italy, all the political parties must perforce take account of the 'barons' who control their major strongholds, and must try to satisfy internal factions (such as those within the Christian Democrat organization) that are themselves to a large extent territorial. Furthermore, the preference vote, which makes a personal choice possible, counterbalances the party influence, at least in the cases of those who are seeking re-election. In West Germany, among the members of the Bundestag elected within the constituency framework (half of the total), the advantage goes to local candidates who can count on strong support in their own electoral areas. Finally, in Britain, local selection committees still play an important role.[18] It is true that both parties draw up official lists of candidates (indeed, the Labour Party system involves a double list that is ratified by the National Executive Committee: List A for candidates proposed by the Trade Unions; List B for the rest). However, it is still possible for local committees to impose their own choices (in the case of the Conservative Party) or at least to bring strong influence to bear upon the national organizers (in the case of the Labour Party, which also insists upon reselection for sitting Members of Parliament).[19]

The formal procedures set up by the parties mask a more fundamental reality. To a large extent, the selection of candidates has already taken place very early on, and the jockeying for position within the political parties is simply the last stage in a sequence of more subterranean processes of elimination.

Those processes are partly of a political nature. The first point to note is that, in the major European parties at least, the competition is limited to a small fraction of citizens, namely voters who are also party activists. In other words, while it is true that election to parliament often leads to those elected becoming political 'specialists', that election is itself very often preceded by a period of training that turns the candidate into a party or political professional. Giuseppe Di Palma and Maurizio Cotta have produced an interesting study of this phenomenon. It takes the form of a longitudinal analysis of the Italian Parliament from 1948 to the end of the 1970s. It shows that the number of Deputies without any previous party experience fell sharply (from 22 per cent up to the third legislature to 11 per cent up until the 1970s, and thereafter to 4 per cent). Meanwhile, an increasing number of Deputies had held some party post before the age of 25 (50 per cent each in the case of the Christian Democrats and the Socialists, 76 per cent in that of the Communists). Given that the average age of election had not dropped since 1948, the study gives some idea of the length of the path that might eventually lead to the goals of selection and election. The authors conclude as follows: 'The average deputy is increasingly often an individual who has completed a long party apprenticeship.'[20] The same phenomenon is to be found in many other countries, particularly in left-wing parties, where selection is the ultimate reward for party activism.[21]

Finally, long before it ever comes to official procedures, selection is also a social matter. The importance of the position of a member of parliament is such that all candidates are expected to possess special qualities and attributes, or at least ones that are *judged to be so* by all concerned, from the parties and candidates themselves down to the party activists and the voters. The fact is that, unlike working-class parties, which seek to identify their representatives with those represented, most political parties and voters have a more or less hierarchical concept of political representation. The representative is expected to possess qualities and skills that render him *worthy* to be put forward. On top of all this, the voter has a traditional (if stereotyped) image of a 'good' candidate for parliament or the presidency.[22] A mysterious alchemy is at work here, in which objective, structural, and historical elements are complemented by subjective views, and the latter frequently make all the difference.

Elected Representatives

The modes of recruitment for Upper House members of parliament are so varied that it would be pointless to try to compare the Italian and the French Senates, the Bundesrat, and the House of Lords. On the other hand it *is* possible to sketch a rough portrait of a 'typical' Western member of parliament. For despite the diversity of national electoral systems, there are striking similarities in the sociological profile of those elected, similarities that are, furthermore, progressively being reinforced. The typical Lower House member of parliament in a European democracy reappears everywhere, with remarkably few variants: he is male, mature, middle-class, well educated, and nowadays increasingly likely to be a professional politician.

Female members of parliament are few and far between. Despite growing public sensitivity to this state of affairs due in particular to the efforts of the feminist movement, women are making hardly any headway in parliamentary Assemblies. (Indeed, in France, for example, even fewer women Deputies have been elected under the Fifth Republic than under the Fourth.)

In West Germany, the number of women elected to the Bundestag rose from 6.8 per cent in 1949 to 10 per cent in 1983. It increased significantly in 1987 (rising to 15 per cent of the total), due to the Greens elected, 25 out of 44 of whom are women. In France, women represented 8 per cent of the total number of Deputies in 1946, but barely 5 per cent in 1981. The situation is similar in Britain,[23] where in 1983 only 23 out of 650 members of the House of Commons were women, that is, 3 per cent; and also in Italy where, from 1946 to 1976, the Chamber of Deputies included on average no more than 8 per cent of women.[24]

European members of parliament are mostly mature. The youngest citizens (18–25) and the oldest are absent from parliamentary Assemblies, most of the elected members falling into the 40–60 age group. Half the German Deputies are less than 40 years old, 44 per cent are between 40 and 55. In France the average age of elected representatives in 1978 and 1981 was, respectively, 51 and 49 (while the average age of candidates was, respectively, 46 and 48: yet another illustration of the preference given to the older men in this career).

Identical situations obtain in Italy and Britain. In Britain, however, there was for a long time a marked difference between Conservative and Labour Members of Parliament. Conservatives, who came from privileged circles, won their seats in Parliament at an earlier age and were, on average, seven years younger than their Labour counterparts. For the latter, as Monica Charlot has pointed out, a seat in Parliament was 'in most cases the accolade granted in return for previous activism'.[25] However, the process of change amongst the political personnel of the Labour Party over the last ten years has virtually eliminated that difference.

From the point of view of their level of education, members of parliament differ greatly from the citizens whom they represent. Their qualifications are no doubt particularly important in a profession that has traditionally depended largely on an ability to communicate and be articulate. In any event, politicians are not only educated but increasingly well educated. In 1976, Robert Putnam published a study of élite groups in Europe.[26] On the basis of the sample studied, it shows that 88 per cent of the members of Congress in the United States, 65 per cent of English Members of Parliament, 76 per cent of Italian Deputies, and 69 per cent of members of the Bundestag in West Germany hold university degrees. All the studies, whether based on wider samples or on parliamentary groups alone, come to the same conclusions, even if the results show a few variations. Furthermore, all the evidence points to a rising level in the education of members of parliament, so far as can be seen from the examinations that they have passed. In 1951, only 57 per cent of British Members of Parliament held university degrees. But that figure had risen to 68 per cent by 1979 and to 79 per cent by 1983 (when 36 per cent held degrees from either Oxford or Cambridge). In the Bundestag, the percentages of members with a university education rose from 52.3 per cent in 1953 to 70.5 per cent in 1980.[27] Roland Cayrol *et al.*[28] have revealed a similar situation in France, as has Maurizio Cotta in Italy.[29]

This continuous progression is to a large extent a result of the increasingly homogeneous nature of the circles from which members of parliament are recruited. In other words, what Giovanni Sartori has called the 'rule of distance' (meaning the distance that disadvantaged citizens have to cover before they can be selected as parliamentary candidates) has progressively narrowed. Thus in Italy, Maurizio Cotta, who estimates the number of Italian Deputies between 1946 and 1976 to have attended a university at 73 per cent, goes on to draw attention to inter-party disparities. 70 per cent of the Socialists and 84 per cent of the Christian Democrats held university degrees, as against 43 per cent of the Communists. A similar imbalance was noticeable between the Conservative and the Labour parties in the British House of Commons up until the mid-1960s, at least. However, among the Italian Communists, the British Labour Members of Parliament, and the German Social Democrats alike, the percentage of representatives with no university education has fallen. In 1970, for example, 53.7 per cent of Labour representatives as against 63 per cent of Conservatives held university degrees, whereas up until the late 1950s a difference of 20 per cent had separated the two parties.

Given the high level of education of members of parliament, it is not surprising to find that most belong to the highest socio-professional categories. This holds good for the Western parliaments in general, all of which—we are bound to recognize—are almost totally inaccessible to the most disadvantaged social categories. Manual workers, in particular, are noticeably absent from the parliaments of the Western democracies. In the Bundestag, the political personnel comprises an estimated 1 per cent of workers;[30] in France 2–3 per cent of Deputies come from the working class.[31] However, worker representation is higher in Italy, thanks to the Italian Communist Party, and also in Britain, thanks to the Labour Party. Maurizio Cotta estimates Italian Deputies of working-class origin to account for 17 per cent of the total (36 per cent of Communist Party representatives) in the 1946–76 period. In this respect, Britain is the only country to present a striking contrast to the other continental democracies since in the early 1970s manual workers still accounted for 25 per cent of Labour Members of Parliament (but only 1 per cent of Conservatives). Under-representation of manual workers and of the working class as a whole is thus a general and constant phenomenon for, except in Britain from 1930 to 1950, this section of the electorate has never found its place in any of the Western parliaments.

On the other hand, it is fair to draw attention to the political decline of the highest social classes, in particular the aristocracy and the *grande bourgeoisie*. In West Germany and Italy they have virtually disappeared, partly as a result of their compromises with these countries' totalitarian regimes, but in France, too, their decline has been continuous ever since the nineteenth century, and in Britain it has been particularly rapid since Lords have had to renounce their titles in order to sit in the House of Commons. The House of Lords is certainly a bastion of the aristocracy but its political role is extremely limited. The same goes for the other two groups that used, in the past, to be dominant: the military and the clergy. Both are ineligible in Britain (unless they resign their positions); but they are also virtually absent from other Western parliaments, even if the Church and the military continue to wield considerable influence.

Most members of parliament come from what Colette Ysmal calls 'categories with a high social status'.[32] The profile of this group is certainly by no means sharply defined, but the description at least identifies the category as a whole better than even vaguer terms such as 'middle class' or 'bourgeois'. Analyses of the composition of the parliamentary group show that its members are essentially drawn from what might be called the 'privileged' professions. The 'privileges' involved are of many kinds and also vary in degree from one political system to another, but we can at least survey them rapidly. Some, of course, are financial privileges, but others are social (membership of the social élite), professional, or to do with status (membership of the Civil Service). The profile of members of parliament varies from one system to another depending on the dominant values and the scope of the privileges involved, but the essential point is that most come from well-to-do categories. The following socio-professional categories stand out among the dominant groups.

Civil servants constitute a major group in the parliaments of mainland Europe, especially if teachers are included in this category. This is true particularly of West Germany, where the percentage of public employees rose from 16.8 per cent in the first legislature to 49.8 per cent in the eighth.[33] In France, on average 30 per cent of Deputies came from the public sector between 1958 and 1978, a percentage that has continued to rise: 31.5 per cent in 1973, 40.7 per cent in 1978, 53.1 per cent in 1981. In both countries, the increasing strength of public employees may be partly explained by the statutory facilities (leave with job security and sometimes a salary) available to civil servants, but it is also due to the prestige of the higher echelons of the bureaucracy. On the other hand, in Italy, where public employees enjoy similar facilities, the percentage of civil servants is lower and on the wane, chiefly due to the poor reputation of the Italian bureaucracy.[34] They account for barely 2 or 3 per cent of the total number of parliamentary representatives, but to this should be added the 18 per cent of professors, whose numbers are also falling. However, this relative weakness of the public sector is made up for by the increasing number of professional politicians who have emerged from the various parties and trade unions. They are truly the bureaucrats of the political apparatus and their entire careers have evolved within these organizations. During the sixth legislature, 89 per cent of the Communist Deputies, 81 per cent of the Christian Democrats, and 66 per cent of the Socialists had begun their careers with duties at a local level[35] (and 60 per cent of Deputies had been party activists before the age of eligibility, which is 25).

In Britain, in contrast, the presence of civil servants in Parliament is negligible, for strict rules bar civil servants and members of the Armed Forces from engaging in political activity. Many, obviously, are discouraged by the stipulation according to which they are obliged to hand in their notice in order to become a candidate.[36]

Industrialists, businessmen, and members of the liberal professions. This is the second most important group, somewhat heterogeneous, but its members possess at least one common characteristic, namely, assured economic independence. In 1981, for example, the French National Assembly included 6 per cent industrialists and businessmen (17 per cent in 1978) and 16 per cent from the liberal professions (28 per cent in 1978).

In West Germany, in the ninth Bundestag (1980–3), professional nomenclature makes it difficult to establish any precise comparison with France. However, of the members of the Bundestag 5.6 per cent came from the legal profession, 9.6 per cent from independent professions, and 2.3 per cent from the world of journalism. In Italy, roughly one-third of parliamentary representatives come from independent professions (the liberal professions or industry and trade). In the United Kingdom, the liberal professions and the world of business are dominant (about 40 per cent) among the Conservatives, but are virtually unrepresented among Labour Party Members of Parliament (7–8 per cent).

Professional politicians. In West Germany and Italy, the number in this group is on the increase. One-third of Italian and German parliamentary representatives may be classed in this category. The proportion is probably lower in France and Britain (by reason, in particular, of a voting system that is more uncertain for candidates who have emerged from the political apparatus), but here too there is a marked trend towards political professionalism.

The sociological profiles of the elected members of parliament in the various Western democracies thus present more similarities than profound differences. The first feature to note is an increasing professionalism that calls for those elected to devote themselves full-time to politics. Nowadays, an elected member of parliament lives *for* and *by* politics. This is a consequence of the growing importance and influence of the political parties, but meanwhile the parties themselves are strengthened by the professionalism of their personnel. The age of the 'amateur' in politics has given way to that of the professional. And, more and more, the professional politician is required also to be an expert in the field of communications, capable of operating within the media and making the most of the means of political marketing.

One area in which the European democracies differ from one another, however, is the local affiliations of their politicians and the avenues open to them to achieving national election. In Britain, a local political career and a national one are not generally complementary. Rather, they develop along parallel lines. Those elected to the House of Commons have tenuous links with their territorial bases and the weakness of those links in part explains the radicalism of local government reforms and the apparent ease with which they are accomplished. A Member of Parliament does not feel particularly bound by local loyalties, only by his party's political programme. The chief link between him and his local base is manifested through the party structure and organization (in the shape of the local electoral committee for the selection of candidates). However, constituency work is more and more necessary if MPs wish to maintain support among the local electorate.

A system more different from that which obtains in France would be hard to imagine, for here, on the contrary, the accumulation of elected offices (*cumul des mandats*) constitutes one of the most solid cultural and political conventions of political life. The reforms introduced in December 1985 to check the practice of accumulating elected offices only partially limited the excesses of a phenomenon that remains unique, without equivalent in the other Western democracies, all of which either prohibit such practices legally or discourage them culturally. The practice of accumulating responsibilities can certainly be advantageous: it provides an antidote to the excessive centralization of power, makes it possible to reconcile the antagonistic views that may be held by the centre and by the periphery, and encourages the consideration of local views at the level of parliamentary and governmental decision-making. But on balance, its negative points weigh heavily. Too much power and influence are concentrated in a few hands; real power tends to be transferred to technical experts or non-elected right-hand men, since the Deputy himself cannot manage to be in two places at once; the *deus ex machina* type of local boss, who constitutes the linch-pin between local and central affairs and between the political and the administrative spheres, acquires an exaggerated importance.

Such is the strength of these local leaders, deeply entrenched in their local strongholds, and discharging a series of interdependent functions, that attempts to introduce reforms that might threaten their status have all failed, including plans to reform the Senate, to merge communes, and to reorganize department boundaries. The fact that the limitations set on the *cumul des mandats* were eventually unenthusiastically accepted can only be explained by the coincidence of two factors. One was the creation of a fourth electoral level (the region), which made it impossible for local Deputies to discharge every single function at every single level; the other was the need, in 1985–6, for many Socialist Deputies to make sure of a few seats at regional level, in default of seats in Parliament.[37]

Such accumulation of responsibilities is extremely rare in Italy and West Germany, since here the general system of proportional representation and the control over the political system wielded by the various political parties make it necessary for electoral rewards to be distributed as widely as possible among party activists at both local and national levels. Political careers thus evolve under the aegis of the party and in progressive stages, moving on from the local to an intermediate level (province, region, or *Land*, as the case may be) and in some cases from there to the national level. In West Germany, particularly, many representatives tend to have deep local roots, since half the members of the Bundestag are elected within the constituency framework, where it is possible for the voters to indicate their choices for particular individuals. However, careers at local and national levels develop successively, never simultaneously.

5

Parliaments

If there is one symbol that stands for a representative system, it is
certainly that of the Assembly, a collegial body through which the will
of all (or part) of the population is expressed. As such, it is indissoci-
able from the liberal democracies: all are constructed around the
Assembly or on the basis of it. Any attack against the organization,
composition, or functioning of the representative Assembly is seen as
an attack or blow against democracy. We should remember that, in
France, the right of dissolution lapsed under the Third and Fourth
Republics until 1955, because it was considered to encourage potential *coups d'état*. Nor should we forget the way in which classic
parliamentary structures have been debased or eliminated under
Fascist, Nazi, Francoist, and other authoritarian regimes. However,
while the fundamental place of parliament in democratic symbolism
may be undisputed, its real role and influence are more debatable.
John Locke's opinion was that parliament 'holds the supreme power
of the commonwealth', but that view no longer seems appropriate
even in Britain, where the saying 'Parliament can do anything except
change a man into a woman' survives more out of habit than any desire
for accuracy. So should parliaments now be regarded purely as 'rump'
Assemblies, theatres of illusion, or even mere 'rubber-stamp
chambers'? Or ought we, rather, to take Pierre Avril's[1] view that the
transformations undergone by Western parliaments constitute a
realignment, an adaptation to the new political and social conditions
that obtain in the Western democracies as a whole?

The latter seems a more accurate and realistic interpretation than
those that emphasize the inexorable decline of Western parliaments.
For we should recognize that the decline to which they point is a
relative one. It is true that today many of the laws that parliaments
pass have been prepared by the executive. But parliaments possess
other means of influence: they can introduce amendments, apply
pressure through the majority party or coalition, mobilize public

opinion, and so on. Admittedly, their powers of control over the executive appear to have declined. But are we not here confusing the issues of agitation and instability with that of democratic control? In France, in particular, diagnoses of her Parliament's decline are too often based on comparisons with the Third and Fourth Republics, despite the fact that these can hardly be claimed to provide satisfactory models. Furthermore, comparison with what some consider to have been the Golden Age of parliamentarianism, that is to say, the nineteenth century, is not convincing either. Given the changing modes of electing Assemblies (limited suffrage, incomplete universal suffrage, the existence of rotten boroughs in England, non-secret voting, the exclusion of women: all are features of the past) and the differences in means of communication and in economic and social structures, any comparison in this area calls for extreme prudence. It would, after all, not occur to us to bewail the decline of modern executives on the grounds that they have become less authoritarian than they used to be in the nineteenth century. Parliaments have undeniably changed and evolved. But, as we assess the transformations that have taken place, we should take care not to compare them to an idealized version of the past.

In the theory and practice of the representative system, parliaments have been assigned three functions: representation, decision, and control over the executive. Each of these functions have gone through considerable changes during recent years and within each country.

THE FUNCTION OF REPRESENTATION: ONE OR TWO CHAMBERS?

In principle, the theory of representation seems incompatible with the idea of more than one chamber of representatives. How is it possible for the people as a whole to be represented by two or three different Assemblies? Yet, in fact, a large number of Western States organize their parliamentary representation using two chambers: the United States, West Germany, Switzerland, Holland, Britain, Italy, Spain, France, etc. However, the origin, justification, and powers of the second chamber differ. By and large, it is possible to distinguish between two groups: on the one hand States in which the second chamber is a product of a federal or regional structure, on the other those in which the upper house is a survival from the country's constitutional past (Britain and France, for example). Generally speaking (as in France and West Germany), the powers of the second chamber are far less extensive than those of the lower (sometimes to the point of being virtually non-existent, as in the House of Lords in Britain). In Italy, in contrast, the powers of the two chambers are identical and the modalities by which their members are elected are so similar that neither could claim to be any more representative or more democratic than the other. In the United States, the situation is the reverse (and, it must be said, exceptional). Here the Senate possesses not only the same powers as the House of Representatives, but also specific responsibilities in the domain of foreign policy and the appointment of high-ranking federal officials.

The chambers whose existence is justified purely by constitutional tradition are, generally speaking, hardly representative. The recruitment system for the House of Lords, for example, is somewhat curious. Not one of the Lords sits there as a representative of the popular will yet, once appointed, he retains his seat for life. The survival of such an anachronistic and unrepresentative institution results in large part from its own policy of 'self-restraint' and the application of what, since 1945, has been known as the 'Salisbury doctrine', so-called after the then Conservative leader of the House of Lords. According to Lord Salisbury, it would have been unseemly, after the Labour victory of 1945, for the Conservatives to use their majority in the House of Lords to oppose the policies of the Labour Party, which held a majority in the House of Commons. To adopt any other attitude would, in point of fact, have been suicidal.

However, the French Senate, whose representative character also leaves much to be desired, did not adopt the same attitude. Senators are elected by universal suffrage, but only at one remove: their major electors are themselves elected locally, but the rural areas are over-represented and most of the major urban electors are selected by local representatives, in other words by local élites or by the party apparatuses. Furthermore, Senators, who are elected for a period of nine years, survive politically despite the changes that may come about in the electoral college. In this domain, change certainly comes about 'at a Senator's pace'. Yet the fact that the representative nature of a senator's mandate is progressively diluted by reason of the very length of its duration is an issue that is seldom raised. Some historical accidents (such as the seven-year tenure of a French President) end up by becoming unchallengeable facts of life.

Historical survivals are also detectable—but in a more marginal fashion—in the Italian Senate which, alongside the Senators elected according to a system of proportional representation, includes five Senators appointed for life by the President of the Republic. The fact that the Senate is representative and possesses powers similar to those of the Chamber of Deputies creates political and constitutional difficulties comparable to those posed by the Senate of the Third Republic in France. Furthermore, its very existence and *raison d'être* are in question. After all, what is the point of having two chambers which, apart from the minor differences in the modalities of electing their members and the greater ages required both for voters and for candidates for election, are bound to be identical? There have been many proposals on ways of giving it a function and complexion of its own that would mark it out from the Chamber of Deputies. Attempts have been made to turn it into a Senate for the regions, a territorial chamber that would constitute the apex of the regional structure established durng the 1970s. But none of these proposed reforms has transformed the Italian Senate into the kind of senate that is to be found in federal States.

It is worth pointing out, though, that the composition of the upper chambers of federal States varies considerably from one system to another. In the United States, Senators are elected by direct universal suffrage, in the same way as Representatives, two for each state. Alaska, with its 400,000 inhabitants, has the same number of elected Senators as California, with its 24 million citizens, so as to maintain strict equality between all the members of the federal State and to prevent domination by the most highly populated states.

In West Germany, on the other hand, the members of the Bundesrat are not 'Members of Parliament' in the *strict* sense of the expression. Article 51 of the Constitution stipulates that they should be 'members of the *Länder* governments'. Their mandate comes to an end when their governmental functions do. The composition of the Bundesrat thus changes in step with reshuffles, resignations, and changes in the majority of coalition governments. Seats in the Bundesrat go to all *Land* Minister-Presidents, *Land* Ministers of Finance, Home Affairs, and Justice, *Land* representatives to the Bund, and any

Land Minister affected by a problem being debated by the Bundesrat. However, regardless of how many of its representatives are present, each *Land* also has at its disposal a number of votes calculated on the basis of the size of its population and fixed by the Constitution: 5 each for Bavaria, Baden-Württemberg, Lower Saxony, and the Rhineland of Northern Westphalia; 4 each for the Palatine Rhineland, Hesse, and Berlin; 3 each for Saarland, Bremen, and Hamburg. The presidency of the Bundesrat is subject to equally strict regulations. It is assumed for the period of one year by the Minister-President of each of the *Länder*, according to a system fixed by the Königstein agreement of 30 August 1950. Like the United States' Senate, the Bundesrat has an important role to play in the legislative process. But, as the Federal Constitutional Court pointed out in 1974, it does not possess the full legislative powers that are held by the Bundestag. Depending on the issue in question, the Bundesrat may hold either an absolute power of veto or merely the power to suspend proceedings. During the 1970s, the role of the Bundesrat increased in importance, as the CDU–CSU made the most of their majority in the Upper Chamber to mount as energetic as possible an opposition to the policies of the SPD–FDP coalition, in power from 1969 to 1982. In this fashion, the Bundesrat's role of territorial representation for the federated states was in part superseded by a more classically political kind of representation in which the clash of interests between the majority and the opposition is played out.

Except in Italy, the lower house is, to a greater or lesser degree, pre-eminent, by very reason of its strictly representative character. Because it is the best means of expression for the democratically declared will of voters as a whole, the lower house holds wider powers and prerogatives that always afford it the final word. This is certainly the case in France and of course Britain, where the official two-chamber system masks what in effect virtually amounts to a one-chamber system.

The 'privileges' of the lower chambers are justified by its representative character. In reality, the quality of that representativeness may vary enormously. Quite apart from the fact that in the nineteenth century the masses were almost totally excluded from the process of selecting representatives, we are bound to recognize that the lower chambers approximate no more than imperfectly to the ideals of liberal philosophy. The one-ballot majority voting system virtually excludes the possibility of changing the British two-party system, even when a third party or a coalition (for example, the Alliance, in 1983) obtains one-quarter or one-third of all votes. In France, the combination of a two-ballot majority voting system and constituency boundaries which have remained unchanged through twenty-five years of intense urbanization has helped to distort the manifestation of the popular will under the Fifth Republic just as, in the 1951 elections, the electoral law on *apparentement* constituted an outright violation of political and electoral deontology.

Should we conclude from the existence of such differences in the representativity of elected members of parliament that in reality these Assemblies are not truly representative, despite what is generally believed of them? There are two opposed views on this subject. Some people claim that Assemblies should 'mirror' the real political, or even sociological, situation of the country as accurately as possible. Feminist movements (e.g. in France and in the United States, chiefly in the Democratic Party) are particularly insistent that women should be better represented both in party leadership and in elected Assemblies as a whole.

This mimetic and increasingly sociological view of representation stands in opposition to the ideas of those who, while also seeking as adequate as possible a representation of the popular will, do not see the matter in terms of an ideal arithmetic. For them, it is equally important that elected Assemblies should not betray the aspirations of the electorate once the elections are over. They emphasize that it is just as important, if not more so, that voters should have a clear understanding of the consequences of their choices in terms of the composition of the government for which they vote and the policies that it will pursue if elected. Despite all their faults, the British and (under the Fifth Republic) the French systems do make it possible for the voters, in electing their representatives, to choose those whom they wish to govern them. In West Germany, the matter is less clear since, if a majority is to be established, the small FDP is bound to be given a measure of influence and may use it to tip the scales either to the right or to the left without necessarily having given the voters any clear idea of its future strategy. But in this respect it is the situation in Italy that is the most open to criticism for here, despite—or perhaps because of—proportional representation, the voter has no way of knowing what impact his choices will have or what interpretation the political parties will put upon them.

LEGISLATION

The decision-making role of Assemblies stems from a rational concept and a notion of the division of tasks inspired by anthropomorphic images. According to the democratic concept of representation, sovereignty lies with parliament, which alone has the right to vote on the law. The law is supposed to satisfy a number of essential criteria. It should have priority over every other kind of norm; and it should condition all the decision-making and practical activities of bodies that are inferior or subordinate to parliament, starting with the government itself.

This sublime view of the law finds its fullest expression in the traditions of Britain and France. Here, the supremacy of the law and of any body that administers it are beyond question: no judge or regulation can be placed above the law. Parliament alone has the right to pass laws. Only since the Second World War have these principles begun to receive a more relative interpretation; and such modifications as have been made to the dogma reflect the *de facto* situation rather than revolutionize it. Over the years, the fine edifice of juridico-political theory has lost some of its lustre in Britain, as it has in France and elsewhere. Parliaments nowadays sometimes seem to be hardly more than rubber stamps or, as Gordon Smith puts it, 'The process of legislation may seem to be a surviving piece of symbolic ritualism.'[2]

It is suggested that parliaments have fallen from omnipotence to impotence, leaving the executive to take most of the decisions, with the sole qualification that parliaments exercise certain controls. What is the situation in reality? Is it true that the Fifth French Republic is characterized by an abasement of Parliament, whereas one outstanding feature of the Italian system is the *centralità del parlamento*? Is the British Parliament still the linch-pin of the political system? What is the role of the Bundestag? A comparison of the decision-making role of these various Assemblies may enable us to gain a less simplistic view of their current situation. Let us consider three different aspects: the division of tasks, the organization of work, and the rules of the game.

The Division of Tasks

In the French and British models, the importance of Parliament stemmed from its central character, both functionally and territorially. Parliament was *the* legislator: not only was the executive by definition subordinate to it, but no other authority was empowered to legislate within the national territory. The Act of Union between England and Scotland in 1607 resulted in the abolition of the Scottish Parliament, just as, to lay the ghosts of the parliaments of the *ancien régime*, the French Revolution denied judges any role in the creation of laws. However, a number of concessions have been made where parliamentary supremacy is concerned and a division of tasks has had to be accepted. Today, those tasks are divided in various ways: between the legislature and the executive; within the legislature; and between various territorial levels.

The fundamental flaw in the system of dividing tasks between the legislature and the executive lies in the rational and hierarchical concept of the process of decision that it implies. The legislative authority decides, the government executes; the first operation necessarily conditions the second. As State intervention has increased, that hierarchical vision has turned out to be both impractical and inappropriate. More and more modifications have had to be introduced into the traditional concept of the separation of powers: either tasks are quite simply transferred to the executive, or the executive takes the place of the legislature when it comes to determining the formulation of the rules formally adopted by parliament.

The transfer of powers from the legislature to the executive came about as a consequence of the progressive incapacity of parliaments to cope with crisis situations or, quite simply, with the development of the Welfare State. For example, the Italian Constitution, with some reluctance, makes allowances for that development. It repeatedly makes provision for what is known as a *riserva di legge*, that is, certain areas—particularly those concerned with public liberties—which can only be regulated by law. On the other hand, circumstances in which legislative powers may be delegated are also envisaged, albeit with considerable reserve and circumspection. Delegation can only take place once Parliament has laid down principles and guidelines in relation to the delegated material. A time limit is set and an objective carefully defined. Finally, if the government does wish to adopt certain rules, giving them the force of laws, it must bring them before the Chambers on the very same day (but may only do so in cases of absolute necessity and emergency). Such decrees lapse if they are not converted into laws within 60 days of their adoption. But in practice constitutional safeguards have been progressively swept aside. The number of law-decrees has been increasing rapidly: from 29 during the first legislature to 124 during the sixth, 167 during the seventh, and 265 during the eighth. Moreover, the limitations imposed by the Constitution have either been rendered pointless or adroitly side-stepped. For example, in order to avoid its decrees lapsing when the 60-day period is up, the government simply adopts a new, identical decree, to postpone the fateful day for another two months. Similarly, the 'necessity' or 'emergency' required by Article 77 of the Constitution is frequently a matter that goes unverified.

Let us recall the principles involved. In theory, parliament holds overall power. But, despite that power, checks and delays tend to accumulate. For example, in the matter of transmitting community directives, Italy constitutes an almost pathological case. In 1981, one-third of the directives were not applied because Parliament never incorporated them into Italian law. To resolve the problem, on 9 February 1982, Law no. 42 was passed, authorizing the government to take the necessary steps for applying ninety-seven directives. So it is Parliament's own inability to come to decisions that causes it to be dispossessed of its powers. Its theoretical rule—of that famous *centralità del parlamento* so often invoked by the Communist Party at the time of the *Unione nazionale*—is replaced by an admission of impotence. Similarly, activism on the part of the government[3] is partly provoked by procedures that prevent it from fully exercising the powers that the Constitution recognizes it to possess. Although it may take the initiative in proposing laws, the fact that the Assemblies control the agenda places the executive in the same position of weakness as that of the government of the Fourth French Republic. It accordingly uses its law-decrees as a means of forcing Parliament to discuss government proposals. They may be treated to a rough ride in the course of the debates on ratification, and if they are rejected this may lead to a governmental crisis. But at least they will have been discussed. As a result, Parliament's supreme authority over both the content and the form of its agenda is doubly undermined. This is the price that has had to be paid for an exaggerated and outdated concept of Parliament's powers of decision.

The situation explains the interest shown in Italy in a 'rationalization of parliamentarianism' of the type introduced in France under the Constitution of the Fifth French Republic. The distinction that it makes in Articles 34 and 37 between legislation and regulations, and delegation by means of a system of ordinances, have all been closely studied with a view to possibly transposing them into the Italian constitutional system. So far, however, no such proposals have been successful, partly because the French system was considered to give too much power to the executive, and partly because it appeared inaccurate. As Pierre Avril has recently pointed out, the separation of the sphere of law from that of regulations was presented as the corner-stone of the normative system of the Fifth Republic until it was noticed that the declared revolution of Articles 34 and 37 had never, in fact, taken place.[4] At any rate, in respect of the cumbersome workings that safeguard the impression of sovereignty given by Parliament, the Italian system is more or less in line with the other systems of Western Europe. Nearly everywhere—with a few exceptions, such as Sweden and Denmark—the executive plays an essential, if not dominant, role in the elaboration of laws. Indeed, in West Germany, for example, where members of the Bundestag certainly play an important role, 70 per cent of the laws are proposed by the government. The practice of Western parliamentary systems generally is thus broadly comparable with that of the 'mother' of them all, namely, the British Parliament.

In Britain, the essential legislative initiative has for long lain with the government. Over 95 per cent of the bills proposed by the executive are adopted and 82 per cent of all laws are initiated by the government.[5] The 'rationalized parliamentarianism' of the Fifth French Republic (95 per cent of the laws are government bills) is thus not at odds with the parliamentary model constituted by Britain: quite the contrary. Nevertheless, British parliamentary procedure differs in some respects, particularly where British traditions are involved. Alongside public bills (proposed by the government) and private members' bills, another form of legislation is available to public or private individuals or bodies (such as local authorities). It is known as 'private legislation'. The bills must be proposed, according to procedures fixed by the House of Commons, by non-members of the House, who must be prepared to defend their bills when challenged. These 'hybrid' bills[6] are thus the product of two procedures, for they can only be proposed in accordance with the procedure followed for 'public' bills, but all 'private measures', that is to say those that affect specific interests, must also undergo an examination in the course of which those 'for' and those 'against' more or less fight it out in debate (as happens, for example, in the case of nationalizations).

Nevertheless, over and above all these formal distinctions, the executive still holds the real power of initiative, either directly or through Members of Parliament who are persuaded to support the government. We should remember, furthermore, that the executive exercises a crucial influence within Parliament itself: the members of the government constitute a close-knit group of about 100 (almost one-third of the majority), all of whom, by definition, support all government proposals.

Finally, through the device of 'delegated legislation', important prerogatives are made available to the government. The expression masks a relatively heterogeneous mode of intervention that corresponds in part to the classic regulatory powers of executives. The legislation is said to be 'delegated' because the fiction of Parliament's omnipotence has prevailed for so long, at least at the level of terminology. But this attribution of regulatory activities to Parliament is more the result of the absence of any rigid hierarchy of norms such as exists on the Continent, than of any real transfer of the domain of law to the government, in the sense in which, for example, the French and the Italians would understand it. These conceptual and organizational differences account for the apparently extensive use of 'delegated legislation' (which has produced, on average, 2,000 Rules and Orders each year since the Second World War). But it would be mistaken to liken the system to the *ordonnances* of the French or the law-decrees of the Italians, even if the vocabulary makes it tempting to do so.

According to political rhetoric and juridical definition, full legislative power lies with parliament or, in some cases, with the lower chamber. Over and above such interventions on the part of the executive as we have considered above, the following question arises: does the business of legislation truly correspond to the way that it is represented in political discourse or to formal juridical definitions? The answer must be 'no', even in the United States, which is the country where it comes closest to doing so. Commissions and committees are often considered simply as a more or less important phase in the adoption of laws—just an instrument used in the organization of parliament's work. This is not a totally erroneous picture, but it does not adequately reflect the measure of autonomy that many of these committees and commissions have acquired *vis-à-vis* their respective Assemblies.

The principal function of commissions is that of *drafting* or *redrafting* laws. Plenary assemblies are ill-adapted to the delicate work of elaborating laws, even if they have the power to do so and, in principle, they alone have the right definitively to adopt the amendments that are proposed to them. The task of 'drafting' laws consequently usually devolves upon commissions. The most obvious example is provided by Britain where, in the course of two 'readings', the House of Commons debates only the general problems presented by a bill and decides whether or not to pass the text on to a specially created standing committee (the only fundamental rule governing its composition being that it must reflect the balance of forces within the House of Commons). The committee thereupon undertakes the real task of legislation, discussing the text, article by article, line by line, with the opposition systematically attempting to substitute its own proposals for those of the government. Thus, the essential task of legislation is carried out by standing committees, which are subject to pressure from two quarters: the opposition, seeking to substitute its own text; and the parliamentary majority, which sometimes tries to amend the government bill. In this respect, the situation in France is analogous. Paul Cahoua's study of 'committees as legislative workshops'[7] gives a clear account of the position of the committees of the French National Assembly. He writes as follows: '26.2 per cent of the amendments registered are proposed by committees. They represent 64.4 per cent of all amendments adopted, and 88 per cent of the proposals made by committees are adopted.' Yet this virtually 'decision-making' role of the committees is not recognized by the fundamental constitutional texts. All that the committees are expected to do, in principle, is make proposals.

However, committees may perform a second function: they quite simply exercise *legislative power*. This happens in Italy, where parliamentary commissions can adopt the famous *leggine* (or 'little laws'), on the basis of Article 72 of the Constitution, subject to two restrictions. First, the Constitution does not allow them to intervene in matters of constitutional or electoral reform, legislation relating to finance, the ratification of international treaties, or in connection with the delegation of legislation. Secondly, either the government or one-tenth of the members of the Chamber, or one-fifth of the members of the Commission itself may, so long as the bill has not yet been finally approved, require that the whole text be returned to the plenary Assembly. It is interesting to note the political effects of this combination of factors: in the first place, Italy is in the paradoxical position of being able to 'produce' many laws but few 'reforms', since most of the texts are given limited application. Secondly, the fact that

special commissions hold decision-making powers particularly encourages systematic intervention on the part of interest groups, since
their influence is thereby brought to bear upon a restricted circle of
individuals (whose inclusion in a particular commission in the first
place results from pre-existing interests in the sector concerned),
besides which their debates usually receive minimal publicity.
Thirdly, the fact that it is at any point possible to return a text to the
plenary Assembly for further discussion turns the whole procedure
into a system of complex bargaining and negotiation between the government and the other Members of Parliament, the majority coalition and the minority (essentially the Communist Party), and within
the coalition. It is significant that, during the 1970s, the Italian Communist Party voted in favour of three-quarters of the *leggine*, abstained
in 5 to 10 per cent of the cases, and opposed the remainder. What this
shows is that, while it is in the plenary sessions of the Assembly
that the major dramas are played out, the committees, thanks to
their decision-making powers, act as the system's 'clearing-houses'.

In France and Britain, regional and local authorities do not possess
any legislative power, and few concessions are made to these
countries' strictly centralized systems. In the case of France, certain
territories and regions (essentially the overseas possessions and
Corsica) are allowed to express their opinions and desires and in some
cases adaptations are made—but always by centrally controlled
means. In Britain, the loudly proclaimed sovereignty of Parliament
may be modified by certain pragmatic concessions: a virtually federal
system operated in Northern Ireland up until 1972; particular
arrangements, including special parliamentary commissions, exist for
Wales and Scotland; and a large measure of autonomy is granted to the
various small offshore islands. However, the ideology of national
sovereignty together with the solemnly proclaimed sovereignty of
Parliament have ensured that these palliatives stop short of recognizing federal or regional Assemblies to possess any legislative powers.
    In contrast, Italy and West Germany have, to varying degrees, and
using their own particular methods, taken steps to divide the tasks of
legislation territorially. In Italy, the Constitution recognizes the
legislative authority of all the regions but grants wider powers to the
five with special status (Sardinia, Sicily, Alto-Adige, the Aosta Valley,
and the Friuli–Julian Alps–Veneto region) than to the fifteen regions
with ordinary status which were established later, after 1970. The

Constitution recognizes the latter to possess legislative powers in all matters as defined in Article 117 (in particular those relating to agriculture, local crafts, tourism, town planning, and so on), always providing they respect 'the fundamental principles fixed by the State laws' and providing 'they do not conflict with the national interest or that of other regions'. For several years, the central apparatus's reluctance to get these 'law frameworks' adopted paralysed activity in the regions. Now, however, the Constitutional Court has ruled that, despite the absence of any specific law on the matter, the 'principles' of the arrangement were implicit in the existing body of legislation; and this has made it possible for the ordinary regions to pass laws within their particular fields of competence. The laws are subject to the 'supervision' of a regional commissioner (or prefect) appointed by the government. If he withholds his approval, the government informs the region of his reasons for opposing the proposal and requires it to make the appropriate changes. If the region persists in its attitude, the government can refer the matter either to Parliament or to the Constitutional Court, depending on whether the clash is of a political or a juridical nature. Seeking to avoid political clashes, the government has in practice tried to turn political conflicts into juridical ones and has transferred to the Constitutional Court the responsibility for pronouncing on all conflicts.[8]

West Germany was spared the hesitations and procrastinations that bedevilled Italy's progress in its construction of a regional State. Both the Allies and the political forces present favoured a system in which powers were apportioned on a territorial basis, for some thought that this would prevent a repetition of dictatorial developments, while others (in particular the French occupying forces) reckoned that the German State would thereby be weakened. The basic law provided for a system in which the *Länder* hold a residual measure of legislative power. Article 70 lays down that the *Länder* have the power to pass laws in areas where the present constitutional law does not specifically assign legislative power to the Federation. Furthermore, even where the Federation does hold such powers, the *Länder* have the right to legislate 'so long as and to the extent that the Federation makes no use of its right to legislate' (Article 72). The basic law recognizes the Federation's right to take over from the *Länder* in three sets of circumstances:

- if a question cannot be settled satisfactorily by the various *Länder*,

- if the legislation of one *Land* may affect the interests of others,
- if it is necessary to protect the juridical and economic unity of the country.

As may be imagined, these 'limitations' are not very rigorous and it is hard to see how any area could, in the long run, elude intervention from the Bund. However, the *Länder* do carry exclusive responsibility for education, the organization of local communities, and policing. The fact that these areas are 'reserved' for the *Länder* can, on occasion, cause problems, particularly when *Länder* policies clash with undertakings made by the Bund (particularly at international level). For example, in 1955, the federal government appealed to the Constitutional Court, claiming that the educational legislation adopted by Lower Saxony was incompatible with the Concordat concluded in 1933 between the Vatican and the Third Reich. In 1957, the Court decided that, in view of the *Länder's* exclusive powers in the domain of education, the federal government could not apply the Concordat regulations, despite the fact that they were still in force.

The Rules of the Game

In the past, parliaments could, no doubt fairly, be defined as bodies responsible for making laws. Nowadays it would be more accurate to call them instruments for converting bills (elaborated elsewhere, as often as not) into written laws. The decision-making powers of parliaments lie not so much in their initiating—or sometimes blocking—legislation, but rather in their revision of drafts that have been prepared elsewhere.

The degree of a parliament's autonomy largely depends upon the procedures through which the work of legislation is organized. Let us now try to assess the degree of autonomy possessed by each of the parliaments that we are discussing, by examining the principal stages of their respective parliamentary processes.

Fixing the agenda. In Britain the work of Parliament is quite strictly organized, in such a way that, while the rights of the opposition are guaranteed, government action is effective. In principle, the House of Commons meets from 2.30 to 10.30 p.m. (except on Fridays, when the hours are from 9.30 a.m. to 3 p.m.), and its business is organized so as to avoid night sessions as far as possible. The hours between 3.30 and 10.30 p.m. are reserved for 'public business', that is, both projects decided by the government in Cabinet meetings and presented by it, and Private Members' bills. In the case of the latter, priority goes to the twenty Members of Parliament whose motions head the ballot taken at the beginning of each session. However, the number of these bills that are both registered and subsequently adopted is relatively low. In the course of the 1979–83 Parliament, for example, 379 Private Members' bills were introduced, of which only 44 were passed (13 per cent), whereas over 95 per cent of government bills were successful. Furthermore, the government can organize debates before making their proposals, for example, by scheduling sittings after the normal closing time of 10 p.m.

The French Constitution of 1958 was influenced by British parliamentary procedure but imposed even stricter discipline upon the Assemblies. Under the Third and Fourth Republics, the Assemblies had been responsible for determining their own agendas, but Article 48 of the present Constitution reverses that situation, ruling that the government takes priority in determining agendas. Whatever time remains—if any—is organized by a President's conference attended by the Presidents and Vice-Presidents of the two Assemblies, the presidents of committees and parliamentary groups, and the general spokesman for the budget, in the form of a complementary agenda. As a result, laws of parliamentary origin are subject to both qualitative and quantitative limitations. They represent barely 10 per cent of all laws, and most are of secondary importance.

West Germany and Italy both allow a large measure of autonomy to their Parliaments, but it is applied differently in the two countries, since their political party structures differ. In West Germany, the agenda is decided by a 'council of elders' (Ältestenrat) composed of the President and Vice-Presidents of the Bundestag together with a number of delegates from the various parties in proportion to their respective strengths. Up until 1969, the rulings of this council had to be agreed unanimously, but since the parliamentary reforms adopted in that year, that is no longer the case. Nevertheless, the procedure for fixing the agenda remains largely consensual and makes it possible to respect the rights of the opposition. The relative autonomy of the Bundestag—which the personal prestige of its President sometimes reinforces—is reflected in a greater openness towards Private Members' bills, although, as everywhere in Europe, the supremacy of the executive remains the rule. According to Alfred Grosser, 'of the 2,395 laws passed during the five parliaments between 1949 and 1969, 34 came from the Bundesrat, 535 from the Bundestag, and 1,826 from the Government'.[9]

In Italy, where Parliament enjoys an institutional role of central importance, the agenda and scheduling of parliamentary tasks are fixed by a conference of parliamentary party group presidents, whose decisions must be unanimous. When such agreement proves impossible to reach, the agenda is fixed by the President of the Lower Chamber (or of the Senate). But, as Antonio Baldassare points out, the President 'must not refuse to attempt to mediate between the various positions expressed in Parliament'.[10] The supremacy of the Italian Parliament's role certainly affects legislative 'input' and 'output'. Laws proposed by Parliament are more numerous (but often of less importance) that those of government origin and, to get round the obstacles of access and delays, the Government has increasingly been forced to resort to the practice of law-decrees some, but not all, of which are subsequently ratified by Parliament.

Parliamentary committees. This is where the essential work of legislation is accomplished, sheltered from media attention and publicity in general. Often enough, political antagonisms are overcome, making way for collaboration between technical experts, all keen to draft as good a text as they possibly can.

In France, the 1958 Constitution limited the number of committees to six, but other parliamentary and presidential systems leave their Parliaments free to organize their own committee work and hence also to decide how many committees are necessary. In West Germany, for example, the number has tended to vary depending upon political considerations. For example, the first Bundestag set up 39 committees, the second 36, and their membership varied by a factor of four. The most 'sensitive' commissions (for example, those concerned with European security) were also the smallest, so as to avoid having to include the smaller parties, in particular the Communist Party. After the marginal parties began gradually to disappear and a *de facto* three-party system developed, the number of committees has oscillated between 15 and 20. One of the most unusual of them is the 'petitions committee', which receives the complaints that citizens may address to Parliament under Article 17 of the Constitution.

In Italy, the Chamber of Deputies includes 14 permanent committees, the Senate 12, and special committees may also be created. As they are quite large (about 45 Deputies and 25–30 Senators to each committee), they are divided into internal committees, permanent *ad hoc* Chamber committees, and Senate committees and sub-committees, sometimes supplemented by other study groups. As a result, close liaison is established both with the ministerial departments that the committees follow and also with the interest groups involved, each of which is represented by a spokesman with specialized knowledge of the situation. By contrast, Britain's standing committees[11] are neither permanent nor specialized. They are set up by the House of Commons as and when need arises and are given no specific names, being known quite simply as Committee A, B, C, and so on. Each is generally composed of eighteen members, all appointed by a selection committee.

Finally, Britain sometimes employs a special type of committee known as a 'committee of the whole House'. When it is decided to set up such a committee, the House no longer observes the rules that apply to plenary sessions. The Speaker leaves his seat and places his mace under the table, thereby indicating that the procedures that usually apply have been suspended. For instance, in these circumstances, a Member of Parliament is allowed to speak more than once on a single subject. It is a procedure that is used particularly when the problem under consideration is too extensive for a single committee to handle on its own and, above all, when the government commands only a small majority that would be further reduced by the few members engaged in standing committees.

The composition of Italian and German committees, like French and British ones, is proportionally representative of the various political groups. However, in France, the majority tends to monopolize the chairmanships. In Germany, the composition of committees is proportionally representative of the various political groups but, as we have already noted, it has sometimes proved possible, by juggling the numbers of members, to eliminate the smallest and most undesirable groups (*Fraktionen*) from committees that are considered to be of crucial importance. The chairmen of these committees are appointed by the Ältestenrat on the basis of a consensus that respects the political equilibrium: the Christian Democrats and the SPD divide the lion's share between them, in accordance with the election results. However, the FDP has never been excluded—not even when its support was not indispensable to the formation of a coalition. In Italy, the rule of proportional representation applies to the composition of committees, but the political groups themselves decide upon which of their members to appoint to which of them. None can belong to two at once (except members of the Senate, where the smaller parties are allowed to appoint the same Senator to sit on two commissions at the same time). Posts of president (or chairman) are allotted in relation to the existing balance of political forces and reflect the consensus that prevails in Italian parliamentary life whatever political quarrels and passions are current.

In Britain, the rules are dictated by the traditional two-party system and the relationship between the majority and the opposition. The chairman of a standing committee is appointed (in the case of each separate law) by the Speaker in collaboration with what is known as a 'chairman's panel', that is to say a group of about ten Members of Parliament whom the Speaker selects at the beginning of each parliamentary session. The role of a committee chairman is of considerable importance, for since 1907 he has held the right to close debates, and since 1934 also that of choosing which amendments to table. Given that committee debates are not public, it is easier for committee members to collaborate and there is less pressure from party whips. However, except in the case of a marginal or non-existent government majority (as from 1974 to 1979), the government may be assured of its own view prevailing.

The committees to which bills are submitted by the executive, parliamentary groups, or other Assembly members have two essential functions: to gather information, the better to legislate; and to amend and revise the drafts that are submitted to them.

The gathering of information may be done by organizing hearings. The practice of holding hearings[12] has been increasingly successful in West Germany and in Italy. Apart from their normal sessions, which are not public, German committees may organize meetings that are open to the Press and the public, during which experts and the representatives of interest groups may have their say. Up until the 1970s, such hearings were relatively exceptional; but since then the Bundestag has increased their number. Similarly, in Italy, the 1971 reform of Assembly regulations (in particular Article 143 of the Chamber of Deputies' regulations and Article 47 of those governing the Senate) opened up the possibility of more hearings in the American style. As a result, many more hearings and inquiries are now conducted by permanent parliamentary committees. As in the United States, the way in which the presentation of problems is staged has become as important as the collection of information.[13] In Britain, where such practices are less general, select committees responsible for monitoring the administration organize hearings, but the standing committees set up to discuss bills do not. In France such hearings rarely take place and, even when they do, their importance is no more than marginal and symbolic.

The second task of committees is to table amendments and in some cases to redraft bills. However, their powers vary from one political system to another depending on the degree of authority enjoyed by the executive through its control over the parliamentary majority. In Britain especially, but also in West Germany, Members of Parliament are expected to amend but not to destroy government bills. In Italy, in contrast, Members of Parliament may completely reconstruct government proposals, in such a way as to render them unrecognizable.

In France, the right of amendment is strictly controlled. In particular, the government can reject all amendments as a result of which funds would be depleted or public expenditure increased. A rule such as this enables a hostile government to reject virtually all amendments that are not to its liking. Furthermore, having rejected them, it can request its majority to adopt the law as drafted, using the 'blocked vote' procedure. The governments of the Fifth Republic have, however, over the years, adopted a more conciliatory attitude, particularly where amendments are tabled within commissions. In the privacy of these meetings closed to the public and to journalists, true co-operation has developed between the government and its majority, and in some cases even between it and the opposition.[14] On the other hand, the purpose of tabling amendments in plenary sessions is frequently to attract attention to the proposals and criticisms of the opposition. These are thus more of a 'filibustering' nature.

Parliamentary debates. The organization of the debates of parliamentary plenary sessions poses various problems. The first is of a purely practical nature, and the order of debates varies from one country to another. The second relates to the Assembly's right to table amendments and also to engage in obstructive policies or filibustering.

Italy's approach to the method of discussing legislation resembles that of the French Parliament. Once the committee representatives have had their say, a general debate is held, followed by a discussion of the bill, article by article, in the course of which amendments may be tabled by parliamentary groups or even by individual Deputies or Senators. The Assembly then proceeds to adopt the overall text. It should be noted that the regulations governing the two Italian

Chambers make it possible, at this stage, through an operation of 'final co-ordination', to correct any contradictions that have crept in as each article of the bill was voted upon. It is a useful procedure that is clearly necessary, but it sometimes lends itself to dubious interpretations and manipulation.

Somewhat different from the procedures described above are those adopted by Britain and West Germany, and they have much in common. Once a motion is entered on the agenda, a general debate is organized on the legislation as drafted. The draft is then passed on to the committees appointed to discuss it, then debated once again on the basis of the amendments proposed by those committees. At this stage amendments may be introduced both by the government and by members of parliament.

The right of members of parliament to table amendments is particularly important, especially in the European parliamentary democracies, where Assembly members have virtually lost the power of legislative initiative, whether they belong to the majority or to the opposition. The tabling of amendments affords the majority party or coalition a chance to 'correct' government proposals, and the opposition an opportunity to make its voice heard or even to put forward counter-proposals by a systematic tabling of amendments.

In Italy, the practice of parliamentary obstructionism has given rise to some particularly tense situations, albeit with a peculiarly Italian style. Because the tabling of amendments is often the surest means of obstruction, the regulations governing the Italian Assemblies have, since 1981, stipulated that there should be one discussion only to cover all the amendments to a single article. Furthermore, in the course of this, each Deputy may speak once only, even if he is the author of a whole series of amendments or additional articles. This rule is part of the arsenal of regulations that the Italian Assemblies have introduced in order to guard against the obstructionism of determined parliamentary groups, such as the Radicals, who in the late 1970s managed on several occasions to block the legislative machine. Up until 1971, the rules allowed the Assembly to bring debates to a close with a vote. In that year, a reform introduced two corrections, limiting the time allowed for each intervention and, in some debates, allowing only one speaker from each group. But that same reform undermined its own effectiveness by opening up the possibility of more flexibile methods. In 1981, the Chamber rules were again made more rigorous: now, each speaker was in theory allowed no more than 45 minutes (although, it is true, he could overrun his time, providing he did not exceed 90 minutes). These measures made it possible to put an end to the most flagrant abuses, in particular the obstruction engineered between 1976 and 1980 by the Radicals, who became champions of filibuster and of amendments. However, it is not possible, nor indeed advisable, to prevent all obstructions, for these remain the last weapon of the minority. In view of the degree of power held by the political parties within the Italian political system, a compromise between democracy and efficiency has been devised. It involves transferring to the parliamentary groups part of the responsibility for their own self-discipline: the rule of 'one spokesman per group' makes it possible to limit abuses and to appeal to the sense of responsibility of the parties that are represented in the two Assemblies. But none of these have been willing to submit themselves to too many restrictions, knowing full well that at some time or other they have all needed to resort to obstructionism—the left in 1949 and 1953 against the Atlantic Pact and the infamous electoral law proposed by Minister Scelba, the right in 1970, when the regional institutions were finally being set up.

As the 'Mother of Parliaments', Britain has considerable experience in the matter of controlling amendments and limiting obstructionism. When the British House of Commons discusses a text that has been amended by the relevant standing committee, the government resumes its full powers and can force its majority to accept either its own amendments or, alternatively, the elimination of the amendments adopted by the committee. Of course, every government must take account of its own majority party and the moods of its back-benchers, but an analysis of the legislative process in Britain shows clearly how limited an impact ordinary Members of Parliament make. A study of the three parliamentary sessions of 1967–8, 1968–9, and 1970–1 has shown that, of the thousands of amendments tabled, no more than thirty-nine (of which only nine were relatively important) were successfully forced through by the opposition or by back-benchers.[15]

The government's control over the processes of Parliament is equally firm when it comes to attempts at obstruction on the part of a minority. There are three instruments for avoiding filibusters. The first device is a motion to close the debate, first used by Gladstone in 1881, to counter the filibusters of the Irish Nationalists. According to this procedure, which is now the subject of Standing Order no. 31, a member of the Commons, usually a whip, can request that a motion to close the debate be put to the vote. With the proviso that the Speaker agrees that there has been sufficient debate (to some extent a guarantee for the minority), the motion is proposed. To be adopted, it must obtain a majority, collecting a minimum of 100 votes.[16] A similar procedure is followed in France. A second means of preventing possible blockages in the work of legislation is constituted by the so-called 'kangaroo' technique of selecting for discussion only the most important of the amendments in cases where it looks as though debating every single one will take too long. The selection is made by the Speaker (or the committee chairman, as the case may be). The third instrument is the guillotine procedure (also introduced in 1881), which allows the government to close debate on any individual item in a bill. When the government considers a bill to be particularly important and the debate over it drags on, it can decide to allocate a limited period of time for the discussion of each item of the bill still to be debated. The government can thus impose a strict schedule upon the debate. When the period of time allotted has elapsed, the debate is halted and the House must vote on the bill, including articles that have not yet been adopted and all government amendments, but not those tabled by ordinary Members of Parliament. The parties—in particular the opposition—are forced to make a drastic choice: either to slow down the process at the risk of debating only a small part of the bill, or to co-operate with the government by debating only the most important points and limiting the time allowed to each speaker.

In this area, too, the French Constitution has followed the British example and provided the government with extremely effective deterrents, which were brought into use even before the advent of truly filibustering behaviour. Parliamentary obstructionism only became a serious problem in the late 1970s during Giscard d'Estaing's presidency. At this point the Socialists became experts in the art of filibustering, but the right also learned from their example and, in its turn, adopted the same techniques after Mitterrand and the Socialists had come to power. The opposition has a number of means of slowing down the legislative process. It can claim that the proposed legislation is inopportune or unconstitutional (declaring it to be unacceptable, raising preliminary questions, tabling motions of adjournment or of censure, appealing to the regulations, demanding public votes or that the session be suspended, etc.) and once these preliminary obstacles are cleared away, it can table quantities of amendments. In 1983, for example 2,204 amendments were tabled when the law on higher education was debated; in 1984, 2,598 on the proposed law relating to the Press. The government, for its part, has three principal means at its disposal: the blocked vote on a bill (that retains only the amendments accepted by the executive); refusing to consider amendments that have not been tabled in committee; and invoking Article 49.3, which authorizes the government to take full responsibility for the bill. The draft is considered to be passed if no motion of censure is voted by a majority of the Assembly within 48 hours. This is an absolute weapon that makes it possible for even a minority government to get its own way, for the opposition is seldom sufficiently strong and united to get a motion of censure adopted. Between 1958 and 1981, this article was called into use only 15 times, but between 1981 and 1986 it was used 6 times. The Rocard Government established in June 1988 declared itself hostile to excessive use of this procedure, but since it does not control an absolute majority in the National Assembly, it is nevertheless forced to resort to it.

The effects of bicameralism. The existence of two chambers complicates the legislative process, since the bills must be studied, and some of them approved, in exactly the same terms by Assemblies whose modes of recruitment, social composition, and ideological affiliation are—or may be—quite different. The relations between the two branches of the legislature vary depending on whether the two chambers involved stand on an equal or an unequal footing.

In France, Italy, and Britain, government proposals may be tabled before either chamber, but the lower chamber is usually the first to discuss the draft prepared by the executive. Indeed, this is obligatory for finance bills. Proposals are generally laid before the Senate or the House of Lords either as a matter of courtesy or for reasons of timing and, in Britain in particular, the House of Lords tends to receive such drafts as are not likely to give rise to much disagreement, a fact that eases the pressure in the Upper House as the parliamentary session draws to a close. The West German Constitution, in contrast, stipulates that 'the Federal Government's legislative proposals *must* in the first instance be tabled before the Bundesrat, which has the right to take three weeks to decide what should become of them'.

When bills have been debated and adopted by the first Assembly to receive them, they are passed on to the other chamber which, in its turn, examines them. It is at this stage that any disagreements between the two chambers must be resolved on the basis of the superiority of the one or negotiation between the two. The British

House of Lords is undoubtedly in the weakest position of all the upper chambers, since it cannot oppose the will of the Commons or the government majority, and has no powers at all in financial matters. Nevertheless, by refusing to adopt a bill, the House of Lords plays a decisive role, for if a bill is to be adopted by the House of Commons on its own, this can only be done in the next parliamentary session. Several months may thus elapse between the two debates, during which time it may prove possible to mobilize opposition and cause the proposal to founder. The risk is even greater when the Lords express their opposition at the end of the parliament: if the subject is a controversial one, the government is wary of forcing the draft through come what may, for if it is defeated in the elections, the bill will disappear along with it.

In France, agreement between the two Assemblies is effected by means of shuttling the proposed text between the two for repeated examination, for such time as it takes to obtain complete and definitive unanimity. If the government wishes to block a text proposed by one Assembly, all it has to do is manipulate the other so as to avert a compromise: the proposal then founders. Furthermore, *only* the Government has the power to unblock the situation when the two Assemblies fail to reach agreement. Once a proposal has been given two readings in each Assembly (or just one, if the government declares the matter to be urgent), the Prime Minister can convene a mixed committee of seven Deputies and seven Senators in all, to represent both the majority and (since 1981) the opposition. This committee must endeavour to elaborate a compromise text that the government is at liberty to put to the vote in both Chambers, including only such amendments as it finds acceptable. If the two Chambers fail to agree over this compromise text, the government is empowered to request the National Assembly to pronounce definitively either upon the text produced by the committee or upon the latest version adopted by the Assembly (which may be revised in the light of amendments made by the Senate). This mechanism is ingenious, for it makes it possible for the government to block or unblock the process at will, choosing, according to the prevailing political circumstances, either to give the Senate parity with the National Assembly or to make it subordinate. In 1958, for instance, General de Gaulle reckoned that he would not obtain a majority in the Assembly but that the Senate would support him. (As it turned out, the reverse was true, for from 1962 to 1969 the Senate opposed de Gaulle.) However, in any event, the government is in a winning position since it can either block the National Assembly with the aid of the Senate or, alternatively, dispense altogether with the Senate's approval. In other words, the two-chamber system provides the executive with an extra means of implementing its own decisions.

The position of the West German Bundesrat is strong in some respects, weak in others. If the bill being debated concerns the federation as a whole, opposition from the Bundesrat constitutes a veritable veto. In other strictly federal matters, opposition from the Upper Chamber can be overridden by a Bundestag vote with an absolute majority of its members (or with a two-thirds majority of voting members if more than a two-thirds majority was obtained in the Bundesrat). In Italy, on the other hand, the matter may continue to be shuttled between the two Assemblies, with neither gaining the upper hand. The only constraint imposed upon the two Chambers is of a procedural nature: at a second reading, each can only pronounce upon the amendments tabled by the other, and only amendments that have undergone such modifications may be accepted. The hope is that, by restricting the field of discussion, piecemeal agreement may eventually be reached between these two strictly equal Assemblies. Curiously enough, no formal arbitration procedure has ever been established although mixed commissions are frequently set up, either through the Constitution (e.g. the commission for regional questions) or as a result of ordinary legislation (e.g. committees for radio and television, and for southern problems).

In West Germany, by contrast, as in France, mixed committees are used to settle differences between the two Chambers. A mediation committee. (*vermittlungsausschus*) is composed of eleven members of the Bundesrat and an equal number of Deputies chosen for their personal qualities. Such committees have no powers of decision. All they can do is propose compromises that seem honourable and acceptable to both Chambers. However, since the rejection of such compromises usually (in the case of federative laws, at least) means that the bill in question will be quashed, the suggestions made by these committees are usually followed.

CONTROLLING THE EXECUTIVE

From the point of view of constitutional theory, the modes of control of a classic parliamentary system and those of a presidential regime have nothing in common. In the former, members of parliament may topple the government by refusing it a vote of confidence or voting a motion of censure, whereas in the latter model two forces, the executive and the legislature, counterbalance one another, blocking each other's moves, without involving the political responsibility of any ministry. Thus, the United States and parliamentary systems seem to represent two strongly contrasting models which apparently share virtually nothing in common. This may be a true opposition at the level of constitutional theory and political philosophy, but it bears little relation to reality or to the manner in which parliaments' modes of control over their executives have evolved ('executives' being, in truth, a misnomer, given the degree of authority that they have acquired). The ambiguity is reflected in the move made, under the Fifth French Republic, to maintain ministerial responsibility of the classic type, even though true power (except from 1986 to 1988) was concentrated in the hands of a President whose actions could not be challenged by Parliament. The function of parliaments has changed, as have their means of control over their executives. It is from this point of view that we shall now examine the evolution and transformation of the ways in which parliaments and governments interact.

The Persistence and Limits of Traditional Forms of Control

The Western parliamentary democracies possess one major instrument for controlling their governments: the vote of confidence or of no confidence. It is a means of control that is still in use and that has been considerably improved, but its importance, in real terms, has been considerably diminished.

In parliamentary systems, parliaments theoretically hold the power of life or death over governments. In practice, however, even if the procedures that constitute the very essence of parliamentarianism do still exist, they are used less and less. For example, Britain, which 'invented' the principle of ministerial responsibility, seldom uses a House of Commons vote of no confidence to unseat a Prime Minister or government. And on occasions when it does do so (as in 1979, when the Labour Government was beaten by a single vote), the fact is that the party in power commanded only a composite or extremely small majority anyway. In general, political crises and the implementation of the principle of responsibility manifest themselves not in constitutional forms but internally, within the majority party. When a government finds itself in difficulties, following repeated defeats and disagreements with its majority, it is sometimes forced to resign without any vote of no confidence (e.g. Chamberlain's Government, in 1940). The dissatisfaction of its back-benchers is expressed through pressures within the party and by acts of 'rebellion' (such as abstentions or hostile votes), which seldom amount to a defeat of the government in strictly constitutional terms. Nevertheless, the government is bound to take account of the restive mood of its troops and in some cases to accept the ultimate consequences and resign. Eden was obliged to do so in 1956 (over the Suez affair), as was Macmillan in 1963 (over the Profumo scandal).[17] In other words, the classical principle of political responsibility before Parliament has been replaced by a mechanism that allows the party in question to make its own choices and to keep its leader under surveillance.

In Italy, we find a similar discrepancy between constitutional theory and practice, albeit for different reasons and taking different forms. In principle, the government may be called into question whenever a vote of confidence or a motion of no confidence occurs (Article 94). The remarkable solemnity of these procedures is manifested in particular by the fact that every individual Deputy is called upon to cast a public vote. This is no doubt one reason why, to date, only two Italian governments have been toppled by these means. Political crises tended to become manifest when disagreements arose over secret votes on government bills (eliminated for the most part in 1988 by a parliamentary reform). The *franchi tiratori* (the deputies of the majority who vote against the government in secret ballots) made the most of such situations to record either their own personal disagreement or the unacknowledged misgivings of their party as a whole. For example, in 1980 the Cossiga Government was forced to resign after two hostile votes on bills that it was proposing when it had barely managed to secure an absolute majority of votes. In June 1986, Bettino Craxi suffered the same fate. In this respect a comparison between Britain and Italy is particularly interesting, for both systems possess mechanisms to facilitate the formation of governments; but in the one case they reinforce government stability while in the other they undermine it. In Britain, the government comprises about 100 members (one-third of the majority), who automatically vote in its support. In Italy, in contrast, governments have a habit of resigning even when they are not constitutionally obliged to do so, and this plays into the hands of those who seek to obtain a minister's portfolio by devious means. However, in both cases the situation may be said to be 'extra-parliamentary', as the Italians put it, in the sense that it becomes an internal problem to be faced by the majority party or coalition. Accordingly, the solemn techniques for registering confidence in the government are increasingly often deflected from their initial objective. Votes of confidence, in Italy, and Article 49.3 in France, for example, are increasingly employed to halt obstructionism on the part of the opposition, thereby becoming the functional equivalents of the motions to close debates, or the guillotine, that are used in Britain.

Italian governments have also been known to come into being and survive on the basis of a *non sfiducia* (a non-no confidence vote). The Andreotti Governments (claimed to be Governments of National Unity) were supported by the entire constitutional spectrum of political parties, with the exceptions of the MSI on the right and the Radicals and the PDUP on the left. All the parties involved supported a vote of confidence in the Government, with the exception of the Communist Party, which abstained, thereby helping to stabilize the Government and actively collaborating in the elaboration of its policies.

Only one motion of no confidence has been passed in Italy since the war, only one in Britain (in 1979) since 1945, only one in France (in 1962) since 1958. The use of the 'absolute weapon' has become so exceptional that it can no longer be called a parliamentary means of controlling the government. Even in West Germany, where the mechanisms for expressing confidence and no confidence have been elaborated in a sophisticated fashion, the Constitution has been deflected from its original intentions. Article 67 establishes an unusual mechanism frequently described as a 'constructive vote of no confidence'. According to the Constitution, the Bundestag can only censure and bring about the fall of a government if an absolute majority of its members votes for a new Chancellor to succeed the one just toppled. It is a procedure only used in exceptional circumstances (for example, in 1982, to topple Chancellor Schmidt and replace him by Chancellor Kohl). The truth is that, as in Britain and Italy, many political crises arise and are resolved outside the parliamentary framework. Adenauer's departure in 1963 was largely due to pressure applied by the CDU and the FDP; and his successor, Ludwig Erhard, suffered a similar fate in 1966, having failed to imbue his party with the new impetus that it needed. Brandt's resignation in 1974 was connected with the discovery of an East German spy in his immediate entourage (the Guillaume affair) and consequently had nothing to do with any hostile vote on the part of the Bundestag. But the Chancellor had in any case lost his influence over both his party and his Government and it would have been impossible for him to remain in power. A similar 'deflection' of the constitutional rules takes place if Parliament is dissolved following a vote of no confidence. Even when a majority is so weak or a coalition so divided that it is reduced to impotence, it may still prove impossible for the opposition to appoint a new Chancellor. For example, in April 1972, Barzel, the CDU candidate, obtained only 247 of the necessary 249 votes. In such cases, Article 68 of the Constitution allows the Chancellor to call for a vote of confidence and, if he is defeated (by an absolute majority), to ask the President of the Republic to dissolve the Bundestag within three weeks, if a new Chancellor is not elected within that period. Thus, on 22 September 1972, the Bundestag passed a motion of no confidence in the Brandt Government by 248 votes to 233. That vote was only obtained because of the organized defection of a few members of the majority, which made it possible to satisfy the juridical conditions for a dissolution of Parliament. Similarly, in 1983, although the Kohl Government had enjoyed a comfortable majority since the CDU –CSU–FDP coalition had been set up in the autumn of 1982, it resorted to a dissolution of Parliament to enable the German electorate to ratify the political changes that had taken place following the resignation of the FDP ministers of the Schmidt Government. As in 1972, it proved necessary to 'organize' a vote of no confidence within the majority itself in order to meet the constitutional conditions for a dissolution as laid down by Article 68.

A Reversal of the Traditional Hierarchy: The Primacy of Unsanctioned Controls

Modes of control other than motions of censure and votes of no confidence do not necessarily immediately lead to that highly symbolic event, the fall of a government. For that reason, they were for long—and often still are, even today—considered to be instruments of secondary or minor importance. The role played by these mechanisms of control varies from one country to another, but everywhere the tendency now is to reinforce them, and those countries with the richest panoply of methods of this kind now tend to 'export' them. Let us consider three of the major ones: parliamentary questions or request for information, committees of inquiry and control, and hearings.

The institution of 'Question Time' developed in Britain in the second half of the nineteenth century, at a time when Members of Parliament were less rigidly controlled by their parties. During Question Time (which usually lasts for one hour each day), Members of Parliament may ask up to two questions each, per day, provided they have given the relevant ministers 48 hours' notice of their intention to do so. Questions that have not been answered orally by the end of the session subsequently receive a written answer. As in France, the technique of putting questions may have either a practical purpose (to find out more about the administration's position *vis-à-vis* a particular subject) or a political one (to embarrass the government). In West Germany, the technique of asking questions is also much in use. About 5,000 questions are asked each year, most of which receive a written reply, the procedure being similar to the British one. Every plenary session (of which there are sixty each year) includes one hour set aside, during which ministers answer about twenty questions. However, in West Germany, the role of questions seems on the whole less important than in Britain (although there have been exceptional instances: in 1962, the Minister of Defence, Herr Strauss, was obliged to resign following questions put to him over the Spiegel affair). In 1965, 'current questions' (*aktuelle stunde*) were introduced, making it possible for the Bundestag to debate the most pressing problems of the moment for one hour every day.

In France, there are two kinds of oral question, those that are not accompanied by a debate and those that are. In the case of the former, the Deputy asks a brief question (lasting no longer than 2 minutes in the Assembly, 5 in the Senate). Following the relevant Minister's answer, he is allowed a maximum of 5 minutes in which to respond. In the case of oral questions accompanied by a debate, the restrictions are less stringent. To explain the problem put before the government, the speaker has between 10 and 20 minutes in the Assembly, 30 minutes in the Senate. Following the Minister's reply, in the Senate each registered speaker is allowed 20 minutes, in the Assembly as long as the President of the session deems fit. The limiting nature of these procedures has provoked two types of reaction. In the first place, in order to secure more time for discussion, the opposition may table a motion of censure even if it has no chance of being adopted, with the sole object of obtaining a debate worthy of the name. Secondly, in 1970 in the Assembly, 1982 in the Senate, a time for 'current questions' was introduced, to give more animation and interest to the dialogue between the executive and the legislature. In 1974, these came to be known as 'Questions for the Government'. This Question Time takes place on Wednesday afternoons in the Assembly. As the session is televised, it produces flights of oratory and dramatic skirmishes which may give the public a somewhat distorted impression of the normal behaviour of Deputies. Wednesdays, furthermore, are the days when the level of attendance is at its highest. In general, the level of parliamentary absenteeism is deplorably high on account of the tendency for Deputies each to accumulate a whole collection of responsibilities at both national and local levels.

Oral questions unaccompanied by a debate are frequently asked (an average of 200 per year), but questions accompanied by a debate are very rare (only 5 in the course of the seventh legislature, which lasted from 1981 to 1986). It is also worth noting that many written questions are asked (17,000 to 18,000 in the Assembly, 5,000 to 6,000 in the Senate, each year). But these questions hardly constitute a means of control over the government. Essentially, their function is practical: to obtain from the Minister an official interpretation of a text or an administrative practice that may then be imposed from above upon his administration as a whole.

In Italy, the practice of Question Time is also much in use and, since the reform of the Chamber's regulations in 1971, Deputies have been able to put their questions not only during plenary Assemblies but also in commissions. The number of questions put orally in the Chamber of Deputies rose from 5,458 during the first legislature (1948–53) to 7,886 during the eighth (1979–83), while the number of written questions increased from 12,472 to 20,204 over the same period. But the rate at which replies are forthcoming is low (only 23 per cent of oral questions received a reply in the course of the eighth legislature, chiefly because there were altogether too many to cope with and because of the system of collecting connected questions into a single group). In Italy, as in France, Britain, and Germany, the Chamber of Deputies organizes times for 'current questions' once a week, on Wednesdays. During these sessions, the questions are answered immediately and the exchange between the Minister and the

Deputy is replaced by a real dialogue. When the Minister concerned has made his reply, five Deputies from different groups are allowed to request further explanations. This practice thus constitutes an intermediate procedure between that of a traditional Question Time and that of what is known in the French Parliament as 'interpellation'.

The practice of interpellation was prohibited under the Fifth French Republic, but is still much in use in other parliamentary systems. In Italy, interpellations, unlike questions, are limited to sessions of the Assembly and are not allowed in commissions. If the author of an interpellation is not satisfied by the reply given by the Minister, he is allowed, according to Article 138 of the Chamber's regulations, to move that there be a 'discussion on the explanations provided by the government'. As with questions, the relatively low percentage of replies received by interpellations (between 12 and 49 per cent, depending on different legislatures) may be partly explained by the increasing use of this procedure (2,546 instances between 1979 and 1983) and by the 'self-sufficient' nature of the parliamentary interpellation, which may be formulated not so much in order to elicit a response and a debate, but rather to sound out public opinion on both the issue concerned and the standing of the Deputy involved.

In West Germany, the formula of the 'minor interpellation' (*Kleine Anfrage*) has been extremely successful. It differs from other forms of interpellation in that it is constituted by written questions posed by at least twenty-six Deputies (the minimum required to make up a parliamentary group or *Fraktion*). A reply must be given by the Minister or government within a fortnight, and is usually expected to contain detailed answers, the purpose of which is not to give rise to a debate but to provide the parliamentary group concerned with as much information as possible. While as many as 400 to 500 minor interpellations are made each year, the number of interpellations in the classical form (*Grosse Anfragen*) is tending to fall.[18]

In Britain, the interpellation takes the form of what is known as a 'motion of adjournment' made by the opposition. When Question Time is up and before Parliament turns to the matters listed on its agenda, any member of the House of Commons has the right to table a motion to debate 'a specific and important matter that should have urgent consideration'. However, he must have the backing of forty other members and convince the Speaker of the interest of such a debate. Since the reform of Standing Order no. 9, in 1967, the

Speaker has been relieved of all constraints of precedence and must simply decide whether the subject is 'proper to be discussed'. If the motion is accepted, the debate is organized for the following afternoon and is brought to a close after a maximum of three hours. In all these possible circumstances which (with certain variants) are common to all parliamentary systems, the control exercised by the chambers depends not so much upon the sanctions that they may impose, but rather upon the continuing pressure that they apply to the government and the administration, and the publicity that this attracts. These new modes of control have acquired a progressive importance due to the work of the media that publicize them and possess the power to turn any question raised by a member of parliament into a national debate. It is the formidable impact of the media that makes these controls without sanctions so powerful.

Committees of inquiry are part of the parliamentary tradition but, as a result of American experiments and practices, here and there other forms of parliamentary monitoring have been developed, in particular taking the shape of investigations and hearings.

France is probably the country in which committees of control or inquiry possess the least influence. In the first place, as we have seen above, the National Assembly may set up no more than six permanent committees, the effect of which is to turn them into veritable mini-Assemblies comprising, on average, about 100 members. The only possibility left for Deputies is to set up temporary committees of inquiry and control (whose duration is limited to six months). These committees, composed on the basis of proportional representation of the various party groups, are in effect dominated by the majority, which generally seizes the key posts of chairman and 'spokesman' and is thus in a position to draw up the report that suits it, while the minority has no chance to express its views in a dissenting report. Under the Fifth Republic, this bipolarization has undermined the credibility of these inquiries to such a degree that, in some cases (the *Rainbow Warrior* affair of 1985, for example), the opposition has given up pressing for the creation of special committees. It is, for example, significant that between 1981 and 1986, a period marked by considerable political tension, only 3 committees of inquiry were set up (though 61 were requested) and not a single committee of control (2 were requested). It should also be noted that the proceedings of these committees are secret and the committees may decide not to publish their reports. Furthermore, they may not be set up (or must cease their activities) when a judicial inquiry is set up to deal with the same question. As can be seen from all these restrictions, committees of inquiry or control in France play no more than a marginal role. Only the senatorial committees of the 1960s (a period when the Senate was opposing de Gaulle) truly fulfilled the functions of monitoring and inquiry that one might expect from a parliamentary Assembly.

In Britain, the 1979 measures taken to reform committees created fourteen select committees to follow up matters connected with their respective areas of responsibility. The number of these committees and the degree of their specialization makes it possible for them to keep a close eye on the functioning and policies of each of the various Ministries, and their power of control is strengthened by the fact that the Ministers themselves and their parliamentary private secretaries, that is to say the Members of Parliament who assist them, are excluded from the relevant committees. The back-benchers consequently play a considerably more important role in these committees than they do in the business of legislation, particularly since the parliamentary 'prima donnas' who are not in the government tend to rule themselves out through lack of time. These select committees may hear all persons necessary for the completion of their tasks and produce reports which give a general account of the information received in the course of these hearings. However, no more than a tiny minority (less than 5 per cent) of their reports are ever debated in the House of Commons. Despite these limitations, the reform introduced important changes into the British parliamentary style. As Philip Norton notes: 'For over a century, Parliament has not been a policy-making legislature. Instead, it has been a policy-influencing legislature.'[19] The new changes underline the British Parliament's function of control, but in a less formal fashion than in the past (since the absolute sanction of a vote of censure is nowadays seldom used).

West Germany seems to have had difficulty in putting the commissions of inquiry (*Untersuchungsausschuss*) prescribed by the Constitution to positive and intensive use. In his study of Western Germany, Gordon Smith[20] interprets this relative weakness on the basis of the peculiar characteristics of the Bundestag, which are indeed very different from those of the House of Commons. As he sees it, whereas the House of Commons is essentially a forum, the Bundestag is a legislative body. It is an *Arbeitsparlament*, which devotes most of its time to committee work rather than to plenary Assemblies, and most of its energies to drafting and amending laws rather than, strictly speaking, monitoring the administration. We should also note that Germany's extremely strong juridical tradition, which includes juridical controls, makes parliamentary monitoring less essential.[21] Consequently, no more than a score or so of commissions of inquiry have been set up since 1949 and few of these have reached any satisfactory conclusions, probably because they are over-politicized. From this point of view, the situation resembles that of France, where the majority frequently seeks to prevent inquiries of an embarrassing kind from taking place, and where the opposition sometimes settles for a boycott rather than participation.

Article 82 of the Italian Constitution rules that every Assembly may conduct inquiries into affairs of public interest through commissions formed on the basis of proportional representation of the parliamentary groups and 'holding the same powers and subject to the same limitations as those of the judicial authority'. In practice, special laws are passed to set up these commissions, in which both Chambers are usually represented. It is a way of extending the powers attributed by the Constitution. (For example, certain secrets that may not be divulged even to the judiciary must be revealed to a commission established by the Constitution.) The enhanced role of these commissions of inquiry is a consequence of the political and social trauma that Italy suffered during the 1970s. The proliferation of scandals, terrorism, and Mafia operations underlined the degree to which the political, administrative, judicial, policing, and financial apparatus had become corrupt. In the course of the eighth legislature, for example, the two Chambers had to set up inquiries into affairs such as the assassination of Aldo Moro, the Sindona scandal (tragically concluded in March 1986, when the banker was discovered poisoned to death in his cell), and the P2 Masonic Lodge. Some of the inquiries were so extensive as to involve years and years of investigation, and even so the questioning of hundreds of individuals did not always lead to altogether conclusive results. The P2 affair, for example, which had exploded so publicly, was wound up correspondingly discreetly, but no clear conclusions were ever reached, no action ever taken (despite the most insistent protests from the Italian Communist Party). Furthermore, the existence of these commissions poses certain delicate problems regarding their relations with the judicial authorities—problems that were only partially resolved by Decision no. 231 made by the Constitutional Court in 1975. The Court was of the opinion that the commissions should agree to pass on to the judiciary all the evidence and information that they had collected, except for those that they considered it necessary to keep secret in order to be able to fulfil their tasks. Furthermore, the increasingly penal nature of these commissions raises the problem of what guarantees to offer to the individuals interrogated. It has been agreed that those interrogated on matters that could lead to penal sentences for them may claim legal assistance, but also that the commission may proceed to arrest a witness in a case of false evidence or a refusal to collaborate. This shift from the political to the legal domain is risky, for a good system of justice needs serenity, rules, and guarantees that the commissions of inquiry can provide only partially, if at all. The developments in Italy nevertheless underline the importance that commissions of inquiry have acquired, following the model provided by the American tradition.

CONCLUSION

How should we evaluate the role of contemporary parliaments and their place in the institutions of their respective countries?

To answer this question, we must start by dismissing the myth that usually obscures the issue, namely, that there ever was some kind of parliamentarian Golden Age when parliaments which expressed the democratic will were the corner-stone of the constitutional system, exerting effective control over the government and dominating the legislative process. It is true that the power and influence of Parliaments have been greater in particular periods and in particular countries (Britain, the United States, and France, in particular). However, a number of qualifications are called for. In the first place, the power of parliaments has frequently been exaggerated, for strategic reasons, by those seeking to create a freer, less authoritarian society. In France, for instance, the myth of British parliamentarianism has been fostered in the interests of certain political groups or parties. Secondly, even when they were powerful or appeared to be, parliaments no more than imperfectly fulfilled their first duty, namely, to represent the people as a whole: limited suffrage, rotten boroughs, electoral corruption, pressures exerted by the existing authorities, etc. were not the exception, but the rule. Thirdly, it is all too often forgotten that the 'decline' of parliament that is nowadays so much lamented has been going on for an extremely long time. It has been pointed out that Bagehot's classic work *The English Constitution*, celebrating the British Parliament, describes a situation that no longer obtained even at the date of its publication (1867). In similar fashion, the critics of the Fifth French Republic are evoking largely mythical parliaments when they contrast the 1958 Parliament to the Assemblies of the Third and Fourth Republics. All too often they confuse unrest with influence, and the ability to topple governments with that of bringing some influence to bear upon the course of events. There can be no better illustration of the parliamentary decrepitude of the Third and Fourth Republics than their respective capitulations, in 1940 and 1958, when the Assemblies placed themselves totally in the hands of two men of destiny, first Pétain, then de Gaulle, in order to set up new institutions. If we recognize that the erstwhile so-called power of parliaments is illusory, the present-day situation appears less dramatic than it is often made out to be.

The first point to emphasize is that parliaments have seldom been more representative than they are today. Suffrage is more or less universal, guarantees to ensure that elections are free from corruption are constantly being improved, and the drawing of constituency boundaries, while not always perfect, is also becoming fairer and better monitored in the European democracies.

Secondly, parliaments remain the forums of political life *par excellence* and, seen from this point of view, their audience, far from shrinking, has increased, thanks to the Press, television, and radio, all of which are mediators and broadcasters of the parliamentary debate.

Thirdly, parliaments, in Europe at least, are still the places where government members tend to be recruited (or at the very least legitimized). In Britain, Italy, and West Germany (and elsewhere too), nobody becomes a Minister until he has proved himself as a member of parliament. Even in France, where General de Gaulle tried to separate the functions of Ministers and Deputies, tradition proved stronger than his political will. Only the United States differs in this respect. Furthermore, the ever-increasing importance of the political parties helps to consolidate the links and interchanges between governments and parliaments, encouraging the professionalism of politicians and making for the reconciliation of the antagonistic views of different groups.

The fact is that the 'input' of a parliament cannot be reduced to the passing of bills. At an earlier stage, it also involves deciding upon party programmes, fixing the political agenda, and negotiating with the executive over legislative proposals. For governments cannot afford to ignore parliamentary advice and opinions, even as they prepare their own proposals. Indeed, very often government bills are the fruit of a synthesis of legislative proposals that have already been tabled (one example in France being the proposals to legalize abortion).

Finally, parliamentary decline is often claimed to be particularly dramatic in the area of controls. But, while parliaments frequently do find it extremely difficult to exercise control, here, too, the scale of parliamentary decline has been exaggerated as a consequence of the prevailing notion that control boils down to votes of confidence or motions of censure. Yet it is quite possible for controls to be effective even without involving any 'political responsibility' in the parliamentary sense, as the example of the United States reminds us. And meanwhile the case of Italy makes the point that the game of toppling governments in which its Parliament indulges is really more a way of paying off old party scores than a means of imposing effective control over the actions of the executive. Nowadays, parliamentary control is genuinely exercised in conjunction with public opinion, and has never been so effective. With the support of the latter and by appealing to it and guiding it, Parliament can now play a new role.

The pluses and minuses are thus much more evenly balanced that may at first sight appear, if we bear in mind that parliaments today avail themselves of their modes of intervention within an institutional, political, and social framework that is very different from that in which Assemblies were originally conceived. As Polsby[22] observes, parliaments are more than ever 'multi-purpose organizations' with a role of central importance to play in democracies of the Western type, and their influence is by no means limited to the closed space of the formal political arena.[23]

6

Presidents and Governments

While the political systems of the democracies may all be founded upon common principles such as the separation of powers and popular representation through Parliament, there are substantial differences between one country and another in the procedures of constitutional machinery set up to achieve these objectives. The purest and, at the same time, most strongly contrasting systems are those of Britain and the United States. Britain represents the model of a parliamentary system, the United States that of a presidential one. Between these two extremes of constitutional classification, there exists a whole range of variants which are the delight of typology specialists. In view of all the profound organizational and structural differences that even a cursory examination reveals, to attempt to compare government institutions may thus seem a risky venture. Nevertheless, one fact is bound to strike the observer over and above the many marked institutional differences: namely, the central character of the function of government virtually universally. This is as true of primitive societies as it is of the most developed ones, and of liberal democracies as well as of the most bloodthirsty dictatorships. No other political institution is so common a feature of all political systems: a government is, as it were, the very incarnation of power. Henri Lefebvre has spoken of the 'catholic' nature of the State, underlining the formidable expansion of this particular form of organized power, and Jean Blondel, in his turn, similarly points out the remarkable 'universality of the phenomenon of government'.[1]

The fact is that, over the above the diversity of institutions in different countries, a fundamental need for command and coercion emerges, even if the Western translation of that need has led to a differentiation and limitation of the organs of power (a separation of powers). Beyond the differences engendered by different histories and cultures, common objectives and functions truly do seem to exist. Besides, we should not exaggerate the importance of institutional differences between the various Western systems, for they are often more formal than substantial and tend to become less striking as a result of 'contamination' from one system to another. Furthermore, similar constitutional structures (for example, those of West Germany, Italy, and Britain) may coexist with highly varied political practices. Consequently, it is only through a more detailed analysis that we may seize upon the ways in which the European executives differ from or resemble one another and the roles they play in their respective political systems.

THE EXECUTIVE

There is no unanimously accepted term to denote the function of government. Montesquieu used the expression 'executive power' but, following Rousseau, the lustre of that expression was dimmed by France's Revolutionaries, who resorted instead to anthropomorphic images, assimilating an executive to a simple executor: the legislature was the head of the system, the executive simply the hand that executed its orders. In the United States, the term 'executive' applies to the President and his collaborators, but de Gaulle insisted that the adjective 'executive' applied solely to the government. In Britain, the word 'executive' generally refers not only to the government itself, but also to the administration placed under it. On the other hand, the term 'government' may equally apply to the whole collection of institutions, rules, and procedures by which the country is run. Here, it is the word 'Cabinet' that most closely corresponds to the French *gouvernement* or the Italian *governo*. However, neither in France nor in Germany nor in Italy does there exist any expression that adequately conveys the dual nature of an executive power that is divided between a President and a head of government.

In parliamentary systems, dual executives are the end-product of a slow evolution in the course of which the prerogatives of the monarch have been transferred to the government and the Prime Minister. The transformation of the role of the monarchy, which has become increasingly symbolic and ceremonial, has made it possible to transfer to a system in which the Head of State embodies the continuity of the State and its institutions, without holding the power or means to devise or implement policies of his or her own. Moreover, by avoiding even a formal concentration of power within the hands of a single executive figurehead, the dual solution incorporates both political and constitutional advantages which may well account for its success among European democracies such as Greece, Spain, and Portugal that have recently emerged from dictatorships.

The Head of State

To borrow the words of Michel Debré, de Gaulle's Prime Minister from 1958 to 1962, the Head of State is the 'keystone' of the institutions of the Fifth French Republic. In the context of a formally parliamentary administration, the importance of his functions constitutes something of an anomaly. It is even fair to say that, from 1958 to 1986 (which saw the beginning of the 'cohabitation' between the right and the Socialists that lasted up until 1988), no Western Head of State or Prime Minister—not even the President of the United States —held such extensive powers. These powers were reinforced by the fact that, since the 1962 reform,[2] the French Head of State has been elected by universal suffrage, which confers upon him greater legitimacy than that possessed by any other politician, a legitimacy as great as that of the National Assembly itself. The mechanisms of election were indeed deliberately elaborated in order to reinforce that legitimacy. Candidates must be put up by 500 'sponsors' hailing from thirty departments (Deputies or local elected officials). In the first ballot of the election, they compete freely. However, to be declared the winner it is necessary to obtain an absolute majority of votes. If no candidate obtains such a majority (and since 1965 none has), only the two candidates who head the poll may stand for a second ballot. This guarantees that, whatever the outcome, the victor will have been elected by an absolute majority of all votes cast. In France, the political consensus is too fragile to allow the appointment of a minority President (as has been known in the United States), or for a President elected by a small fraction of the population to be politically acceptable.

Armed with his prestige (in the case of de Gaulle) or 'consecrated' by the vote, a President of the Fifth Republic holds considerable powers even though he carries no political responsibility and is elected for a very long term of office (seven years), the only justification for which is the tradition established under the Third Republic. The Constitution bestows numerous powers upon him: he appoints the Prime Minister, presides over the Council of Ministers, signs decrees and ordinances, appoints three members of the Constitutional Council (including its President), and also senior civil servants. But in addition, he is Commander-in-Chief of the Armed Forces and head of the Diplomatic Service; and he can call a referendum and dissolve the National Assembly. Finally, in exceptional circumstances (war or rioting), Article 16 gives him the right to exercise a kind of 'legal dictatorship': for such time as he deems necessary, he may assume all powers necessary for dealing with the situation. (These measures were clearly prompted by President Lebrun's inability, in 1939–40, to manage events when de Gaulle, for his part, announced his intention of continuing the struggle from a London base.)

As listed above, these powers are already startling enough. But it should also be noted that, from 1958 to 1986, they were further extended by two factors: the 'conventions' created by the practices of de Gaulle and his successors; and the combination, over almost thirty years, of the presidential and the parliamentary majorities. The Head of State thus had at his disposal a generally docile majority and also a government completely at his service, and was thereby in a position to adopt an extremely wide interpretation of his powers. In practice, there was no limit to the problems to which the President could address himself: agricultural negotiations in Brussels, fiscal policies, decisions regarding one particular group or another. There is probably no other Western country where a President could have the last word on the route to be taken by a regional line of the Paris Underground (de Gaulle), or decide to create a cultural centre (Pompidou), a Parisian museum (Giscard d'Estaing), or to undertake a whole series of major public building projects (Mitterrand). In effect, the Elysée has often operated as a substitute for the Matignon (the seat of the government) to the extent that technical councillors and the heads of presidential missions had systematic access to the files of every Ministry and frequently also the last say in decisions on these matters. One of the characteristics of the French system is that the *éminences grises* (the high-ranking civil servants in the various Ministries, that is, the staff of the President, the Prime Minister, and other Ministers) often have far more influence and power than the political or administrative personnel who are in principle responsible for devising and elaborating policies.

This quasi-monarchical and extremely delicate shared system was disrupted by the victory of the right in the parliamentary elections of 1986, at a time when François Mitterrand, the Socialist President, was to continue as Head of State until 1988. This was the start of the period of what journalists and politicians refer to as 'cohabitation'. It was the first time that such a situation had arisen under the Fifth Republic and it looked like being an explosive one, since relations between the majority and the opposition in France have in the past traditionally been atrocious. Ever since 1789, a series of governments have collapsed or ended abruptly as a result of *coups d'état* or civil wars, having failed to convert the Constitutional text into a political and social pact. As it turned out, however, the prospect of an impending presidential election and the fact that the two main protagonists were both potential candidates made it possible for this constitutional experiment to run its course without too many upsets.

Compared with the way in which institutions operate during periods of agreement between the President and the Assembly, cohabitation considerably reduces the powers of the Head of State.

Once the President has entrusted the premiership to a Prime Minister from the opposite 'camp', he is obliged to leave him a large measure of freedom in the choice of his Ministers. Between 1958 and 1986, the composition of governments was affected more by the choices made by the President than by proposals coming from the Prime Minister. In a period of cohabitation, however, it is the Prime Minister who forms his government (as the Constitution states he should) to a large extent at his own discretion. All the same, it was noticeable that in the Chirac Government of March 1986, the appointments of two Ministers (Foreign Affairs and Defence) resulted from a measure of consensus between the President and the Prime Minister, a fact accounted for by the sweeping powers that the Constitution allots to the President in these two areas. Furthermore, in periods of cohabitation, when the government and the National Assembly stand in opposition to the President, it is difficult for the latter to call for a referendum or to institute a revision of the Constitution; for the Head of State may only take those two decisions when the government or Parliament proposes that he should do so.

Apart from the power to dissolve the Assembly, that of implementing Article 16, and the right to tender his resignation, a President in a period of cohabitation thus loses most of the freedom of manœuvre available to him in a period of consensus, for he is deprived of the support afforded by a government appointed largely by himself and that of a majority in the Assembly. In these circumstances, it is well and truly the government, on the strength of its majority in the

Assembly, that 'determines and directs the policies of the nation' (Article 20 of the Constitution).

The constitutional and political influence of the Head of State is much weaker in the other parliamentary systems. In Britain, the Head of State, who is also Head of the Church of England, is designated according to the rules of primogeniture. In West Germany and Italy, the President of the Republic is elected according to a procedure that confirms both the national and the federal or regional nature of the political system. In West Germany, the electoral college is composed of members of the Bundestag and an equal number of delegates elected on the basis of proportional representation by the various *Landtage*. Each *Land* contributes a number of delegates in proportion to its population, but, unlike the system for the Bundesrat, in which the *Länder* representatives represent the existing *Länder* governments, in a presidential election the delegates are representative of the various political forces (CDU, SPD, etc.). The relative strengths of the parties are thus crucial, even if this is, in principle, tempered by the fact that voting is secret. However, neither in Germany nor in Italy have party disagreements ever upset the expected results: at the most, they may have made it necessary to hold more ballots.

Italy displays the same preoccupations as Germany, although the modalities of selection are somewhat different. A President of Italy is elected by the two Chambers in a common Assembly chaired by the President of the Chamber of Deputies. These Deputies are joined by three delegates from each region (but only one from the Aosta Valley) at least one of whom, usually, does not belong to the regional majority. In all three countries, the modalities of acceding to power condition the extent and nature of the responsibilities and functions involved. These may be summarized under three headings: the symbolic function, the function of providing a constitutional guarantee, and the function of maintaining balance.

1. The symbolic function may seem the least significant, but in reality it probably constitutes one of the most important elements of a Head of State's powers, since it is this that authorizes and legitimizes his or her intervention in domains in which, in principle, the powers are no more than nominal. The Heads of State who possess the widest room for manœuvre are those who have most successfully managed to symbolize the country's identity, being seen as the incarnation of all the public and private virtues of their people. It is that identification

that makes it possible for the British sovereign to symbolize the unity and permanence of the State (the Crown) over and above all political divisions. The Queen is so totally neutral that she speaks as is demanded, as the mouthpiece of either the Labour or the Conservative Party when she delivers the Queen's Speech, which is written by whoever is the current Prime Minister. Her position is far above party and parliamentary antagonisms: Her Majesty's Government has to coexist alongside Her Majesty's Opposition. Her international prestige is what provides the tenuous but nevertheless solid link between the various components of a widely disparate Commonwealth. She is also the Head of the Church of England. All these attributes combine to make the British sovereign the model for all monarchs and even for parliamentary Heads of State. In the republican States of Italy and West Germany, the mission of the President of the Republic is analogous, but is subjected to additional constraints. Given that the parties play such an important role in selecting the Head of State, the political nature of the candidate and the appointment inevitably weaken his position as a symbol of national unity to some extent. Every newly elected President is obliged to try to erase the memory of his erstwhile party allegiances. That requirement is not always an easy one to fulfil, particularly when the elected President's past gives rise to polemics (Lübke in 1967–8, Leone in 1978, and Waldheim, elected President of Austria in 1986). The personality of a Head of State and his general *savoir-faire* are thus essential ingredients in the construction of the presidential image. The first President of West Germany, Theodor Heuss, and the popular Sandro Pertini of Italy are both remarkable examples of Presidents who had the ability to create a powerful presidential image.

2. In parliamentary democracies, Heads of State also stand as guarantors of the country's institutions. This function is to some extent a counterpart to their declining role as effective focuses of power, for, as can be seen from the example of the Fifth French Republic, this function of guardian of the country's institutions is materially guaranteed by the measures that assure the Head of State a longer term of office than other institutions (in particular, Parliament). The Italian President is elected for seven years, the two Chambers for only five; the West German President for five years, the Bundestag for four; and the British monarchy is clearly the very epitome of a continuity symbolically expressed by the cry of 'The King is dead. Long live the King!' Given the weakness of their

powers, it seems fair to wonder whether these Heads of State really do effectively guarantee the continuity of the State. In light of the 1939–40 disaster in France and Lebrun's attitude at the time, de Gaulle's response at the Liberation was negative; and in 1958, René Coty, in his turn, contributed to the move towards a change in the political system rather than defend the Fourth Republic which, it must be admitted, was already moribund.

However, the attitudes of French Presidents from 1939 to 1958 and their individual failures in their fundamental mission could not, on their own, justify the establishment of a President with extensive powers. The German and Italian experiences of the inter-war period would indeed warn against such a move. Neither the considerable powers nor the strong influence of the Heads of State in the Weimar Republic and the Italian monarchy were capable of preventing the corruption of their countries' political systems, nor the rise of Hitler and Mussolini.

3. Heads of State have a third, equally delicate mission: to act as arbiters. In Britain, this function is seldom called upon, although in difficult circumstances the monarch may make his or her influence felt. This happens when a general election results in no absolute majority and, discreetly, sometimes in other circumstances too. In 1945, for example, Attlee acted on the 'advice' of George VI, and chose Bevin as Foreign Secretary rather than Hugh Dalton: and in 1986, the British Press suggested that the Queen, as Head of the Commonwealth, may have tried to persuade Margaret Thatcher to adopt a firmer attitude towards South Africa. This role of maintaining balance, by 'exerting influence', as President Vincent Auriol of France was so often claimed to have done under the Fourth Republic, also depends more upon a Head of State's personality than upon the specific powers allotted to him by the Constitution. For example, the first President of the Italian Republic, Luigi Einaudi, managed to create for the post of President, for which there was no historical precedent, an autonomous political 'space', particularly when it came to appointing members of the Constitutional Court, dissolving Parliament, and even choosing a President of the Council. (Pella, for example, was chosen without any consultation.) Between 1948 and 1955 the parties had a chance to assess the importance of the post of President and that was no doubt what sparked off the ferocious battles to gain control of it. Gronchi tried, unsuccessfully, to make the double post of Head of State and President of the Council approximate more

closely to that of an American-style President, while the election of Segni, President from 1962 to 1964, was the price that the left wing of the Christian Democrats (who favoured a centre-left government) had to pay to the party's conservative wing. For that very reason, and also because he did not approve of the existing coalitions, Segni, in two short years of office, made more use than any of his predecessors of the Head of State's power to refuse to ratify adopted laws when the funds necessary for their application had not been voted.

His successor, Giuseppe Saragat (1964–71) took his role as a guarantor of the centre-left formula so seriously that he steered the formation of all governments in that direction, thereby exceeding the strict terms of his institutional mandate. The subsequent election of Giovanni Leone (1971–8) marked both a return in force of the centre-right and at the same time a more discreet interpretation of the role of President. Leone was obliged to tender his resignation six months before the end of his presidential term (as a result of being compromised in the Lockheed scandal), but while in office he had helped to give the post of President a lower profile that was more in keeping with the model envisaged by the Constitution. The election of Pertini meant a return to presidential activism and independence for the Head of State. Pertini, who was elected by a combination of all the parties included in the constitutional spectrum (that is, the parties that had emerged from the Resistance), revealed himself, like Einaudi, to be extremely independent of the influence of all political parties. Unlike the first President of the Italian Republic, however, he could depend upon widespread popularity. He manipulated public distrust of the political parties to his own advantage in a sometimes demagogic fashion; exploited his past as a member of the Resistance, and his great age; and spoke up against things that no other politicians dared to mention. He took both the government and the political parties to task, admonished both the left and the right, and filled the role of 'father of the country / father of the family' in all the many assassination attempts, catastrophes, and national calamities by which Italy was beset. Politicians were secretly exasperated by this inconvenient figure, whose exceptional popularity allowed him to play the iconoclast, and they were becoming alarmed at the prospect of a second term (which they were powerless to prevent) for an aged and intractable President who would continue to stir things up. But Pertini spared them, and stepped down in favour of Cossiga, a supporter of the policy of reconciliation with the Italian Communist

Party, at a time when the historic compromise was in fashion. The present President, who was elected in 1985, acts far less as an intermediary, with the result that there is now a danger of the parties regaining their lost ground. So much is suggested by the so-called La Staffeta (hand-over) agreement, following which the Christian Democrats and the Socialist Party in 1985 arranged between them to replace the Socialist Premier, Craxi, by a Christian Democrat. In this whole business, the President of the Republic, theoretically responsible for choosing and appointing the President of the Council, looked more as if he was simply there to be informed of a *fait accompli*.

The experiences of West Germany also underline both the limits and the potential of the role of Head of State as a constitutional arbiter. In reaction against the excesses of the Presidents of the Weimar Republic, the formal powers of the Head of State have been largely whittled away, and the political evolution of West Germany has more or less precluded any informal modification of those limitations. Indeed, the trend is rather the reverse: for example, the Head of State is in principle supposed to choose a candidate for the post of Chancellor and to put his name forward to the Bundestag. But in fact he does no more than pass on to the Bundestag the name proposed to him by the majority party or coalition. As would be expected, the same goes for the appointment of Ministers and senior civil servants. When Heinrich Lübke tried to dismiss Gerhard Schröder from the Ministry of Foreign Affairs in 1965, his intervention was condemned almost unanimously as being misjudged and contrary to the Constitution. The President's powers are equally limited when it comes to the dissolution of the Bundestag. In this domain, the powers of the President, conferred upon him by Articles 63.4 and 68 of the Constitution, are in practice subordinated to the decisions reached by the parties and (in the case of Article 68) by the Chancellor. Thus, in 1983, when Chancellor Kohl organized an artificial crisis so that the voters would ratify the new alliance between the CDU–CSU and the FDP, the President expressed his misgivings over what amounted to a distortion of constitutional procedure, but ended up by bowing to the Chancellor's request. It is thus only in a state of crisis that the West German Head of State might be in a position to play a significant role. The Presidents of West Germany have in general performed their functions with dignity. (The one who attracted the most criticism, Lübke, retired several months before his time was up, ostensibly so as to avoid a clash between the presidential and the parliamentary elections, but really because his position during the Second World War was giving rise to more and more controversy). However, their principal role has been to act as the embodiment of the State. From that point of view, and in this limited perspective, the Presidents of West Germany have performed their function correctly. But to discover where the real power lies, we must turn to the complementary element in the system, that is, the government and its leader—known either as the Prime Minister or (in Italy) as the President of the Council.

The Government: The Selection and Appointment of Ministers

The process of selecting and appointing Ministers is more complex in parliamentary systems than in the American presidential system, since one essential stage must first be completed—that of the choosing of the Prime Minister by the Head of State. That expression 'choosing' is, however, ambiguous, for the freedom of choice of a Head of State is limited to varying degrees, depending upon the country's Constitution, the prevailing political circumstances, and so on.

Today, it is exceptional for a Head of State to enjoy total autonomy in the procedure of choosing a Prime Minister, and very few examples of such a situation can be found. Up until the mid-eighteenth century, the British monarchs certainly chose their Prime Ministers to suit themselves, but in 1746 and 1757, George II was forced, whether he liked it or not, to call upon Pitt, the majority leader. In France 120 years later, MacMahon learned to his cost of the limits of a Head of State's powers in a parliamentary system. King Victor Emmanuel III in Italy and Hindenburg in Germany failed to oppose the rise of Fascism and Nazism by refusing to appeal to the respective leaders of those two movements—a fact that was later held against them. Today, no Head of State holds discretionary powers in the choice of a Prime Minister, for the limitations to which he is subject encapsulate the very principle of the parliamentary system: namely, to replace the arbitrary authority of one individual by the popular will as expressed by the parliamentary majority.[3] In this respect, the history of the Fifth French Republic is significant. It has often been said and written that the President could choose whoever he liked. That seems fair comment given both the nature of the political system (not strictly parliamentary) and also the practice of a succession of Heads of State: the Prime Minister chosen was never the leader of the majority, but became it; sometimes he had been elected to Parliament, but even that was not obligatory, as is shown by the appointments of Georges Pompidou in 1962 and Raymond Barre in 1976. However, that freedom of choice was only made possible by the coincidence of the presidential and the parliamentary majorities, and by the fact that the Prime Minister chosen was generally acceptable to that existing majority. Moreover, certain taboos could not be violated. After his defeat at the polls in 1967, Maurice Couve de Murville was not appointed Prime Minister. And by 1978, Valéry Giscard d'Estaing was making it clear that he would call upon François Mitterrand to be Prime Minister in the event of a victory for the left. In 1986, there was no alternative. Despite the 'suspense' engineered by the sybilline pronouncements of the Head of State, no sooner was the victory of the RPR–UDF coalition announced than Mitterrand appointed Jacques Chirac, the leader of the principal political group. The Fifth Republic thus found its way back to the strict canons of classic parliamentarianism. Of course, Mitterrand could have appointed someone else, but only at the risk of the appointment being turned down by the man of his choice or, worse still, by the new majority.

The opposite extreme is the situation of a Head of State who has absolutely no room for manœuvre at all, but is obliged to appoint the Prime Minister chosen, *de facto*, by others. The most remarkable example of such subjection for the Head of State is represented by Britain, where the monarch's 'choice' amounts to no more than the ratification of a double process of pre-selection: first by the party, which chooses its own leader; then by the electorate, which gives victory to one particular party together with its leader. Nevertheless, a Head of State's lack of autonomy is also affected by the coincidence of specific circumstances: the presence of a leader whose position is uncontested, and an electoral victory that is indisputable. If either or both of these factors is missing, the Head of State regains some of the monarchy's old powers of influence. For example, in 1923, when the Prime Minister, Bonar Law was obliged to retire for reasons of health, George V called upon Stanley Baldwin to head the Government, although he had been expected to choose Lord Curzon. In 1931, George V again played a significant role in choosing Ramsay Mac-Donald, the Labour leader, who thus became Prime Minister in a minority government. When he resigned as a result of dissension within the Labour Party, which was divided over the measures to be taken to deal with the economic crisis, the King consulted the

Conservative and Liberal leaders and then decided to call upon Ramsay MacDonald to form a Government of National Unity. This 'class collaboration' caused a crisis in the Labour Party; but in October 1931, the country ratified that option by giving 554 seats to the supporters of the National Government, as against 52 to the hard-line Labour candidates. In general, though, the role of the British monarch is extremely limited and the sovereign can only affect the choice of Prime Minister in quite exceptional circumstances.

The situation of West Germany is, in this respect, very similar to that of the sovereign of the United Kingdom. Each party is headed by a leader who, in the event of his political group winning the election, is naturally destined to become Chancellor. Alfred Grosser underlines this point, recalling to mind how, in 1959, Adenauer, prompted by a desire to thwart the chances of his Deputy Chancellor, Ludwig Erhard, to whom he was antipathetic, briefly stood as candidate for the presidency of the Republic. Adenauer left for his holidays, telling journalists that his bedside reading would consist of the Constitution, in which—as Grosser ironically suggests—he no doubt discovered the bitter truth: namely, that, as President, he would no longer be in a position to impose his own choice for the post of Chancellor. This marginalization of the Head of State's role was prompted by the unfortunate experience of the Weimar Republic. In response to what Von Beyme has called 'the Hindenburg allergy' and to prevent the Chancellor from becoming what Gordon Smith calls the President's 'scapegoat' and avoid a repetition of untimely presidential interventions and dissolutions in the style of the Weimar Republic, the Constitution of the Federal Republic insists that the Chancellor be elected by the Bundestag, leaving to the Head of State a purely formal role in this domain.

Between these two possible extremes, there are some cases in which the Head of State, either as ruled by the Constitution or as a result of a fluid political situation, does enjoy significant powers: in the Fourth French Republic, for instance, and in the Italian Republic today, particularly when the Head of State can rely on the support of public opinion. Vincent Auriol and Sandro Pertini both, in the absence of a political majority, used their own personal popularity to influence the choice of Premier. They did so either by organizing consultations very much under their own aegis or by proceeding to 'nominate' a potential Prime Minister who would only be appointed if he managed to form a government. Practices such as these sometimes made it possible to make use of certain potential but controversial candidates before eventually settling upon the one whom the Head of State secretly favoured all along. The situation in the Fourth Republic nevertheless differed from that which obtained in Italy at least up to the election of Sandro Pertini in 1978. In contrast to the situation in almost all the other parliamentary democracies, in France the President of the Fourth Republic was never bound by any rule stipulating that, in the absence of an absolute majority, the Prime Minister (called, at the time, the President of the Council) must be chosen from amongst the members of the largest party, the party holding a relative majority. The picture established by Jean-Claude Colliard in his study of contemporary parliamentary democracies shows quite clearly how unusual the French situation was: not one of the twenty-one Presidents of the Council came from the largest political party, namely, the Communist Party, considered to be 'beyond the pale'. Colliard comments as follows:

In other countries, as a rule, the higher the position of a party (on a classificatory scale ranging from 1 to 8, and based on the relative size of the various parties), the more chance it has of forming a government. In the case of the Fourth Republic, the reverse appears to have been true and the most propitious position for becoming President of the Council seems to have been membership of a small party ranking fourth or fifth on the scale.[4]

In Italy, on the other hand, the Head of State has been allowed less room for manœuvre, despite the appearance, there too, of the procedure of 'nomination' (*presidente incaricato*). Until Sandro Pertini's election, the convention—always hitherto respected—was that the Premier should be selected from the party which held a relative majority, in other words from the Christian Democrat group. And, even within this framework, the President's hands were tied except when the Christian Democrats had failed to put forward any specific suggestions. It became possible to flout the convention only when the development of a more fluid political situation (as a result of the decline of the Christian Democrats) coincided with the advent of a President of Pertini's charisma. Having called in vain upon first the Republican La Malfa, then the Socialist Craxi to form a government, the Head of State turned to Giorgio Spadolini, who thus managed to become the Italian Republic's first Prime Minister from one of the secular parties (although Parri had also qualified for that description during the transition period of the Liberation). After the 1983 elections, the President appealed to Craxi, the leader of the small Socialist Party (with 12 per cent of the vote), who eventually broke the record for longevity for a government leader: not until April 1987 was he obliged to tender his resignation. It may seem surprising that the Christian Democrats of the 1980s should have tolerated the flouting of a constitutional convention so favourable to them. Two explanations may be adduced for this, apart from the strength of Pertini's personality. In the first place, the Christian Democrats saw this retirement from the centre of the stage as a possible period of sorely needed rejuvenation. Secondly, the Italian Communist Party, pressing hard upon the heels of the Christian Democrats, was gaining strength, even emerging from the European elections of 1984 as the leading party. If that situation were confirmed and the constitutional convention maintained, it would be necessary to select a Prime Minister from the ranks of the Communist Party. Rather than draw attention to the *conventio ad excludendum*, the Christian Democrats accepted what they hoped would be no more than a temporary setback, until the return of better days. In 1985–6, the Christian Democrat Secretary General, De Mita, was already pointing out the advantages of 'rotation'. And the La Stafetta agreement of July 1986 did indeed envisage the post of President of the Council passing to a Christian Democrat. However, that was reckoning without Craxi's Machiavellian manœuvrings and his proposal to hold referendums in future. This split the majority so deeply that the next parliamentary elections had to be brought forward to June 1987.

In the parliamentary democracies that we have considered, it would thus appear that the Head of State's role in selecting a Prime Minister has become marginal. Only France stands out as an exception. But if the coexistence of a President with an Assembly whose opinions diverge from his becomes a more frequent phenomenon, the Fifth Republic will fall more closely into line with neighbouring democracies. And in that case, as in Britain, West Germany, and Italy, the choice of Ministers would similarly become a prerogative of the Prime Minister rather than of the President of the Republic.

When it comes to the appointment of Ministers, whoever the formal authority belongs to (the Head of State, for instance), essentially the power belongs to the Prime Minister. The only real exception is constituted, once again, by the Fifth French Republic, by reason of its bicephalous executive system. However, as a result of the experience of cohabitation between 1986 and 1988, the situation in France has fallen more closely into line with those of its neighbours.

In the American presidential system, Ministers are always chosen from outside Congress, and are the 'President's men'. In France, where the system is a hybrid one, a considerable proportion of government Ministers, including two Prime Ministers (Pompidou and Barre), have been selected from outside Parliament. It has even happened that Ministers who, after appointment, have tried their luck at the polls (Messmer and Couve de Murville in 1967) have been retained in their ministerial posts despite having suffered humiliating electoral defeats. However, tradition demands that most 'experts' recruited in this way should, sooner or later, enter the political arena to receive confirmation in their posts from universal suffrage. There is nothing of this kind in purely parliamentary systems, for here it is an unwritten rule that a Prime Minister should choose his Ministers from the ranks of Members of Parliament. Here and there, one could cite cases where appointments have gone to individuals outside Parliament, but they are certainly exceptional. There have been scarcely a dozen instances in Italy since the war, while in West Germany experts are easily turned into members of the Bundestag because of the system of electoral lists and proportional representation. In Britain, a few individuals from outside Parliament have from time to time been appointed as Ministers, but they have had to stand for Parliament (and be elected) at the next by-elections held in the country.[5] The convention is an implicit but natural consequence of ministerial responsibility, both individual and collective. How could Parliament possibly exercise political control over Ministers who had no connections with it? The rule becomes even more stringent and specific in countries where the government is responsible to both Chambers, as in Italy. The President of the Council is bound to allocate a few portfolios to Senators. Similarly, in Britain, despite the minor role played by the House of Lords, there is still a rule that a Minister may only address the House of which he is a member. In practice, this means that the British government is bound to include a few Lords so as to be in a position to present and defend its policies before the Upper House. For example, in July 1978, the Callaghan Government was composed of 113 individuals, only 97 of whom were members of the House of Commons, and in February 1984, the Thatcher Government numbered 101 individuals, only 79 of whom were members of the Commons.

But the essential constraint in any parliamentary system can be summed up in one word: balance. Whether the parliamentary majority is composed of a single party or emanates from a coalition, the Prime Minister must take account of internal equilibrium, factions, and rivalries, and, contrary to what a rapid and simplistic assessment might suggest, the correct balance is not necessarily easier to achieve in a single party than in a coalition. Jean-Claude Colliard, who has made a systematic study of this question in connection with the practices of Western parliamentary democracies, emphasizes that although 'the key to allocation is, in principle, a simple arithmetical rule', in practice the situation is far more complex. He distinguishes five different patterns for the allocation of ministerial posts where coalitions are involved: proportionality, over-representation for the larger parties, over-representation for the smaller parties, over-representation for the Prime Minister's own party, and parity for all the parties concerned. In actual fact, the first and the last options are seldom used, for rigid arithmetic is hardly compatible with the subtleties of politics. Thus Colliard cites only one case of proportionality in France under the Fourth and Fifth Republics (the third Pompidou Government, composed of 22 UNR and 3 RI), and only one instance of parity (the Barre Government). In Britain and West Germany, no such situation of strict proportionality or egalitarian balance in a single coalition has ever arisen.

In Italy, on the other hand, the allocation of posts (both at party and at State level) corresponds to a relatively strict arithmetical calculation.[6] In this connection, Portelli writes

the famous Cencelli handbook on the allocation of posts—both generally and specifically within the party—institutionalizes this practice. The various posts are distributed proportionally on the basis of the results of each faction at the last national party congress: the posts of President of the Republic and President of the Council, Ministers and Under-Secretaries of State, the Presidents of the two Chambers, and posts of responsibility within the party. When the first Craxi Government was set up, the rule was applied to the letter, producing a spectacle in which one of the minority factions of the Christian Democrats blocked the formation of the Government until such time as it got its own way. When it is also remembered that the Cencelli handbook—itself a Christian Democrat creation—is now generally applied to all the factions and sub-factions of all the parties that go to make up the majority, it becomes clear just how unfair the apportionment of power has become.[7]

The other patterns noted by Jean-Claude Colliard all constitute situations of imbalance that favour either one dominant party or, alternatively, the party or parties whose support is necessary if a majority is to be obtained. In situations such as these, the political balances achieved bear little relation to strict arithmetical calculations. The number of ministerial posts allocated to particular groups reflects the degree of pressure and influence that they can respectively bring to bear, as does the *quality* of those posts (the titles and importance of the various portfolios and the opportunities they afford for patronage). There is one particular pattern that often applies to coalitions in which one or several small parties are absolutely indispensable if a parliamentary majority is to be obtained. This was the case, quite spectacularly, of the second Adenauer Government (1958), in which the CDU–CSU held only 11 of the 19 portfolios (despite having won over 45 per cent of the votes), while the FDP with 9.5 per cent obtained 4 posts, the BHE 2 posts for its 3.9 per cent of the vote, and the DP also 2 posts for its 5.9 per cent of the vote. However, the distribution of posts does not necessarily convey a true picture of the balance of power, as is shown by the Christian Democrat/FDP coalition of 1961: the FDP certainly obtained a slightly higher proportion of posts than their electoral score allowed them to hope for, but above all they managed to impose two draconian conditions: first, that Adenauer should retire before the end of the legislature; and secondly, that a 'coalition committee' should discuss government proposals before the Cabinet adopted them, to prevent FDP Ministers from being manipulated or overwhelmed by the Chancellor's blandishments.

Similarly, in Italy the smaller parties have managed to capitalize on their strength as necessary partners: the second Moro Government, for example, distributed most posts between the PSI, the PSDI, and the tiny Republican Party, so that it would be possible to continue the centre-left experiment started six months earlier, in December 1963. The same phenomenon was frequently to recur and was a feature of the second Craxi Government, formed in August 1986. In this, the tiny Liberal Party obtained 2 portfolios, the PRI and the PSDI 3 each, and the PSI 6, as against the 16 that went to the Christian Democrats. In other words, dominant parties have to pay for the collaboration of minority parties, and the latter sometimes subject them to a veritable process of blackmail. This has seldom happened under the Fifth French Republic, as the secondary partners of the majority have possessed no more than limited means of exerting pressure upon the coalition as a whole since this has been clearly dominated by the principal party, that of the President. On the other hand, when the President came from one of the smaller parties, as did Valéry Giscard d'Estaing from 1974 to 1981, the 'dominant' party found itself in a weaker position and was less heavily represented in government in both the Chirac and the Barre Cabinets. However, in some situations, the pressure from the smaller parties is not at all unwelcome to the leader of the dominant party, especially if the latter is of a hetero-geneous or even composite nature, as in the case of the CDU–CSU. Brandt and Schmidt were quite glad of the pressure exerted by the FDP as this tended to keep their left wings in check. Similarly, Chancellor Kohl must certainly have been relieved that the absence of a homogeneous majority spared him a resounding individual clash with Franz-Josef Strauss, the 'Bull of Bavaria'.

All the variants described so far underline the advantages that pivot parties are adept at deriving from the necessity of coalitions, for they are in a position either to use their power of veto (since without them no government can possibly be formed) or their destructive powers (since if they resign they bring down the government). However, in certain circumstances small parties that take part in government nevertheless derive scant advantage from this. A relatively exceptional situation of this kind arises when the small parties concerned are in no position to exert pressure on the dominant party. One case in point, in France, was that of the Independent Republicans from 1962 to 1968. Had they engineered a crisis, it would have resulted in the Assembly being dissolved and elections, in which they, as a party, would probably have foundered. Small parties are even more clearly in-capable of exerting pressure on a dominant party when the latter, no doubt partly due to the voting system, itself controls an absolute majority. Then, the reason for its forming a coalition has nothing to do with the needs of parliamentary arithmetic; rather, it is because it is seeking a majority consensus in the country as a whole. Neither the Gaullists in 1968[8] nor the Socialists in 1981[9] were obliged to share power with, respectively, their Giscardian and Communist allies. But de Gaulle and Pompidou, and, similarly, Mitterrand, were well aware of all the difficulties that would face a majority party that attempted to govern on its own without having received an overall majority of votes. In circumstances such as these, it is the minority party that finds itself in a delicate position: virtually the only choice open to it is between knuckling under or resigning, as the Communists discovered between 1981 and 1984.

Nevertheless, the above remarks, based on quantitative data, need correcting from a qualitative point of view. In the first place, distributing appointments of Ministers and Secretaries of State is but *one* of the means by which a head of government can satisfy factions and parties. On a qualitative level he can also play upon the degrees to which a purely honorific or, alternatively, an essential value is attached to those appointments. Hence the creation of the posts of Deputy Prime Minister (not always provided for by the country's Constitution) and of new Ministers of State with or without portfolio, and the proliferation of Secretaries of State and Parliamentary Secretaries, all of which are a means of distributing many small satisfactions at no great cost. Furthermore, a subtle and detailed examination would be needed to gauge the real impact of the smaller parties, or at least of their leaders. Should the influence of the Independent Republicans (supporters of Giscard), in France, be measured by their number or by the position of their leader at the Ministry of Finance? Should we concentrate upon the size of the German FDP Party, or its influence upon economic policies, or the decisive parts played by Scheel and Genscher in the domain of foreign policy, in particular *Ostpolitik?* From the opposite point of view, the diminishing number of Italian Christian Democrat Ministers under the Socialist leadership between 1983 and 1986 was perhaps not as significant as the figures and the loss of the Presidency of the Council might have suggested. After all, the Christian Democrats had retained not only the Vice-Presidency, the Ministry of Foreign Affairs, the Home Office, the Ministry of Justice, and the Treasury, but also the Ministries most involved in clientship, in particular those concerned with large numbers of jobs, or whose social and economic impact was particularly important: Education, the Postal Service, Health, the Civil Service, State-Run Industries, Southern Italy, etc.

Secondly, we have so far only considered the constraints affecting the choice of individuals to fill certain posts, not those that affect policy-making. But we should not forget that this aspect is often crucial and that parties upon which the majority is dependent may well be influential even if they do not formally belong to the government. For example, the devolution policy for Scotland and Wales was proposed by Callaghan's Government in order to retain the support of the nationalist parties. Similarly, from July 1976 to August 1979, the minority but homogeneous Christian Democrat Government in Italy was supported by every party in the constitutional spectrum, most importantly the Communist Party, whose influence upon the country's major economic and social reforms during this period was crucial.

Governmental Cohesion

The problem that confronts all governments, whether presidential or parliamentary, is how to reconcile each Minister's autonomy in discharging his departmental responsibilities with the unity necessary for all government action.

In parliamentary systems, Prime Ministers hold two essential trump cards that the American executive lacks: the constraints that stem from ministerial responsibility and the existence of firmer and more disciplined party structures. The archetype of this kind of executive leadership is constituted by the British Prime Minister. The parliamentary system invented by Britain requires, in the name of the government's collective responsibility before Parliament, that the Cabinet should present a united front so as to maintain the cohesion of its majority. This institutional constraint has certainly undergone considerable modification over the years, but it was extremely useful at a time when the Prime Minister was still considered simply as 'the first among equals' in the government.

In Britain, the principle of collective responsibility no longer welds the executive together as it did in the past (although the notion of the individual and collective responsibility of Ministers remains far stronger than on the Continent). The task of maintaining cohesion now falls to the Prime Minister, who truly has become the keystone of the Cabinet. In the post-war period, the role of the Prime Minister has assumed such importance in the institutions of Britain that it has sparked off considerable controversy over the apparent transformation of Cabinet government into 'presidential government'. All Prime Ministers since 1945 have made full use of their freedom, in effect, to hire and fire their colleagues. In July 1962, Macmillan carried out a veritable purge in order to resume a firm hold over his Government, sacking seven Ministers, including the Chancellor of the Exchequer and the Ministers of Defence and Education. Yet despite being his first victims, the Ministers affected were the first to recognize the Prime Minister's 'life or death' powers.[10] With Margaret Thatcher's accession to power, any doubts remaining on the role of the Prime Minister as leader of the government were soon dispelled. The 'Iron Lady' has not only exploited to the full the prerogatives granted her by the Constitution and by convention; she has imbued the role of Prime Minister with her own personal decisive and authoritarian style, engineering successive reshuffles in such a way as to promote those loyal to her (the 'dries') and ease out the Ministers classed as 'wets', who do not invariably share her views. According to Michael Lee,

> Mrs Thatcher seems to have extended the authority of the Prime Minister beyond the limits respected by her predecessors. . . . She does not simply take the initiative in Cabinet discussions, but also tends to 'short-circuit' it by organizing external pressures when she comes up against internal resistance. Furthermore, the Ministers responsible for economic and industrial questions feel obliged to consult her on a regular basis.[11]

In July 1989, she reshuffled her Cabinet, replacing twelve out of twenty-one Ministers after the Conservative losses in the June European elections.

The role of the British Prime Minister is the product of a long political and constitutional evolution whose peculiar nature becomes easier to understand when it is compared to those of its German and Italian counterparts. These two countries have adopted the framework and canons of the parliamentary system but, in the absence of all the ingredients used in the British recipe, they have introduced a number of differences inspired by their own particular histories or designed to allow them to evolve in new directions. Both Germany and Italy constructed their political systems in the aftermath of the war, upon the ruins of their dictatorships. Yet the institutional consequences that they have drawn from their past experiences differ substantially. In Italy, a decree issued as early as 1944 introduced the expression 'President of the Council of Ministers' as a replacement for the title 'Head of Government', which had been established by a law passed in 1925. The semantic change reflected not only a rejection of an authoritarian style of government leadership but also a desire to prevent a recurrence of such mistakes by introducing *ad hoc* institutional mechanisms designed for that purpose. The President of the

Council, deprived of power and means and unable really to choose and fire his Ministers, was supposed to be no more than the first of the Ministers, and on the face of it that reform appears to have proved successful, to judge—that is—by the titles of two books by specialist observers of the Italian political scene, the British Percy Allum's[12] *Italy, Republic without Government* and the Italian American Giuseppe Di Palma's[13] *Surviving without Governing*. Italy and France (in 1945) both learned the same lesson from their experiences of authoritarian and non-democratic governments: weaken the executive and make Parliament the central point of the Constitution and political life in general.

The reactions of post-war West Germany were different. While the country sought to guard by every means against any resurgence of Nazism, it was aware that it was the deficiencies of the Weimar Republic that had in part been constitutionally responsible for the birth of the Nazi regime. In the light of past experience, it was clear that until Hitler arrived upon the scene, the Chancellor had been made (to borrow Gordon Smith's expression)[14] the 'scapegoat' of the Reichstag and the President of the Reich. To prevent such an erosion of the Chancellor's role, the Federal Constitution switched to the Chancellor powers that were essentially transferred from the former domain of the President. It also conferred pre-eminence upon the position of Chancellor by stipulating that the Bundestag itself should elect him, thereby reinforcing his position as leader of the executive. As in Britain, the mechanisms of ministerial responsibility have been largely deflected from their original purpose. Nevertheless, in Germany too the executive as a whole is subject to similar parliamentary constraints that operate to the advantage of the Chancellor. For even if the Bundestag, *as an institution*, does not have much say in the choosing of a Chancellor, the majority party or the parties in the coalition must come to an agreement on a candidate, and if they should eventually come to disapprove of the one whom they elect, the mechanisms of 'constructive no confidence' still constitute a serious limitation to any rebellious inclinations they might have. Consequently, once elected, the Chancellor finds himself in a strong position and, furthermore, a seldom-flouted convention requires that he be appointed for the duration of the legislature. With the exceptions of Adenauer's retirement in 1963 and the resignations of Brandt and Schmidt, it is certainly by now traditional that the government is headed by the same leader throughout the duration of each legislature. Between 1949 and 1990, West Germany has known no more than six Chancellors: Adenauer, Erhard, Kiesinger, Brandt, Schmidt, and Kohl.

This institutional characteristic of West Germany was further reinforced by the strong influence that Adenauer had in the shaping of the style and role of the Chancellor, an influence that, particularly until the late 1950s, rested upon his extraordinary popularity. As Grosser notes, 'The real political impact of the Head of Government has varied considerably, depending upon individual personalities and circumstances.'[15] Nevertheless, the lack of leadership provided by his successor, Erhard, did not result in any loss of prestige for the post of Chancellor; indeed, for a long time ironic remarks about the *Kanzlerdemokratie*, the 'Chancellor's democracy', continued unabated. All the same, as Gordon Smith points out, the circumstances that had permitted the exceptional political longevity of the first Chancellor, Konrad Adenauer, soon disappeared. In Smith's opinion, Adenauer's pre-eminence had been promoted by three elements: the role that he had played in constructing the CDU, the particular nature of the electorate, most of whom owed their first acquaintance with democracy to the Christian Democrat leader, and the international status of West Germany, whose evolution had been largely determined by the actions of Adenauer. With these elements gone, the Chancellor's role as leader of the Government became more subject to institutional and party factors and less a matter of personal charisma.

A head of government's power to lead his team is still determined by what are, in effect, political factors connected with the party system and the role played by the parties in the interaction of institutions. If we compare the three 'pure' parliamentary systems of Britain, West Germany, and Italy, it becomes immediately clear that, although these three systems in principle belong to the same 'family', the political conditions in which they operate are substantially different. In the period since the war, Britain has never had a single coalition government (though the Callaghan Government from 1976 to 1979 was a minority government dependent upon the parliamentary support of the Liberals or the Scottish and Welsh Nationalists or both). In contrast, *every* German government has been a coalition, even when it was not arithmetically necessary that it should be. In Italy, despite the continuing Christian Democrat dominance ever since the war, single-party governments have been the exception rather than the rule, and most governments have included small right- or left-wing groups to support the dominant party. It is accordingly impossible to gauge a Prime Minister's freedom of movement in leading his government without taking into account his relations with his own party and with the other groups included in the coalition.

British Prime Ministers owe their dominant position to the party that chose them as leader, and as such they are automatically considered as the person to head the government if the party wins the election. Moreover, while in opposition, a party leader acts as the head of a 'shadow cabinet', and this by anticipation places him in the position of head of a future government team. However, the ways of choosing a party leader and hence also a possible future Prime Minister vary from one party to another, and to a certain extent determine his room for manœuvre in government. In the Conservative Party it is the Members of Parliament who are chiefly instrumental in choosing their leader, whereas in the Labour Party the trade unions are extremely powerful and may make it possible to choose a leader who is more radical than the Labour members of the House of Commons themselves are. More importantly still, whereas a Conservative leader can freely choose the members of his shadow cabinet, a Labour leader must collaborate with whichever Members of Parliament the parliamentary group selects. Even if they never come to hold a post in government equivalent to the one that they had in the shadow cabinet, the situation creates expectations and lays extra constraints upon the Labour leader, obliged as he is to surround himself with colleagues whose views may be at odds with his own. Divisions in the ruling Labour Party (and hence in the Labour Cabinet) reached a climax in 1974–5, when the party and the Government, unable to reach agreement over whether to remain in the Common Market or to withdraw from it, tried to get round the difficulty by organizing a referendum. Onlookers were presented with the ridiculous and unusual spectacle of a Government in which some Ministers were campaigning for a 'yes', others for a 'no'. To Harold Wilson, who was Prime Minister, the easiest way to cope with the situation seemed to be to assign the principle of collective solidarity and responsibility to the 'back burner' for the time being, thereby forgoing the possibility of providing the firm lead and drive sorely needed by a Government already weakened by internal rifts. Such problems certainly appear to be more acute for the Labour Party, with its strongly defined ideology and its organized factions; but the Conservatives are not spared them either. Margaret Thatcher's Cabinet was deeply split over the Westland issue and, in the past, the leaderships of both Alec Douglas Home and Edward Heath were strongly challenged.

The role of a Prime Minister who heads a coalition would seem to be even more problematic. However, it is hard to generalize since his or her ability to lead the government successfully is bound to depend upon the nature of the coalition. In the 1950s, Adenauer governed with the support of small right-wing parties (in particular, the Refugee Party), which were virtually extensions of the dominant party and could always be counted upon to support the Chancellor. In 1961, the situation was quite different: only three parties now remained in the Bundestag and the FDP was in a position to lay down, as a condition for their participating in a coalition Government, that Adenauer should retire half-way through his term of office. Kiesinger, Chancellor of the grand coalition of 1966–9, was more concerned to mediate than to lead from the front, particularly since some of his Ministers (Schiller and Strauss, for example) disagreed over policy and were on execrable personal terms. Similarly, the last two years of Helmut Schmidt's Government were marked by arguments between the Social Democrats and the FDP that increased in intensity until the latter changed allies in 1982.

Furthermore, the Chancellor frequently has to cope with divisions among his own troops over particular aspects of his policies. Adenauer was forced by his majority to accept an 'Atlantic' clause, as a condition of their ratification of the Franco-German treaty. When Brandt was elected Chancellor for the second time after his party's triumphal success in the 1972 elections, he failed to make the most of this chance. His hesitations allowed a certain vacillation to creep into the party and deprived the Government of an assured leadership (a situation for which he tried to compensate by increasing the politicization of the higher echelons of the Civil Service, in the hope of ensuring efficient execution of government decisions). Helmut Schmidt, for his part, appeared to be a victim of the FDP defection in 1982; but his fall was also brought about by deep rifts within the SPD, divisions that the head of the Government had been powerless to overcome since they were, by their very nature, irreconcilable (ecologists against trade unions, pacifists against militarists, and so on).

In other words, however strong the position of a German Chancellor, it depends upon his own personality, the nature of the coalition, and the prevailing political circumstances. And, except during the period of Adenauer's chancellorship, the Chancellor's power has never smacked of the authoritarianism that the Presidents of the Fifth French Republic have led the French to expect (and perhaps to relish). A German Chancellor has to enter into discussions, negotiate, and accept such compromises as the institutions and the parliamentary majority impose upon him. For the Chancellor's leadership is always modified and held in check by the rule of *Ressortprinzip*, according to which each Minister is solely responsible for his own department.

The 'Italian miracle'—to use the expression fashionable in the 1960s (albeit at the time applied to the economy)—is a quite different matter. As we have seen, initially the President of the Council in principle had only a minor role to play. His Ministers were generally imposed upon him by the parties, his authority over them was virtually non-existent, his powers for co-ordinating the government team were minimal, and his means of operation laughable—on paper at least. However, the paradox is that the Italian President of the Council, like the Third Estate of 1789, from being 'nothing' has definitely become 'something'. Although he enjoys very few of the powers and means at the disposal of his foreign counterparts, he has progressively strengthened his position 'not by reason of his own functions', as Cassese points out, 'but because he is situated in a position where he is able to influence and reconcile all the different fragmentary subsystems'.[16] Cassese goes on to describe him as 'the catalyst for all the other elements that need to be united'.[17] In a system as fragmented as the Italian one, the President of the Council becomes the key piece in the political game and also the point from which the interplay of the many administrative and para-administrative agents may be co-ordinated. In a sense, his role rises above the chaos engendered by the theoretical autonomy of each of the many centres of decision-making, the constant conflicts between various political or bureaucratic lobbies, and the external need for a central reference point. It is true that the powers of an Italian President of the Council are a far cry from those possessed by Prime Ministers in other parliamentary systems. However, quite apart from the fact that his role has grown considerably more important since the war—without any institutional changes being made—it is necessary to gauge the 'performance' of a President of the Council on the basis of the characteristics of Italian political life and the processes by which political decisions are made. Italian politics are a long way from the politics of authoritarianism, *decisionismo*, and radicalism. They proceed via endless debate, compromise, consensus, and piecemeal reforms. Transformism, that is, the ability of political groups to absorb ideas and even people from other, hostile groups, is part of the tradition of united Italy: the country was developing the art of 'incrementalism' long before British and American scholars popularized the expression. In short, only the vices and virtues of Italian political life can provide a yardstick by which to gauge the evolution of the role of the President of the Council. The Craxi phenomenon provides a good illustration of the changes that have taken place over the past forty years. Despite the fact that, during the 1970s, Craxi's Socialist Party represented no more than 13 per cent of the electorate, its leader has managed to turn the post of President of the Council into the central pivot of the whole system. It is symptomatic that Craxi (who has beaten the records for political longevity, since his Ministry has been the third longest in the entire history of united Italy) strengthened his personal position as a political leader through the role that he played as President of the Council, and thereby helped his party to strengthen its position to over 14 per cent in the elections of June 1987.

Even in the context of the heterogeneity and diversity of the experiences of the Western democracies as a whole, the French situation stands out as one of the most unusual, since here the government leadership has, practically speaking, been shared between the President of the Republic and the Prime Minister. The situation, which is in principle a cumbersome one, was to some extent created by the Constitution, but was subsequently shaped and reinforced by practices that de Gaulle introduced and that his successors have maintained. For the most part, potential conflicts have been stifled by the supremacy of the Head of State (considered to be the country's guide or captain), whose strength has rested on his strong claim to legitimacy and his two majorities, the one parliamentary, the other presidential. Conscious of the conditions necessary to preserve partnership and harmony in the government leadership, politicians and the public alike continued for a long time to view the prospect of an antagonistic diarchy with alarm, the effect of which was no doubt to defer any change in the situation. However, following the Socialists' defeat in the elections of 1986, a new balance was struck. The President's role shifted. From being the quasi-monarch that practice over recent years had made him, he became more of an arbiter, as prescribed in Article 5 of the Constitution. His powers were reduced to the veto (over ordinances), the purveying of advice (the guide became an oracle), and arbitration (the power to dissolve Parliament). His role in government leadership was now limited to the fields of defence and foreign policy; and it should be remembered that, even in the realms of 'high politics', nowadays more and more of the agreements concluded are of a technical or sectorial nature. A President can certainly give a lead on general lines of orientation, but much of contemporary international relations is largely a matter of agreements on transport, taxation, the immigrant work-force, and so on, and these are the province of the Ministries with technical expertise rather than the presidency. In all other respects, government leadership passed, in accordance with Article 20 of the Constitution, into the hands of the Prime Minister. It was he who decided and implemented the policies of his government. This situation, which turned out to be less awkward than most observers predicted, probably gained acceptance from the various protagonists only because it was regarded as provisional, the prelude to a return to the 'natural' order of things, that is to say pre-eminence for the presidency where leadership of the executive is concerned. Most French politicians would probably describe cohabitation in much the same terms as those that Paul Reynaud applied to de Gaulle at the beginning of the Fifth Republic: 'a tricky moment to be got through'.

Determining Policies

As we have noted above, a head of government's powers as leader of his team are particularly crucial when it comes to determining choices, co-ordinating policies, and supervising the way in which decisions are implemented. In other words, a government may be considered either as a team or, alternatively, as a collection of individual Ministers each essentially responsible for his own department.

The most formalized system in this respect is that of West Germany, whose constitution makes arrangements—somewhat conflicting, in some cases—relating to the collegial or autonomous position of Ministers. Article 65 of the Constitution allots to the Chancellor what Article 20 of the French Constitution, under the Fifth Republic, attributes to the government ('the government determines and directs the nation's policies'). According to this provision, the Chancellor has the right to decide upon 'the general political line'

(*Richtlinienkompetenz*). Of course, this theoretical duty varies according to the nature of the coalition, the personality of the Chancellor, and the influence of certain of his Ministers. Adenauer certainly played a determining role in tying Germany to the West, just as Brandt was responsible for opening up relations with the East. But Erhard's influence was probably greater when he was simply the Minister credited with creating the German miracle than when he became an increasingly controversial Chancellor. Similarly, the SPD–FDP coalitions frequently produced scenes of stormy disagreement over economic and foreign policies. On the whole, observers of German politics agree that Chancellors from 1949 truly were in a position to direct the policies of their country, but they point out that the power of the German Chancellor is now on the wane and the steering of the governmental vessel is an increasingly difficult task.[18] The fact is that the Constitution also states that Ministers should manage their own portfolios autonomously, which seems somewhat at odds with the other provisions of Article 65. We shall examine later how, and by what means, potential clashes have been avoided.

In Italy, in contrast, the President of the Council is in no way empowered to direct the policies of his Ministers. According to the Italian Constitution the 'king' is stripped bare, so the President of the Council can only influence the activities of his Government by *political* means: that is, by referring it to the programme negotiated with the other parties in the coalition, by making full use of any collateral support forthcoming from Parliament or the media, by playing off the disagreements between one Minister and another, by employing the powerful brake constituted by the Treasury, and finally, in the most difficult cases, by using his veto[19] to block certain moves on the part of his Ministers. Over the past decade, the gravity of the problems facing Italy has afforded the President of the Council the chance to strengthen his influence over policies, particularly through financial control of public bodies and semi-public ones and through the crucial role that he has played in the area of security and public order (particularly since 1977). However, the increasing importance of the role of the President of the Council is limited by the decisional powers of the Italian politico-administrative system.[20] There can be no doubt, for example, that many of the reforms introduced during the 1970s constituted no more than implementations of the measures dictated by the Constitution that had been 'frozen' ever since its adoption, while the sweeping projects announced when the Ministries were set up were in reality more a matter for debate than for practical implementation.

In this respect, the situation in Britain is the opposite of that in Italy. In Italy, the parties lay before the voters programmes that, without a single-party majority, they are likely to find it hard to implement; the voter has no way of knowing what kind of post-election alliances will be formed or what their composition will be. By contrast, British voters are presented with programmes, frequently clearly defined, which the victorious party, by virtue of its theoretical 'mandate', considers itself committed to implementing. Some observers have regarded this commitment to the party programme to be the source of many of Britain's difficulties: they have pointed out how ridiculous these radical swings sometimes appear, particularly in the economic sphere. The Prime Minister is thus invested with a precise mission which he or she can invoke in the event of his or her Ministers proving recalcitrant. In return, when it is the Premier who drags his feet in the implementation of party policy, the party has a right to remind the executive of its electoral promises. Such situations are quite common in the Labour Party, in which, up until the 1980s, the unions exercised a dominant influence. Tension between the demands of grass-roots activists and the constraints to which a government party is inevitably subjected has clearly been growing, and the party's decline is in part a consequence of its failure to attract votes from the centre. It is a typical instance of the dilemma that faces all left-wing parties faithful to the ideals of reforming society and standing by their commitments. Another example was the French Socialist Government's 1984 schools reform. An initially prudent bill was radicalized by a series of strongly secularist amendments which the Prime Minister, Pierre Mauroy, had found it impossible to refuse. This revived the spectre of the historic schools conflict, dominant in French politics since 1959, and led to the massive right-wing demonstrations of June 1984. The pragmatism displayed by Mauroy's successor, Laurent Fabius, indicated a switch to a 'party-government' attitude: that is to say, to more flexible practice that allowed the Prime Minister to steer his government's policies bearing in mind present or future needs in so far as these could be assessed, always in the light of changing circumstances.

In France, the direction of government activity under the Fifth Republic has, as we have seen, been decided for the most part by the Head of State. This had always been the case in areas considered to be of essential importance (decolonization, defence, foreign policy, and European affairs), and even in more technical or less crucial sectors in which presidential arbitration was deemed necessary. From 1958 to 1986 and since 1988, given the coincidence of the presidential and the parliamentary majorities, the Head of State's interventions into government affairs were subject to no check apart from his own discretion. Between 1986 and 1988, in contrast, the government was in a position to make full use of its powers without subjection to the President, except in the areas of defence and foreign affairs. Since June 1988, Mitterrand has adopted a less interventionist line, relinquishing to the Prime Minister responsibility for most policies (and also for their possible unpopularity). The division of tasks thus depends essentially upon contingent conventions rather than constitutional rules. It varies according to the protagonists involved, the circumstances, and, in the last analysis in most cases, the President's own decision on whether or not to intervene in government action.

For a long time, the Prime Ministers of parliamentary systems were more or less without means of either an administrative or a financial nature, or in terms of personnel. To have at his disposal at least a minimal infrastructure, it was traditional for the Prime Minister or President of the Council to combine his functions with those of another Minister, usually that of Finance or Foreign or Home Affairs. In France, it was not until the emergence of the Popular Front in 1936 and the premiership of Leon Blum that the leader of the government began to acquire the trappings of a support system. Similarly in Italy, up until the 1950s, the office of President of the Council was provided with neither staff nor means, not even with an official headquarters. The Presidency of the Council constituted as it were an extension of the Home Office (usually the responsibility of the President of the Council himself), which provided him with the necessary material means of operation. The virtual absence of logistical means at the disposal of the President of the Council corresponds to his theoretically slender responsibilities. But once again, appearances are deceptive. In principle, the presidency of the Council commands no budget or staff of its own. It may call upon the services of up to 340 staff seconded from other Ministries or offices (a significant force) and can make use of Treasury funds for its own expenses. In practice, though, the scene looks rather different: quite apart from this personal staff, usually headed by a Councillor of State, the President of the Council can count upon the services of an Under-Secretary (either a senior civil servant or a Member of Parliament), who has his full confidence and acts as his closest collaborator and spokesman. To understand the importance of this post, we should remember that it is one that has been held by a number of top-level figures such as Andreotti (from the fourth to the eighth De Gasperi Governments) and Giuliano Amato, the powerful and much respected *éminence grise*, to Bettino Craxi. As regards the administrative organization of the President of the Council's office, practice and theory are, again, at odds. In the first place, immediately after the war, the President's staff was about 50 strong; by 1963 it had risen to 300. Since then the number has increased perhaps tenfold. In its report of August 1986, the Audit Office estimated the members of the office of the President of the Council (which also includes the members of the offices of Ministers without portfolio) at 1,586[21] and the total number of staff employed at the Palazzo Chigi at 3,828 (ten times more than the official allocation). Expenses show a similar discrepancy between appearances and reality. The original budget for the Presidency was 1,995 thousand million lire, but in reality expenses have more than doubled (to 5,022 thousand million).[22] However, the Audit Office recognizes in its report that these anomalies are due to the mismatch that has developed between obsolete regulations and financial provisions, on the one hand, and the increasing importance of the Presidency, on the other. In its conclusions, it emphasizes that the bill to reform the Presidency (finally adopted in 1988) would constitute a step forward and 'an important stage in the implementation of the Constitution'.

It would appear that, in Italy, the increasing size of these staffs is an institutional and structural reaction to the constraints of a system that is diffuse, fragmented, and multipolar. This impression is confirmed when we compare Italy to Britain and Germany, where the staffs of Prime Minister and Chancellor are far more modest, despite the key roles that these figures play. In Britain, there is an extra point to take into account: the Cabinet Office is in principle at the disposal of not only the Prime Minister but the Cabinet Ministers as a whole. The Prime Minister is assisted by a staff that is extremely small, even compared to that of a French Minister. Relations between the Prime Minister and the other Ministers depend upon six 'Private Secretaries'. These are chosen from the Civil Service for their ability and also, despite the fact that they are supposed to be apolitical, for their loyalty to the policies of the party in power. The Prime Minister is also assisted by a Press Officer and may call upon political advisers chosen from outside the administration. The team of political administrators grouped around the Prime Minister is thus seldom composed of more than ten people, the remaining hundred or so staff of 10 Downing Street being essentially made up of secretaries and the like. Nevertheless, the limited dimensions of this 'private office' does not prevent the Prime Minister, as leader of the executive, from playing a crucial role that is of far more importance than that of his or her Italian counterpart. For the British Prime Minister, as leader of his party and the parliamentary majority as well as head of the government and its Ministers, holds enough trumps to be able to dispense with a parallel administration that might prove more a source of complications and conflict than an effective instrument of decision. Although it is not exclusively at his individual disposal, the Prime Minister can rely on the Cabinet Office, which in part fulfils the functions assumed, in France, by the General Secretariat of the government. But over and above all this, the Cabinet Office plays a role of fundamental importance in determining policies, since its members loom large in all the ministerial committees in which the various departments try to harmonize their respective points of view. The consensual style of politico-administrative decision-making in Britain explains why Edward Heath's attempt in 1970 to create a Prime Minister's 'office' modelled on French lines hung fire. This Central Policy Review Staff,[23] designed to give the Prime Minister advice unbiased by the interests of the individual Ministries, and to create an overall planning programme for government action was, under Margaret Thatcher, first consigned to a secondary role, then, in the autumn of 1983, quite simply scrapped. Margaret Thatcher much preferred to rely upon the Downing Street policy unit.

In Germany, the Chancellor's staff is neither as large as those available to his counterparts in the United States and Italy, nor as minimal as the British Private Office. By virtue of the tasks assigned to it and its size, the Chancellor's Office (Bundeskanzleramt) most resembles the office and staff at the disposal of the Prime Minister of France. As in many other areas, the powers acquired by this structure stem to a large extent from the measures taken by Konrad Adenauer. He was so keen to have at his disposal an efficient instrument for implementing decisions that up until 1955 he went so far as to combine his functions of Chancellor with those of the Ministers of both Defence and Foreign Affairs. For ten years, from 1953 to 1963, the Chancellor's office was run by Hans Globke, Adenauer's adviser and a remarkable organizer, whom the Chancellor backed and retained in his post despite his past as a high-ranking civil servant under the Third Reich. Globke left his mark at the organizational level just as Adenauer left his at the political level, and the Chancellor's Office has retained all its importance despite the subsequent presence of secretaries in whom less confidence was placed and who lacked Globke's managerial skills (Grabert, for example, appointed by Brandt at the beginning of his second Government). The Office is organized into six functional divisions, each one under the management of a senior civil servant (a ministerial *Direktor*), appointed at the discretion of the government. These are the only appointments, apart from the Secretary of State[24] or Minister who is the Head of the Office, that can be described as political, for although successive Chancellors have managed to politicize the Office when new appointments were being made,[25] their opportunities to do so more generally are limited, since most of the civil servants who man the Office are appointed on a permanent basis. In other systems this situation might produce tensions, but in this case it does not give rise to too many difficulties because of the political consensus, the tradition of coalitions, and a concern to appoint first and foremost civil servants of high calibre. At present, the Chancellor's Office comprises a staff of roughly 500, of whom about 100 belong to the highest echelons of the Federal Bureaucracy. A measure of flexibility is introduced into the personnel management by the presence of many contractual staff (about 40 per cent of the total).[26] Apart from being served by the Office itself, the Chancellor has at his disposal a Press Office with a huge staff (of about 800), described by Grosser as 'gigantic as compared to what exists in other pluralist states'.[27] The Chancellor is thus provided with an efficient instrument to promote co-ordination and collegiality. In contrast to the British Cabinet Office, however, its staff is stable and more loyal to the Chancellor than to the Ministry from which they may be seconded. Moreover, despite the fact that the West German system is a fragmented one due to its federal structure and the persistence of coalition governments, the Chancellor's Office has so far—apart from the Press Office—resisted the inflationary trends displayed by the American Executive Office and the Italian Office, both of which have now assumed the dimensions of veritable central administrations.

The limited expansion of the Chancellor's staff is partly explained by the wide powers held by the *Länder*, which are responsible for virtually all administration. But the chief reason for it is the strong measure of autonomy possessed by the various German Ministries (*Ressortprinzip*), which prevents the Chancellor from direct intervention into the current business of each of them. Although he must verify and guarantee the application of the measures announced in his general policy statement (*Regierungserklärung*), he is not expected to interfere in his Ministers' handling of their respective sectors. This is totally different from the situation in France, where it has sometimes been known for an adviser to the Prime Minister (or the President) to overrule a Minister. Such a state of affairs would be inconceivable, even scandalous, in West Germany.

It is true that in France, under the Fifth Republic, the services at the disposal of the executive have presented two unusual features. In the first place, both the President's staff and the Prime Minister's wield considerable influence over the actions of Ministers and the administration. Secondly, the staff of both heads of the executive always comprise two different groups, the one more concerned with political action, the other responsible for steering and co-ordinating the administrative machine (although, in practice, the two functions often appear inextricably intermingled). The presidential Secretariat (composed of between 15 and 30 people) and the General Secretariat of the government (about 100 strong) are the principal cogs in the administrative machine. But whereas the latter is an extremely venerable institution with long-standing links with the parliamentary system (and, indeed, with monarchical roots), the former was set up in its present form by General de Gaulle, his predecessors of the Fourth Republic having been served by no more than a handful of individuals with little influence. The main tasks of the General Secretariat of the government are to organize meetings of interministerial councils and committees, to supervise the preparation and implementation of legislation, and to ensure the co-ordination and continuity of ministerial action—in short, to assist the Prime Minister in his general functions as leader and as head of the 'college' constituted by the government. Some members of this secretariat may be appointed at the discretion of the Prime Minister, but the general stability of these civil service posts, which constitutes a guarantee of State continuity, is considerable, even in the case of the one that is most in the public eye, namely, that of the Secretary-General to the Government. When, in 1986, Jacques Chirac dismissed the Secretary-General who had been appointed by the Socialists in 1981, this was regarded as a break in what had become a well-established tradition of the Republic. In 1988, on the other hand, Michel Rocard retained the Secretary-General whom his right-wing predecessors had appointed. At the Elysée, where no such traditions exist, the President himself appoints his men at his own discretion, and here the turnover is far more rapid (two or three Elysée Secretaries in the course of a seven-year presidential term of office). The importance of these posts is attested to by the fact that many of their incumbents (Jobert, Balladur, François-Poncet) have been appointed to major ministerial duties following a period working at the Elysée.

The other component of the Elysée and Matignon staffs, that is, the directly political element, consists of offices (*cabinets*) whose members, for the most part senior civil servants seconded from the most prestigious departments of the public sector (the Council of State, the Audit Office, and the Inspection des Finances), operate as *chargés de mission* or technical advisers. The members of these *cabinets* are recruited on the basis of their sympathy for the existing authorities and, in theory, their duties are to advise the Prime Minister or Head of State and to supervise the activities of the sectors for which they have special responsibility. In reality, they are frequently more influential than the Minister in charge of the sector concerned, if only because they are afforded constant access to the decision-makers at the top (whereas a Secretaire d'État, for example, may only come face to face with the President once or twice a year). However, the power of these *éminences grises* varies according to the ability of the Minister in question to impose or defend his own views and also the conceptions that the President or Prime Minister may entertain of their respective roles. At all events, conflicts and 'guerrilla' operations abound, including some between the two *cabinets*. The hostility of Georges Pompidou and his closest advisers towards the members of Jacques Chaban-Delmas's *cabinet* was one of the causes of the sacking of Chaban-Delmas in 1972.

The collective work of government is organized in councils or committees. Constitutional literature and political symbolism represent the council of ministers or the Cabinet (in the English sense of the word) as the centres, *par excellence*, of collective decision-making and policy determination. But in fact that is seldom a true picture, for the discussion and determination of government policies cannot possibly be limited to brief weekly or fortnightly meetings lasting two or three hours and with fifteen to thirty participants. In reality, in parliamentary systems a Council of Ministers is a symbol of the principle of collegiality sanctioned by ministerial responsibility. Accordingly, it is at these meetings that the government's essential actions are approved or 'decided': the adoption of bills and regulations, budgetary decisions, the orientation of internal or foreign policies, personnel appointments, and so on. But the meeting itself is hardly more than a final formality in a long process of decision-making, which has taken place elsewhere involving negotiations between the various partners in a coalition, internal arbitration within the party or parties in power, interministerial compromises and decisions, and policies adopted by the administration. However, the processes leading to these collective decisions and the extent of the head of the executive's authority in the resolution of conflicts vary from one country to another.

In France, the Council of Ministers formally ratifies decisions taken elsewhere. It is unusual for the Head of State chairing the meeting to consult each Minister present and even rarer for the meeting to provoke any clash (as happened in 1967, when Edgar Pisani tendered his resignation in protest against the use of ordinances). The meetings of the Council of Ministers are preceded by smaller and more informal meetings of Ministers and senior civil servants, and it is in these that most decisions are taken. Up until 1986, ministerial or interministerial committees were presided over by the Prime Minister or his representative, except when the President called meetings at the Elysée, in which the general policies of the government tended to be determined. Meanwhile, permanent interministerial councils were presided over by the Head of State, and it fell to them to deal with problems considered to be either of crucial importance (e.g. Algeria, or African or Madagascarian affairs) or areas of potential sensitivity at the time (e.g. the Central Planning Council created in 1974 or the Nuclear Policies Council in 1976). Jean Massot has illustrated the progressive presidentialization of the system by showing the extent to which councils (based in the Elysée) took over from committees (based in Matignon).[28] But between March 1986 and June 1988, the situation was totally reversed since now it was the Prime Minister who held the essential power to call and chair committee meetings. The Head of State was reduced to chairing the Defence Committee and the Council of Ministers (the latter being a more or less formal role).

It is in West Germany that rules for organizing the work of

government are the most strictly codified. Although every Chancellor can impose his own style upon the management of government, the essentials are determined by legislation adopted in 1951 (and revised in 1970) on the basis of Article 65 of the Constitution. It is this that determines the procedures of decision-making, in particular the rules applying to Cabinet voting. But it is relatively rare for the Cabinet to take a vote. Often, disagreements are resolved and decisions taken in a context that is more informal and also, given the prevalence of coalitions, more party dominated. For example, during the period of the grand coalition led by Kiesinger, rifts were frequently repaired and contradictions resolved at Kressbronn, near Lake Constance (hence the name 'the Kressbronn Circle' given to these periodic meetings). But conflicts cannot always be resolved politically, for many of them are not specifically related to the parties. As Renate Mayntz[29] points out, some antagonisms are 'structurally determined, reflecting the conflicting interests and inclinations of Ministers and their respective clienteles'. In such situations, only the Chancellor's personality and his gifts of mediation and persuasion can produce agreement over policies that accommodate the different views of his Ministers. By reason of the Constitution and the practices established by Adenauer, the powers that the Chancellor possesses are thus far from negligible, but they are limited by the increasingly important part played by the parties in the formation of coalitions and the determination of government policies. His prerogatives are restricted by the general policy declaration that he makes to the Bundestag, a declaration that is itself conditioned by the agreements reached between the various parties included in the coalition government (*Koalitionsvereinbarung*). Finally, in accordance with the Constitution, which allows Ministers a very large measure of independence (*Ressortprinzip*) in the running of their Ministries (as regards both political decisions and the organization of their departments), the Chancellor only has the right to intervene if a Minister's decisions do not seem to conform to the general orientation of government policies. As can be seen, especially if the Chancellor is weak, the head of the West German executive does not enjoy such sweeping powers as his French and British counterparts.

In Britain, as in other parliamentary systems, 'full Cabinet' meetings give official expression to a more important process of decision-making that is already completed. Essentially, this takes place in Cabinet committee meetings, whose importance is such that they are sometimes said to constitute the fundamental element in the United Kingdom's process of governmental decision. These committees fall into two main categories, the permanent (or 'standing') committees, which deal with questions such as foreign affairs, defence, and so on, on a regular basis; and *ad hoc* committees. The creation, composition, and agendas of these committees are decided by the Prime Minister, who also chairs the most important of them. In theory, the list of committees, their composition, and the decisions that they make are kept secret, for reasons of confidentiality, but also so as to maintain the fiction of collegiality and ministerial solidarity. The committees are not supposed to take decisions that are the province of the 'full Cabinet'. Obviously, this excessive secrecy is impossible to maintain: not only can lists of all these committees together with those of their members be found in academic works on political science, but also the Press takes mischievous delight in publishing all kinds of information and reporting on many controversies that are in theory cloaked in secrecy. In a sense, the greater the extent of politico-administrative secrecy and the more limited the consensus reached over political decisions, the greater number of 'leaks' there tends to be. Within the Cabinet, the Prime Minister provides strong leadership, not so much as a result of his (or her) constitutional prerogatives but rather of his position as head of the majority party. Occasionally, the Prime Minister may call for a vote, but only does so in very exceptional circumstances (although the procedure was more common under recent Labour Governments, on account of the internal divisions that existed within the party). Usually, decisions are reached by consensus, possibly after the Prime Minister has consulted each Minister individually. The object is to avoid crystallizing the existence of a minority within the government by taking a formal vote.

In Italy, as we have seen, the President of the Council is both weak, by reason of the role that the parties play in coalition governments, and, at the same time, central to the system, in that he is one of the few cogs in the machine in a position to free some of the others in the system and thus to make it run more smoothly. The position of the President of the Council is seen rather differently by different observers. Some, Merlini, for example, stress that all too many ministerial committees are placed under the authority of one or other of the Ministers themselves.[30] Others, such as Cassese, point to the progressive extension of the powers of the President of the Council. (For example, the co-ordination of regional affairs and the regions' conference have recently been placed under his direction.) What should also be pointed out is that, as in all countries, but particularly in Italy, the President of the Council must always reckon carefully with whoever is in charge of the Treasury, especially if the latter happens not to belong to the same party or faction as the President of the Council himself.

However, as in all systems, more or less formalized procedures have been devised to improve the processes of decision. One case in point has been the attempt to associate party secretaries with the government so as to resolve crises from the inside rather than from outside the Cabinet. Another has been the constitution of very small crisis Cabinets. (For example, to cope with the Achille Lauro affair, Craxi conferred with the Ministers of Defence and Foreign Affairs.) This is also fairly common practice in Britain, where 'inner Cabinets' are frequently set up (either to deal with ongoing problems or in crisis situations such as the 1982 Falklands War). In such situations, the Prime Minister presides over a group of Ministers selected either on the grounds of their particular responsibilities and skills or because of the confidence that the head of government places in them. Thus the crisis Cabinet set up during the Falklands War included Cecil Parkinson, not—obviously enough—because he was Chancellor of the Duchy of Lancaster, but as Chairman of the Conservative Party and a faithful ally to Mrs Thatcher. All these processes and structures provide added proof of the gap that has developed between constitutional theory, according to which the Council of Ministers or Cabinet is the central organ of decision, and current political practice, which is remarkably different.

CONCLUSION

The government today, whether parliamentary or presidential, is the central element of a political system. The centrality of its role stems from a number of factors. In the first place, as has already been emphasized, governments and the apparatuses that they control have benefited from an expansion of functions, means, and staff that is unparalleled in other 'branches' of power. In the early nineteenth century, in Britain, the number of staff employed by the central government was roughly equivalent to that employed by Parliament. Today, any comparison between the two would be pointless, except to stress the vast discrepancy between the means available to the legislature and those enjoyed by the executive.

Secondly, contemporary processes of decision-making, which call for rapid action and reaction often kept secret until they are officially reported, render the roles played by the political parties and their leaders more important and reinforce the power of teams that are kept small, or even of individuals, to the detriment of decision-making machinery such as Parliaments. Even in Italy, where the executive (except for a few exceptions) is weak and unstable, the expression *centralità del Parlamento* reflects only one side of the political reality: Parliament, as everywhere, certainly remains the primary forum for political debate, but even the formal power of decision-making is increasingly slipping from its grasp and passing to the government (which can pass law-decrees) and to the administration.

Thirdly, the reciprocal checks that legislatures and executives used to be able to impose upon each other have become more and more unbalanced. Ministerial responsibility is no longer an issue or, when it is (taking forms that are frequently semi-constitutional), as in Italy, it is not so much a matter of Parliament attempting to apply controls as of disagreements between the parties or between different factions within a party. Ministerial responsibility in the classic sense of the expression plays such an insignificant role that, beneath all the turbulence caused by the rapid succession of governments, Italian Ministers in fact continue to display a remarkable degree of political stability. In contrast, the means of control and constraint available to the executive are both powerful and widely used. They include, for instance, procedures to expedite decisions (such as Art. 49.3 in France and the guillotine in Britain), as well as other constitutional constraints.

Finally, the growing power of party leaders and the increasingly important role played by the political parties provide Presidents and heads of government with extra trump cards. Ordinary members of parliament are more likely to be dependent upon the executive than vice versa. This reversal of roles can be seen quite clearly if we look back at the situations in which leaders of the executive have found themselves in difficulties over recent years: Nixon and Brandt were undermined by revelations in the Press, de Gaulle by a referendum; Eden, Macmillan, Adenauer, and Erhard were all, more or less unceremoniously, put out of action by their own parties, while (with the exception of Jacques Chirac in 1976) French Prime Ministers have suffered the same fate at the hands of their respective Presidents but not those of Parliament as such, and so on. Only the Italian situation is (to some extent) an exception to the rule.

However, it would be excessive to conclude that the executives of today have become all-powerful. They continue to be subject to both internal and international constraints and to pressures exercised by the political parties, other groups, and their own administrations, all of which constitute so many considerable limitations to their authority. Nowadays, particularly in the West, societies are complex and unwieldy entities that in many cases can only be steered into making changes of a marginal nature. Notwithstanding the undeniable charisma of certain leaders (Reagan, Thatcher, and Mitterrand, for example), governmental power is limited by the plurality of the agents involved in all policy-making and the recalcitrance of facts. It is altogether in accordance with the logic of things that it should be the very elements supposed to possess the most power and authority (the government and its administration) that should be the most subject to *external* pressures, now that internal limitations upon the exercise of power have been eroded or have become obsolete.

Local and Central Bureaucracies

The sector that has changed the most over the last century in the Western democracies is probably that of central administrations. The change is primarily one of size, reflecting the remarkable expansion of the functions assumed and the services rendered by the various branches of the State apparatus. The 50,000 officials of the Italian central administration at the end of the nineteenth century have increased fortyfold and today number almost 2 million.[1] Britain, which in the early nineteenth century employed only 20,000 in the central administration, today employs about 500,000.[2] The figures are slightly lower in West Germany (just over 300,000 in 1980)[3] on account of the essential administrative role of the *Länder*, but overall the tendency is the same. It is extremely difficult to establish statistical comparisons between different countries, on account of the differences between their respective staffs and functions (public in some countries, private in others). It is nevertheless clear that, once the various levels (central and local) and fragmentations of the administrations concerned have been taken into account, the ratio of civil servants to members of the public works out to be remarkably similar in all the Western countries.

The changes that have taken place also concern the functions assumed by administrations. Here, expansion has been continuous ever since the nineteenth century. The formidable explosion of the Welfare State and 'Big Government' was checked (but not totally halted) only by the economic crisis of the 1970s. Today, European democracies use, on average, over 40 per cent of the gross national product for running costs and the redistribution of national wealth. The management of taxation and redistribution and of investment in the State requires a whole army of staff, massive funding, and increasingly numerous and sophisticated regulations and procedures. For the tasks of bureaucracies have not only proliferated; they have also changed in kind, calling for new methods, instruments, and modes of management. And in cases where the traditional adminis-tration has not proved capable of encompassing the necessary changes, new structures have developed alongside, using the new methods that the many new functions demand.

Other transformations have been of a more fundamental nature. First, in every case, the body known—for the sake of convenience —as 'the administration' is extremely heterogeneous. When necess-ary, the whole conglomeration presents a united front to the external world and is sometimes believed by the public to be indeed united. However, in reality it constitutes a severely divided world of separate departments in which much energy is devoted to pre-empting one's neighbours, empire-building, angling for judicial guarantees for or-ganizational or functional claims of one kind or another, and defend-ing one's own responsibilities and prerogatives. There is nothing particularly scandalous about that, nor is the phenomenon peculiar to public organizations. However, it is all a far cry from the myth of a united administration under the control of the political authorities or from the Weberian model of bureaucracy. The internal conflicts of administrations are recognized to varying degrees in different coun-tries: in Italy, they are an integral part of the politico-administrative scene; in Germany, the force of *Ressortprinzip* to some extent legiti-mizes the autonomy of the different departments. In France, where the Revolution, using materials left by the monarchy, built such a fine theoretical edifice, the majesty of power is less prone to such cracks in its façade. Nevertheless, in reality the situation is no different from elsewhere.

But it does not follow from this heterogeneity that all the agents involved stand on an equal footing. Everywhere, the financial admin-istrations dominate: their strategic position, their direction of taxation and finance, which gives them control even over the policies of each government that enters office, and the strength and calibre of the élites who make up their staff are all factors that combine to turn the Ministries of Finance into 'States within States'. The fortunes of other Ministries depend upon current circumstances, political decisions taken by the government, and social pressures. Ministries in charge of technology, the education sector, and culture (in France and Italy) have greatly expanded. Defence retains its important position, par-ticularly in countries such as France and Britain where it is concerned with issues that are diplomatic and political as well as military, and with strategies that have global implications. On the other hand, some

Ministries are currently in a relative state of decline (Foreign Affairs) or have yet to establish themselves firmly (the Environment). Within each individual Ministry, furthermore, technical staff sometimes clash with general administrators, as do political appointees with personnel recruited on the grounds of personal merit, 'insiders' vie with 'outsiders', and so on. In short, there could be no better way of debunking the myth of the 'State' with a capital 'S', be it that of the Jacobins, the Marxists, or the *philosophes*, than by noting the multiform, fluctuating, and antagonistic nature of Western States.

There is a second point to make that also applies to all the Western democracies. Nowadays, each of their administrations plays a role of crucial importance in public policy-making. According to Western tradition, and also to the Cartesian view of the processes of decision-making, the role of administrations is to implement decisions taken elsewhere, usually by the political authorities. But, as many studies have shown, that view has not for some time corresponded to the real state of affairs. Nowadays, bureaucracies are involved at every stage in public policy-making.

1. They help to shape the political agenda, that is, they elicit demands of which the political authorities have been unaware, suggesting bills, reforms, and changes to them. Or, alternatively, they help to set aside demands that are 'fantastic', 'unrealistic', 'too expensive', or 'completely impractical'. Thus, they operate as 'sifting agents', even if they do not monopolize that function and if, in most cases, they allow the political authorities to appear to be active in that capacity.

2. They help to determine the substance of political decisions by drafting bills conceived or accepted by the political authorities. Policies are frequently initiated by a written text (a law or a ruling), a financial grant, an *ad hoc* choice of instruments, or the selection of particular procedures. At all these levels, bureaucracies are necessary, indeed essential partners. Only they can provide the expertise to enable the political authorities to realize their plans. But this 'assistance' from the civil servants often places the authorities formally responsible for decision-making in a position of dependence: as is frequently acknowledged, 'it is impossible to govern against one's bureaucracy'.

3. Bureaucracies are, furthermore, responsible for implementing the government's policies. This, indeed, is normally considered their *raison d'être*. As we have noted, their function extends far beyond what

is frequently and simplistically claimed for them, namely, that of executive agents. Moreover, the way in which a policy is implemented may have very little to do with faithful execution of the plans of those who conceive it. All policies affect not only those whom they immediately concern and those who benefit from them, but also those who apply them. Policy implementation invariably involves adjustments, distortions, unexpected effects, and changes that are quite beyond the control of whoever originally decided upon the policy. Long before the 'policy studies' of today abundantly confirmed the fact, Tocqueville, in his *L'Ancien Régime et la révolution*, noted that 'Rules are rigid, but practice is flexible.' The truth is that the dichotomy between decision and execution is quite artificial. 'Execution' involves the juxtaposition and/or accumulation of a whole set of 'decisions' not recognized as such and in many cases neither formalized nor legitimized, yet which effectively transform the original decision. Execution means decision 'continued by other means' and with other decision-makers, however much philosophical, political, and juridical discourse persists in turning a blind eye to that mutation.

4. Finally, bureaucracies, as the instruments and means of expressing the continuity of the State, have an inherent interest in pursuing and maintaining the policies to which they have committed themselves. Institutional and structural pressures 'justify' this. Everything combines to encourage them in doing so: the guarantees afforded by the status of civil servants, the techniques for renewing the funding of services that have been approved, competition between one Ministry and another, and pressure from 'clients' (the regulated) working in unison with them. These links often constitute 'policy networks' committed to defending the policies that they initiated and from which they benefit. Recent neo-liberal policies may have brought into question such conduct, amplified as it has been by the Welfare State. However, it has proved extremely difficult to put the clock back, to 'roll back the State'. In both Britain and the United States it has been proved that in the course of a decade of governments determined to reduce public expenditure, it has been possible to do no more than block any escalation.

The principle according to which the continuity of the State should be ensured, whatever the changing fortunes of the political authorities, essentially plays into the hands of the bureaucracies that are technically its servant but in practice its masters. Despite all the rhetoric to the effect that the administrative branch must be subordinate to the political, the experience of the Western democracies inclines one to doubt this. The power of administrations lies in a number of factors: in the limited room for manœuvre (political, financial, and psychological) available to politicians in applying their policies, the difficulties involved in steering this huge apparatus in the desired direction, and the ability of civil servants to organize themselves into powerful pressure groups that are capable of resisting government decisions or of imposing their own views.

There are thus many similarities between the Western bureaucracies, despite all the differences caused by history or by the particular position of each administration within the framework of its country's system as a whole. And today they are complemented by yet another unifying factor: Western democracies all face the same problems, are all subject to similar constraints, and are all engaged in continual interactions which lead them to seek similar solutions. By reason of these common constraints and experiences, there exists today a veritable market in methods of administrative reform, in which ideas are exchanged about new structures, new methods, and new modes of management. National administrative training centres, the use of an 'ombudsman' or independent commissions, means of access to administrative documents, and techniques for combating terrorism are just a few examples of the subjects of common interest to the administrations of the liberal democracies today. And beyond that limited circle, they are also of interest to countries which, for historical or ideological reasons, tend to use the liberal democracies as administrative models.

ADMINISTRATIVE STRUCTURES

Whatever the country under consideration, one general point is clear: bureaucracies are extremely complex and the administrative unity so dear to Weber turns out to be a myth. There have been many attempts to rationalize the situation, many denunciations of the creeping tentacles of bureaucracy, many 'hatchet committees' and other attempt at radical reform. But, for all that, many responsibilities continue to be duplicated, many posts are in reality redundant, and the statuses of different administrative departments are largely unstandardized. However, to give a simplified picture of a complicated situation, let us concentrate our analysis upon four levels which, to a greater or lesser extent, are discernible in all the systems that we are studying: central bureaucracies, peripheral (deconcentrated or decentralized) authorities, autonomous or specialized bodies, and the public economic sector.

Central Bureaucracies

Central administrations are in principle placed under the authority of a Minister and organized as Ministries or Departments. But there are exceptions to that general rule, particularly in the United States, where it has proved difficult to set up Ministries (in 1987, there were still no more than thirteen in all, five of which had been created since 1953), and where the gap is filled by Agencies, Boards, or Authorities. But even in countries with less strong political and psychological reservations about the creation of new Ministries, governments may prefer to resort to structures that are the functional equivalent of Ministries without being formally organized as such. So it was in the cases of regional development (DATAR) in France, the environment (up until 1986) in West Germany, the Commissariat for civil protection in Italy, and so on. Another factor differentiating one country from another is the degree of public interventionism tolerated (a Minister of Culture would be virtually inconceivable in Britain) or national peculiarities (the Commonwealth for Britain, the refugees for Germany, the southern problem for Italy, the Overseas Departments and Territories for France, and so on). Finally, the number and size of Ministries and the services that they provide also depend upon the country's degree of administrative deconcentration or decentralization.

All Ministries are organized hierarchically, on the model of a pyramid, although the various levels go by different names in different countries: bureaux, directorates, divisions, etc. However, the significance and effects of this hierarchical model may vary considerably from one system to another or even within a single administration.

1. Some Ministries are placed under the direction of a single individual, the Minister, who is both a political leader and the head of his department. In other cases, by reason of the size of the Ministry or the political need for a distribution of portfolios, the ministerial department is functionally divided so that responsibility for various sections may be allocated to a number of different officials. Some

Ministries may thus be divided between two, three, or even four Ministers of unequal status. One of them is set above the others, but although he holds superior authority, the running of the department differs from that of one placed directly under a single head. In the European democracies, ministerial authority is frequently divided in this way, essentially for political reasons to do with the proliferation of ministerial posts and those of Junior Ministers (about 100 in Britain and Italy), or the constraints imposed by coalitions (in West Germany, France, and Italy).

2. Communication between the political summit of the pyramid and the bureaucracy may take a direct form or may be effected through an intermediary political office. In the first case, the Minister has direct contact with the officials in his service. But even here variations occur: a British Minister may not choose his own subordinates but must accommodate himself to those already in harness, whereas an American or German Minister can make his own appointments to posts of high responsibility, choosing officials whose views are close to his own (in West Germany), or his own political friends from either the public or the private sector (in the USA). In contrast, in France and Italy, a special office (the *cabinet*) mediates between the Minister, the administration, Parliament, and the various interest groups involved. The office is both political (through the ideological or party affinities between its members and the Minister himself) and administrative (through its composition, since most of the office staff are drawn from the top echelons of the civil service). These *cabinets* have their roots in the historical mistrust—which endures even today—that politicians feel towards the administration, for the latter is suspected of distorting or failing to apply the Minister's directives. But it is worth noting that, in a country such as Britain, where relations between Ministers and the administration rest upon the principle of the latter's strict neutrality, a minority of voices (but a considerable number, for all that:[4] for example, a minority in the Expenditure Committee of the House of Commons for 1977–8) have been arguing for an 'injection' of political appointments within the upper administration.

3. A third organizational difference or variation may stem from the presence (or absence) of a top official (Secretary-General) who heads the administration and is answerable to the Minister. Such an official is responsible for co-ordinating the activity of the various branches of the Ministry, preparing ministerial decisions and supervising their implementation, issuing directives, and so on. Such officials, where

they exist, are very powerful, for they can lay claim either to a stability and experience that lend considerable weight to their authority, as in the case of a Permanent Secretary in Britain, or to a wealth of administrative experience backed up by the trust of the Ministers who selected and appointed them, which is the situation of the German *Staatsekretäre*. In some cases, stability and political confidence can both be there, as when the same coalitions govern in rapid succession (e.g. in France, under the Fourth Republic, or in Italy). In such circumstances, a Secretary-General may become just as influential as his Minister—or even more so: under the Fourth French Republic, the Secretary-General of the Ministry of Education certainly wielded more influence than the numerous Education Ministers who succeeded one another in his time. That is no doubt why the Fifth Republic has gradually been eliminating ministerial Secretaries-General, who are such symbols of bureaucratic power. At the Quai d'Orsay, however, the post of Secretary-General survives and remains a highly prestigious one. In Italy, the Ministries of Foreign Affairs and Defence have also retained this structure.

4. The extremely variable size of ministerial departments constitutes another factor of differentiation between them. The size of an administrative apparatus depends upon the types of tasks and responsibilities allotted to the Ministers concerned. Ministries of the Environment are always tiny compared to the giant structures of Ministries of Defence or the Postal Services (where the latter are set up as Ministries). For example, both in Italy and in France, the Ministry of Education is the major State employer, representing one-third (in France) and one-half (in Italy) of all civil servants dependent upon the central administration. In a comparison between different systems, variations in the size of Ministries provide an interesting indication of the degree to which tasks are dispersed (by assigning them to lateral agencies or organizations of a more or less autonomous nature) or responsibilities are decentralized (by being transferred to local authorities that lie outside the hierarchical central Ministry). When that happens, pyramidal administrations that outwardly resemble one another may, in reality, operate quite differently.

Peripheral Authorities

Implementing decisions and raising finance are activities that employ ever-increasing numbers of administrative staff, who must perform the most diverse functions and remain in constant touch with the public. Governments may opt for one of two main strategies. Either they can make use of a local administration that is dependent upon the central authorities; or, alternatively, they can depend on local authorities that are autonomous but remain under the ultimate control of the central Ministries. The first of these two solutions was—and still is—exemplified best by the French (together with the Italian) model. The second solution is that adopted—albeit in very different ways —by Britain and West Germany.

We should, however, note that in practice neither model is implemented in a pure form: mixed solutions are the general rule.

The French model, on paper at least, is certainly the closest to a hierarchical pyramid. The quasi-military concept of organization and the aim—or illusion—of producing a strategy of general application and transmitting directives and information via a whole series of agents working for the central authorities provides an idealized model of the rationalist and centralist inspiration of the governments of the *ancien régime*, the Revolution, and the Empire. It is a model that has been followed—either deliberately or willy-nilly—by many European States such as Belgium, Italy, and Spain, at one point or another in the course of their histories. The prefect is positioned at the centre of the local organization. He is the representative of the State and is—in theory at least—responsible for co-ordinating all external services. This 'strange animal from the French menagerie' (to borrow the words of a British observer, Howard Machin) was certainly a powerful instrument of a centralized administrative system. However, for different reasons, neither in Italy nor in France does the reality fully correspond to that theoretical description. Italian prefects have never wielded as much power and influence as French ones, if only because of the inadequacy of the external services provided by the State over which, from the very start, they soon lost control. Italian prefects, responsible as they were for organizing elections and for law and order, and consequently compromised by Fascism, have been unable to resist post-war democratic tendencies and the growing influence of the parties. As Sidney Tarrow shows,[5] it is now the latter that have become the true intermediaries between the centre and the periphery.

Virtually the only real justification for the model of a prefect surrounded by external services was the central authorities' claim to control a web-like system that covered the entire territory and encompassed all administrative activities. This system was a powerful instrument in the construction of nation states in much of mainland Europe. The fact that it has survived, in particular in France, is due to the weakness and fragmentation of local systems. However, the system has evolved, under the pressure of two similarly oriented tendencies: in the first place, the prefect and the external State services (or field services), which were in theory supposed to ensure the overall authority of the central government, have been taken over at local levels. Numerous sociological studies undertaken in the 1960s succeeded in demystifying the rhetoric of the supremacy of the central hierarchy and revealed that relations between prefects and the notables surrounding them were on the whole a matter of compromise and collusion. Furthermore, the urbanization and massive expansion of services in towns during the 1960s showed that, while the field services may have been well suited to rural localities, they were certainly unable to cope with the more general development of the Welfare State. Today, public services (apart from education) have for the most part passed into the control of local authorities, although the field State services have preserved certain prerogatives which make it essential for local and the central authorities to collaborate. The 1982 decentralization reform, which transferred power from the prefects to the local élites, was not a revolution but in many instances the legalization of a quasi-*fait accompli*.

A second solution is to rely upon autonomous (and elected) local or regional authorities. Apart from Britain, with its two local levels (county and district), most European countries operate with at least three main strata of local authorities: regions, provinces, and communes in Italy; *Länder*, *Kreise*, and *Gemeinden* in West Germany; regions, departments, and communes in France. But in West Germany, as in France, this pattern is further complicated by many other bodies whose task is to mediate or to organize co-operation.

The degree of importance, numbers, and strengths involved at these major levels is by no means identical in the various countries. The weak link in the chain tends to be the *Kreis* in West Germany, and the region in France. In Italy,[6] a better balance is maintained between on the one hand the 20 regions, which discharge a number of important responsibilities and which afford a haven for the Italian Communist Party (excluded from the central system) and, on the other, the 95 provinces which, in the last analysis, remain the structure upon which the parties and, hence, the political system are based. The provinces are themselves divided into 8,000 communes. The most fragmented system is the French one: 22 regions, 95 departments, 36,000 communes, and in addition several thousand (more than 15,000) *ad hoc* organizations set up to liaise between local authorities. In West Germany, the 10 *Länder* (plus Berlin) are divided into 235 *Kreis* and 8,500 communes (*Gemeinden*), 88 of which operate simultaneously as both communes and *Kreis*. It is worth pointing out that, following the reforms introduced in the mid-1960s, the number of communes was cut by two-thirds. This was a fine example of concerted action in an effort to decentralize, for the movement was a general one, despite the fact that each *Land* was in principle free to decide when, to what extent, and how to introduce reforms.

In Britain too, the number of local authorities has been drastically cut, in fact reduced by two-thirds, as in West Germany. Here, the operation was even more spectacular: of the 1,500 old units in the previous system, the 1974 reform retained in England and Wales only 47 non-metropolitan counties and 6 metropolitan counties, subdivided respectively into 333 and 36 districts. As well as these, there remained the Greater London Council, divided into 32 boroughs, plus the City of London. As from 1 April 1986, and following a long battle between Margaret Thatcher and the Labour Party, the Government abolished the Greater London Council and the 6 metropolitan counties. Thus, today, all that remain are 47 counties (plus 9 regions in Scotland), 369 districts, the 32 boroughs of London (and 53 districts in Scotland, which has its own local system).

Various pressures favouring devolution of responsibilities to infra-State authorities has led to a complex redistribution of tasks virtually everywhere. In West Germany, for example, the *Länder* have been recognized to hold certain legislative powers, but their exclusive responsibilities do not amount to much: the police force, education, and the organization of local authorities. Moreover, in the cases of police and education, the 'exclusive' aspect of the powers of the *Länder* has given way to a system of collaboration and mutual agreement with the federal government. For the rest, the lion's share of power remains with the Bund.

So, to see how the *Länder* can determine or direct policies, we should not look at the legislative level but rather at the processes through which decisions—in particular those taken by the federal government—are executed and implemented. For the *de facto* legislative quasi-monopoly held by the Bund is counterbalanced by the undisputed supremacy of the *Länder* in the administrative sphere. By and large, federal policies and *Länder* policies are all implemented either by the civil servants of the various *Länder* or in a sectorial fashion, under the supervision of a kind of prefect: these *Regierungspräsidenten* are each placed at the head of an administrative area intermediate between the *Land* and the *Kreis* (it is, in effect, composed of a collection of *Kreise*). This important post to a certain extent makes up for the lack of legislative power at *Land* level, but it also means that power and influence is channelled away from local politicians and passes to the bureaucrats: in 1980 there were 1.5 million *Länder* civil servants, as opposed to 300,000 federal ones. In order to make the system work, co-operation between various levels of government is absolutely necessary.

There can, however, be no denying that 'co-operative federalism' has encouraged a centralization of the system that is to the advantage of the federal authorities. It is they who hold the key powers (defence, the Mint, foreign affairs), control the largest funds, and are best placed to respond to citizens' demands for fair treatment and to the concentration of economic forces. The centralization of West Germany is not primarily a political matter. Rather, it stems from a combination of 'the due process of law' or *Rechtsstaat* and imperatives of an economic and commercial nature. The federal institutions that provide the best guarantees for an egalitarian respect for citizens' rights (the supreme courts) and the exercise of economic liberties are also the focal point for pressures exerted by interests of the most diverse nature: trade unions, economic forces, and even institutional interest groups such as local authorities, which frequently band together in competition between the federation and the federated in an attempt to divert power from the central authorities.

Britain might also have evolved towards a quasi-federal system if the 1978 reforms, which envisaged a substantial devolution of powers to elected Assemblies in Scotland and Wales, had been adopted. The British Parliament would have been dispossessed of many of its powers (except in the areas of international affairs, taxation, and economic policy) and an executive similar to a government would have been created in Scotland. (In Wales fewer powers were to be transferred: housing, education, environmental planning, local government—and the executive functions were to be exercised by committee chairmen). Strangely enough, the bills submitted at the referendum 'federalized' the United Kingdom without consulting the country as a whole and without providing for any mechanisms for settling disagreements that might arise between Parliament, the Assemblies, and the central and non-central executives. However, the referendums on devolution having failed, there remain very few limitations to governmental centralization and such as there are stem more from time-honoured practice than from any specific rules governing the organization of the Scottish Office and the Welsh Office.

In both cases, centralization is organized in a particular way (somewhat reminiscent of the methods of colonial administration) that makes it possible to give special treatment to these regional problems, due to mechanisms that combine a horizontal type of centralization under the aegis of a Secretary of State together with much deconcentration of the administrations for which he is responsible. Since 1892 in the case of Scotland, and 1964 in that of Wales, the respective Secretaries of State have handled many responsibilities which, for the rest of the United Kingdom, are normally assumed by their other colleagues in the British government. For example, the responsibilities of the Secretary for Scotland correspond to those of nine Ministers in England, and he also supervises their corresponding decentralized administrations in Edinburgh. But this official role, which might seem like that of the governor of a colonial territory, represents only one aspect of what is in reality a far more complex situation. Just as a French prefect, who also represents the State, becomes the spokesman for the interests of the department or region for which he is responsible, similarly, within the Cabinet, the Secretaries of State for Scotland and Wales act in defence of their territories in a way that is unparalleled in the other Ministries. Although this function of theirs is neither officially required nor laid down by statute, it is an essential element of their political status and helps to make this particular form of centralization advantageous to the 'Celtic fringe'. Furthermore, this territorially based politico-administrative organization is reflected within Parliament itself. Since 1907, the Scottish Grand Committee (and, since 1960, the Welsh Grand Committee) of the House of Commons debates (usually in London, but sometimes in Edinburgh) bills that especially affect the region. Since 1966, Select Committees (on whose role see Chapter 5) have also been set up to supervise policies being carried out in Scotland and Wales, and these, too, help to strengthen regional pressure groups by reinforcing territorial divisions to the detriment of functional ones.

The scope of the administrative tasks that fall to the *Länder* and the legislative powers that remain to them make the responsibilities and means of the Italian regions—and, *a fortiori*, those of the French ones—seem very modest indeed: the latter look extremely lightweight in comparison. The legislative powers of the Italian regions are generally slight, but greater in the five with special status (Sicily, Sardinia, the Trentino–Alto Adige region, the Aosta Valley, and the Friuli–Veneto–Julian Alps region), particularly in the economic and cultural sectors. However, in both the regions with special status and those with ordinary status, the quantitative proliferation of statutes has not always been accompanied by any qualitative improvement in the standards of government. Nowadays, regional laws can frequently be seen to be quite simply subject to a time-lag, compared with national laws or other regional laws adopted in the past. This is not really surprising, for the regions' small measure of autonomy restricts their means of adaptation. Furthermore, the responsibilities allotted to the regions by the 1947 Constitution relate to relatively secondary sectors: commune boundaries, social assistance, crafts, tourism, hunting, fishing, and so on. The more important sectors are those concerned with health and agriculture, but the regions have no autonomous financial means to cope with health problems and have to a large extent been 'relieved' of their responsibilities as regards agriculture by the transfer of agricultural policy-making to the EEC. The regions have had to fight tooth and nail to prevent the transfer of responsibilities, which has been taking place since 1970, from totally whittling away their means of intervention in the various areas attributed to them by the Constitution. For example, Article 117 of the Constitution is worded in such a way as to make it easy to manœuvre the introduction of restrictive interpretations. It runs as follows: 'In the following matters, the region fixes the legislative rules *within the limits of the fundamental principles fixed by State law, and on condition that those rules do not oppose the national interest or that of the other regions*' (my italics). Given a measure of ill will on the part of central institutions, it is clearly easy to play games with such dispositions. This is exactly what happened in the early 1970s: either isolated powers were excised from the 'body of responsibilities' attributed to the regions, leaving them with no autonomy at all (an operation known as *ritaglio*, 'redefinition'), or the adoption of the general principles that were supposed to make it possible for the regions to act on their own initiative was quite simply blocked. The first of those two obstacles was removed, due to the political climate of 1977, particularly as a result of pressure from left-wing regions and the Communist Party (whose tacit support the Christian Democrats were courting in connection with their policy of what was known as 'National Union'). The second was swept away by the Constitutional Court, which ruled that, in default of a specific national law, the general principles mentioned in the Constitution could be regarded as following from the whole body of legislation already in effect.

The Italian regions are also active at the administrative level, although that is not the purpose for which they were originally designed. According to the Italian Constitution and the national legislature, the regions were originally conceived as intermediaries, centres of co-ordination and initiation, operating between the central and the local levels. Accordingly, the regions ought to have delegated most managerial tasks to the provincial and communal levels. But that never happened since, given an institutional climate in which they were at a disadvantage, the regions were anxious to hang on to whatever meagre powers they might possess. That is why the regions, originally planned as quite light structures, today employ some 60,000 officials. At the same time, it is only fair to point out that this body represents no more than 2 per cent of civil servants as a whole, despite the fact that the regions manage around 10 per cent of all public expenditure. But in this area, too, regional autonomy is limited, since 90 per cent of the resources available to the regions are provided by the State, and most of them come already earmarked for specific purposes. The room for manœuvre is thus extremely limited. This last point helps us to compare the degrees of regional autonomy in Italy and in France. The French regions have limited funding and discharge relatively few responsibilities (in comparison with the massive central institutional apparatus) and the staff available to serve them is extremely small (2000). Yet their action is far from negligible, for up until 1984–5 most of their income was devoted to subsidizing investments made by other authorities. This afforded them a certain amount of leverage out of all the sums involved, which in turn enabled them gradually to strengthen their position.

Given the interdependence between central and local authorities regarding the implementation of policies, the choice of solutions is a relatively simple one: either to adopt an authoritarian and centralizing policy so as to ensure that decisions taken at the top are carried out satisfactorily; or, alternatively, to set up instruments of collaboration designed to promote consensus and interdependence. Margaret Thatcher deliberately chose the first course, and it has led her into an increasingly repressive and centralizing spiral. The metropolitan counties (London and six elsewhere) were recalcitrant and considered to be overspending. The solution was simple: as from 1 April 1986, the Government abolished them. To reduce local spending, Margaret Thatcher forced through the Local Government Planning and Land Act (1980) and the Local Government Finance Act (1982), strengthened controls (in particular by creating the Audit Commission in 1983), and forced local authorities to put out to tender for public services through the Housing Act (1980), the Education Act (1980), and the Health and Social Security Act (1983). Localities that overspend are subject to financial penalties by having their central government subsidies cut. Furthermore, for the first time since the creation of rates in 1601, the Rates Act authorizes the government to fix the levels of all local rates (rate-capping). All these controversial measures were considered justified in the name of expediency. After her third consecutive victory in 1987, Margaret Thatcher radicalized her policies still further. In the Queen's Speech, written by herself and delivered by the Queen on 25 June 1987, Margaret Thatcher announced a redistribution of responsibilities, channelling them towards central government in the domains of education and housing. Citizens can now request that local schools be placed under the authority of the Minister of Education rather than under that of the local council. They can also ask for the management of public housing to be taken over by independent organizations rather than the local authorities. Finally, the Government announced its intention to do away with the rates first in Scotland, then in England and Wales, and to replace them with a community charge (often called 'poll tax') to be redistributed by the government. Conflict between the central and the local authorities is thus much exacerbated in Britain, which now constitutes the principal and most striking exception to the tendency towards 'co-operation' which seems to prevail in most of the other Western countries.

In the United States and West Germany, the term 'co-operative federalism' has been used to refer to the increasingly close collaboration that has taken over from the principle of classic federalism in which each separate level was autonomous. But it is a phenomenon that is not restricted to strictly federated systems. Non-federated systems also resort to a similar type of co-operation, using specific

methods and instruments of their own but not differing fundamentally from those used by federal systems. These administrative, financial, and sometimes political instruments may be formalized to
varying degrees from one country to another, but in all cases their
overall effect is to substitute co-operation for the traditional situations
of separation or supervision.

1. In West Germany, particularly numerous and important formalized instruments of co-operation have been introduced. One of the
most long-standing forms of collaboration evolved in the Conference
of Education Ministers, an institution that comprises a whole collection of structures (a plenary assembly, various committees, and a
general secretariat). It is chaired by each of the *Länder* Ministers in
turn, and the chairman also acts as spokesman and representative,
most importantly in the Bund and in meetings with foreign counterparts. Similar conferences operate in other ministerial sectors, above
all at the level of the *Länder* Prime Ministers.

Furthermore, hundreds of committees of every kind have been set
up to enable the Bund and the *Länder* to discuss, negotiate, and come
to agreement on problems of common interest. Among the best
known of these are the Science Council (Wissenschaftsrat), the
Education Council (Bildungsrat), and the Council for Economic
Affairs (Finanzplanungsrat). Frequently, the consensus reached is
formalized by treaties or agreements of a political or administrative
nature, which have full juridical force.

A further step in this process of institutionalization was taken
in 1969 with the revision of the Constitution that recognized and
'authenticated' these practices by introducing the concept of 'common tasks' (*Gemeinschaftanfgaben*) in a number of sectors such as the
building of universities, regional economic policy, agricultural policy,
and the construction of dikes. The federal government was authorized
to intervene and co-finance projects, thereby contributing to a better
distribution of resources and fairer treatment for the less advantaged
Länder. This reform, introduced under the Grand Coalition in power
at the time (the CDU–CSU–SPD) has since given rise to much
criticism and many members of the Bundestag (especially from
southern Germany) have urged the suppression or modification of
these 'common tasks'. But the system has survived, as has the more or
less formalized co-operation established at all levels.

Italy and France have not set up such a comprehensive body of
formal agreements, but both countries also make use of mechanisms

designed to make for co-operation between central and local authorities. In France, the means most favoured has been contracts—not that they are always concluded between perfectly equal partners, but at least they betoken a switch to dialogue instead of relations of a hierarchical nature. They constitute agreements between the State and local authorities on planned spending programmes over a period of years. Over the last fifteen years, all kinds of contracts have been drawn up and have multiplied: contracts with various localities, with medium-sized towns, with suburbs, and other planning contracts too. The juridical validity of these agreements is by no means assured, but that is not the important point. First and foremost, these agreements between the centre and the periphery testify to a new mode of government and a new relationship. In Italy, the modalities of co-operation between the State and the regions are, according to Sabino Cassese, similar to the practices adopted in West Germany, but on a rather more modest scale. He writes:

In many different sectors, which range from aid for financing the building of universities to cultural measures, employment, agriculture, health, housing, and so on, committees composed of representatives of both the State and the regions are at work. There are at least a hundred of these bodies, many with their own staff, and they operate in sectors that are the responsibility of the State as well as in those that are the responsibility of the regions. Their functions are to mediate between interests, to avert conflict, to exchange information, to deliberate, and so on.[7]

2. These formal agreements are reinforced (or in some cases superseded) by informal relations which may not be as solid and stable but nevertheless constitute essential links between the central and the local authorities. They take many forms: the intertwining of responsibilities and the politico-administrative so-called 'honeycomb structure' in France; communication between the centre and the periphery established by party organizations, in West Germany and Italy; the appointment of local or regional spokesmen to keep in touch with the central or federal authorities (associations of mayors, or regional presidents, in France and Italy respectively); 'Missions' from the *Länder* in Bonn, each one headed by the *Minister für Bundesangelegenheiten*, that is to say the Minister for co-operation with the federal government. More specifically, what have been called 'policy networks' or 'policy clusters' are set up on a sectorial or vertical basis. These are groups which include representatives from certain departments of the central or federal authorities, and from various

states or localities, and economic and social groups that are concerned by the particular policy in question (for example, the Minister of Industry, the areas affected by the steel crisis, the employers seeking aid, and the trade unions anxious to preserve jobs). Moreover, collaboration of this kind tends to be made easier by the fact that, despite all efforts at rationalization, the distribution of responsibilities is never altogether strict and clear. Overlaps and confusions are the rule rather than the exception and occasion countless problems that can only be resolved through co-operation, unless, that is, increasingly authoritarian solutions are adopted; but these are not necessarily effective anyway.

3. Finally, co-operation between central and local authorities involves funding from both sources, subsidies, and other fiscal and financial devices that create interdependence. For one important fact needs to be recognized: with very few exceptions, local fiscal autonomy is an illusion in the contemporary world. As Rémy Prud'homme has remarked, 'there are no good local taxes', for the simple reason that local resources never match local needs, particularly when, as in France, the country is divided into so many separate units. There are several possible ways of resolving this problem. One is to 'nationalize' all revenue, as is done in Italy and Holland; but the danger is that the process of redistribution may turn into something of a free-for-all. Another is to make various adjustments and piecemeal arrangements, as in France and the United States. Yet another is to rationalize the system and make it more equitable, as in West Germany, where the best balance of central and local resources has been achieved, although even this system has provoked criticisms within the country. The system depends upon each of its various levels dividing up virtually all its fiscal revenue on the basis of percentages that may be revised when necessary. With this system, everyone benefits or suffers from the general economic situation, since every level receives a fraction of the revenue as a whole, whether it comes from high- or low-yielding taxes, from taxes that are elastic or taxes that are not (whereas in other countries the central governments tend to retain a monopoly over the most modern and high-yielding taxes, leaving what amounts to the crumbs to the lower levels). For example, in 1982, the Bund obtained 48.7 per cent of the revenue, the *Länder* 34.6 per cent, the communes 13.2 per cent, and the remainder went to the EEC. This is probably the model towards which the archaic and complex French system will eventually evolve, but it will mean first overcoming the extra problem

of the country being divided into an excessively large number of local authorities.

Thus, despite profound institutional differences between the various States, it is possible to detect a number of meaningful convergences. In the federal States, the politico-administrative processes are certainly undergoing a measure of centralization, for the reasons mentioned above. The most centralized States are equally certainly moving towards decentralization and regionalization. An inextricable mixture of rules, conventions, and practices has evolved, tending mutually to compensate for or correct each other's excesses, and creating a system of complex relations in which central and peripheral power are not in truth separate, as the metaphor would suggest, but are on the contrary linked through mechanisms, some formal, some not, devised to encourage co-operation, interaction, and joint or mixed processes of decision and finance. Only Britain is an exception in this general evolution. Here, centralization has been reinforced to the point of becoming a fetish. Tension between the central and the local authorities is growing, constituting one expression of the deepening antagonism between the majority and the opposition. The consensus and conventions that traditionally used to link the local authorities to the government and Parliament have been dislocated by the radicalism of Thatcherite policies and the no less radical reactions of Labour local authorities. The traditional political and administrative centralization of the United Kingdom is no longer counterbalanced by its 'local government'. And it is the Conservatives, the traditional defenders of local autonomy, who have brought about this evolution, first through their 1974 reforms (which reduced the number of local authorities by two-thirds, making it easy for the government to impose its own control over each that remained), and subsequently through the reforms of the 1980s, which have had the effect of tightening the Government's grip on them.

Specialized Bodies

All Western bureaucracies share a proliferation of *ad hoc* organizations and parallel institutions whose statutes, structures, and modes of action are extremely diverse. The reasons for this state of affairs are simple enough. On the one hand, the distribution of increasingly specialized services has produced a need for better-adapted means of intervention. On the other, given the difficulties of undertaking a radical reform of the cumbersome classic administrative machinery, the tendency has been to set up parallel structures.

Here again, at the risk of over-simplification, it is possible to distinguish three main types of specialized administration: regulatory and monitoring bodies; those responsible for the management of public services; and those engaged in productive activities—although these do not, strictly speaking, constitute true administrations.

Regulatory and monitoring bodies are a new type of autonomous administration which has been most widely developed in the United States (where it is sometimes referred to as the 'headless fourth branch' of the government). It takes the form of what are generally known as Independent Regulatory Commissions.

The relative depoliticization of these regulatory bodies—or, at the very least, their emancipation from government or party control—was attractive to the European States, which had hitherto experimented either with classic modes of State regulation or with the more controversial methods of corporatism. In France, a number of commissions have thus come into being which, although less powerful and less autonomous than their American counterparts, nevertheless adopt a similar approach: the Commission des Opérations de Bourse, the Commission Informatique et des Libertés, the Commission de la Communication des Documents Administratifs, the Haute Autorité de l'Audiovisuel, which later became the Commission Nationale de la Communication et des Libertés, then, in 1989, the Conseil Supérieur de l'Audiovisuel.

In Britain too, commissions with either regulatory or consultative powers play a similar role: the Monopolies and Mergers Commission, the Commission for Racial Equality, the Civil Aviation Authority, etc. Others, conversely, more closely resemble the corporatist model of organizations designed to serve specific interests: the University Funding Committee, the Research Councils, and the Arts Council. In West Germany, the past two decades have been marked by the spread of organizations of this kind, despite the reservations expressed—as in France—by the German juridical establishment in relation to this 'dismemberment' of the State. In particular, the Commission responsible for commercial competition and monopolies (Bundeskartellamt) in principle holds considerable powers in the sphere of commercial mergers.

Fewer examples spring to mind in Italy, but two of them are CONSOB, responsible for monitoring Stock Exchange activities, and the Istituto per la Vigilanza sulle Assicurazioni Private. As can be seen, one of the characteristics of contemporary administrations is the transfer of regulatory tasks to autonomous organizations. This process of fragmentation is a feature every bit as important as the practices of 'deregulation' that tend to attract so much more attention.

Regulatory and monitoring bodies generally carry national or federal status and are few in number. But organizations responsible for the management of services are present at all levels of administration and defy statistical measurement. The most we can do is make a few approximate estimates. For example, there are estimated to be several thousand public organizations of this kind in France, about 40,000 *enti pubblici* in Italy, and about 500 quangos (quasi-autonomous non-governmental organizations) at national level in Britain.

To get some idea of the complexity of the situation, one has only to think of the vast miscellany, in France, of public administrative or industrial and commercial establishments, the mixed-economy companies, the agencies, commissions, and offices, not to mention the thousands of organizations funded with public money and camouflaged by their anodyne appearance as associations set up under the law of 1901.[8] It must be pointed out that this seemingly uncontrollable proliferation is the price that has had to be paid for administrative, budgetary, and financial procedures quite unsuited to the realities of the contemporary world and today's need for efficient management.

The confusion is further compounded by the absence of any logical relation between function and status. For example, in France and Italy, the description 'public establishment of an economic nature' in many cases has very little to do with the said establishment's activities. (It is simply a device to leave it with a free hand.) This gives rise to quarrels of Byzantine complexity, the juridical resolution of which frequently simply leads to further confusion. Why, for instance, should an administrative judge consider the port of Genoa to be an *ente pubblico economico* when the port of Naples is classed as an *ente pubblico non economico*?[9]

Finally, it is worth pointing out that the degree of autonomy possessed by all these agencies, establishments, and quangos varies considerably, ranging from subjection through strict supervision to almost total independence. It depends upon the conditions in which the organization was created, the source of its funding, the type of tasks it is supposed to carry out, and the ability of its managers to shake off supervision from other quarters.

Public Management of Productive Activities

The public economic sector is not a part of the administration in the strict sense of the expression, for the problems, the management methods, and the status of the personnel involved are different from those of the classic type of administration. It would therefore be natural enough to exclude from the administrative domain firms that are nationalized or that are controlled by the national or local public authorities. However, such an exclusion would not necessarily make sense in countries such as Britain which, unlike France and Italy, do not assign all public agents a body of rules and guarantees that confer upon them the status of civil servants. The gap that exists in France between a salaried employee in a nationalized industry and a local or State civil servant does not exist in Britain, where the majority of these employees are bound by contractual rules that resemble those of the private sector. Only the situation of part of the Civil Service bears comparison with the circumstances of the French public sector.[10] Furthermore, the distinction between 'service' and productive activities is becoming increasingly blurred in economic systems that create intermediaries between the two and are characterized by the establishment of increasingly close links between them. However, some productive activities, whether at local or at national level, are organized according to methods that are closer to those of the administration than to those of the private sector, although this is becoming less and less common. For example, the situation of an employee of the EDF or the RATP resembles that of a civil servant more closely than that of his counterparts in the private sector. Finally, the historical aspect is also important. Economic sectors taken over by the State some time ago are much closer to administrations than those nationalized more recently. The postal services and the railways are in many cases tantamount to administrations, despite efforts to render their management more flexible, whereas nationalizations of more recent date have had no more than a limited impact upon the running of the businesses concerned.

Having said this, it is only fair to point out that in this sector the situation varies considerably from one country to another. The public sector is particularly developed in Britain, France, and Italy, but much less so in West Germany. The most developed productive industries in the public sector are to be found in Britain, France, and Italy. As well as military munitions factories, the postal services, and the railways, which were the first sectors to be taken over by the State, they now include radio and television, electricity, banking, the motor industry, coal, steel, air transport, etc. In Italy, furthermore, State shareholdings (either a legacy from Fascism or acquired mainly in the 1960s) involve the State right across the board, including the sector of food supplies. Critics of this rough-and-ready interventionism have frequently made fun of the *panettone dello stato* (the State bread roll) and have emphasized the desirability of limiting State participation to sectors that are truly strategic. Following the waves of insidious or official nationalization (and renationalization in the case of Britain) that have taken place not only in Britain but also in Italy (e.g. the nationalization of Enel in 1962) and France (e.g. the unrecognized nationalization of steel in 1979 and the official nationalization of major industrial and banking companies in 1982), the movement is now on the ebb and privatization is taking over. Massive privatization has taken place in Britain and France, but it is also happening, less spectacularly, in Italy. Here, since the businesses concerned are not nationalized in the strictly juridical sense of the term, it has been possible to sell off State holdings in the IRI, which has been managing them, in a more pragmatic fashion. Romano Rodi, the president of IRI (up to 1989), thus proceeded to offload a number of holdings[11] (the most spectacular being the sale of Alfa-Romeo to Fiat), not without provoking considerable polemics between the Christian Democrats, who supported him, and Craxi's Socialist Party. At present, the trend everywhere is for State disengagement and criticism of 'State-managed economies', probably because administrations have failed to prove that they can do better than the private sector in this area.[12]

THE CIVIL SERVICE

The development of modern bureaucracies has been characterized by a progressive but incomplete abandonment of notions of hereditary posts and practices of clientelism, involving patronage and corruption. Instead, a legal-cum-rational model has been adopted, one of the most important aspects of which is that the recruitment of staff, their training, and their promotion obey specific rules that are generally applied. This way of organizing the bureaucracy was initiated in France at the time of the French Revolution which, while taking over the administrative heritage of the monarchy, modernized it and conferred a new legitimacy upon it. Prussia also undertook a 'revolution from above', following the defeats that it suffered from Napoleon. This was known as the Stein-Hardenberg Reform and it established an administrative system that managed to survive all three of the political disasters of 1918, 1933, and 1945. Britain and Italy were slower to take steps to eliminate corruption, clientelism and political control over the administration. Britain did not introduce reforms until 1855, following the Crimean War (which revealed that the administration had attracted only men 'without ambition, indolent and incompetent') and Northcote and Trevelyan's extremely critical reports urging that the principles still observed today in the Civil Service should be brought into operation. In Italy, it was not until 1908 that Giolitti, under pressure from civil servants, agreed to a 'status' that would put an end to 'the monstrous coupling' of politics and the administration and would provide guarantees (regarding employment and careers) for employees whose southern origins no doubt—in view of the dearth of other employment—explained their anxiety and claims.

Today, the principles that govern the recruitment, training, and careers of civil servants tend to create similar situations in all the Western countries. Recruitment is meritocratic; there are guarantees concerning careers, rights, and duties, and these, substantially or formally, constitute a definite 'status' that is different from the situation of employees in the private sector. Differences nevertheless remain from one system to another, on account of their respective histories and traditions.

There are thus both similarities and differences not only in the manners in which public administrations are organized but also in the relations between the bureaucrats of the various systems and their politicians, particularly those in positions of top responsibility in the State.

Recruitment, Training, and Careers

Before attempting to compare the existing systems in the Western democracies, we must define their respective interpretations of the expression 'public employee'. In France and Italy, it tends to include the entire body of civil servants, whether national or local, and despite differences in status. However, the equivalent expressions in general have a more restricted meaning in the other countries, if only because of the greater degrees of autonomy possessed by peripheral bodies in West Germany, and the distinction that exists between central and local employees in Britain.

The second point to be taken into consideration has to do with the internal differences between one 'public administration' or 'Civil Service' and another. Even in its most limited sense, the concept of a public administration may cover a wide variety of employees: permanent ones, contractual ones, clerks, manual workers, etc. For example, the 300,000 public administration employees of West Germany are divided into three groups: civil servants in the strict sense (*Beamte*), clerks (*Angestellte*), and workers (*Arbeiter*). In Britain too, over one-third of Civil Service employees is made up of 'industrial workers'. In Italy, the 450,000 employees of the *Aziende Autonome* (autonomous public companies) must be included with the 1,500,000 State officials, and so on.

Thirdly, it should be stressed that the particular traditions of each country and the existence or absence of a distinction between Private Law and Public Law result in the establishment of different mechanisms. The countries of mainland Europe offer their civil servants constitutional and statutory guarantees and generally fix the terms of their employment according to the techniques of public law. On the other hand, Britain, the land of common law, resorts in the main to rules and procedures that are close to those used in the private sector (e.g. contracts). But there are other points of similarity: English civil servants nowadays also benefit from guarantees that increasingly resemble those that affect public administrations on the Continent, while the latter are, in turn, adopting practices followed by the English and American administrations. (For example, in Italy, contracts have now been introduced (*contratti del pubblico impiego*) especially for the purpose of determining salaries, and nearly everywhere wages are negotiated with the public authorities.)

In all the Western democracies that we are considering, the recruitment of civil servants is based upon the merit system, in particular upon competitive examinations. However, the significance and procedures of this type of selection vary. In Italy, France, and Germany, the competitive mode of selection tends to favour those with particular kinds of training (particularly legal training). Tests of an abstract and general nature are followed by probationary periods (in West Germany) or by oral tests and interviews designed to evaluate the candidate's personality. But there are many exceptions to this process of selection (as the Constitution in Italy indeed recognizes) and alongside the standard competitions there are many other methods of recruitment that allow the administration considerable discretionary room for manœuvre. (They can organize competitions for particular posts, make temporary appointments, draw up contracts, etc.) In practice, in Italy and in France, at both national and local levels, a large proportion of civil servants gain security of tenure when their contractual posts are confirmed, without ever having entered any real competition. In Britain, more emphasis is laid on tests, exercises, and interviews designed to reveal the candidate's aptitude for his future functions. Needless to say, only those with the required qualifications may present themselves as candidates for these posts.

Systems also differ with regard to the degree of centralization that characterizes the processes of selection. In Italy and West Germany, recruitment is essentially organized by the various Ministries (or other specialized public bodies) on the basis of their own particular needs. In France, on the other hand, since the Second World War, centralization in the recruitment of ministerial personnel has been the rule (although there are many exceptions). In particular, the competitions held by the ENA (École Nationale d'Administration) and the IRA (Regional Institutes of Administration) are major instruments for interministerial recruitment placed under the aegis of the Minister of Public Administration. In Britain, the selection process is also extremely centralized, being placed under the exclusive authority of the Civil Service Commission.

What training do civil servants receive before and, if they are successful, after they take up their duties? In general, there are two main categories of civil servants: those who have received a 'general' training and those who have received a 'specialized' one. Those with a general training, who are responsible for decisions and management, outnumber the rest and assume the most traditional of the administration's tasks. Methods of recruitment (through competitive examinations) are in most countries still marked by a preference for generalists. However, these fall into two groups: the French, Italian, or German type, most of whom have received a legal training; and the English type, whose university degrees are usually in the humanities. For example, in the early 1970s, civil servants who had been trained as lawyers represented 54 per cent of the total in Italy, 67 per cent in Germany, but only 4 per cent in Britain.[13] Sometimes described as an 'administration of amateurs', the British Civil Service has often been criticized for its lack of technical experts and the poor career prospects held out to such people. The Fulton Report (1968) declared, 'The Civil Service is not a place for amateurs. It must be composed of men and women who are true professionals.' Similarly, in Italy, the formalistic and idealistic legal training of Italian civil servants has often been denounced as being—at least in part—the source of the Byzantine complexity and inefficiency of the country's administration.[14] However, the lack of technical expertise of the Italian and English administrations (and, to a slightly lesser extent, West Germany's) needs qualification. In the first place, in Britain and West Germany, most administrative services, in particular those for which a technical training is necessary, are organized at the local level. (In the United Kingdom, for example, the civil servants of the central administration may be called amateurs, but those employed by the local authorities are often described as 'professionals'.) Furthermore, when administrations lack the necessary technical experts, they can either themselves provide the specialized training needed (as often happens in West Germany, for instance) after recruiting their personnel, or else turn to parallel specialized institutions (and this is common practice in most countries). Some countries, like France, allow more room for specialists (chiefly drawing upon the *grandes écoles* such as the Polytechnique, the École des Mines, the École des Ponts, etc.). But this does not necessarily make for a clearer distinction between generalists and specialists. Very often, the functions of management and administration, which are in principle the major domain of generalists, are assumed by technical experts, particularly in France, where the division of territory between graduates from the ENA and those from the Polytechnique give rise to covert but intense struggles for influence.

The French schools responsible for preparing the administrative élite (the ENA, the Polytechnique, etc.) or the intermediate personnel (the IRA) have no counterparts in the other Western countries, which rely essentially upon the universities for the training of their future public administrators. In West Germany, for example, the Speyer School of Administrative Sciences, founded in 1947 in the French zone under the Occupation, was partly inspired by the example of the French École nationale d'administration, but its functions and methods are very different.[15] It is much more like a centre for the continuing training or perfecting of the skills of civil servants already in office than an instrument for selecting, training, and classifying candidates, in the manner of the ENA. The Scuola superiore dell'ammistrazione pubblica in Italy plays a similar role to that of Speyer's Hochschule, but has never acquired a reputation sufficiently prestigious for it to be considered the equivalent of one of the French *grandes écoles*. The Civil Service College created in Britain in 1970 on the recommendation of the Fulton Committee is also a centre providing continuing and intermittent training for civil servants. It offers courses of 4, 12, and 28 weeks, designed for civil servants from the upper echelons when they first enter the Service and during the third and the fifth years of their appointments.

Unlike in the private sector—in theory, at least—the careers of civil servants follow a relatively smooth and predictable evolution. Practically speaking, three main questions arise: how are civil servants' careers organized? How much vertical and horizontal mobility can they expect? What rights and guarantees do they enjoy?

1. The answer to the first of these questions is that in general there exists a (variable) balance between promotion on the grounds of merit and promotion on the grounds of seniority. Nearly all countries provide a body of statutory or conventional rules guaranteeing promotion in line with seniority. That is certainly true of mainland Europe, where the matter is strictly codified and institutionalized (by commissions to establish parity, and superior councils in France; committees on federal personnel in West Germany; hierarchical and jurisdictional controls, etc.). But it also applies to countries such as the United States, which is often unfairly represented as being a province of discretionary, or even arbitrary power. To regard it as such, however, is to forget that, as a reaction to such abuses as do occur, the principle of seniority is defended with particular vigour and tenacity. It should also be pointed out that, even when merit does override seniority,

strict procedures have to be followed: internal competitions (in France and Italy), or promotions made on the basis of profiles made by the hierarchy. But these strict regulations are applied mainly at the lower or middle levels of the bureaucracy (except in Italy, where the principle of seniority tends to be strictly observed right up to the top of the ladder).

For top civil servants, the principle of promotion on the grounds of merit applies more generally. That is certainly the case in Britain, where the 'high-flyers', mostly products of Oxford or Cambridge, enjoy a series of rapid promotions right at the beginning of their careers. Later, however, promotion comes more slowly, and political preferences are excluded, so that most of the top civil servants employed as heads of departments are relatively mature (generally about 50 years old). In West Germany, the situation is quite similar, except that the possibility of promotions or sackings for political reasons sometimes upsets the bureaucratic pecking order.

2. The problem of vertical and horizontal mobility is partly connected with the question of merit. Incentives for mobility are clearly less strong the more the system is based upon seniority. A comparison between the various countries underlines the lack of mobility, either horizontal or vertical, that exists in most administrative systems. In France (and, since 1980, in principle also in Italy), vertical mobility is ensured through internal competitions. The procedure presents the advantage of an incorporated quota system (civil servants who already hold appointments are sure of obtaining a number of the new promotions). Its drawback, though, is its inflexibility, not to mention the fact that it is sometimes deflected from its object of social promotion (as in the internal competitions of the ENA). In Britain, following the criticisms of the Fulton Committee, a single-tiered structure was introduced (to replace the tripartite division into administrative, executive, and clerical classes). Its purpose was to make it possible for any competent civil servant, regardless of his or her initial grade, to get to the top. By authorizing 'leap-frogging' in the case of the most able, this was supposed to introduce a considerable element of democratization. However, the scheme would appear to have been less successful in this respect than its promoters had hoped.

The opportunities for horizontal mobility are hardly any better. A study carried out in Britain revealed that, in 1971, 72 per cent of the upper administration had spent their entire careers working in the same department. The situation is much the same in West Germany and even worse in Italy. In France, the career of a top civil servant will as a rule unfold in the same Ministry, but here there are two qualifications to be made. In the first place, all administrators are expected to move around somewhat (although their mobility is in some cases more apparent than real, as they move no further than some institution attached to their original Ministry). Secondly, the most brilliant careers are invariably marked by considerable mobility inside—and sometimes outside—the administration. In some countries (France being the main exception), this relative immobility of public officials is offset by some movement between the national and the local administrations. In West Germany, this type of exchange is quite common between all levels (local, *Land*, federation), but it is rare in France (despite a few exceptions, particularly since 1981, and a number of new measures introduced to facilitate mobility between the national and the regional public sectors), and exceptional in Britain and in Italy (despite transfers of staff to the Italian regions following the 1970 reforms). As for mobility between the administrative, political, economic, and other sectors, this is strongest in France (as a result of the interpenetration of élites and the role played by the State *grandes écoles*), rarer in West Germany, and almost non-existent in Italy and Britain (the rare exceptions here being mainly the Treasury civil servants, known as the 'Treasury knights' (see below).

3. The rights and duties of civil servants are sometimes solemnly established in Constitutions and general laws (Italy, 1957; France, 1958–9; West Germany, 1965), sometimes in isolated written texts, and sometimes through 'conventions' that are more important than the few written rules on the subject. In practice, the anomalies that appear between one system and another are real, but are probably less important than they may seem at first glance. The disorder and multiplicity of regulations in France and Italy lead to just as much confusion as the apparent complexity of the German federal system.

(*a*) The principal rights of civil servants fall into several categories. First there are those related to remuneration and tenure. The first point to note is that everywhere, even in the most 'legal and regulated' situations, contracts play a part of some importance, varying in degree from one case to another. Salaries and conditions of work are sometimes subject to contract in France, Italy (where collective contracts are negotiated every three years),[16] and Germany, but especially in

Britain. Guarantees of employment vary in strength according to whether or not the relations between the administration and its employees are determined by contract but the mechanisms of dismissal or demotion are seldom used. The situation of employees is, in principle, less securely guaranteed when it is a contractual one, but in practice guarantees of employment are considered an important factor.

Rights affecting trade union and political affiliations depend upon the dominant ethic and specific concept of public service in each country. The right to form trade unions has by now been won in every country, and as a result many more civil servants now belong to trade unions, even in countries where membership used traditionally to be low. Today, one-third of civil servants are trade union members in France, 45 per cent in West Germany, and between 50 and 60 per cent in Britain and Italy. But everywhere certain limits to trade unionization are imposed, in relation either to particular categories (the police, the army, the secret services) or to the modes of collective action.

Particularly affected is the right to strike—traditionally the most effective weapon available to trade unions. The right to strike of German civil servants is not recognized, and everywhere it is denied to categories responsible for maintaining the security of the State (the army, the police). However, even where this is the case, public employees are frequently organized into associations that constitute powerful 'lobbies' and that may, furthermore, resort to forms of action (such as the protests of the Paris police and the appeals made by telephone to the Ministry of Defence in Rome by the military, etc.) which make the same kind of impact as a stoppage of work (e.g. the go-slow strikes of customs officials or air traffic controllers). Finally, the right to strike is subject to a range of 'conventions' and limitations: advance notice is obligatory in France; wild-cat strikes are banned in Italy (by the law of 29 March 1983); and in Britain there is a tradition of no striking in the essential State services. Here, the right to strike is linked with the right to form trade unions and does not constitute an infringement of contract provided the legal obligations have been observed (the Trade Union Act of 1984).[17]

Political rights are guaranteed most generously in West Germany, France, and Italy with regard both to embracing an ideology or joining a party, and to the possibility of standing as candidate in an election. The regulations at present in force are so generous in France that some observers, such as Ezra Suleiman, consider them positively to encourage members of the administration to take part in politics, and the same applies to West Germany. Moreover, French and German civil servants have certainly made the most of the situation, making a point of 'colonizing' the political parties and Parliament. In Britain, on the other hand, civil servants are subject to severe restrictions. About 200,000 central civil servants are forbidden to take part in party activities and national politics and may only become engaged in local politics if they obtain special ministerial authorization. The choice before them seems simple enough: either resign from public service or give up political activism. However, as we shall see, the situation is in reality more complex in the case of members of the upper echelons of the administration.

(*b*) The duties of civil servants. Set against the rights that are granted them within the limitations noted above are a number of duties that civil servants are bound to accept. Some are fundamental, others of a more formal nature. Let us confine ourselves to two examples: the obligation to serve the State with loyalty, and the obligation of discretion.

The obligation to serve the State with loyalty may be understood in a more or less sweeping fashion. All countries declare that civil servants are employed in the service of the State, the nation (e.g. Article 98 of the Italian Constitution and the law of 1965 in West Germany), or the Crown, not that of any political party that happens to be in power. But the implications of such declarations may vary. In France, the Constitution states bluntly that 'the administration is at the disposal of the Government'. Yet the Fifth Republic was the first regime not to embark upon a purge when it was set up.[18] But in a less obvious way, the administration can always limit the right to compete for employment of those whose opinions (and the ways in which they are given expression) are considered too extreme. Nevertheless, the Council of State (in the Barel decision, 1954) introduced limitations to those possibilities, a step that made the French system more liberal, since it ruled out insistence upon ideological conformism. The situation is much the same in Italy and Britain, even if their methods are different. In contrast, West Germany insists upon total loyalty to the established institutions. In the name of the obligatory loyalty of civil servants towards the federal Constitution, certain candidates for employment in the public sector and certain types of civil servant were banned from the administration from the start, at the moment when the Federal Republic was being set up, but no more drastically than in other States. The problem became more pressing when the extreme left decided that the moment had come for their 'long march through the institutions', that is to say their subversion. To cope with this, the Ministers of the Interior of both the Bund and the *Länder* agreed upon certain methods of inquiry and for the elimination of these subversive elements. They were announced in a document entitled 'Discussion on Radicals' (*Radikalenerlass*) but better known as the 'professional bans' (*Berufsverbot*). Although relatively few bans were passed—a few hundred—it provoked considerable political and legal debate. (The Federal Constitutional Court twice pronounced on the matter, in 1975 and 1977, favouring acceptance of the ban.) The matter assumed the proportions of a veritable national problem (or even an international one, given the involvement of the extreme left, mainly in France and Italy).

In Britain, political activities may be denied to certain civil servants, but at least they are in principle allowed to belong freely to a political party. Up until 1985, nevertheless, 'the Government, supervised by a three-man commission, could dismiss from any employment considered vital to State security, any civil servant who was a member of or sympathized with either the Communist Party of Great Britain or a Nazi party'.[19] But in 1985, Margaret Thatcher extended these rules to cover all public service employees (not simply members of the Civil Service) and set about applying them to 'subversive groups' (defined as such by the government itself).

A second duty that affects civil servants relates to the expression of their opinions not only on political matters but also on the running of the service or the administration. It involves the duty of being discreet and of maintaining confidentiality and secrecy (see the Official Secrets Act, 1989). This last constraint is imposed very strictly in Britain[20] the major effect of this seemingly being to multiply leaks and scandals in the Press. In other countries, it is imposed more flexibly.[21] Generally speaking, it is fair to say that, in countries where parliamentary commissions have an active role to play (Italy, Germany, and Britain), combining secrecy with the obligation to divulge any information that members of parliament require is becoming an increasingly acrobatic feat.

Senior Civil Servants and Politics

The embarrassed relations—even clashes—that arise between administrations and politicians in the liberal democracies testify to the difficulty of reconciling the contradictory principles upon which they are founded and harmonizing the dogmas of the past with the realities of today. Let us briefly recall a few major points. All the liberal democracies place politics first: the principle of the majority will, and respect for the opposition, expressed in free and competitive elections. In other words, the administration is the servant of the political authorities inasmuch as the latter represent the will of the people. But, over and above this, the administration must respect another principle of liberal democracy, namely, that all citizens should receive equal treatment and hence that the administration must be impartial.[22] This is where the first contradiction surfaces, between the principles of representative government (according to which a majority implements its programme using an administration which, whatever its status, is *obliged* to accept the Government's policies and decisions) and the principles of the liberal charters defined by the American and French Revolutions (including that of equality, which implies the rejection of partisan treatment). The obvious solutions to this clash of principles are essentially determined by the particular historical contingencies and politico-social structures of individual countries. Each system to some extent clings to its own national concepts of neutrality, politicization, loyalty, etc. But the particular features of individual systems also tend to be muted as a result of pressures from phenomena that are common to all States, in particular the 'administrative explosion' that has affected not only the Western States but also those of the Third World and the Socialist countries.

Similarly, one way to escape from the impasse created by arguing about the respective merits of these democratic principles or the bureaucratic evolution of different systems is to undertake a sociological analysis of the élites concerned and the positions that they hold.[23] For although the problem of relations between administrations and politicians may be a general one, and although the question of the politicization of local administrations appears particularly important in certain countries (particularly where the level of local or regional autonomy is high), the essential problem concerns the highest echelons of the State, where decisions, whether political or administrative, are taken.[24] A study of administrative élites, the methods of their recruitment, and the extent to which they circulate between the public and private sectors may make it possible, if not to discover the key to the problem, at least to gain a better understanding of the relationship between the administration and the political sector, and to seize upon the disparities between principles loudly proclaimed (neutrality, independence, etc.) and the realities of the situation. The relations between the political and the administrative spheres may thus be better revealed by studying the ability of each élite group to influence and penetrate the other than by any amount of abstract or formal analysis of the rules by which their relations are officially codified. In this way, we may be more successful in locating the various models of relations that apply in some of our liberal democracies on a spectrum that ranges from independence to subordination.

The authorities in more or less every liberal democracy have been attracted by a policy of separation between the political and the administrative spheres, as if contamination between the two would be bound to produce negative effects. To call a civil servant 'politicized' or describe him as a 'politician' is seldom considered a compliment. Similarly, although perhaps to a lesser degree, the bureaucratic nature of certain political functions tends to give rise to unflattering or even critical comments ('the permanent staff' or the 'professionals' of the political sphere). Yet the temptation to seal these two worlds off from one another completely must be interpreted in different ways in different countries, in the light of the process adopted by each one in constituting itself as a State and of its subsequent democratic development.

In some cases, as in Britain, the democratic process antedates the creation of an administration. By the beginning of the nineteenth century, Britain already manifested most of the features of a liberal democracy. On the other hand, its administration was no more than embryonic and did not really exist as such until 1854: not until the Northcote–Trevelyan Commission produced its report in that year were the principles adopted that still underpin the British Civil Service. For civil servants, promotion and access to high public office is a matter of time and selection by their senior colleagues. There is no ENA to set the seal of approval upon young people freshly turned out by some *grande école*, no classificatory grades that bestow a particular status to last until retirement. High flyers, two-thirds of whom are products of Oxford and Cambridge, have to go through the hoops. Recruited as 'administrative trainees', talented young civil servants in their thirties become 'Private Secretaries' to some Minister, in which capacity they act more or less as the head of an office, with the proviso that they never involve themselves in political or party business, this being the preserve of a 'Parliamentary Secretary' (a Member of Parliament close to the Minister). The next step could be to become an Assistant Secretary, then at long last possibly a Permanent Secretary. A British senior civil servant thus depends for his promotion upon the judgement of his superiors, that is to say, the 'Senior Appointment Selection Committee', chaired by the Head of the Civil Service. In practical terms, what this means is that a civil servant needs to get himself noticed by his superiors for his qualities as an administrator (which implies considerable moving about from one post to another within the various Whitehall departments), and that he is unlikely to reach the top of the administrative hierarchy until he is relatively old.[25] Until quite recently (more or less until Margaret Thatcher came to power), it would have been unbecoming and counter-productive for a civil servant to attempt to exploit his working relationship with a Minister in an effort to obtain more rapid promotion. As Richard Rose writes: 'Civil servants have a long-term stake in their career, and any attempt to use party political contacts for short-term advantages would jeopardize their long-term prospects.'[26] However, over the past few years, the Civil Service's self-management and the convention of independence from the political authorities have suffered interference from Margaret Thatcher and some of her Ministers, and this has provoked such protest and polemics that some observers today even speak of the end of the apolitical Civil Service.

The rule of the mutual isolation of the political and the administrative spheres, despite the necessary close and continuous collaboration between the two, clearly imposes a certain strain upon civil servants. For the convention of neutrality to be credible, British civil servants must, like Caesar's wife, be above suspicion. Hence the restrictions which limit their party, political, and trade union involvement, the absence of any policy of secondment for political reasons so far as they are concerned, the obligation to resign if they wish even to stand as a candidate for parliamentary election, the requirement to seek permission to accept a sinecure even after their retirement, and so on.[27]

The upshot is that there are *no* civil servants in the House of Commons, and no more than a negligible percentage of ex-civil servants. But the recent upheavals produced by the policies of the Conservative Government suggest that the balance established since the mid-nineteenth century is a fragile one, dependent to a large extent upon a political consensus and a measure of give-and-take and moderation in the political struggle.

As soon as these are undermined and that balance is impaired, the 'apolitical' nature of the Civil Service is affected. What this reveals, furthermore, is the true nature of the neutrality of the Civil Service. It is not so much a matter of a median position that would make it possible for efficient and skilful civil servants to steer a successful course between the reefs to the right and the left. Rather, what is at stake is what the French would call *loyalisme*, that is, a double commitment: to serve the State unswervingly, regardless of one's own party or political views; and to treat all those under one's administration with total impartiality. To expect the success of such a balancing act may seem unrealistic. It was only possible to maintain in Britain by reason of the long-standing dominant political consensus, the modest dimensions of the central administration (500,000 civil servants in all), and the minimal cross-fertilization that takes place between the Civil Service itself and the nationalized industries (where party favouritism is more likely to occur).

In Italy, the mutual isolation of civil servants and the political sphere is part of a radically different historical, political, and social context. In Britain, the separation between the political and the administrative spheres is essentially a matter expressed through rules and conventions, all of which by no means prevent the administration from playing an essential determining role in the elaboration of policies and the taking of decisions. In Italy, in contrast, the isolation of the senior civil servants is a sign of their limited ability to affect the process of decision-making and their desire to protect themselves from involvement in political and party matters.

The Italian administration that was established after the unification of the country was based on the Piedmontese model, itself a reflection of the Napoleonic system.[28] The first senior civil servants (prefects and ambassadors) were men from the north, mostly drawn from the Piedmontese bourgeoisie and aristocracy. But little by little, this political administration of a quasi-colonial nature was superseded by a meritocratic administration, recruited increasingly from south of Rome. The Liberals and the Marxists thought alike on this score: the unification of Italy must be bought at the price of integrating the intellectual *petite bourgeoisie* of the south since, for them, the sole opportunity for a career lay in administration. Today, the public sector is still 'colonized' by southerners and bears the imprint of their particular brand of education: idealist, formalistic, and juridical. As Sabino Cassese emphasizes, the preponderance of southerners (roughly two-thirds of all officials) is not just a territorial phenomenon, and would not be a serious problem if it were. It is also a cultural matter in which the 'productive' north is set in opposition to the 'unproductive bureaucracy' of the south.[29] The cultural characteristics of the south are also reflected in the pervading nepotism at work in the allocation of administrative jobs. Political string-pulling is certainly not avoided in the business of securing posts in the public sector (particularly at the lower levels, where there is more room for manœuvre for operations of political clientage); but, as careers advance, it is totally rejected, judged inopportune, and prevented by many laws and regulations. An Italian civil servant seeks to obtain maximum legal and statutory guarantees that will enable him to pursue his career safely out of the way of interference from the political parties and the politicians. In other words, he counts upon the principle of promotion by seniority.

The situation is the same even at the level of high public office. It is here that the flow of recruitment and promotion is controlled, in an extremely corporatist fashion. The upper echelons of the public sector (*la dirigenza*), which comes under pressure from sectorial associations and trade unions, is constantly expanding (about 8,000 individuals at present) and civil servants in posts of authority tend to be elderly. Sabino Cassese shows that in 1979 only 10 per cent of these 'directors' fell within the 35 to 50 age group; 33 per cent were between 51 and 55 years of age; 29 per cent between 56 and 60; and 28 per cent between 61 and 65—and these figures were virtually the same in 1960.[30] Despite reforms introduced in 1980 but whose impact remains limited, the Italian system is characterized by a *corporatist* type of isolation. The separation between the political and the administrative spheres is not prompted by the same objectives (neutrality) and necessities (give-and-take) as the British Civil Service. It is not the product of any theory, nor founded upon any system of values. Its only excuses are historical (the Piedmontese domination, Fascism) and pragmatic (the prevailing 'partitocracy'). Nor is the separation between the senior public administration and the political sphere one-way. Senior civil servants certainly resist interference from the political sphere, but at the same time they themselves seldom venture into parliamentary or ministerial arenas. Italian civil servants enjoy statutory advantages that are essentially identical to those of their

French counterparts with regard to freedom to take part in trade union and political activities (in other words, conditions that are extremely favourable). Yet the number of employees from the public sector (not counting teachers) elected to Parliament has never exceeded 5 per cent and, in the entire history of the Republic of Italy, no more than three or four senior civil servants have ever become Ministers. The consequence of this inward-looking attitude (also manifested in other ways which we cannot dwell upon now) is that Italian senior civil servants find themselves relatively marginalized. Instead of producing ideas, they simply execute them; instead of making decisions, they adopt a preventative, blocking role: as a result, it is hard to consider senior officials of the Italian public sector as belonging to the country's élite. However, perhaps this picture of mutual distrust calls for some modification, for one way or another the political and the administrative spheres must coexist, if not co-operate.

This situation of distrustful alienation would hardly be viable were it not for a whole collection of palliatives designed to overcome the difficulties. In the first place, the Council of State and the Audit Office play the role of an intermediary in establishing communications between the bureaucracy, in the strict sense of the term, and the political system. These two jurisdictional institutions, particularly the former, provide a reservoir of advisers for Ministers anxious to gather competent men around them. Roughly one-third of the members of ministerial offices come from the Council of State alone, equalling the number of civil servants drawn from the Ministries for which those offices are set up. Because the former group consists of able men who are willing to play an active role on the edge of the political arena, obtaining the position of director of a ministerial *cabinet* may, according to Storchi,[31] lead to a 'veritable career', for some remain in their posts for as long as ten or fifteen years, following the fortunes of 'their' Ministers as these move from sector to sector. But the Council of State and the Audit Office may also be used for quite the opposite purpose, as fields where individuals whose careers are on the wane, rather than on the rise, may tactfully be put out to grass. They constitute ideal dumping grounds for staff directors whom Ministers wish to be rid of. Cassese reckons that about 10 per cent of the members of these two jurisdictional institutions are former office directors who have been pensioned off in this way. The situation of the two institutions is thus comparable to that of their French counterparts, except that the latter tend to be used more to reward old friends than to get rid of undesirables.

Another way of improving the situation is to turn to the semi-public sector or the universities in order to get round the administration's unwillingness to become involved with politics. The Italian administration, with all its inefficiency and its obstructions, thus finds itself left on the touch-line when it comes to filling the most dynamic posts in the *enti pubblici* and also appointing staff for them, for preference goes to men from the rest of the public or semi-public sectors. University teachers, for their part, display none of the reticence of administrators. There are few jurists, political experts, or historians of any stature who have not ventured out into the sea of Italian politics in one way or another. In general, the political roles played by Italian university teachers are probably unparalleled elsewhere in the Western world. They become councillors, *éminences grises*, local representatives, Deputies, members of all kinds of commissions, editors of newspapers associated with the various political parties, and so on. Their presence in the political sphere is further encouraged by the general consensus and tolerance of Italian society: it has room for all sorts, whether from the left or the right, and all can claim the rewards that are handed out in the political world (prestige, publicity, and means of both an institutional and a personal nature).

In conclusion, some comment is perhaps called for upon the apparent paradox of the isolation of the country's administration, given that Italy is always presented as an example of clientship and patronage, the country of *lottizazione*. In truth, the beneficiaries of the political sinecures handed out are not civil servants (apart from some exceptional cases, in particular at regional level). The allocation of 'jobs for the boys' is a minor phenomenon, which above all concerns office directors in the Treasury. Others affected by it tend to be administrators of the public or semi-public sector, but they are not civil servants in the strict sense of the term. *Lottizazione* and patronage chiefly benefit what could be called the party or trade union bureaucracies. Nor is it any exaggeration to speak of bureaucracies in this connection: after all, the parties and trade unions employ several thousand individuals, mostly paid out of public funds either directly, through wages or grants provided for by the law, or indirectly, through the distribution of salaries also drawn from public funds. Political life and the public sector are thus funded by a huge, systematic hand-out, distributed proportionally. Up until the 1970s, the Christian Democrats were both the arch-devisers and the major beneficiaries of this policy of distributed funding. Since then, the secular parties have obtained their slice of the cake, and even the Communist Party gets a share. Needless to say, the allocation of funds engenders furious battles. The administration of every bank and savings bank is the object of constant haggling, and for three years the board of the RAI failed to get itself renewed. In Italy, this is the level at which an osmosis takes place between the bureaucracy and the political sphere.

In the two cases of Britain and Italy, the separation of the administration from politics clearly has different causes and radically different effects. In a two-party system, the British administration has managed to avoid the dangers of purges carried out by each succeeding government by proclaiming its neutrality at the same time as retaining effective and virtually exclusive control over policy-making. Senior civil servants do not venture into the sphere of party politics but they do remain the indispensable shapers of policies. In contrast, the Italian upper administration has put itself beyond the reach of dreaded political interference but at the cost of being relegated to the sidelines. The most it can do is be obstructive—and it takes every opportunity to do so—and meanwhile manage its own 'financial interests', in other words preserve its methods of recruitment, its status, and its careers.

At the other end of the spectrum, political and bureaucratic élites belong more or less to the same world. There is more than one way of interpreting confusion between the political and the administrative sectors. At first sight, such an osmosis would seem to be characteristic of totalitarian States. The monarch's religion is forced upon his subjects, the administration must identify with the values, creed, and strategies of the politicians in power.

That is exactly what the embryonic administrations of the late eighteenth century were conceived to be: simply an extension, an arm of the executive. But such a monolithic system could only survive over a long period of time within a dictatorial framework, and its natural corollary, in the event of political changes, would be a purge. That is why no liberal democracies have political administrations, as certain underdeveloped or socialist countries do, however strong the temptations to establish them may have been at some point or other in their histories.

Germany, Italy, Spain, and Greece—to name but a few—are all countries in which, during the twentieth century, attempts have been made to politicize the administration within the framework of a Fascist dictatorship. France, for its part, had already experienced purges first with the bloody episode of the Convention, and later, after each revolution or change in the regime, from the army. Few bureaucracies have undergone so many serious upheavals in the last two centuries—a fact that testifies both to the political sector's distrust of civil servants and also to the ease with which it has been able to penetrate the French administration.

But there is another way of regarding an osmosis between the political and the administrative sectors, and this emphasizes the democratic virtues of such a process. This point of view rests upon a belief that an administration is dependent not only upon the Government and the country's elected representatives, but also upon those under its administration. What better way of ensuring this kind of dependence than the election of administrators? This notion was embraced by the first French Constitution of 1791, which instituted the election of civil servants, and it still applies widely in America at the level of individual states and localities. In France, election as a mode of recruiting civil servants has completely disappeared, but a few traces of this concept of administrative democracy are still detectable both within the administration itself (with all its committees to monitor parity and so on) and in sectors that have not been completely taken over by the traditional administration (social security, professional sectors under 'shared management', etc.).

Here the 'politicization' of the administration and its elected employees is particularly ambiguous. It is neither monolithic nor uniform. The degree of politicization achieved is bound to depend largely upon the links that candidates for administrative posts and those who are elected maintain with the political parties. Such tends to be the situation in particular in systems known, sometimes disparagingly, as 'consociational',[32] that is, countries in which civil peace and political equilibrium result from a meticulous sharing-out of responsibilities in all sectors—economic, cultural, political, administrative, etc. Consensualism in these cases is in reality usually the product of the pacification of many antagonisms. The Netherlands, Israel, Belgium, and Austria have all been or still are prototypes of States in which political and social equilibrium was or is maintained by dint of a judicious and complex system of allocating spoils. In Belgium, for example, where an artificial unity was for a long time guaranteed and maintained by an élite, part Walloon, part Flemish, but totally francophone, the system exploded, revealing all the territorial, linguistic, political, and trade union-based cleavages that have now become familiar.[33] In Austria, a *proporz* system based on an agreement between the Socialist Party and the People's Party quite literally divides up all political and administrative posts between the two main political groups.[34]

To judge from these experiences, it would seem that total separation between the political and the administrative sectors may come about in two different sets of circumstances. Either it is part of a national situation of such a specific nature that it is impossible to 'export' unless many precautions are taken; otherwise it becomes a source of serious malfunction (as in Italy). The opposite solution, involving osmosis between the political and the administrative spheres, usually leads to one of two impasses: totalitarianism in its blackest guise, or a dismantling of the State in which parties, factions, and interest groups all gain in power. The only remaining possibility is to steer a difficult middle course, attempting to come to terms with the situation by recognizing the ineluctable nature of the links between the two spheres and trying to adapt accordingly. That is the course for which West Germany and France, each in its own way, have opted.

The merit of the West Germany system is that it tackles the problem of the politicization of the administration by containing it within quite strict limits. Positioned between the political sector and the topmost echelons of the administration are a number of senior civil servants generally known as *politische beamte* (political civil servants). These high-ranking civil servants, who act as the Secretaries-General of Ministries or as directors of ministerial offices, emerge from the ranks of the administration but are selected (and dismissed) on the basis of political criteria. The political aspect of their status stems essentially from the procedure through which they may be appointed and dismissed at the discretion of the government in power. If dismissed, the senior civil servant concerned receives a 'pension',[35] the size of which depends upon his rank and seniority.

In a system that produces many coalitions, this procedure makes it possible to guarantee that the Ministers will be aided in their tasks by reliable civil servants,[36] while the latter, for their part, benefit from statutory and financial guarantees that are by no means negligible. In many respects, and with only a few variations, the position of senior civil servants in Germany resembles that of those in France. Despite the fact that in both countries the administration is claimed to be at the service of the public rather than of any political party, the neutrality of civil servants, particularly in the upper echelons of the administration, is not always as complete as bureaucratic discourse would suggest.[37] The impingement of politics is manifest in the first place in the requirement that civil servants should support the values of the federal constitutional order. It is thought that, in the course of the 1970s, about 1,000 civil servants or candidates for appointments in the public sector were fired or rejected, while as many as 700,000 employees had their personal files scrutinized by the Office for the Protection of the Constitution.

But connections between the political sector and the administration are also evident from the influence that the political parties in power bring to bear upon the appointment and careers of senior civil servants. In Germany, as in France from 1958 to 1981, the politicization of the upper echelons of the public sector until 1969 attracted less attention as a result of the domination of the CDU–CSU. When the Social Democrats came to power (with the FDP) in 1969, they managed to ease out a number of senior civil servants whom they regarded as hostile or lukewarm. In October and November 1969, 11 *Staatsekretäre* and 8 directors of ministerial offices were replaced, as were 70 other senior civil servants whose sympathies lay in the other direction. Between that date and 1982, many more changes have taken place, provoking considerable criticism from the Christian Democrats (not that this prevented them from acting in a similar way as soon as they returned to power).

Notwithstanding the precarious nature of these top posts in the public sector, civil servants have not been discouraged from aiming for these levels that are subject to the Government's discretionary powers. On the contrary: many of them have even become actively engaged in politics either in the parties or in Parliament itself. Kenneth Dyson[38] estimates that 41.9 per cent of the members of the Bundestag have emerged from the public sector (about half of them being teachers) and in some of the *Land* Assemblies that proportion exceeds 50 per cent. He also records that in 1978 civil servants accounted for 12.3 per cent of the members of the CDU, and in 1977 for 13.2 per cent of the CSU, 10 per cent of the SPD, and 14 per cent of the FDP.[39] This close coincidence between politicians and civil servants[40] is encouraged by a whole collection of protective rules that are mostly to the advantage of the civil servants: for five years they can make themselves politically available and still draw 75 per cent of their salary; they can be reintegrated into the civil service without difficulty, or move freely between the two spheres; up until 1975, they could be paid as a member of the Bundestag as well as drawing 60 per cent of their civil servant's salary or pension, etc. In short, Ezra Suleiman's[41] appraisal of the situation in France might be equally well applied to the German system: the statutory and financial advantages enjoyed by the public sector in effect subsidize the political system, to the advantage of one particular social group and the parties to which its members belong. The only major difference is that, unlike France, West Germany has set up a more strictly codified basis for the relations between the administration and the political sphere and has officially ratified the political status of the civil servants at the top of the State hierarchy.

It is certainly in France that osmosis between the political and the administrative spheres is the greatest, not only because senior civil servants there play a political role, but especially because the civil service is the breeding ground for a large proportion of political personnel. However, the movement of élites between the political and the administrative worlds is but one aspect of a more general phenomenon, namely, the interconnections between the élites that move in and control all sectors: both the public and the private sectors of industry, banks, and insurance companies, cultural activities and international posts, Parliament and the government. Setting the situation in its historical context may help to illuminate the crucial role played by the upper administration and its politicization. The importance of the French upper administration stems from the way in which the élites over whom the State established a virtual monopoly have always been educated and selected. Already under the *ancien régime*, the 'cream' was selected in specialist schools that catered for the needs of the State. The system was further organized and systematized by Napoleon Bonaparte: the École normale supérieure, the Polytechnique, the École des mines, and the École des ponts et chaussées have channelled the most brilliant individuals of each generation into the administration. In 1946, the École nationale d'administration was created, vitually all its students being drawn from the Institut d'études politiques in Paris and the former private École des sciences politiques (nationalized in 1945). This brought individuals with a general education in the humanities into the same State-dominated orbit as other specialists and technical experts produced by the *grandes écoles*. The long-standing supremacy of these State schools would not have been so unassailable if their former students had been confined solely to the administration. In reality, being one of the 'happy few' and part of a 'super élite' made one eligible for major posts of responsibility in both the private and the public sectors. The most significant development in recent times is that of the Polytechnique. It was originally set up for the training of military officers, but nowadays this is no more than a marginal function. The 'Polytechnique Mafia', to borrow the title of a book written by one of its former students, now controls many important posts both in the Ministries and in industry.

The other key factor in the politicization of senior civil servants was the creation in 1815 of ministerial *cabinets*. These streamlined structures designed to provide Ministers with advice and assistance were the brain-child of monarchists under the Restoration, who distrusted the Napoleonic administration, which was still in place. The government wanted to be able to turn to reliable, committed advisers, not civil servants who owed their eminence to their loyalty to the fallen Emperor. These small groups of about a dozen individuals, appointed at the discretion of each Minister, were originally composed of dependable civil servants temporarily seconded from their departments in the administration, together with men drawn from outside the administration. Gradually however, they came to be recruited solely from the administration, for civil servants, with their inside knowledge of the workings of the administration, turned out to be more useful than individuals brought in from outside and, besides, they determined to corner for themselves the advantages that accrued from service in these offices. After two or three years of 'worthy and loyal service', these civil servants were indeed—and still are—generally well rewarded: they would either be promoted within the administration, appointed to some prestigious position in the semi-public sector, or else acquire some sinecure in the private sector, unless, that is, they developed a taste for politics and decided to stand for Parliament themselves. Political swings and roundabouts and changes of government render posts in these offices unstable and precarious, but the most prestigious groups in the administration have more or less colonized them. In other words, the *esprit de corps* working to the advantage of each administrative group involved (Polytechnique men, those from the Council of State (Conseil d'État) or the Audit Office (Cour des Comptes), and so on) compensates for the effects of politicization. Civil servants may be divided by their personal political or party loyalties, but they close ranks when it comes to defending the privileges, posts, and strongholds that each of these bodies has managed to make its own.

But it is under the Fifth Republic that the politicization of senior civil servants has reached its peak. General de Gaulle's overt hostility towards politicians as a whole was expressed in particular by his appointment of a whole host of senior civil servants to posts of major importance, starting with some in the government itself. Between 1959 and 1981, on average 41 per cent of French Ministers were drawn from the upper echelons of the Civil Service[42] and about 30 per cent were appointed to the government without being elected Deputies. A similar preponderance of civil servants is noticeable in Parliament. Between 1958 and 1978, 31 per cent of all Deputies came from the bureaucracy, and in 1981 that percentage rose to 53.1 per cent (but in this instance chiefly professors). All the political parties (apart from the Communist Party and the National Front) were affected by this rise of the civil servants: whether governments are left-wing or right-wing, they are all dominated by the technocrats from the *grandes écoles*.[43] The system is fuelled and perpetuated by the considerable facilities that the Civil Service makes available to its employees to enable them to take part in politics, the prestige and influence that accrue from being part of an extremely interventionist State and, finally, the considerable career advantages that stem from political collaboration with government Ministers. The phenomenon became even more noticeable, seemingly almost caricatured, when the Socialists came to power in 1981, to be followed by the right in 1986. Many were replaced, and the criterion for such decisions tended to be party affiliation rather than professional ability. As a result, too many staff purges took place, non-political civil servants began to feel a certain discouragement, and increasingly severe criticisms were voiced about the political sector's grip over the administration, a grip that was making itself felt ever lower down in the hierarchy (and in local administration, too). The spoils system *à la française* may not have disappeared entirely since the left's return to power in June 1988, but it has certainly been considerably toned down.

This rapid survey shows that, while nobody disputes the ability of civil servants to initiate and implement public policies, because of an unreal notion of their neutrality, they are often criticized for becoming involved in party politics. But in truth the terms of the argument are somewhat obscured, since the accusation of 'politicization' made against the civil servants is so vague. The term can mean different things at different levels:

1. Politicization may be an ideological concept. That is to say it refers to a system of values to which civil servants subscribe in the same way as other citizens. This kind of politicization is little noticed and seldom criticized provided the civil servants subscribe to the system of values that is dominant or the society concerned is an extremely consensual one. Only parties or groups 'outside the system' attack this kind of involvement in politics on the part of civil servants.

2. Politicization may be to do with the *political parties*: in this case, the fact that individual civil servants support particular political parties is either explicitly or implicitly recognized. But this kind of politicization takes many different forms. In some countries it leads to practices associated with spoils systems, as different governments succeed each other, and this tends to extend to the upper strata of the administration all the antagonisms that arise in political life in general. Such is certainly the situation in the United States, but it is also produced, in specific forms, in Germany and France. Elsewhere, party politicization constitutes a deliberate functional response to the conflicts and rifts that divide the country. In these cases, posts in the public sector are literally shared out between the various political elements of which the country is composed (as in Belgium and Austria). This provides a consensual solution for coping with deep conflicts and antagonisms in a peaceful manner, but it sometimes has the effect of generating even greater tensions, since the agreement achieved concerns not so much means of reducing these divisions, but rather methods that extend them to all aspects of social life.

3. Finally, politicization may be of a structural nature. In this case, politicization is not so much a matter of the choices that individual civil servants make. Rather, it is an effect of the organization of the service as a whole. It would be illusory to imagine that organizations such as the Conseil d'État in France and the individuals who run them can be apolitical or neutral when their very structure and/or their functions are deeply affected by politics.[44] There is nothing shocking or surprising about this. But it is better to face facts and draw the inevitable conclusions—both deontological and organizational—rather than avoid the issue.

It is the party politicization that gives rise to the most acute polemics. Other forms tend to pass without comment. This somewhat incomplete appraisal of politicization tends to produce considerable pressure in favour of depoliticizing the public sector. But the idea of eliminating politics from the upper administration is probably utopian. Even in Britain, where the Civil Service is the least open to party influences, the illusion of a 'pure' administration is frequently challenged. Richard Crossman, the former Labour Minister, wrote, 'There is nothing like a civil servant for being a politician and denying that he is one,'[45] and Léo Moulin points out that

mechanisms of politicization are also at work in this somewhat imaginary England that tends to be used as a model but where moving in certain social circles, having been educated at particular schools, speaking with a particular accent, and dressing in a particular style all constitute social criteria that are just as specific and effective as belonging to one political party or another.[46]

The administration's neutrality *vis-à-vis* the political authorities is one of the founding myths of liberal democracy. And they are impressive myths, for they have made it possible to limit the power of the ruler and guarantee as fair and equal treatment as possible to every citizen, thanks to the progressive mutual dislocation and independence of the two spheres.

But the close and continuous collaboration that takes place at their upper levels is likely to make it inevitable that administrative personnel change along with governments, and this raises problems that cannot be side-stepped merely by expressing disapproval. The way to keep the politicization of civil servants within reasonable bounds is to make changes in the political system rather than in the administrative sphere. Administrations are noticeably more highly politicized where the political sector serves as a clearing-house between various separate spheres. The best route for transferring from the administrative sector to the economic seems to be by way of the political, at least in the United States, West Germany, and France. On the other hand, in Britain and Italy (despite the fact that in both countries important semi-public sectors exist, just as they do in France), the relative separation between the administrative and the political spheres makes it difficult for civil servants *stricto sensu* to move on to conquer neighbouring domains. The fact that so many differences exist between the various systems suggests that the variable that accounts for the degree of politicization in different civil services should be sought not so much in the characteristics peculiar to each of these administrations, but rather in the structure and organization of the political systems themselves.

CONTROLLING THE BUREAUCRATS

Administrations started as servants; but have they now assumed the role of masters? The question is justified by the formidable expansion of the tasks, means, and staff of administrations, an expansion that neither politicians nor citizens seem able to control or check. Means of control do not seem to have kept pace with the quantitative and qualitative evolution that has overtaken bureaucracies. Methods of control have in many cases remained unchanged since the beginning of the century: essentially they are either of a juridical nature or else they amount to no more than 'self-monitoring' systems that are unquestionably necessary but by now quite inadequate. As for strictly political controls, virtually everywhere they play no more than a marginal role.

Political Controls

In principle, political authorities can control their administrations in a number of ways. They can make sure that the policies carried out are firmly in line with their directives and with established regulations; they can control the extent and use of the financial means available; and they can often call for the resignation of civil servants in posts of responsibility. Furthermore, liaison between the political authorities and the administration set up to implement their directives is underwritten and reinforced by the fact that the political responsibility of the Minister who heads the administration is at stake when the service is found to be deficient or at fault.

But in all these respects, political controls have been and continue to be of limited effect. The deflections that the intentions of the decision-makers undergo in the course of their implementation are not noticed until too late and, once habits and interests are established and the situation becomes a *fait accompli*, they are hard to rectify—not to mention the fact that frequently the political authorities responsible for initiating a particular policy are no longer there to react to the unexpected effects of their initial decisions or the distortions that these have suffered. Besides, generally speaking, political authorities show little enthusiasm for retrospective evaluations to determine the results and impact of their policies.

The same applies to financial controls, although these could and should constitute a powerful weapon in the hands of the political authorities. Governments and Parliaments are usually content at least to renew the budget of the previous year and in most cases are prepared to increase it without any proper inquiry into the need for funds or the proposed way of using them.

Internal checks can also constitute a way of the executive retaining control provided, that is, there is a genuine desire to make proper use of the existing machinery. Thus, the audit procedures in Britain and the monitoring of the Inspection of Finance and other supervisory bodies in France help to keep a check on the quality and propriety of administrative operations.

There is one other way in which political authorities can retain control over their administrations. It is through the appointment and dismissal of senior administrative officers. This is a sanction used frequently in the United States and also, on occasion, in France and West Germany, but often for political rather than administrative reasons. The administrative 'fuse' blows when it comes to protecting political officials (as happened in 1985 in the *Rainbow Warrior* affair in France). It is also worth pointing out that often—particularly in France and Italy—the sanctions imposed by politicians on civil servants look remarkably like promotions. This is an indication of the extent of the political authorities' timidity where influential administrations are concerned. In truth, in mainland Europe, civil servants are seldom held responsible *de facto* (the administration as a whole tends to assume responsibility for the mistakes of its individual agents). In England, however, civil servants are more likely to be held personally responsible, particularly in civil matters. Finally, in Britain, the responsibility of Ministers—who are accountable in theory for all the actions of their respective Ministries, including all their faults and errors—is more firmly established.

Controls through the Courts

Everywhere, the administration's responsibility towards the political authorities was established at the outset, but not its responsibility towards citizens. It was only quite late on (the late nineteenth century in Germany, France, and Italy, and not until the twentieth century in Britain) that true control became available to citizens, who could now seek redress by bringing court actions. Through a bizarre historical irony, the very States that strove the hardest to protect themselves against interference from the judiciary by setting up special laws and special tribunals for the administration were the first to have to accept the most stringent controls. But since the Second World War administrative laws and tribunals have also been established in the countries with systems of common law, that is, the United States and Britain (where the influences of both the Scottish juridical system and continental law have made considerable impact).

The model for controls imposed by administrative and financial tribunals was provided by the French Council of State (Conseil d'État) and more recently by the conversion of prefectorial councils (*conseils de préfecture*) into regional administrative tribunals. In Italy, the system is virtually identical: the Consiglio di Stato (which became more or less a court of appeal) was to a large extent supplemented by newly created regional administrative tribunals. In West Germany, the model was somewhat complicated because of the State's federal structure. Here, there are three separate levels: the tribunals at local level, the administrative tribunals of the *Länder*, and the administrative tribunal of the Federation as a whole, which sits in Berlin (Bundersverwaltungsgericht). In West Germany, administrative tribunals are complemented by specialized ones (which, unlike the French specialized tribunals, are not subject to the control of the supreme administrative Court and which are thus autonomous at their own level). Also worth mentioning are the fiscal tribunals (the *Finanzgerichte*), which only exist at *Länder* and Bund levels, and the social tribunals (*Sozialgerichte*), which deal chiefly with social security cases and are organized at three levels, as are the general administrative tribunals. It is interesting to note that France, which provided the original inspiration for this structure, is today, in its turn, adapting to the German type of system in order to cope with its overload of cases. As from 1989, five courts of appeal will in part take the place of the Conseil d'État, which will thereafter limit itself to pure legal supervision and to checking the most important decisions of central government.

What with the growing number of cases in all countries, these courts are now facing problems, for the dearth of judges is producing a veritable legal bottle-neck so that exercising one's right to seek redress from the administration and obtain due compensation is becoming increasingly fraught with uncertainty. French administrative tribunals are considered to be overstretched (with 9,600 cases brought in 1986 before the Conseil d'État and 59,000 before the regional administrative tribunals justifying the creation in 1989 of five Courts of Appeal on the German model). But in Italy the situation is even more serious (15,000 cases for the Consiglio di Stato and 40,000 for the regional tribunals),[47] and it is worse still in West Germany (in 1978, 98,000 appeals at local level, 14,500 at *Länder* level, and 2,400 at the level of the federal administrative tribunal). However, West Germany has many more judges, and this helps to expedite the judicial processes.

The extent of the tasks facing all these administrative tribunals tends, however, to mask the quite substantial differences between them. In France and Italy, in particular, many of these tribunals' energies are devoted to litigation within the administration itself (47 per cent of all cases in Italy) or to very specific areas of the administration (especially town planning and finance). There are thus many disparities between different sectors, and this throws a rather different light on the role of monitoring the administration that is generally ascribed to the administrative tribunals. Finally the force or quality of the sanctions that a judge may impose depends upon the degree of independence that he has managed to establish for himself in relation to the administration. In this respect, Italian and German judges generally adopt a less deferential attitude towards their administrations than do their French counterparts, who are more intimately linked with theirs (either by reason of their common training in the ENA or through being appointed from within the administration's ranks). German judges and—to a slightly lesser degree—Italian ones are judges of legality rather than judges of the administration (in both senses of the expression) and this has the effect of putting them in the position of essential partners in the administrative process. Paradoxically enough, the relative timidity of French administrative judges towards the administration tends to marginalize their position and get their decisions discounted.

Only the Conseil d'État is unaffected in this respect, but this is not so much on account of its status as a court of appeal but rather because of its position as 'adviser to the throne' and the fact that a proportion of its members (albeit a changing one) is active in both the political and the administrative spheres.

In these three countries, the administrative tribunals are complemented by Courts of Accounts, whose functions are consultative and monitorial. In Italy, for example, all administrative decisions of the State that involve some expenditure must be submitted to the Court for approval. However, given the avalanche of decisions with which it is unable to cope, the effect of this is to render its control illusory or purely formal. In West Germany, the Federal Court of Accounts[48] concerns itself only with federal expenses; the *Länder* are monitored by special courts of their own (similar to the new regional audit offices in Italy, except that in Germany these are not subject to the federal Audit Office). The German Federal Court of Accounts plays a similar role to the French one and, like the latter, is obliged to produce a report, which it submits to the Bundestag. Also, as in France, the impact made by the Court of Accounts seems somewhat weak, partly because by no means all its recommendations are put into effect and also because its monitoring means are to some extent ill-adapted to the contemporary functions of the administration. The sanction of legality—which in any case could only be a partial one—turns out to be relatively ineffective because it is applied too late. As for managerial monitoring, as in France this remains limited and hesitant, for the judges have few weapons at their disposal and are, moreover, reluctant to impose methods of control that would go beyond their role as judges.

In Britain and the United States, the concept of 'public law' has emerged since the Second World War and special institutions exist for settling disputes between the administrations and individual citizens. Thus Britain nowadays has over 2,000 administrative tribunals that operate in a wide range of sectors (taxes, social security, pensions, etc.). Their name, 'administrative tribunals', is designed to distinguish these first-level institutions from the normal judicial system (where the term 'courts' is used), for the principles on which they are based, their procedure (which is far more informal and less dependent on precedent), and their composition all mark them out from courts of the classic kind. Furthermore, as in the United States, any appeals against the decisions of the administrative tribunals must, in the last resort, be made to the courts. As can be seen, the British administrative tribunals have much in common with the specialized courts at the lowest level in France (such as the Social Security Appeals Commission) (Commission de recours de la sécurité sociale). But the pro-liferation of these tribunals now taking place and the development of public law should lead to further changes and tighter controls. How-ever, the problems involved in incorporating these new tribunals into the traditional juridical system are reflected in the creation, in 1958, of a Council on Tribunals, its purpose being to keep an eye on their progress, methods, and results, with a view to suggesting to Parlia-ment what reforms should be introduced. Meanwhile, for the time being, both in the United States and in Britain, the controls through the courts upon the administration remain necessary and important.

In countries subject to common law, the inadequacies that justified the establishment of embryonic administrative tribunals are to some extent offset by the comparative boldness of judges towards the administration and by the more efficient means that exist for control-ling it. The administration has no 'natural judges' of its own, in the first instance, and is subject to the same constraints as those imposed in litigation between private individuals. Furthermore, in the United States in particular, proof of responsibility on the part of the administration[49] may result in its having to pay damages that are not limited (as they are in France) by any concern to preserve public funds. Finally, the courts wield very real powers of constraint over the administrations in these countries: powers of injunction, forbidding or ordering them to proceed (or not to proceed) to issue writs (writ of mandamus, prohibition, or *certiorari*) which, if ignored, may occasion charges of contempt of court followed by increased financial penalties.

Even the most effective juridical controls have their drawbacks: in general, even in the best of circumstances, they are extremely time-consuming and expensive. (The right to dispense with the services of a lawyer in administrative tribunals, in France, is somewhat illusory and tends to look more like a privilege for jurists than a facility for ordinary citizens.) Consequently, despite an increase in the number of appeals, many problems have remained unresolved, or badly re-solved, by juridical means. The fact that so many citizens, ill-equipped to defend themselves, were appealing to their Deputies for help constituted one of many indications that litigation was failing to operate satisfactorily in situations that, without being particularly

serious, certainly needed to be rectified. The solution seems to have
been provided by the Scandinavian countries. They created a new
institution to deal with this type of problem: the Ombudsman.
Following their example, in 1972 France set up a Mediator, Britain a
Parliamentary Commissioner for Administration. However, these
two 'mediators' are not as powerful as the model that inspired them,
for account had to be taken of the pre-existing mechanisms of
litigation and also of the reluctance of members of parliament to
relinquish their own traditional function as mediators between ordinary citizens and the administration. Consequently, applications to
the French Mediator and the British Commissioner can be made only
through members of parliament. Italy and West Germany have not
introduced any mediators at national level. But it is worth noting that
in 1950 West Germany did set up an Ombudsman for military affairs
and that some *Länder* (including the Rhineland Palatinate, which, in
1973, was the first to institute a *Bürgerbeauftragte*) did so at *Land* level.
In Italy, eight regions have set up *difensori civici* at regional level, but
their powers have been limited both in written texts and in practice
and, to date, the results have not been particularly impressive.

CONCLUSION

Western administrations bear the imprint of abstract Weberian
models of rational-cum-legal organization. But they have also undergone profound changes that affect both their internal structure and
their relations with other organizations or with citizens. In conditions
such as these use of the term 'administrations' is justifiable only by
virtue of its convenience value. For all administrations have been
affected by a fundamental qualitative and quantitative explosion and
their modern evolution is characterized by:

- an unprecedented number of public employees;
- a wide range of new kinds of employee, to cope with the
  increasing diversity of the needs of both the administration itself
  and the citizens who benefit from its services;
- the heavy public cost of administrative activities, and their
  increasing inflexibility;
- the trade unionization of civil servants (trade union membership
  is frequently higher than in the private sector);
- the fragmentation and heterogeneity of administrative bodies,

(leading to discrepancies in status, organization, and funding and to rivalry between different departments);
- the growing autonomy of many departments, each committed to its own particular logic;
- increasingly blurred distinctions between the public and the private sectors as a result of the growing mutual interpenetration of various interests and administrations, and of a high degree of organizational and methodological mimetism.

8

Constitutional Courts

In Montesquieu's triad of legislative, executive, and judicial powers, the third element has long been the weakest. This imbalance in Western institutions, or at least in the European democracies, results from the fact that the democratic principle (of national or popular sovereignty) and the representative principle (that Parliament rules supreme) have long been regarded as more important than the third liberal principle underlying Western political systems, that of the moderation and separation of powers.

In France, the hostility of the Revolutionaries towards the judiciary caused them to go so far as to deny it any control over the administration. The formulation of that hostility in the law of 17–24 August 1790 is well known: 'Judicial functions are distinct and will always remain separate from administrative functions. On pain of breach of faith, judges may not in any way at all upset the operations of administrative bodies nor summon administrators before them for reasons connected with their functions.' This hostility to intervention by an over-mighty judiciary in decisions reached by, or under the aegis of, a Parliament that was the expression of popular sovereignty persisted until 1958.

In Britain, the relative weakness of the judiciary does not result so much from a fundamental antagonism of this kind (inspired, in France, by the Revolutionaries' desire to break the reactionary opposition of the judges that was so patent in the last years of the monarchy). Rather, it stems from the undisputed supremacy of Parliament, of which the other powers are, so to speak, emanations. The government is derived from Parliament, and the judicial system is crowned and supervised by the House of Lords, which is also the highest court in the land. It took some time for the judicial function, at present implemented *de facto* by nine Law Lords (who also have the right to sit in the House of Lords) to become truly autonomous.

The absence of any constitutional court in Britain does not mean that no system of checks and balances exists. In the first place, faced with the law, British judges proceed by means of interpretation ('construction') and have always made determined use of this faculty, even to the point of 'rewriting' parliamentary law or changing its meaning. Secondly, very many regulations, particularly in the domain of civil liberties, are not instituted by Parliament. Instead, they are a part of the common law evolved by judges. For instance, much of British penal law stems from jurisprudence. Thirdly, the role that judges play in the protection of liberties has been strengthened by Britain's ratification of the European Convention on Human Rights. Finally—and herein lie both the greatness and the weakness of the system—respect for the Constitution and fundamental rights result more from guarantees of a political or moral nature than from legal ones. For example, the introduction of identity cards would be considered no more than a formality were it not that public opinion would regard it as the sign of a violation of fundamental liberty and has up to now blocked any moves in that direction. Effective public opinion is the sole barrier, for Britain has no written Constitution, no Declaration of Human Rights, no Supreme Court. The superiority of constitutional rules stems not from their solemnity or from any procedural guarantees expressed in a document considered to be paramount, but from the consensus on the part of both élites and the general public regarding norms that have emerged in the course of a long political history. However, this edifice displays detectable cracks. The use of referendums, the implicit recognition that the sovereignty of Parliament is limited by Britain's participation in European Community treaties, the question of public liberties in grave situations (such as the troubles of Northern Ireland), and the example set by the other European democracies, all of which have introduced constitutional controls, are all factors that have prompted some, as yet isolated, voices to suggest that a Constitutional Court should be set up in Britain.

Thus, in both Britain and France, for reasons both historical and ideological, the principle of a separation of powers has been no more than partially respected, and the supremacy of Parliament long went unchallenged. The law has been credited with all the necessary virtues (regularity, justice, perfection) by very reason of the standing of its creator, namely, Parliament.

To find a different tradition one must look to America. Not only was the US Constitution the first to implement the separation of powers and establish the fact in a written document; it also declares itself to be the product of a popular consensus and a social pact, and hence to constitute the supreme law of the land. But while the Founding Fathers were democrats of a kind, they were primarily liberals, wary of popular pressures and their expression as law. This explains Hamilton's words in the *Federalist*: 'The Constitution is the fundamental law . . . And when the legislative will, expressed as laws, finds itself in opposition to the will of the people as declared in the Constitution, judges . . . must bring their decisions into line with the laws that are fundamental, not with those that are not.' However, that interpretation in the *Federalist* was still no more than wishful thinking: as yet, nothing in the Constitution subjected judges to the check of constitutionality or granted the last word to the Supreme Court. That had to wait until 1803, when the Supreme Court's famous ruling in the *Marbury* v. *Madison* case, under the inspiration of Chief Justice Marshall, did uphold the superiority of the Constitution to which all are subject—including courts and tribunals, which are thus bound to uphold it. Thirteen years later, in the *Martin* v. *Hunter's Lessee* case of 1816, the Court confirmed that decision by ruling that it was itself the guarantor of the uniformity of judgements throughout the territory of the United States. The interpretations of the lower tribunals, including the Supreme Courts of individual states, were subordinated to those of the highest court in the Union.

We are thus presented with two strongly contrasting situations, two interpretations of the principle of the separation of powers and of the hierarchy of values and norms. Until the mid-twentieth century, the American concept, which stresses the virtues of 'constitutionalism' and the pre-eminent role of constitutional judges, was an isolated and marginal one. The American experience seemed alien to the history, myths, and mores, not just of Britain and France, but of the whole of the old continent. Europeans disregarded the analyses of Tocqueville, preferring Édouard Lambert's lapidary formula of 'government by judges'.[1] But the collapse of classic parliamentarianism in mainland Europe, the trauma of Nazism and Fascism, and the eventual demystification of law as such after the Second World War brought home the truth of Lammenais's lucid but bitter conclusion that 'the law can be oppressive'. In such a context, it was not surprising that West Germany should have a Constitutional Court by 1949, Italy by 1956, and even France by 1958.

Nor, though, is it surprising that the European countries have sought different solutions, many of them inspired by the doctrines of the Austrian jurist Kelsen,[2] to the problem of constitutional checks and balances from those of the United States. Europe's constitutional courts had to be grafted on to traditions and a legal apparatus that were already solidly established, whereas in the United States, constitutional supremacy was established at more or less the same time as all the other national institutions and on the heels of a judiciary and a legal system very different from those of Europe.

The importance of the institutional and organizational role played by constitutional courts in most Western States (Britain being the major exception) explains and justifies their hybrid, semi-judicial, semi-political nature. They are certainly institutions that interpret laws and pass judgements, and on that account may be described as organs of jurisdiction. But because they operate as mediators, implementing a system of checks and balances, because of the nature of their powers, and because of the manner of their composition, they are also highly political bodies. This description is often rejected, the term 'political' carrying negative connotations of politicians, parties, discretionary or even arbitrary powers, partiality, favouritism, and every sort of corruption. Some strong defenders of constitutional courts claim their functions are strictly judicial; while their critics accuse them of being mere political tools. These simplistic and reductionist views are neither realistic nor borne out by the evidence. Law constitutes an expression of political aims, decisions, and value systems. It is produced mainly by avowedly political bodies such as parliaments and governments whose legitimacy rests upon universal suffrage. But administrations, judges, and other social agents, too, have a hand in law-making, in their cases without the sanction of universal suffrage. This dimension has to be fully recognized if we are to understand these institutions placed at the frontier of law and politics.

POLITICS AND THE JUDICIARY: ORGANIZATION AND INTERCONNECTIONS

The way in which the Courts operate should be considered from both an external and an internal point of view. What is their position in the juridical and political organization of the State? And how does their own internal organization reflect their twofold nature and function?

The Courts in the Juridico-Political System

The hybrid nature of Constitutional Courts is, at least in part, a consequence of the ambivalence of their terms of reference. Their first role is to 'declare the law' at the very highest level, that of the Constitution. That function could be analysed as pertaining to the traditional role of a judge, and at first sight appears to do so. But the Courts are also supposed to be (or to have evolved into) the instruments of a system of political checks and balances designed to prevent other bodies from exceeding their powers and to ensure that the values expressed in the Constitution are respected. The position of the Courts, as described in constitutional texts, in a sense reflects the initial uncertainty of the Constituents and the difficulty of establishing priorities regarding their twofold functions. For example, the Constitution of West Germany ascribes to the Constitutional Court a type of organization and powers that indubitably stem from a 'political' point of view, but goes on to set out its rules and functions in chapter 11, 'Judicial Power', where Article 92 states: 'Judicial power is entrusted to the judges; it may be exercised by the Federal Constitutional Tribunal, by the federal tribunals provided for under present fundamental law, and by the *Länder* tribunals.'

By contrast, the provisions of the French and Italian Constitutions reflect a more directly political bias. The 1958 French Constitution contains no suggestion that any real judicial powers should be recognized, let alone that a proper Constitutional Court should be set up. Instead, the primary function of the new Constitutional Council was to shield the executive from parliamentary encroachment. Although this function might adopt juridical means and forms, it was essentially political; the legislative aspect is patently far less important. In the 1948 Italian Constitution, provisions relating to the Constitutional Court were grouped together in Section 6 (magistrates courts being the subject of Section 4), under the heading 'Constitutional Guarantees', a fact that underlines the particular character of what was, at the time, a new institution in the Italian political system.

If they are to perform their essential role correctly, Constitutional Courts must possess the means to make other constitutional bodies and lower courts respect their decisions. This would appear to be better guaranteed in a system such as that of the United States, where the Supreme Court is recognized as the highest authority within a comprehensive juridical order.

Although the politico-constitutional context of the French Constitutional Council (Conseil constitutionnel) is very different, its evolution presents certain similarities with that of the American Supreme Court. The French Constitution recognizes that the Council's decisions 'must be observed by the public authorities as well as by all administrative and jurisdictional authorities', but initially this provision was limited in scope: it applied almost exclusively to Parliament; the executive was not affected. As for the Court of cassation and the Council of State (Conseil d'État), they could refuse to accept the decisions of the Constitutional Council, since there were no means of enforcing the supremacy of its judgements. Although no institutional changes have been made to rectify the Constitutional Council's relative impotence, it has, solely through its jurisprudence, been able to convert its position into one of strength. Its 1971 decision on the freedom of association enabled it to increase its powers of control considerably, by including in the constitutional texts the Preamble to the 1958 Constitution which referred to both the 1946 Preamble and the 1789 Declaration of Rights. From an unexpansive Constitution of ninety-two Articles, the Council now became the guardian of a body of rights and concepts the content, meaning, and scope of which need constant interpretation if the policies of the legislature (or rather, essentially, the government) are to be satisfactorily monitored. At the same time, the Council's chief purpose now became, not so much to guarantee constitutional limits and procedures, but rather to rule on whether government action was compatible with the fundamental principles enshrined in the Constitution of the Republic. By so doing, the Council has increasingly determined the *content* and limits of the decisions of the legislative, administrative, and judicial authorities, although it has not acquired any extra powers to enforce respect for its judgements. In this respect the French Constitutional Council suffers by comparison with the American Supreme Court, which holds general, centralized powers of control. But, more and more, the devices of liberal democracy operate to the advantage of the French Council. The rules of the Constitutional State (*l'État de Droit*) and the principle of the limitation of powers are the best possible assurances that its judgements will be respected.

Between the two extremes of the centralized control of the American system on the one hand, and the fragmentation of the French one on the other, there are a number of relatively effective intermediate solutions, as can be seen from the Italian and, especially, the German examples. It would have been perfectly possible for the Supreme Courts of Appeal and the highest administrative tribunals of Europe to acquire as large a measure of control over the constitutionality of their States as that assumed by the Supreme Court of the United States. However, the firmly established principle of the supremacy of the law, the 'timidity' (as Mauro Cappelletti puts it) of judges, and the dual nature of the Courts, each of which is supreme in its own order, all combined to prevent Judge Marshall's illustrious example from being followed in Europe. The problem that remained to be resolved was thus how to guarantee the effective supremacy of a Constitutional Court that had to be fitted into a pre-established judicial system.

Setting up a Supreme Court, as such, would have upset too many deeply rooted traditions and juridical mechanisms, so the Italians and Germans tried to establish bridges between judicial and administrative Courts and constitutional jurisdiction. The first bridge involved deciding that 6 out of the 16 constitutional judges in West Germany and 5 out of the 15 in Italy should be drawn from the ordinary courts (as is also traditional in the United States, where a certain number of federal judges are invariably appointed to the Supreme Court). The second bridging device, which we shall consider in more detail later, meant empowering the magistrates of civil, penal, administrative, and financial courts to appeal to the Constitutional Court to rule on all questions of constitutionality that might arise in the course of any lawsuit.

It remained possible to go further. The German example shows that, despite the deep differences between the German and the American modes of monitoring constitutionality, it is possible to achieve equivalent effects. Article 93 of the West German Constitution enables it to monitor the application of laws. The Court may pronounce, in particular, 'upon constitutional appeals that may be brought by anybody who thinks that any of his fundamental rights or any of the rights guaranteed by Articles 20.4, 33, 38, 101, 103, and 104 have been infringed'. Since the Constitution states that fundamental rights are binding upon all legislative, executive, and judicial authorities, this means that a citizen may attack any legislative, administrative, or court decision that *directly infringes* any of his rights. In practice, this provision affects mainly administrative or Court decisions, for it is quite rare for a law in itself to cause such *direct* infringement. Since the Court insists that all other avenues for seeking redress should have been exhausted, essentially the appeals that private individuals can bring before it are those against the injustice of either administrative or judicial decisions. In 1984, there were over 3,000 appeals and about 100 judgements were made. That may seem a low figure, but it is enough to guarantee strict respect for the jurisprudence of the Constitutional Court on the part of all civil, penal, and administrative courts and tribunals.

The Juridical–Political Interface

Another illustration of the hybrid nature of Constitutional Courts is provided by their composition. In France, as in West Germany and Italy, the modes of recruitment and the general characteristics of their judges show that, while Constitutional Courts are not purely political bodies, at the same time nor are they quite the same as other courts.

The *political* aspect is manifest chiefly from the nature of the authorities responsible for making appointments. In France, the nine judges are appointed by the President of the Republic and the Presidents of the two Assemblies (and the only individuals to be members of the Council as of right, namely former Heads of State, are of course eminently political figures). In Italy, of the fifteen members of the Constitutional Court, one-third are chosen by the Head of State, one-third by the two Assemblies in a joint session, and one-third by the supreme, ordinary and administrative magistracies (three by the Court of Cassation, one by the Council of State, and one by the Court of Accounts). If the political nature of two of the three appointing authorities in Italy needed any stressing, we might point out that the process for setting up the Court was blocked for eight years (not until 30 November 1955 did Parliament manage to agree on five names) and that there was a violent clash between those who favoured discretionary powers for the Head of State (i.e. that he should be free to choose whoever he liked) and those who considered that he should simply ratify the government's choices (a suggestion which Einaudi, the first President of the Republic, and his successors successfully resisted).

In West Germany, finally, the rule is that of the sixteen members of the Federal Constitutional Tribunal half should be appointed by the Bundestag and half by the Bundesrat. In practice, the Bundestag elects a proportionally represented commission of twelve, which chooses eight of the sixteen judges. To be elected, a candidate must obtain eight out of twelve of the commission members' votes, and this can only be achieved if the two major parties (the CDU–CSU and the

SPD) come to an agreement, to the detriment of the smaller parties. (The Liberal Party can usually elect only one judge, the Greens not even one—at least, as things stand at present.)

The political character of the Constitutional Courts is also evident from the past (and in some cases, future) careers of the judges: in 1987, twelve of the sixteen German judges belonged to a political party or were closely involved with one, and in Italy the same applied in the case of the judges appointed by Parliament and the President of the Republic. In France, these appointments are also politicized, not only by reason of the authorities who make them, but also because the Constitution lays down no conditions at all, not even regarding the judges' professional qualifications.

In these circumstances, and in view of the prestigious standing of the Courts, it is not surprising to find many leading political figures among the judges: the French Constitutional Council has included a future Prime Minister and President of the Republic, Georges Pompidou, among its members; the last president but one of the Italian Court, Leopoldo Elia, was tipped for Christian Democrat candidate for the Presidency of the Republic; both the German Constitutional Court and the French Council number Ministers of the Interior and Justice among their presidents. And if judges are lucky enough to have been appointed while still sufficiently young to be able to continue their careers when their appointments lapse, many return to political life, particularly in West Germany and Italy (Bonifacio, the president of the Italian Court from 1973 to 1975, later even became Minister of Justice).

The *juridical* aspect of the Constitutional Courts is manifested in the nature of the conditions that are sometimes set upon appointments. France does not insist upon any professional qualifications and consequently in principle leaves the way open to politicians. The Council is thus in part composed of 'amateurs'. However, this is an anomaly that is likely to be progressively corrected, for the scope of the Council's jurisprudence is now such that political and party authorities will be increasingly disinclined to regard the function of judge as a sinecure fit to crown a career or as a way of pensioning off politicians considered to be in the way. In Italy and Germany the guarantees of professional competence are stronger. In Italy, the judges are chosen from the ranks of magistrates (or retired magistrates), professors from Faculties of Law, and lawyers who have been in practice for over twenty years. Professionalism here is thus well guaranteed, as it is in federal

Germany, where three of the eight judges appointed by each of the two Chambers are recruited from amongst the members of a supreme federal court. The remaining five must possess the qualifications specified for judges by German law. In Italy and West Germany, constitutional justice is thus entrusted to professionals; and, furthermore, the appointment procedures guarantee that these will be more than merely technical legal experts.

This balance of the juridical and the political seems a good compromise for the exercise of constitutional justice, for this cannot satisfactorily be entrusted purely to politicians, amateurs, or legal specialists in the narrow sense of the expression. The dream of a Constitutional Court with no political links at all is certainly unrealistic, so, in view of the necessity for a combination of the juridical and the political, we must reject the position adopted by René Chiroux when he writes: 'As regards the—crucial—problem of the appointment of members, the foreign models are not really satisfactory. The choice of constitutional judges in the United States, federal Germany, and Italy reflects political as well as juridical motivation. How can such a Court conceivably be above suspicion?'[3] It is not so much the modes of appointment and recruitment adopted by these countries that should be regarded with suspicion, but rather the absence, in France, of any rules either written or unwritten that would help the Council to function better. Besides, is it not unfair to the judges to suspect them of partiality simply because they were appointed by political authorities? Of course, the possibility is not altogether ruled out, but it is all the greater when the judge owes his appointment purely to favour, without being professionally qualified for the post. If, on the other hand, those selected can rely on their own solid professional capacities over and above political preferences, they will find it easier to resist political temptations and to serve the institution to which they belong, rather than dance to the tune of their original sponsors. How, otherwise, should we explain the illustrious example of Judge Marshall in 1803, that of the French Constitutional Council in 1971, and the even more impressive behaviour of the Italian Court which, though still scarred by the political polemics that surrounded the appointment of its members, had the courage to make its very first judgement a historic one?[4] Or, again, how to explain the fact that Earl Warren, Eisenhower's own nominee in 1953, was nevertheless the architect of one of the most revolutionary policies ever produced by the Supreme Court?

The autonomy that the judges, due in part to their professional abilities, can assert *vis-à-vis* their political partners is reinforced by the independence that they are guaranteed by the tradition of autonomy of the judiciary as a whole—an independence that is structured by the obligations to which they are subject. As they are appointed for a relatively long period (nine years in France and Italy, twelve in Germany), their positions are secure and, as a result, they may, if they wish, enjoy total freedom of decision. On the other hand, it would no doubt be helpful to introduce stronger regulations with respect to incompatibility between the functions of a constitutional judge and certain other functions of a political, public, or private nature. In particular, it would be desirable, in France, to ban not only combining the functions of judge with any elective functions (including those connected with local politics) but also standing for election without first resigning (as members of the Civil Service have to do in Britain if they wish to stand as candidates in general elections). In other words, while the political and the juridical aspects of constitutional law are intertwined so closely that the notion of absolute 'purity' is impractical and utopian, it is, at the same time, fundamentally important to eliminate, through law or convention, all possibilities of the kind of political manœuvring that still all too frequently takes place in France. The appointments to the Council of former Presidents of the parliamentary Assemblies by their successors are examples of the kind of political 'facilities' that amply justify some people's dream of a pure juridical world.

POLITICAL OR JURIDICAL? SUBMISSIONS, PROCEEDINGS,
AND JUDGEMENTS

When defining Constitutional Courts, should the emphasis be placed on the noun or the adjective? Are they first and foremost tribunals, or part of the constitutional machinery? This is not a purely formal question for, logically, the procedures for referring cases to the Courts, the pattern of proceeding, and the style of judgements ought to be determined or at least influenced by the answer. But in practice, logic has very little to do with the matter and, yet again, the conclusion must be that Constitutional Courts are rather like the bats of fable—sometimes mice, sometimes birds.

Modes of Submission

Of all the systems operating in Western countries, the French solution is by far the most political and the least judicial in character, as regards both applications and patterns of procedure. Initially, submissions to the Constitutional Council could only be made by four authorities: the Presidents of the two Assemblies, the President of the Republic, and the Prime Minister. Obviously enough, such a restriction and the nature of the authorities that were empowered to refer were hardly conducive to judicial activism on the part of the Council: between 1959 and 1974, neither the President of the Republic nor the President of the National Assembly had ever appealed to it. The President of the Senate had done so only three times and the Prime Minister only on six occasions, on questions of whether particular laws were or were not in conformity with the Constitution.

The fundamental change was introduced by the constitutional reform of 29 October 1974, which authorized 60 Deputies or Senators to appeal to the Constitutional Council. At the time, the opposition scoffed, calling it a *réformette* (or 'mini-reform'), despite the fact that it was they who were likely to benefit from it (since the majority was unlikely to appeal to the Council over any law that it had itself passed). In practice, however, the 1974 revision proved to be of crucial importance—possibly as important for the long-term stability of State institutions as that of 1962, which had ruled that the Head of State be elected by universal suffrage. The number of applications made to the Council now rose markedly with first the Socialists, then the right, and—after March 1986—the Socialists again, seizing almost every opportunity to appeal to the Constitutional Council. Between 1974 and 1981, 67 appeals were made, 63 of which emanated from Parliament; between 1981 and March 1986, there were 101, 99 of which emanated from Parliament. Quantitatively, the change was thus considerable. But qualitatively, the political nature of the operation remained unaffected, and it is reinforced by the required timing for applications to the Council, which must be made between the final passage of a bill and its promulgation by the President.

The procedures for referring bills to the Constitutional Council lead to a means of control that is both abstract and a priori (since appeals against a law must be made before it has come into force by being promulgated). It is a means of control that is generally favoured by

French jurists, who value its simplicity. In 1981, Jean Rivero cogently summed up this attitude as follows:

To my mind it [the procedure] has one virtue, only one, but of prime importance: it is simple . . . Parliament approves a bill; before it becomes law, the Constitutional Council is requested to pronounce on it; if the bill is declared not to be in conformity with the Constitution, it disappears from the scene, through a trapdoor. It is still-born; the matter is settled.[5]

These methods of appeal in France certainly possess the significant advantages of simplicity and dispatch. On the other hand, the drawbacks involved offset the benefits. The briefness of the interval of time between the adoption of a bill and the pronouncement of the Council's judgement (between a week and a month) has the effect of turning the Council into a kind of 'third chamber' to which the political minority can appeal and which thus has, at it were, 'the last word', while passions and polemics are still raging. In these circumstances, the Council's decisions tend to be regarded not so much as judgements, but rather as expressing either rejection or approval of the policies that the Government has persuaded Parliament to adopt. However, this drawback may be mitigated by the attitude and behaviour of the judges themselves, for the systems used by other countries show that the Courts are not always unaffected by polemics.

Both in West Germany and in Italy, modes of application to the Constitutional Court are sometimes political, sometimes juridical. Appeals of a political nature are, however, limited to certain specific questions. For example, in West Germany, appeals may be made to the Constitutional Court by the federal government or by the *Länder* governments in cases of disagreement over the interpretation of their powers (since 1951 there have been thirty or so appeals of this nature), and by constitutional bodies recognized by the Constitution to possess this right, if a clash arises with another constitutional body (twenty-seven such appeals between 1951 and 1983). The Court may also receive from the Bundestag, the Bundesrat, and the federal government appeals aiming to ban a political party for violating the principles of the Constitution. But in none of these cases is it a matter of pronouncing on the constitutionality of laws. The only possibility of a political appeal in this domain is to be found in Article 93.1, which states that the Court may receive appeals from the federal government or from a *Land* government 'in cases where clashes of opinion or doubts arise over the formal and material compatibility with constitutional law of a federal law or a *Land* law, or over a *Land* law's compatibility with any other federal law'. This type of control, known as an abstract control (*abstrakte Normenkontrolle*) is applied relatively infrequently: since coming into being, the Court has been requested to deal with only about fifty cases of this kind.

Similarly, in Italy, the Constitutional Court may receive appeals from the government when regional laws appear to contravene the correct division of tasks between the State and the regions; and it may also be requested by the regions to pronounce upon State laws which appear to infringe their own powers (although the Court has no power to suspend the laws in question). The Court may also pronounce upon disagreements that may arise between different constitutional bodies but, as in West Germany, the Court's activities in this area remain marginal.

The essential activities of both the West German and the Italian Courts concern appeals of a judicial nature. In both countries, the judges of any court may (whether or not at the request of the parties involved) appeal to the Constitutional Court to rule on the question of any law's constitutionality.[6] Thus, in Italy, over 90 per cent of the appeals heard concern concrete litigations that have been referred to the Court, as do a large number in West Germany (765 between 1951 and 1983).

Finally, in West Germany, when the fundamental rights of an individual have been infringed, any citizen concerned may appeal to the Constitutional Court. The appeal may either be lodged directly against a law within one year of its promulgation (this is relatively uncommon), or against an administrative or judicial decision concerning the application of the law within one month of the publication or notification of the decision, but only after first seeking satisfaction from all other courts of appeal. There are more appeals of this nature than any other kind (several thousand every year, 3,382 in 1984) and they threaten to overwhelm the Court. To cope with this rising tide of direct appeals, it has been obliged to delegate to a Committee of three judges the task of sifting requests, which they can reject by declaring them to lack motivation. This leaves the Court itself with no more than 100 or so decisions to make on individual appeals. However, this procedure still has considerable significance, for the Court's decisions on concrete litigation and, in many cases, on the judgements involved in it make an important contribution to the task of maintaining the real supremacy of constitutional values and ensuring that they penetrate every branch of the law and every aspect of social life.

As this survey shows, in some countries the modalities of appeal are mixed (West Germany and Italy). In others such as France, they are not exactly in conformity with the role that these Courts ought to play or that they claim to play. The political nature of the appeals made to the French Constitutional Council is increasingly at odds with its growing function of pronouncing on the constitutionality of laws.

Procedures

The procedure followed in such actions also testifies to the hybrid nature of constitutional lawsuits. In some respects, it resembles that for normal litigation. But a number of peculiarities are occasioned by the political nature of the Court. Even so, the political nature of the composition of a Court is not directly reflected in the procedure that it follows. This heterogeneity is one of the most unusual peculiarities of Constitutional Courts.[7] The differences between one country and another are most marked in respect of the opportunity for debate (or lack of it) and the degree of secrecy by which actions are affected.

It is in France, where the Council is often accused of being a third Chamber, that the procedure for constitutional 'trials' least resembles the normal practices of Courts. Despite a few slight improvements introduced recently, the procedure remains characterized by its secrecy and the limited opportunities that it affords for hearing both sides of the question.[8] Until Badinter took office as President of the Council, those appealing were allowed to present their own observations but were not informed of any written comments that had been passed to the Council, in particular those formulated by the Prime Minister's office. Since 1986, the notes produced by the government's General Secretariat have been passed to the applicants, and in response they may present their own arguments, to which the General Secretariat is invited to reply. This undeniably constitutes a measure of progress. But secrecy remains the general rule, from start to finish, as is manifested by the fact that decisions are given collectively, with no hint of dissenting views. On this subject, Laurent Cohen-Tanugi writes as follows:

In order to protect itself against accusations concerning its 'political' nature, and to take up a firmly 'juridical' stance, the Council usually presents its decisions in the traditional manner for conveying judgements in French

Courts of Justice: arguments are syllogistic, judgements peremptory, and all underlying disagreements, all considerations of juridical policy, and all dissenting opinions are concealed . . . Yet constitutional law, by its very nature, lends itself even less than other branches of law to arbitrary claims of absolute truth couched in a correspondingly formal style. The Council's determination to express its decisions in the formal language of the French juridical tradition thus sometimes produces *precisely the opposite of the desired effect*, in that it conveys an impression of arbitrariness to the public.[9]

Symptomatic of this confusion was the Council's reaction in 1986 to the criticism that its decisions were provoking. On 12 August it issued a statement that sums up all the ambiguity of its interpretations of the terms 'juridical' and 'political'. The Council drew attention to the fact that 'the Constitution had entrusted it with the *juridical mission* of verifying that the laws submitted to it were in conformity with that Constitution. It therefore declined to become involved in the current argument since this fell within a *political context*'[10] (my italics).

In Italy, on the other hand, the procedure does allow for contradictory debate. All parties involved in the litigation which has given rise to the prejudicial question, and, similarly, the *Avocattura dello Stato*, may submit memoranda and relevant information up until twelve days before the hearing. The hearing is open to the public and, to date, the presiding judge has never needed to close the Court to the public, as he is legally authorized to do—not even in the most polemical of cases, for example, that of the law on abortion. The Court then retires for its deliberations (which may necessitate several meetings), and a vote is taken. Once the decision is made, the President entrusts one judge with the task of formulating it and, as in France, it is considered to have the approval of the Court as a whole.

The German version is an even better example of the hybrid nature of constitutional action. Klaus Schlaich writes as follows:

Procedures before the federal Constitutional Tribunal are characterized by the fact that the circle of individuals empowered to make declarations before the Tribunal is much wider and more flexible than in other judicial procedures. One peculiarity of Constitutional Law . . . is that the business of interpreting, changing, or perfecting Constitutional Law is also part of the political process, in which everyone participates and by which everyone is affected.[11]

However, that participation varies according to the type of appeal and monitoring action involved:

- In the case of the abstract monitoring of laws, the constitutional bodies concerned can only make statements.
- In the case of constitutional appeals made by individuals, the plaintiff and the body affected by the appeal (the legislature, the administration, or some other court) can present all the evidence, statements, and information necessary for an examination of the matter.
- In the case of the concrete monitoring of laws, the Bundestag, the Bundesrat, the federal government, and (if necessary) the *Länder* governments and Assemblies may all take part in the procedure and make their own statements.
- Finally, the court may, on its own initiative, invite any expert or qualified person (e.g. politicians, party representatives, or jurists) to state their views.

In principle, oral debate is the rule, but in practice this is reserved for the most important and most political cases (in which hearings sometimes last for several days), a fact that further strengthens the political image of the Court. On the other hand, the fact that it is possible to challenge a judge strengthens the juridical aspect of the action. At the end of the action, the Court announces its decision and, in some cases, also reports any dissenting opinions.

Judgements: A United Front or Room for Dissent?

This is a particularly delicate point upon which we must briefly dwell, for the countries we are considering resolve the question of concurring or dissenting opinions in quite different ways. France and Italy take shelter behind the principle of secrecy and collegiality. In contrast, West Germany has, since 1971, opted for transparency and open debate. In France, demands for the recognition of dissenting opinions have been few, and meanwhile the secrecy of Council deliberations is in general well maintained (at least, the leaks that occur do not spread beyond a limited circle of initiates). In Italy, by contrast, there exists a strong movement in favour of dissenting opinion and the judges themselves have entered into the debate. For example, in 1971, Leopoldo Elia suggested that minority judges should be able to express their disagreements. However, when he was on the point of being elected President of the Court in 1976, he adopted a much more reserved line on the matter. Furthermore, quite frequently Italian judges who favour the introduction of dissenting opinion make their own opinions on Court decisions known in articles or interviews, thereby implicitly indicating how they will vote. These 'reasoned confessions', as they have been called, are individual and partial substitutes for the expression of dissenting opinion, and at the same time bring pressure to bear in favour of changing the present rules. What disadvantages and what advantages would accompany the recognition of dissenting opinion?

The three main disadvantages may be summed up as follows:

1. Dissent would introduce doubt as to the correctness of decisions and undermine them by diminishing their dignity, solemnity, and authority. To some extent, dissent constitutes 'a worm i' the bud'.

2. Dissent would strengthen the politicization of the Court, for the parties or groups involved would make use of the debate in Court to further their own polemics. As a result, the Court would, as the Italians put it, be 'instrumentalized' by the political forces.

3. By making the judges votes public, the recognition of dissent would expose them to all kinds of more or less hidden and heavy pressures from many quarters, ranging from the authorities who appointed them, through political parties and interest groups, to public opinion in general as expressed, in particular, by the Press. Secrecy and collegiality, on the other hand, are more likely to guarantee their serenity and independence.

However, the advantages of recognizing dissent are by no means slight:

1. It would improve the technical quality of judgements. In the first place, the existence of a majority and a minority would make it unnecessary to look systematically for compromise decisions, designed to give offence to none (the French Constitutional Council's decision on the law establishing new constituency boundaries might fall into this category). Secondly, the existence of a minority opinion certainly makes for more vigorous and better-argued majority decisions. At the same time it rules out amateur judges. As Michel Fromont writes in connection with the German Court, 'it seeks to convince by painstakingly arguing and justifying its decisions; and that presupposes its acceptance of the discussion and criticism in which it frequently engages or for which it paves the way'.

2. Dissent keeps the public informed. It demonstrates that the rule of law—especially in this area—is not inscribed in stone, but is

instead the product of an interaction of norms, values, and principles with contingent concrete situations for which there *could* be a different interpretation—and indeed *might* be in the future. The clash of opinion also makes the point that agreement over results takes into account differing views on the means of achieving them. The recognition of dissent involves relying on the intelligence of citizens, who are presented with all the complexities and difficulties inherent in any clash of ideas rather than with the simple virtues of an edict.

3. The expression of dissent may encourage the Courts to produce dynamic jurisprudence, for it constitutes more than simply 'throwaway' remarks on the part of the minority judge or judges. It manifests the kind of cogent and strictly argued debates that stimulate and enrich constitutional reflection. Furthermore, it often constitutes a stage in the evolution of jurisprudence, for with the passing of time a minority view may gather to it enough judges to constitute a new majority.

4. Finally, dissent constitutes a concrete reflection of the reconciliation of the rule of law and democratic principles, at the very highest level, that of the Constitution. Because the Courts are positioned on the borderline between the juridical and the political spheres, within the framework of systems that aim to be democratic, they cannot restrict themselves to pronouncing on the law through some mysterious alchemy that is beyond the understanding of the public. The debate that arises out of a plurality of opinions may prove very beneficial to constitutional jurisdiction. In the first place, it shifts discussion from the field of political suspicions and polemical accusations that may or may not be without foundation to the more fundamental area of values and the more technical one of juridical argumentation. Secondly, judges may derive from the organization of open and pluralistic debate of this kind a substitute for the 'democratic legitimacy' that will never be theirs. Thirdly, the attention that the public pays to the decisions of the Court, and the ensuing debate, framed by the variety of opinion that exists within the Court, constitute the best possible guarantees against tendencies toward 'government by judges'. 'Who will guard the guardians?' is the question often asked, to underline the dangers that the existence of supreme judges might introduce were they subject to no controls at all. And there is really only one answer to that question: the public, the media can guard the guardians, but only if debate and reflection continue to be enriched and fuelled by a plurality of opinions instead of withering

away under the onslaught of sniping attacks and sarcasm, as all too frequently happens.

THE JURIDICAL AND THE POLITICAL: ABSTRACT OR CONCRETE CONTROLS?

The monitoring of laws, whether undertaken a priori or a posteriori, is described as 'abstract' when it does not arise from any litigation over the application of a particular law. The type of monitoring known as 'concrete' (always a posteriori) takes place when a lawsuit or some kind of litigation has arisen. It would certainly be misleading to assimilate abstract monitoring to political controls and concrete monitoring to juridical ones, for the experience of Constitutional Courts amply demonstrates the extent to which the juridical and political aspects are intertwined in both cases. All the same, it is true that abstract controls tend to be more political, concrete ones more juridical. Abstract monitoring is the rule in France, the exception in West Germany and Italy, and unknown in the United States. In the last three countries, it is through the concrete monitoring of laws that the Courts generally operate, so the French model is an unusual and isolated case.

There are two possible variants of concrete monitoring:

1. The question of unconstitutionality may be a preliminary issue that any judge whose function is to arrive at the facts of the case himself settles, under the supervision of superior courts or, if necessary, the Supreme Court. That is what happens in the United States.

2. Alternatively, the question has to be settled by the Constitutional Court, to which the judge whose function it is to establish the facts of the case may make application by tabling a preliminary question. This is the solution adopted by West Germany and Italy.

Both these solutions have been rejected by the majority of French jurists, even though Italy and Germany have demonstrated that 'teamwork' and collaboration between ordinary courts and the Constitutional Court are perfectly possible.

The French advance various arguments to justify this rejection:

1. They contrast the complexity and slowness of concrete monitoring to the simplicity and speed of the French system of abstract and a priori controls.[12] This argument does not lack force, but a fair

rejoinder would surely be that, in the first place, there is no reason why the two modes of control should be mutually exclusive; indeed, if they were both in use, the safeguarding of constitutionality would be considerably strengthened. Secondly, if too much store is set by the virtues of simplicity, the genuine *complexity* of *real* problems may be missed and a simple system confused with what may actually be an inadequate and rudimentary one.[13] Furthermore, even if the problem of slowness (particularly in Italy) is undeniable, would it not be preferable to try to put that right, rather than to forgo the advantages of a better method of control?

2. Concrete monitoring would choke the Constitutional Courts with appeals that are of secondary importance, misguided, or fantastic, whereas, in France at present, 'the responsible and competent authorities whose duty it is to make applications to the Council do not submit to it laws whose constitutionality is not in any doubt'.[14] It is true, of course that abuses do occur, as in all social practice. But why does the answer, once again, have to be a hyper-élitist and paternalistic solution? (Is it that appeals on matters of unconstitutionality are considered too important to be entrusted to ordinary judges or to citizens?)

3. The German and Italian solutions turn the Constitutional Courts into 'super-Supreme Courts of Appeal', which, as Louis Favoreu states, are obliged 'essentially, to devote themselves to examining ordinary affairs in which they have to pick out the constitutional questions and then scrutinize them'.[15] And Favoreu goes on to ask: 'Is that really their role? Have they not somehow been "diverted" from their original function?'[16]

Favoreu's criticism seems curious and in contradiction with his other—perfectly correct—thesis that the process of monitoring constitutionality 'upsets' the law, 'progressively projecting over its other branches the shadow of the Constitutional Council'.[17] For what better way of ensuring that constitutional values do indeed permeate not only the law but also the very lives of citizens than by concrete monitoring of the law *as it is applied*? As Mauro Cappelletti remarks: 'In this way, the question of constitutionality is, so to speak, illustrated and made concrete by the episode in real life that is laid before the judge of a lower court.'[18] Far from a constitutional judge demeaning himself by taking the trouble to examine 'ordinary affairs', he may find this to be a way of bringing his authority and full influence to bear and truly making sure that the rule of law (*État de Droit*) is respected.

4. Finally, it is argued that declaring a law to be unconstitutional several years after its adoption would undermine juridical stability. The repeal of a law is clearly bound to be upsetting to juridical stability. But the question merits further examination. In the first place, is the juridical stability of an unconstitutional law preferable to the discontent occasioned by its repeal? A politician might answer 'yes', but would a jurist?

Secondly, juridical stability is a relative notion in systems that each year adopt numerous new laws (many of which truly do upset the existing situation—for example, where fiscal matters are concerned) and regulations which, for their part, *are* submitted to a posteriori juridical controls. Now, in a formal hierarchy, laws may be placed above regulations, but that does not necessarily correspond to the 'real' situation. In other words, the content of decrees may be just as (or even more) important than that of certain laws, but the former can nevertheless be annulled after being in a force for a few years. So, although the problem of juridical stability is no doubt one that should be taken seriously, let us not delude ourselves: these days, juridical instability is more likely to be caused by volte-faces and instability within the legislature than by any warning shots fired by judges.

Finally, as the German situation shows, it is perfectly possible to correct the drawbacks of total retroactive annulments by resorting to less drastic methods: partial recisions, declaring the law in question to be constitutional provided it is correctly interpreted (i.e. as by the Court), provisional regulations covering a period of transition, declaring a law to be unconstitutional but not retrospectively so, and so on.

Our review of all these arguments has provided an opportunity to indicate the advantages of concrete monitoring. But, as Mauro Cappelletti has pointed out, another of its merits is that it keeps in step with the times: 'This is a modern concept, according to which rights and the law have a life of their own; and it stands in contrast to the static, outdated scholastic concept of a purely a priori system for monitoring laws.' And as Leopoldo Elia, a former president of the Italian Constitutional Court, has pointed out, from a practical point of view this makes it possible to correct old laws that contravene the Constitution. This is an argument of considerable force, when it is remembered that French law still includes dozens of legacies from the past that infringe individual liberties. For the most part they lie dormant but are, unfortunately, always there to be revived for use in particular circumstances. In conclusion, then, it should be emphasized that concrete monitoring makes it possible to revise archaic legislation in a flexible manner that is both in harmony with the problems and spirit of the present age, yet at the same time is based upon superior norms. The use of a concrete and diffused (that is to say, open) system of monitoring to declare antiquated laws to be unconstitutional makes it possible for the legislature to intervene and modernize the legislative apparatus in response to the needs, imperatives, and fundamental values that a particular lawsuit brings to light.

THE POLITICAL AND JURIDICAL TASKS OF CONSTITUTIONAL JUDGES

The tasks of constitutional judges are in part defined by the supreme law of the State but also, as we have seen, to a large extent by the Courts themselves. It would appear from the written statutes and the praetorian directives of the Courts, taken together, that the Courts fulfil three types of function. The first is to guarantee constitutional equilibrium; the second to protect rights and liberties. Their third task (which we shall not be examining here) varies from country to country and seems to be of relatively secondary importance. It includes functions such as those of monitoring the political scene and the organization of national elections.[19]

Constitutional Judges as the Guarantors of Constitutional Equilibrium

This task may be evaluated from two points of view: territorial and functional. I will consider the former first.

There is a territorial aspect to the principle of the separation of powers. Constitutions establish a balance between the powers attributed to central authorities and those guaranteed or granted to local ones. Generally speaking, there is more at stake here than simply the technical means of distributing responsibilities. The division of powers reflects an agreement or consensus reached at some particular point, recorded in the Constitution and (in most countries) guaranteed by a Constitutional Court. However, that guarantee is in general directed more to maintaining the fundamental principles upon which the system is based than to insisting on scrupulous respect for the balance initially established. For it is quite clear that, although Constitutional Courts may have been successful in preserving the basic federal, regional or unitary nature of the German, Italian, and

French systems, they have not stood in the way of the progressive centralization that has been taking place, in various forms, more or less everywhere.

In Germany and Italy, the roles of the Constitutional Courts are explicitly defined by the basic law. The German Constitution (Article 93) makes the Karlsruhe Court responsible for pronouncing judgement on disagreements between the federation and the *Länder* or between one *Land* and another; and the Italian Constitution (Article 134) assigns to the Italian Court a similar responsibility both to monitor regional legislation and also to rule on conflicts between the State and the regions, or between one region and another, over the powers attributed to them. In both countries, the influence of the Constitutional Courts has been useful in preventing excessive inequalities, but has never been anything like as crucial as that of the Supreme Court of the United States. In West Germany, it was originally thought that the Constitutional Court would play a fundamental part in maintaining the balance between the various *Länder* that make up the federation, but in the event this appears to have remained a role of secondary importance. The Court has only had to pronounce judgements on such matters on about thirty occasions, for in general the Bund and *Länder* authorities have preferred to find more practical solutions to their conflicts (special agreements, mixed commissions, negotiation). The famous decision of 28 February 1961, in which the Court denied the federal government the right to set up a national television channel, certainly must have encouraged them to do so. In its pronouncement, the Court drew attention to the unwritten principle of 'friendly behaviour' (*Bundesfreund*) within the federal framework, and specifically declared:

In all cases in which the Federation attempts to set up any agreement with constitutional implications relating to a matter in which all the *Länder* have an interest and by which they are all affected, the obligation to behave in a federal fashion precludes it from acting on the principle of 'divide and rule', that is to say of seeking a solution in dividing the *Länder*, for instance by trying to make agreements with some and then forcing the others to abide by them.

The Court went on to enumerate at length the elements of this code of federal good conduct, which had, in effect, enabled West Germany to construct a new system of co-operative government. On the other hand, the Court did not attempt to discourage the trend toward centralization that has emerged as a result of the overlapping powers of the Bund and the *Länder* in most domains. It has always declined to monitor the (extremely vague) clause in the basic law that allows intervention on the part of the Bund in the interests of standardizing living conditions throughout the federal territory.[20]

The functions attributed to the Italian Constitutional Court in matters concerning the territorial distribution of powers have placed it in a rather difficult position, for in cases of unconstitutionality in regional law (denounced by the regional commissioner for the Republic), the government can make application to the Constitutional Court. At the same time, though for reasons to do with *opportunity* and in cases where conflict arises, the government may also request Parliament to pronounce and decide on the matter. Practice in the 1970s showed that the government manifested a marked tendency to resort to law in its political clashes with the regions, referring to the Court many conflicts that had been artificially dressed up to look like constitutional questions. At the time, the Court was inclined to favour centralization, harbouring reservations regarding the regional experiments then in progress and, as a result, the relations between the regions and the Constitutional Court tended to be marked by distrust. However, as the regional process became more stable and attitudes within the Court changed,[21] the regions came to regard the Constitutional Court as an instrument that guaranteed their autonomy. Their confidence has been increased by instances of jurisprudence that have been more favourable to them. For example, in its decision of 12 October 1983, the Court ruled that even a situation of 'economic emergency' could not justify the violation of a fundamental constitutional principle such as that of regional autonomy.

The question of territorial equilibrium is less acute in France, where the Constitution lays down the unitary nature of the Republic. But even here, the construction of a united Europe coupled with the decentralizing reforms of the Socialists has afforded the Constitutional Council a change to reaffirm and underline the principle of the indivisibility of the Republic (Decision 76.71 of 30 December 1976) and also to clarify the meaning of national unity (in particular in 1982 in connection with the Commissioner of the Republic's powers to monitor territorial authorities and that of decentralization[22] (in 1982, in connection with the special status of Corsica).

Constitutional Courts also take action to rule on certain clashes that arise between one constitutional body and another, or to see that their respective rights to exercise the powers attributed to them are respected. The first point to note in connection with clashes between different constitutional bodies is that constitutional definitions and juridical interpretations of what constitutes such a body vary in scope from one country to another. West Germany extends the concept to include the political parties and, in certain circumstances, the various parliamentary groups, or even members of the Bundestag. But, despite its own wide powers, the German Court has demonstrated considerable prudence, as have the Courts of other countries, whenever it came to intervening in clashes between different public authorities. Between 1951 and 1983, the German Court took action in only twenty-seven cases of this kind. Like the Italian Court, it is careful not to venture too far into the domain of political activities, maintaining that it is not its function to rule upon this type of conflict. Here are a few examples: Despite the fact that the conditions in which the Bundestag was dissolved in 1983 were 'suspect' from the point of view of whether they were in conformity with the spirit of the Constitution, the Court did not take steps to rescind the President's decision (on this point, see Chapter 5). The Italian Court, for all that it is sometimes accused of being a co-legislatory body, has made no pronouncement on the way in which parliamentary parties and groups have interpreted certain constitutional provisions. (For example, it ruled that it was up to the Senate and the Chamber to decide—each possibly adopting a different solution—on how to interpret constitutional provisions regarding parliamentarians' absenteeism.)[23] Many observers have criticized the Council's failure to impose controls on the French President and have deplored his discretionary powers. But had the Council decided that the Head of State *must* sign the decrees and ordinances that the Council of Ministers presents to him, this would have led to a daunting revision of the practices and spirit of the Constitution which would, in its turn, have placed the French President in the relatively powerless position of his German, Italian, and Austrian counterparts. In the final analysis, Courts refuse to enter into head-on clashes with other constitutional bodies or to become involved in exclusively political questions, for example, in which the executive and the legislative authorities are in conflict. It is a policy that makes perfectly good sense, for a judge lacks the credentials of democratic legitimacy which alone could give him the authority to settle purely political conflicts.

However, the attitude of self-restraint that leads all the Courts to accept the privileges of the executive and the rights of Parliament does not reduce the Constitutional Courts to the role of purely passive spectators. In the first place this is because, as has been noted, they have been given specific powers to control the executive or Parliament. Secondly, on the periphery of the exclusively political core of the powers of public authorities, Constitutions have established rules that it is the Courts' duty to guarantee. Thus, all these Courts are particularly vigilant with regard to procedure (the regulation of parliamentary business, the rights of members of parliament, the right to amendment, etc.) and to ensuring that the powers attributed to each of the constitutional bodies are respected. For example, the German Court has censured the Government's practice of exceeding the budgetary limits laid down by Parliament; the Italian Court has ruled that the purely cosmetic reform of a law by Parliament did not justify ruling out the organization of an abrogative referendum; and the French Constitutional Council, responsible for seeing that Articles 34 and 37 are respected, has increasingly acted as the guarantor of all the rights of Parliament (insisting on detailed laws of entitlement, and producing a stricter interpretation of the right of governmental amendment).[24] By indirect means such as these, the Courts are able to keep the activities of constitutional bodies on course and, above all, can prevent excessive imbalances from developing between them.

It is interesting to note that the Constitutional Council, initially regarded as the executive's 'watchdog', is now increasingly seen as the guarantor of the powers of Parliament (even if, for reasons of political expediency, the Presidents of both Assemblies have, on the contrary, declared that the Council was flouting their rights). It has even been successful in spelling out the manner in which certain presidential prerogatives should be exercised. In short, while the functions of Constitutional Courts are narrowly circumscribed to the extent that they may not pronounce on the rights or wrongs of purely political quarrels, the function that remains to them is one of crucial importance, namely, to ensure that the rules of the game are respected and, when necessary, to clarify them.

Constitutional Courts as the Protectors of Rights and Liberties

This major function of Constitutional Courts is often described, using the German terminology, as 'the protection of fundamental rights'. It is a felicitous formula, for it emphasizes the essential importance of the defence of rights and liberties. But it could be misleading, for it might give the impression that 'less fundamental' rights are not (or are less well) protected. In fact though, the guarantee provided by the constitutional judges affects more than purely concrete rights. It is also, indeed above all, a procedural guarantee. Since no right is absolute, it may be permissible to infringe the right of public assembly or the right to property, but only in certain circumstances and when strict rules are observed in so doing. As Judge Douglas eloquently observed of the United States, in the *Wisconsin* v. *Constantineau* case [1971], 'It is significant that most of the provisions of the Bill of Rights are procedural, for it is procedure that marks much of the difference between rule by law and rule by fiat.'

All Constitutional Courts fulfil that function, but the ways in which each of them operates have been largely determined by history and the particular ideological and institutional context. For instance, the French Constitutional Council had to create efficient instruments of control by including in its terms of reference the Preamble to the Constitution which, in its turn, refers back to the 1946 Preamble and the Declaration of 1789. By contrast, the German and Italian Courts were created largely as a result of the Constituents' desire to set up an instrument for the protection of liberties.

Secondly, the duties of the various Courts are laid down by reference to texts that in some cases go back many years (e.g. to 1789) but in others are of recent date (the end of the Second World War)—texts whose contents vary from one country to another. In some, the provisions are so specific as to resemble legislative rules, in others they take the form of far more general proclamations. Article 1 of the German Constitution declares: 'The following basic rights shall bind the legislative, the executive and the judiciary as directly enforceable by law.' On the other hand, in Italy, where the Constitution is less explicit, a long-standing uncertainty exists as to the proper meaning of 'rights' of an economic or social nature which, unlike classic 'rights', might in truth simply represent political aspirations. In the long run, both in Italy and in France, where uncertainty also arose over the implications of the 1946 Preamble, it has proved necessary to include all preambles and proclamations within the terms of reference even if, by reason of their vagueness or generality, it is not always possible to draw the same concrete conclusions from each and every one.

Thirdly, to cope with provisions that are out of date but nevertheless still affect both those who are currently involved in politics and also the circumstances of the moment, a certain amount of interpretation or 'maieutics' (a term often used in Italy) is called for. This interpretative function of constitutional judges has frequently been criticized, for it obviously implies creative powers that sometimes clash with the views and interests of other public authorities. The situation in Italy is revealing in this respect. Between 1948 and 1956, when the Constitution was finally adopted, the Italian Supreme Courts (the Council of State and the Supreme Court of Appeal) persisted in regarding the rights recognized by the Constitution simply as proclamations that carried no positive juridical force. However, with its very first decision, in 1956, the Constitutional Court ruled that those rights constituted its points of reference and its guiding thread. It is not surprising that the interpretative function of the constitutional judges is frequently condemned: it clashes sharply with two notions that are deeply rooted in the Western democracies, particularly in mainland Europe, namely, the principle of parliamentary sovereignty and that of the 'passive' nature of a judge's role: he may declare the law but not create it.

All the Constitutional Courts have nevertheless embarked upon this course of interpretation—a course so perilous that some fear it could lead to the creation of a 'totalitarian' State. The German Court refers to the theory of 'open constitutional norms', which it may interpret, and to the principle of proportionality, according to which, to be constitutional, actions of the State must be 'necessary, appropriate, and not excessive'. The French Constitutional Council has also embarked upon a course of praetorian interpretation that depends upon reference to 'the fundamental principles recognized by the laws of the Republic', principles which Danièle Lochak has described as 'vague' and 'intangible'. Laurent Cohen-Tanugi rejects such criticisms:

By using its judgements to establish the parameters of a definition of French democratic values, the Constitutional Council has, over the past fifteen years, been filling a gap (compensating for the absence of any founding Declaration of Democratic Rights) and correcting a failure to keep up with the times (France's persistence in regarding democracy as a concept established once and for all rather than a continuing process). Since the Constitution was not founded upon any definition of democratic principles, those principles can only be determined *retrospectively*. This is a project that should definitely be on the agenda at a time when so much heart-searching is being devoted to the proper functions of the State, the law, and the market, in the context of the French Social Compact.[25]

The effectiveness and the range of the Courts' protection of fundamental rights depend partly upon the degree of boldness displayed by constitutional judges as they interpret and apply the Constitution. But the procedures for eliciting their judgements and monitoring controls (mentioned earlier) are equally important. The advantages of concrete, a posteriori monitoring undeniably outweigh those of abstract controls that may be either a priori or a posteriori, for concrete monitoring makes for a better understanding of the real juridical and social position and guarantees that greater respect for the decisions of the Constitutional Court is shown by the other authorities (legislative, administrative, and jurisdictional).

CONCLUSION

Throughout this chapter we have been mindful of the ambivalence of Constitutional Courts, and I have tried to show that they can neither be reduced to mere political bodies nor limited to functions of a purely judicial nature. This hybrid situation is clearly a source of tensions and of both strengths and weaknesses. In short:

1. As political bodies, the Constitutional Courts are, as Robert Dahl has pointed out, policy-makers that have gradually evolved methods of their own which endow them with a very real power not simply of reform but also of decision. Not content with the radical but clumsy and unsubtle weapon of outright annulment, they have developed other techniques: partial annulment, declarations of constitutional conformity within the limits of the Court's own definitions, partial and qualitative annulment as in West Germany (the law remains in force, except in certain situations as defined by the Court), deferred annulment (also in West Germany), which renders the law precarious and forces the legislature to intervene, judgements that go on to indicate what action should be taken (in Italy and the United States), and so on. But despite all their ingenuity as policy-makers, the Courts are limited by two constraints that are part and parcel of their position within the institutional framework as a whole. In the first place, they cannot implement their own decisions but must rely on other branches of government to put these into effect. Secondly, the Courts can only *react* to the appeals that are made to them in the guise of either direct applications or preliminary rulings. Unlike Parliaments and governments, they can never initiate policies. To pronounce their

judgements, they are obliged to wait for a favourable opportunity to arise. This may either take the form of a new law (as in France) or of a legislative, administrative, or judicial decision that gives rise to a judgement of unconstitutionality.

2. This inherent weakness of courts in general and Constitutional Courts in particular explains how it is that the judiciary has sometimes been regarded as 'the least dangerous branch' (as Hamilton put it in the *Federalist*, no. 78), despite the fact that nowadays many politicians (from all countries and all parties) and some jurists condemn their praetorian activisim[26] on the grounds either of principle (popular legitimacy and sovereignty) or expediency (regarding the judges as 'trouble-makers'). It is true that, in spite of their weakness, over the past few decades the Courts have managed to confirm their position as essential partners and have imposed their authority, thanks to the force that one major principle carries in the Western democracies: namely, that the rules that currently apply must be respected and the law of the strongest rejected, even if this means the stronger party climbing down. It is solely by virtue of this provision that Constitutional Courts in the past, and the European Communities' Court of Justice today were (or are) able to impose their decisions even upon governments and to do so without weapons and without soldiers: the force of a principle can be enough.

But precisely because the supremacy of the Courts' decisions does not result from force, they have to do their utmost to prevent that reserve of respect and obedience from being eroded. Judges consequently need to be particularly aware that their legitimacy, which stems from their ability to elicit respect for the highest values enshrined in the Constitution, must never be substituted for the democratic legitimacy of other branches of government. This leaves them with scant room for manœuvre but at the same time it makes it possible to replace the Jacobin (and—albeit unwittingly—potentially totalitarian) formula 'You are juridically in the wrong because you are politically in the minority' with another. This is the fine definition of the role of the legislature given by the French Constitutional Council in its judgement of 23 August 1985: 'The law can only express the general will by respecting the Constitution.'

3. A constitutional judge, by reason of his eminent role, operates in a different temporal context from other political protagonists. The body of norms to which he refers is constituted by values that are, so to speak, atemporal (liberty, natural justice, etc.) or at least not confined

to that 'present moment' which so much obsesses other political agents, subject, as they are, to the pressure of society's demands and electoral deadlines. However, the judges are not solely oriented towards the past; they must also guarantee that those values continue to be respected in the future, a fact that accounts for and justifies the prescriptive function of their judgements. Faced with a dictator, they would be useless at blocking his progress; but, by virtue of the way in which they strengthen the bases of democracy, they are essential instruments for preventing any dictator from acceding to power.

But there is another temporal aspect that is peculiar to Constitutional Courts, although variations occur from one system to another. It relates to the length of the judges' mandate and the methods employed for replacing them when it has run out. Constitutional judges are in general appointed or elected for longer periods than the members of other constitutional bodies[27] and they are replaced in batches or gradually, either because that is the rule laid down by the Constitution or because individual judges die whilst in office. A number of important consequences ensue. For one thing, the impact of successive political changes is tempered, but without this leading to stagnation even over a short period, since new arrivals and departures amongst the judges are frequent. For another, the mode of recruitment ensures a certain heterogeneity and pluralism. In other words, the situation combines all the ingredients likely to make for a gradual evolution of policies of a less contingent nature than those of other public authorities. Of course, from time to time jurisprudence is affected by profound changes of orientation, but in general the jurisprudential policy of Contitutional Courts is characterized by incrementalism. Finally, we may emphasize the following point: the Constitutional Courts of the Western democracies work to reconcile democratic, representative, and liberal principles (the principles of the popular will, government through representatives, and powers limited by a system of checks and balances). The Courts can accommodate governments of both the left and the right. Their role is to remind them that in fulfilling their mission they must never cease to respect the Constitution and the values that it expresses. In the last analysis, the judges must have enough power to check power without usurping it; this is the source of both the grandeur and the complexity of their role.

9

Challenges to Democratic Systems

Political rhetoric, legal tradition, and ideological manifestos have often contributed to an abstract and monolithic view of government as 'the State', especially in continental Europe. Such analyses, based as they are upon reductionist theories, preclude any but the most misleading of representations. Admittedly, once 'rational' and 'logical' interpretations are abandoned, doubt and disorder set in: there turns out to be no 'great clock-maker', no puppeteer pulling the strings, after all; nor can any clear dividing lines be drawn between the public and the private sectors, Parliament and government, the centre and the periphery. A quite different picture emerges from an analysis of the concrete functioning of the democracies, for what it reveals are the complexities of the mechanisms of power, the interaction of the agents involved, and the vast number of influences and decision-makers at work. The panoramic view certainly becomes more blurred, the certainties less assured. But that is the price that has to be paid for a more accurate appreciation of the situation. Robert Dahl's question: 'Who governs?' turns out to be more apposite and fundamental than ever. The task of identifying and studying those who hold power is an unending quest for understanding never to be completed.

However, this picture of a multiplicity of agents, a jungle of decisions, and a tangled web of actions should certainly not lead us to unqualified acceptance of the pluralistic theories which regard such dispersal and fragmentation as proof of truly democratic life. True, power is more widely distributed in democracies than in other systems of government, but that is not to say that it is divided equally. All citizens are equal, but some are more equal than others. Is it the case, then, that, in accordance with the iron rule defined by Robert Michels, democracies must inevitably be oligarchies controlled by a handful of political, social, and military élites? The criticism is a serious one, and liberal and élitist schools of thought have been sparring for years over the question of whether the Western political systems are pluralistic or oligarchic. The right position to adopt on this is probably the intermediate one which Dahl, after a long investigation, proposes: certainly it is the élites who govern, but they fall into many different, and competing, groups; and this prevents power from falling into an excessively limited number of hands.

It is not only the essential nature of the Western democracies that is a matter of disagreement. Their contemporary development is also controversial. The stringent criticism of Welfare State democracy produced by economists and philosophers such as Hayek, Friedman, and Nozick in the United States, is particularly pessimistic, sometimes to the point of maintaining that democracy is disappearing altogether from the Western political systems of today. A State with tentacles everywhere, which assumes responsibility for the redistribution of wealth and seeks the well-being of its citizens through interventionism which these critics consider to be of a quasi-totalitarian nature, is regarded by them as the very antithesis of the democratic ideal. For the various proponents of this neo-liberal line, the solution lies in restoring full value and importance to the individual, the only subject who really matters (for society as such has no right to lay claim to a will of its own), and to the market—the only regulatory mechanism capable of respecting the freedom of choice of the individual. This fundamental critique has not eradicated the Welfare State, but it has undermined its standing both in peoples' minds and in the institutions of the Western political systems.

The neo-liberal challenge is not the only one that the Western democracies have had to face. All of them have built themselves up by using institutional and ideological mechanisms to integrate their more or less heterogeneous components; at some time or other in their histories, each of them has sought to extend their frontiers or even to set up empires. Their progress towards democracy has been punctuated by civil wars, internal conquests, colonial expeditions, and the creation and collapse of empires. The 1960s was a period of prosperity and stability for the Western democracies: willy-nilly, internal integration had been achieved; by the time the terrible maelstrom of the 1940s came to an end, frontiers were fixed; the process of decolonization was more or less completed. But the (relative) calm of this period did not mean that there were no 'new frontiers' left to conquer. The democracies no longer needed to control or pacify far-flung provinces, but they were faced with the task of achieving the social, cultural, and political integration of 10 to 15 per cent of their populations who still felt isolated: the immigrants. European nations are now contained within frontiers which history has forced them to consider as 'natural'. But they are now engaged in the discovery of a multipolar, interdependent world in which even the superpowers are sometimes forced to acknowledge their impotence. This phenomenon is particularly strong in Europe, within the European Economic Community, where no single country can decide on important measures unilaterally: there can be no economic policies except those that take into account the situation of neighbouring States, no military policies that disregard the constraints imposed by alliances and the balance of power between the two major world powers. Nation states must now learn to adapt to 'limited sovereignty', whatever the nostalgic regrets of their nationalistic elements.

Today, in the EEC, it is estimated that about one-third of all national legislation and regulation is adopted under constraint, that is to say, with respect to Community rules. It is a proportion that is bound to increase with the advent of a single market in 1993. Entire sections of policy-making are now elaborated jointly, on the basis of an unexpressed theory of 'implied powers'; and even activities in the most sensitive areas (taxation, diplomacy, and defence), considered to constitute the very essence of individual States, are now subject to a creeping expropriation.

However, all this raises daunting problems with respect to the way in which the European democracies function. An increasingly wide gap is developing between those responsible for making major decisions and the citizens who are the source of their legitimacy. This is certainly true at supranational level, where a democratic deficit has been recognized to exist. But it is also—and increasingly—true of each individual country. The democracies were conceived and developed on the basis of the idea that the people afforded legitimacy to the makers of decisions, the latter being ideally embodied by governments and parliaments. It is an ideal that has probably never been fully realized, but it is undeniably true that a widening gap has developed between such mechanisms of classic democracy as are still in place and the real mechanisms of contemporary political systems.

For the sake of argument, we could perhaps allow that, after long years of tentative progress and improvement, political democracy has been more or less achieved: the institutions are accepted, the decision-makers are legitimate, monitored, and subject to the sanction of the people. Administrative democracy, however, has to a large extent yet to be created. True, considerable progress has already been made in this area. The due processes of law now afford the people better protection and more guarantees. But much still remains to be done in order to set up, not an ideal, unattainable perfection, but simply a system that shows more respect for the rights of individuals.

It will no doubt be objected that an excess of democracy tends to kill democracy. And it is quite true that the delicate balance upon which democracy depends is easy to upset. For democracy is never a *fait accompli*, a definitive creation, and—contrary to the beliefs of the Welfare State's detractors—political democracy tends to become increasingly fragile as it loses the ability to ensure social cohesion. Now that the existing democracies reject revolution as a means of change, democratic stability must be sought in a constant process of adaptation and adjustment in which, in default of unanimous agreement on the subject of change, there does exist consensus on the right procedures for bringing about its realization.

And the fact remains that, for all those who are forced to submit to a dictatorial or authoritarian regime, the democratic model—with all its faults—remains an ideal. In the aftermath of the First World War and the great economic crisis, almost all the democracies of Europe seemed threatened. Yet today they are at once internally sound and a subject of fascination to the external world: Chile and Argentina, Hungary and Poland, Algeria and the Philippines are all, with varying success and using various strategies, trying—not to imitate Western democracy slavishly—but gradually to rediscover its mainspring, whether it is economic, social and political pluralism, the separation of powers, or the rule of law. Today, more than ever, democracy remains a challenge.

Notes

Introduction

1. G. Almond and S. Verba, *The Civil Culture: Political Attitudes and Democracy in Five Nations* (Princeton, NJ: Princeton University Press, 1963). On the concept of political culture, see Y. Schemeil, 'Les Cultures politiques', in J. Leca and M. Grawitz, *Traité de science politique*, iii (Paris: PUF, 1985), 394.
2. R. Dahl, *Political Opposition in Western Democracies* (New Haven, Conn.: Yale University Press, 1966), xvii.
3. Y. Mény and V. Wright (eds.), *Centre—Periphery Relations in Western Europe* (London: Allen and Unwin, 1985).

Chapter 1. Politics and Society: Cleavages

1. D. Rae and M. Taylor, *The Analysis of Political Cleavages* (New Haven, Conn.: Yale University Press, 1970). See also R. Dahl, *A Preface to Democratic Theory* (New Haven, Conn.: Yale University Press, 1956).
2. See A. Lijphart, 'Lingua, religione, classe e preferenze politiche: Analisi comparata di quattro paesi', *Rivista italiana di scienza politica*, 8 (1978), 78–111.
3. A. Lijphart, 'Typologies of Democratic Systems', *Comparative Political Studies*, 1(1) (Apr. 1968), 3–33.
4. G. Grunberg and E. Schweisguth, 'Profession et vote: La poussée de la gauche', in Y. Capdevielle, E. Dupoirier, G. Grunberg, E. Schweisguth, and C. Ysmal (eds.), *France de gauche, vote à droite* (Paris: FNSP, 1981).
5. G. Michelet and M. Simon, *Classe, religion et comportement politique*, (Paris: FNSP, 1977).
6. P. G. Pulzer, *Political Representation and Elections in Britain*, (London: Allen and Unwin, 1967), 98.
7. H. Laski, *Parliamentary Government in England* (London: Allen and Unwin, 1948), 63.
8. Ibid. 70, 72.
9. S. E. Finer, *Comparative Government* (London: Allen Lane, 1970), 142.
10. S. Beer, *Modern British Politics*, 3rd edn. (London: Faber and Faber, 1982), 242.

11. D. Butler and D. Stokes, *Political Change in Britain: The Evolution of Electoral Choice* (London: Macmillan, 1974).

12. The question of the class vote is one of the problems most fiercely debated by British political scientists, who disagree about its importance and also its evolution. One recent work emphasizes the persistence of the class vote (A. Heath, R. Jowell, and J. Curtice, *How Britain Votes* (Oxford: Pergamon Press, 1985), but this thesis has been criticized (I. Crewe, 'On the Death and Resurrection of Class Voting: Some Comments on "How Britain Votes"', *Political Studies*, 34(3) (Sept. 1986)), and other recent studies have also underlined the relative decline of the class vote (R. Rose and I. McAllister, *Voters Begin to Choose: From Closed Class to Open Elections* (Beverly Hills, Calif.: Sage, 1986); M. Franklin, *The Decline of Class Voting in Britain* (Oxford: Clarendon Press, 1985).

13. G. Pasquino, 'Il Partito comunista nel sistema politico italiano', in G. Pasquino (ed.), *Il Sistema politico italiano* (Bari: Laterza, 1985), 140.

14. Ibid. 132.

15. A. Lancelot, 'L'Orientation du comportement politique', in J. Leca and M. Grawitz (eds.), *Traité de science politique*, iii (Paris: PUF, 1985).

16. A. Grosser, *L'Allemagne de notre temps*, Coll. Pluriel (Paris: Fayard, 1978), 440–1.

17. Ibid. 453.

18. Lancelot, 'L'Orientation du comportement politique', 394.

19. R. Inglehart, 'Changing Paradigms in Comparative Political Behavior', in A. Finifter (ed.), *Political Science: The State of the Discipline* (Washington: APSA, 1983), 443.

20. G. Smith, *Politics in Western Europe*, 4th edn. (London: Heinemann, 1983), 25.

21. J. Gottman, 'The Evolution of the Concept of Territory', *Social Science Information*, 14 (1975), 29.

22. Lancelot, 'L'Orientation du comportement politique', 404.

23. K. Von Beyme, *Political Parties in Western Democracies* (Aldershot: Gower, 1985), 278.

24. J. Blondel, *An Introduction to Comparative Government* (London: Weidenfeld and Nicolson, 1969), 53.

25. S. M. Lipset and S. Rokkan, 'Cleavages, Structures, Party Systems, and Voter Alignments: An Introduction', in S. M. Lipset and S. Rokkan (eds.), *Party Systems and Voter Alignments: Cross-National Perspectives* (New York: Free Press, 1967).

26. S. Rokkan, *Citizens, Elections, Parties* (Oslo: Universiteit Forlaget, 1970).

27. For an application of Rokkan's model to the European political parties, see D. L. Seiler, *Les Partis politiques en Europe*, 2nd edn., Coll. Que sais-je? (Paris: PUF, 1982).

Chapter 2. Political Parties

1. Edmund Burke, *Thoughts on the Cause of the Present Discontents*, 2nd edn. (London, 1770), 110.
2. M. Duverger, *Les Partis politiques* (Paris: Colin, 1951); L. D. Epstein, *Political Parties in Western Democracies* (New York: Praeger, 1967).
3. J. La Palombara and M. Weiner (eds.), *Political Parties and Political Development* (Princeton, NJ: Princeton University Press, 1966).
4. K. Janda, *Political Parties, a Cross National Survey* (New York: Free Press. 1980).
5. D.-L. Seiler, *Partis et familles politiques* (Paris: Themis (PUF), 1980).
6. Moderate bourgeois and parliamentary monarchy established after the July Revolution of 1830, which brought down Charles X.
7. See G. Galli, *I Partiti politici* (Turin: UTET, 1974).
8. V. Bogdanor (ed.), *Liberal Party Politics* (Oxford: Clarendon Press, 1983).
9. French counter-revolutionary ideologists.
10. A priest who defended Catholic teaching and social policies to favour the disadvantaged.
11. M. Caciagli, 'Il Resistibile Declino della Democrazia Cristiana', in G. Pasquino, *Il Sistema politico italiano* (Bari: Laterza, 1985), 103.
12. Ibid.
13. M. Anderson, *Conservative Politics in France* (London: Allen and Unwin, 1974); J. Charlot, *Le Phénomène gaulliste* (Paris: Fayard, 1970).
14. R. Kirk, *The Conservative Mind* (Chicago: Gateway, 1960).
15. R. E. M. Irving, *The Christian Democratic Parties in Western Europe* (London: Allen and Unwin, 1979).
16. W. E. Paterson and I. Campbell, *Social Democracy in Post-War Europe* (London: Macmillan, 1974); F. Bealey (ed.), *The Social and Political Thought of the Labour Party* (London: Weidenfeld and Nicolson, 1970).
17. M. Thorez, Eighth Congress, Villeurbanne, Jan. 1936.
18. Although the Italian Communist Party is itself suffering from a dearth of ideas at present, its troubles are nothing like as grave as the crisis affecting the Greek and Portuguese Communist Parties, or the decline of the French and Spanish Communist Parties.
19. N. Bobbio, 'La Questione socialista', *Monde Operaio*, (1976), 41–51.
20. Y. Mény (ed.), *Dix Ans de régionalisation en Europe* (Paris: CUJAS, 1982).
21. The spectrum embraces at one end the peaceful anarchist goat-breeder, at the other the high-level technician devising alternative sources of energy and rejecting the nuclear solution.
22. R. Inglehart, 'Post-Materialism in an Environment of Insecurity', *American Political Science Review*, 75(4) (1981), 880–900.
23. D. Boy, *Le Vote écologiste en 1978* (Paris: RFSP, 1981), 394–416.

24. F. Muller-Rommel, 'Ecology Parties in Western Europe', *West European Politics*, 5(1)(1982), 68–74; F. Muller-Rommel, 'New Social Movements and Smaller Parties: A Comparative Perspective', *West European Politics*, 8(1), (1985), 41–55.

25. M. and J. Charlot, 'Les Groupes politiques dans leur environnement', in J. Leca and M. Grawitz (eds.), *Traité de science politique*, iii (Paris: PUF, 1985), 437.

26. 'Le RPR', *Pouvoirs*, 28 (1984), *passim*.

27. P. Avril, *Essai sur les partis* (Paris: LGDJ, 1986), 109.

28. Duverger, *Les Partis politiques*, 10.

29. Ibid. 46.

30. A. B. Wildavsky, 'A Methodological Critique of Duverger's Political Parties', *Journal of Politics*, 21(2) (May 1959), 305 ff.

31. W. Wright, 'Comparative Party Models: Rational, Efficient and Party Democracy', in W. Wright (ed.), *A Comparative Study of Party Organization* (Colombus, Ohio: Merrill, 1971).

32. See F. J. Sorauf, 'Political Parties and Political Analysis', in W. N. Chambers and W. D. Burnham (eds.), *The American Party System: Stages of Political Development* (Oxford: Oxford University Press, 1967).

33. Avril, *Essai sur les partis*, 69.

34. R. Michels, *Political Parties: a Sociological Study of the Oligarchic Tendencies of Modern Democracy* (New York: Free Press, 1962).

35. Ibid. 289.

36. M. Weber, *Wirtschaft und Gesellschaft* (Tübingen: Mohr), 1922.

37. K. Von Beyme, 'I Gruppi dirigenti nella SPD', *Città e regione*, 3 (1983), 21–40.

38. A. Zuckerman, *The Politics of Faction: Christian Democratic Rule in Italy* (New Haven, Conn.: Yale University Press, 1979); G. Sartori (ed.), *Correnti, frazioni e fazione nei partiti italiani* (Bologna: Il Mulino, 1973); G. Pasquino, *Degenerazioni dei partiti e riforme istituzuionali* (Bari: Laterza, 1982).

39. K. Dyson, *Party, State and Bureaucracy in Western Germany* (London: Sage, 1977).

40. V. Ciuffa, 'Rispettato il "manuale Cencelli"', *Corriere della sera*, 5 Aug. 1983.

41. M. Charlot, *Le Système politique britannique*, Coll. U (Paris: Colin, 1976), 41.

42. J. Blondel, 'Party Systems and Patterns of Government in Western Democracies', *Revue canadienne de science politique*, 1(2) (June 1986), 183–90.

43. G. Sartori, *Parties and Party Systems* (Cambridge: Cambridge University Press, 1976).

44. G. Galli, *Il Bipartismo imperfetto: Comunisti e Democristiani in Italia* (Bologna: Il Mulino, 1966).

45. P. Farneti, *The Italian Party System*, ed. S. E. Finer and A. Mastropaolo (London: Frances Pinter, 1985), 184.

46. Ibid. 185.

47. R. D. Putnam, R. Leonardi, and R. Y. Nanetti, 'Polarization and Depolarization in Italian Politics', *American Political Science Association Conference*, New York, Sept. 1981.

48. F. Pappi ('The West German System', *West European Politics*, 7(4) (Oct. 1984), 7–27) suggests that there have been two main phases to the West German system. The first, 1948–61, involved a diminution in the number of parties; the second, 1961–83, the stabilization of a three-party system. Since the 1983 elections, confirmed by those of 1987, it would appear that a four-party system is becoming established.

49. The first Mauroy Government, between the presidential and the legislative elections of 1981, was similarly 'monochrome'. Yet, strictly speaking, both the Mauroy and the Fabius Governments were coalitions, as both included a number of Radicals.

50. E. Pappalardo, *Partiti e governi di coalizione in Europa* (Milan: Fageli, 1978).

51. W. Riker, *The Theory of Political Coalitions* (New Haven, Conn.: Yale University Press, 1962).

52. L. Dodd, *Coalitions in Parliamentary Government* (Princeton, NJ: Princeton University Press, 1976).

53. I. Budge and D. Farlie, *Explaining and Predicting Elections: Party Strategies and Issues. Outcomes in Twenty-Three Democracies* (London: Allen and Unwin, 1983).

Chapter 3. Interest Groups

1. G. A. Almond and G. B. Powell, *Comparative Politics: A Developmental Approach* (Boston: Little, Brown, and Co., 1966).

2. This law encouraged the organization of groups by allowing them to acquire an extremely liberal juridical status merely by declaring themselves.

3. S. Berger, 'Regime and Interest Representation: The French Traditional Middle Classes', in S. Berger (ed.), *Organizing Interests in Western Europe* (Cambridge: Cambridge University Press, 1981), 99.

4. The National Union of Manufacturers, created in 1916, and the National Confederation of Employers' Associations, founded in 1919.

5. H. Weber, *Le Parti des patrons: Le CNPF, 1946–1986* (Paris: Seuil, 1986).

6. A. Grosser and M. Menudier, *La Vie politique en Allemagne fédérale* (Paris: Colin, 1977), 233.

7. P. Self and H. Storing, 'The Farmers and the State', in R. Kimber and J. Richardson (eds.), *Pressure Groups in Britain* (London: Dent, 1974).

8. A. Grosser, *L'Allemagne de notre temps*, Coll. Pluriel (Paris: Fayard, 1978), 346.

9. M. Cammelli, *L'Amministrazione per collegi* (Bologna: Il Mulino, 1980), 240.

10. In Britain, the CBI, in its 1983 Annual Report, mentions that it took part in a wide range of committees, about seventy in all, including the National Dock Labour Board, the Health and Safety Commission, the Commission for Racial Equality, the Genetic Manipulation Advisory Group, etc.

11. Y. Mény, 'La Légitimation des groupes d'interêt par l'administration française', *RFAP*, 39 (1986), 99 f.

12. M. Golden, 'Neo-corporativismo ed esclusione della forza-lavoro dalla rappresentanza politica', in G. Pasquino (ed.), *Il Sistema politico italiano*, Libri del tempo (Bari: Laterza, 1985), 254.

13. In practice, however, the interpenetration of American élites may make board members over-sensitive to the interests that they are responsible for controlling.

14. See E. Suleiman, *Politics, Power and Bureaucracy in France* (Princeton, NJ: Princeton University Press, 1974).

15. J. Hayward, 'The Nemesis of Industrial Patriotism: The French Response to the Steel Crisis', in Y. Mény and V. Wright (eds.), *The Politics of Steel: Western Europe and the Steel Industry in the Crisis Years (1974–1984)* (Berlin: De Gruyter, 1987), 502.

16. A. F. Bentley, *The Process of Government* (Evanston, Ill.: Principia Press of Illinois, 1949), 208. According to Bentley, government and its policies result *purely* from the pressures exerted by various groups. He writes, for example: 'the balance of the group pressures *is* the existing state of society' (pp. 258–9).

17. M. Olson, *The Logic of Collective Action: Public Goods and the Theory of Groups* (Cambridge, Mass.: Harvard University Press, 1965).

18. P. Schmitter, 'Still the Century of Corporatism?', *Review of Politics*, 36 (1974), 93.

19. Ibid. 85–93.

20. A. Cox and J. Hayward, 'The Inapplicability of the Corporatist Model in Britain and France', *International Political Science Review*, 4(2) (1983), 217–40.

21. J. Keeler, 'Corporation and Official Union Hegemony: The Case of French Agricultural Syndicalism', in Berger, *Organizing Interests in Western Europe* (Cambridge: Cambridge University Press, 1981).

22. G. Lehmbruch, 'Liberal Corporatism and Party Government', *Comparative Political Studies*, 10 (Apr. 1977).

Chapter 4. Voters, Elections, and the Elected

1. G. Sartori, *Théorie de la démocratie* (Paris: Colin, 1973), 84.

2. R. Hrbek, 'La Réalité du mode de scrutin allemand', 'La Représentation proportionnelle', *Pouvoirs*, 32 (1985), 67–82.
3. G. Amato, 'Le Système électoral', 'Italie', *Pouvoirs*, 18 (1981), 49–58.
4. Apart from the elimination clause of 5%.
5. e.g. in a department with two seats at its disposal, the votes obtained by all the lists apart from the top two are 'lost'. If the two elected share between them 70% of the votes (40% and 30% respectively), the remaining 30% of voters remain unrepresented.
6. See G. Pasquino, 'I Sistemi elettorali', in G. Amato and A. Barbara (eds.), *Manuale di diritto pubblico* (Bologna: Il Mulino, 1981).
7. F. Lanchester, *Sistemi Electorali a forma di Governo?* (Bologna: Il Mulino, 1981).
8. Amato, 'Le Système électoral, Italie', 52–3.
9. In West Germany, the Constitutional Court monitored the rule according to which a constituency population was not supposed to exceed or fall short of the average constituency population figure by more than 25%. In its decision of 22 May 1963, the Court declared: 'The constituency boundaries have become unconstitutional in that they clearly no longer correspond to the distribution of the population, and it is no longer likely that the distortion will rectify itself. The federal legislator is consequently to proceed to change the constituency boundaries during the present legislature.'
10. The Constitutional Council had already marked out the guidelines for its jurisprudence in a decision relating to New Caledonia in 1985.
11. Decision no. 86.208 of 1/2 July 1986.
12. Decision no. 86.218 of 18 July 1986.
13. M. Beloff and G. Peele, *The Government of the UK: Political Authority in a Changing Society*, 2nd edn. (London: Weidenfeld and Nicolson, 1985), 169.
14. Ibid.
15. M. Charlot, *Le Système politique britannique*, Coll. U (Paris: Colin, 1976).
16. K. Von Beyme, 'The Role of Deputies in West Germany', in E. Suleiman (ed.), *Parliaments and Parliamentarians in Democratic Politics* (New York: Holmes and Meier, 1986), 156.
17. K. Von Beyme, *The Political System of the Federal Republic of Germany* (Farnborough, Hants: Gower, 1985), 28.
18. A. Ranney, *Pathways to Parliament: Candidate Selection in Britain* (London: Macmillan, 1965); M. Rush, *The Selection of Parliamentary Candidates* (London: Nelson, 1969); P. W. Buck, *Amateurs and Professionals in British Politics, 1918–1959* (Chicago: University of Chicago Press, 1963).
19. P. Paterson, *The Selectorate: The Case for Primary Elections in Britain* (London: MacGibbon and Kee, 1967).
20. G. Di Palma and M. Cotta, 'Cadres, Peones and Entrepreneurs:

Professional Identities in a Divided Parliament', in Suleiman (ed.), *Parliaments and Parliamentarians in Democratic Politics*, 57.

21. Charlot, *Le Système politique britannique*, 105.
22. D. Butler and D. Stokes, *Political Change in Britain: The Evolution of Electoral Choice* (London: Macmillan, 1974).
23. P. Norris, 'Women's Legislative Participation in Western Europe', *West European Politics*, 8(4) (Oct. 1985), 90–2.
24. M. Cotta, *Classe politica e parlamento in Italia (1946–1976)* (Bologna: Il Mulino, 1979).
25. Charlot, *Le Système politique britannique*, 105.
26. R. D. Putnam, *The Comparative Study of Political Élites* (Englewood Cliffs, NJ: Prentice Hall, 1976).
27. All these figures are taken from a study of 'The Political Class in European Parliamentary Regimes (France, Belgium, West Germany, Britain)', carried out by J.-P. Caille within the framework of the DEA de sciences politiques of the University of Paris II, Feb. 1985 (unpublished).
28. R. Cayrol, J.-L. Parodi, C. Ysmal, *Le Deputé français* (Paris: FNSP, 1973).
29. Cotta, *Classe politica e parlamento in Italia*.
30. H. Haack, *Die Personnelle Struktur des 9 Deutschen Bundestages: Ein Beitrag Zur Abgeordnetensoziologie* (Bonn: Z Parl, 1981), 185.
31. Cayrol *et al.*, *Le Deputé français*; R. Cayrol, 'Beaucoup plus d'enseignants, moins d'industriels et de paysans', *Le Monde*, 23 June 1981.
32. C. Ysmal, 'Élites et leaders', in J. Leca and M. Grawitz (eds.), *Traité de science politique*, iii (Paris: PUF, 1985), 616 f.
33. H. Neumann, *Zur Machtstruktur in der Bundesrepublik Deutschland* (Munich: Knoth, 1979).
34. Di Palma and Cotta, 'Cadres, Peones and Entrepreneurs', 53.
35. Ibid. 57.
36. Except when it is a case of seizing upon a pretext in order to return to civilian life! However, since the exodus of soldiers claiming to be candidates in order to get out of the army (in the early 1960s), a Commons committee has been set up to verify the credibility of candidacies.
37. J. Becquart-Leclercq, 'Cumul des mandats et culture politique', in A. Mabileau (ed.), *Les Pouvoirs locaux à l'épreuve de la décentralisation* (Paris: Pedone, 1983), 207–39; A. Mabileau, 'La Limitation du cumul des mandats: Illusion électoraliste ou modernisation démocratique', in *Annuaire des collectivités locales 1986* (Paris: LITEC, GRAL, 1986).

Chapter 5. Parliaments

1. 'L'Assemblée d'aujourdhui', *Pouvoirs*, 34 (1985), 9.
2. G. Smith, *Politics in Western Europe*, 4th edn. (London: Heinemann, 1983), 171.

3. F. Cazzola and M. Morisi, *L'Alluvione dei decreti* (Milan: Giuffre, 1985);
   R. Motta, 'L'Attività legislativa dei governi 1948–83', *Rivista italiana di scienza politica*, 15(2) (1985), 255–292.
4. Avril, 'L'Assemblée d'aujourdhui', 5.
5. These figures represent the average since 1945. See J. Dutheil de la Rochère, 'L'Inflation législative et règlementaire en Grande-Bretagne', in C. Debbasch (ed.), *L'Inflation législative et règlementaire en Europe* (Paris: CNRS, 1986), 106.
6. J. Jacob, 'Legislation, Its Background, Functions and Formal Structure', European Science Foundation, Sept. 1985.
7. P. Cahoua, 'Les Commissions, lieu du travail législatif', *Pouvoirs*, 34 (1985), 37–49.
8. See Y. Mény (ed.), *Dix Ans de régionalisation en Europe* (Paris: Cujas, 1982).
9. A. Grosser, *L'Allemagne de notre temps* (Paris: Pluriel, Livre de poche, 1978), 243.
10. A. Baldassare, 'Le "Performances" del parlamento italiano nell'ultimo quindicennio', in G. Pasquino, *Il Sistema politica italiano*, Libri del Tempo (Bari: Laterza, 1985), 313. Intervention by the President of the Chamber of Deputies was made possible by a change in the regulations introduced in 1981. (The President of the Senate had held that prerogative ever since 1971.)
11. It should be noted that the House of Lords has no standing committees, only select committees.
12. D. Truman, *The Government Process* (New York: Knopf, 1953), 372.
13. G. De Vergottini, *Les Investigations des commissions parlementaires en Italie*, i (Paris: RDP, 1985), 37 ff.
14. e.g. in 1984, when tension was running very high between the right and the Socialist Government, 90% of the amendments tabled *in commissions* were adopted.
15. J. A. G. Griffith, *Parliamentary Scrutiny of Government Bills* (London: Allen and Unwin, 1974).
16. The same procedure may be adopted when the House is sitting as a 'committee of the whole House', and also in standing committees (in the latter case, provided the motion is supported by one-third of the committee).
17. The Conservative Party has also been known to force its leaders to resign following electoral defeats. Alec Douglas Home was obliged to resign in 1965 (after the 1964 defeat) as was Edward Heath in 1975 (after the 1974 defeat).
18. See N. Johnson, 'Questions in the Bundestag', *Parliamentary Affairs*, 16(1) (1962–3); A Grosser provides the following figures regarding the *Grosse Anfrage*: 160 during the first legislature; 97, 34, and 45 in the following legislatures (*L'Allemagne de notre temps*, p. 245).

19. P. Norton (ed.), *Parliament in the 1980s* (Oxford: Blackwell, 1985), 17.
20. G. Smith, *Democracy in Western Germany: Parties and Politics in the Federal Republic* (London: Heinemann, 1979).
21. It should also be pointed out that West Germany has particular methods of control that fulfil an important function: among them, the right of citizens to petition the Bundestag (over 12,000 petitions are currently presented each year), the right of all individuals to apply to the federal Constitutional Court over a violation of basic human rights, and the creation, in 1956, of a kind of ombudsman for military matters, etc.
22. N. Polsby, 'Legislatures', in F. I. Greenstein and N. W. Polsby (eds.), *Handbook of Political Science*, v, (Reading, Mass.: Addison, Wesley, 1975), 301.
23. F. Baumgartner, in a recent study ('Parliament's Capacity to Expand Political Controversy in France', *Legislative Studies Quarterly*, 12(1) (Feb. 1987), 33–54) concludes his assessment of the role of Parliament in France as follows: 'The French Parliament is not the center of policy-making by any stretch of imagination. It is the center of politics, however, and politics can have a great impact on policy.'

Chapter 6. Presidents and Governments

1. J. Blondel, 'Gouvernements et exécutifs: Parlements et législatifs', in J. Leca and M. Grawitz, *Traité de science politique*, iii (Paris: PUF, 1985), 355.
2. The 1958 Constitution had initially made provision for the President to be elected by a college of notables (Deputies, locally elected representatives, and representatives from overseas territories), numbering about 75,000 individuals. The system was devised, on the one hand, so as not to be solely dependent upon Deputies and senators (who used to elect the President under the Third and Fourth Republics) and, on the other, to avoid direct universal suffrage. The memory of the *coup d'état* of 2 Dec. 1851 by Louis Napoleon Bonaparte (the only President to be elected by direct universal suffrage until 1962) prompted fears that the same might happen again. It was only in 1962, at the end of the Algerian War, that General de Gaulle was able to hold a referendum to get the Constitution revised and establish presidential elections by direct universal suffrage.
3. E.g. in Britain, ever since the late 19th cent. there has existed a firmly established tradition that the Prime Minister must be a member of the House of Commons. In 1963, Lord Home submitted to this 'convention' by renouncing his hereditary rights and getting himself elected to the House of Commons in a Scottish by-election.
4. J.-C. Colliard, *Les Régimes parlementaires contemporains*, (Paris: FNSP, 1978), 130.

5. Unless they are made members of the House of Lords, which makes things rather easier (e.g. Lord Young).

6. M. Dogan, *How to Become a Cabinet Minister in Italy: Unwritten Rules of the Political Game*, European University Institute Working Paper, 1983.

7. H. Portelli, 'La Proportionnelle et les partis', 'La Représentation proportionnelle', *Pouvoirs*, 32 (1985), 87.

8. The RI obtained three ministerial portfolios and one Secretary of State portfolio in the Couve de Murville Government, four ministerial and three Secretary of State posts in the Chaban-Delmas Government (which also included three Centre PDM Ministers).

9. The Communists totalled only four Ministers in the Mauroy Governments from 1981 to 1984.

10. J. P. Mackintosh, *The British Cabinet*, 3rd edn., London, Stevens, 1977.

11. M. Lee, 'Fonctionnement du gouvernement et rôle du Premier Ministre sous Mme Thatcher', 'La Grande-Bretagne', *Pouvoirs* (1986), 45–57.

12. P. A. Allum, *Italy, Republic without Government?* (London: Weidenfeld and Nicolson, 1973).

13. G. Di Palma, *Surviving without Governing: The Italian Parties in Parliament* (Berkeley, Calif.: University of California Press, 1977).

14. G. Smith, *Democracy in Western Germany: Parties and Politics in the Federal Republic* (London: Heinemann, 1979), 56.

15. A. Grosser, *L'Allemagne de notre temps*, Coll. Pluriel (Paris: Fayard, 1978), 225.

16. S. Cassese, 'Esiste un governo in Italia?', in G. Pasquino (ed.), *Il Sistema politico italiano*, Libri del tempo (Bari: Laterza, 1985), 279.

17. Ibid. 279.

18. See e.g. Grosser, *L'Allemagne de notre temps*; N. Johnson, 'Questions in the Bundestag', *Parliamentary Affairs*, 16(1) (1962–3); R. Mayntz in R. Rose and E. Suleiman (eds.) *Presidents and Prime Ministers* (Washington, DC: American Enterprise Institute, 1980).

19. Of course, the Italian President of the Council has no power of veto in the constitutional sense of the expression. However, in a political context, he has on occasion managed to block various moves on the part of his Ministers. Recently, for example, Craxi prevented the sale to De Benedetti of a firm from the public sector despite this being favoured by both Prodi, the President of the IRI, and also the Christian Democrats.

20. For a disillusioned and pessimistic analysis of the role of the President of the Council, see Stephano Merlini, 'Presidente del Consiglio e collegialità di governo', *Quaderni Costituzionali*, 11th year, (Apr. 1988), 7–32.

21. Report from the Corte dei Conti, cited by *La Repubblica*, 12 Aug. 1986.

22. Ibid.

23. The Central Policy Review Staff was in particular entrusted with correcting two faults frequently imputed to the British government and

administration, namely, insufficient co-ordination between Ministers and inadequate overall long-term planning. It was also supposed to check that adopted policies tallied with mid-term government objectives, and also to serve as a 'think tank' for government ideas.

24. In West Germany, the term 'Secretary of State' refers to civil servants with a status equivalent to that of the Secretary-General of the French Government or Presidency. The Chancellor's Office was placed under the directorship of a senior civil servant up until 1969, and from 1974 to 1989. Between these periods, the role was filled by a Minister, a member of the federal government. The importance of the post may be appreciated from the fact that Karl Carstens, who held it briefly in the late 1960s, became President of the Republic in 1979.

25. The principal changes clearly occurred between 1969 and 1970, when the SPD–FDP coalition came to power after twenty years of Christian Democrat domination.

26. Within the Chancellor's office, overall planning (which includes taking into account and evaluating long-term problems, the analysis of social and political trends, and the management of an organized information system) falls, in part, to civil servants, but also to young university academics who work on specific studies or are appointed on contract for one or two years.

27. Grosser, *L'Allemagne de notre temps*, 240.

28. J. Massot, 'Le Chef du gouvernement en France' (Paris: La Documentation française, 1979), 164.

29. Mayntz, 156.

30. S. Merlini, 'Presidente del Consiglio e collegialità di governo'.

Chapter 7. *Local and Central Bureaucracies*

1. This figure includes teachers and professional soldiers.

2. This figure includes only 'civil servants'. It does not include either soldiers or teachers. It should be noted that the Civil Service has lost 260,000 members since Margaret Thatcher came to power.

3. On European administrations, see F. Ridley, *Government and Administration in Western Europe* (Oxford: Robertson, 1979); J. Armstrong, *The European Administrative Élite* (Princeton, NJ: Princeton University Press, 1973).

4. In its 1985–6 report, the Treasury and Civil Service Committee again suggested experimenting with 'policy units' (the approximate equivalents of French *cabinets*). The Government's response was that Ministers who wished to could do so.

5. S. Tarrow, *Between Center and Periphery: Grassroots Politicians in Italy and France* (New Haven, Conn.: Yale University Press, 1977).

6. B. Dente, *Governare la frammentazione* (Bologna: Il Mulino, 1985).

7. S. Cassese, 'États, régions, Europe', 'Régions', *Pouvoirs*, 19 (1981), 19–26.

8. This is an extremely liberal law that makes it very easy to set up an association with a legal status.

9. S. Cassese, *Il Sistema amministrativo italiano* (Bologna: Il Mulino, 1983); D. Serrani, *Il Potere per enti: Enti pubblici e sistema politico in Italia* (Bologna: Il Mulino, 1978).

10. Note, however, that the Civil Service also comprises a category of 'industrial civil servants' that corresponds to State-employed workers (e.g. in munitions factories). Between 1979 and 1985, their number fell by 39%.

11. Since 1987, the IRI has sold off twenty-seven companies and given up its majority holdings in many others, with the result that five new firms have made their appearance on the Stock Market.

12. See J. Vickers and V. Wright, 'The Politics of Industrial Privatisation in Western Europe', *West European Politics*, 11(4) (Oct. 1988), 1–30.

13. See M. Dogan (ed.), *The Mandarins of Western Europe* (New York: Sage, 1975).

14. See Cassese, *Il Sistema amministrativo italiano*.

15. The Bundesakademie in Bonn also rates a mention.

16. Contracts were introduced in 1968 in the health sector and were extended to public employees generally within the framework of Law no. 93 (1983).

17. But the very fact of forbidding a vital sector to become unionized comes to the same thing as denying it the right to strike.

18. V. Wright, in M. Balluteau, F. de Baecque, D. Lochak, B. Tricot, and V. Wright, 'La politicisation du Conseil d'État: Mythe ou réalité?', *Pouvoirs*, 40 (1987).

19. Y. Fortin, 'L'Administration centrale britannique', in IIAP, *Chronique de l'administration à l'étranger, Administration 1985*, (Paris: La Documentation française, 1986, p. 104, and 1987, p. 99). See also R. Thomas, 'Devoirs et responsabilités des fonctionnaires et des ministres: un défi pour les membres du Cabinet ministériel britannique', *RISA*, 52(4) (1986), 619–653.

20. The obligation of secrecy is laid down by the Official Secrets Act (1911). Following a leak in the Ministry of Defence in 1984 (when a civil servant, Clive Ponting, passed documents relating to the Falklands War to a member of the Opposition), a civil servant was charged in a court of law, but was acquitted. This occasioned considerable friction, which was prolonged in 1986 when the Government attempted to stop the publication in Australia of the memoirs of a former Secret Service employee, Peter Wright.

21. In France, despite the law, access to administrative documents is still

strongly discouraged by the administration. In Italy, there was no follow-up to a report produced in 1984 urging the adoption of more liberal policies.

22. E. Etzioni-Halévy, *Bureaucracy and Democracy: A Political Dilemma* (London: Routledge and Kegan Paul, 1953).

23. G. Timsit and C. Wiener, 'Administration et politique en Grande-Bretagne, en Italie et en RFA', *RFSP*, 30(3) (1980), 506–32; R. Putnam, *The Comparative Study of Political Élites* (Englewood Cliffs, NJ: Prentice Hall, 1976); M. Dogan (ed.), *The Mandarins of Western Europe*; J. Aberbach, R. Putnam, B. Rockman (eds.) with the collaboration of T. Anton, *Bureaucrats and Politicians in Western Democracies* (Cambridge, Mass.: Harvard University Press, 1981).

24. See E. Page, *Political Authority and Bureaucratic Power: A Comparative Analysis* (Brighton: Wheatsheaf Books, 1985).

25. Only one-quarter reach the level of Under-Secretary before they are 50 years old.

26. R. Rose, 'The Political Status of Higher Civil Servants in Britain', in E. Suleiman (ed.), *Bureaucrats and Policy Making* (London: Holmes and Meier, 1984), 151.

27. A. Doig, 'A Question of Balance: Business Appointments of Former Civil Servants', *Parliamentary Affairs*, 39(1) (1986), 63 ff.

28. Cassese, *Il Sistema amministrativo italiano*.

29. S. Cassese, *Questione amministrativa e questione meridionale: Dimensione e reclutamento della burocrazia dall'unità ad oggi* (Milan: Giuffre, 1977). The lower echelons were the first to be taken over, then the entire Civil Service.

30. S. Cassese, 'The Higher Civil Service in Italy', in E. Suleiman (ed.), *Bureaucrats and Policy Making*, 35–71.

31. G. P. Storchi, 'Gli "Incarichi esterni" dei magistrati amministrativi', *Rivista trimestrale di Diritto pubblico*, 2 (1977), 596.

32. See, in particular, Arendt Lijphart's classic work, *The Politics of Accommodation: Pluralism and Democracy in the Netherlands* (Berkeley, Calif.: University of California Press, 1968), 197.

33. L. Moulin, 'The Politicization of the Administration in Belgium', in Dogan (ed.), *The Mandarins of Western Europe*, 47 f.

34. G. Lehmbruch, *Proporz demokratie* (Tübingen: Mohr, 1967).

35. The Germans describe the position of these civil servants as 'a provisional retirement'. The civil servant is allowed to draw 75% of his salary for five years.

36. Up until 1969, Ministers could, if they wished, be represented by senior civil servants at meetings of the Council of Ministers.

37. See N. Johnson, *State and Government in the Federal Republic of Germany: The Executive at Work*, 2nd edn. (Oxford: Pergamon, 1982).

38. K. Dyson, 'West Germany: The Search for a Rationalist Consensus', in

J. Richardson (ed.), *Policy Styles in Western Europe* (London: Allen and Unwin, 1982), 23.

39. J. L. Bodiguel cites the following figures for France: 30% were civil servants in the governments of the Fourth Republic, 65% under the Fifth; 19.5% of Deputies were civil servants in 1958, 20% in 1968, 33% in 1973, 38.8% in 1978, 51% in 1981 ('Les Relations entre administration et partis politiques dans la France contemporaine', doctoral thesis, IIAS, Louvain, 1985).

40. See R. Mayntz, 'German Federal Bureaucrats: A Functional élite between Politics and Administration', in Suleiman (ed.), *Bureaucrats and Policy Making*.

41. E. Suleiman, 'From Right to Left: Bureaucracy and Politics in France', in Suleiman (ed.), *Bureaucrats and Policy Making*, 107–35.

42. D. Gaxie, 'Les Ministres de la V^o', 'Le Ministre', *Pouvoirs*, 36 (1986), 61–78.

43. E. Suleiman, *Politics, Power and Bureaucracy in France* (Princeton, NJ: Princeton University Press, 1974); E. Suleiman, *Élites in French Society: The Politics of Survival* (Princeton, NJ: Princeton University Press, 1978).

44. The discretionary appointment of federal judges by the President of the United States politicizes the federal judicial system just as, in France, the appointment of Councillors of State from inside the bureaucracy does, and the intensive practice of secondment within ministerial *cabinets* contributes towards the politicization of this court, whatever the individual behaviour of its members and whether or not they belong to a political party.

45. R. Crossman, *Inside View* (London: Cape, 1972), 78.

46. L. Moulin, 'The Politicization of the Administration in Belgium', 174.

47. According to S. Cassese, 223,000 applications are pending (18,000 of which are appeals). The average delay is about eight years ('Giudice amministrativo e amministrazione', RTDP section 1/87, p. 113).

48. A law of 20 July 1985 reorganized the federal Court of Accounts, which is defined as a body situated between the executive and the legislature. This is chiefly reflected in the procedures for appointing its President and Vice-President: they are elected by a majority secret vote of the members of the Bundestag, having been proposed by the federal government.

49. However, it should be pointed out that until quite recently in Britain (1977), a judge of legality was not simultaneously the judge of responsibility and this involved individuals under jurisdiction in long, complex and costly litigation.

Chapter 8. Constitutional Courts

1. E. Lambert, *Le Gouvernement des juges et la lutte contre la législation sociale aux États-Unis* (Paris: Giard, 1921).

2. The jurist Kelsen provided the inspiration for the Constitutionality Controls introduced into the Republican Constitution of Austria between the two World Wars (1920–38).
3. R. Chiroux, 'Faut-il réformer le Conseil Constitutionnel?', 'Le Conseil Constitutionnel', *Pouvoirs*, NS 13, (1986), 107–24.
4. In its first *sentenza* of 5 May 1956, the Court decided that it could rule on all laws, whether passed before or after the Constitution. This enabled it to sift through the legislation of Fascist inspiration that was still in effect in many sectors.
5. J. Rivero, 'Rapport de synthèse', in L. Favoreu (ed.), *Actes du colloque 'Cours constitutionnelles et Droits fondamentaux'* (Paris: Economica, 1982), 526.
6. There are, however, a number of important differences between the two systems. In West Germany, the validity of laws from before the Constitution (and not modified by later laws) is investigated by ordinary tribunals, whereas in Italy, the Court is competent to rule in either case. Furthermore, actions brought before the German Constitutional Court lapse when the main case is over; in Italy, in contrast, once a constitutional action has started it is deemed to have an existence of its own.
7. M. Shapiro, *Freedom of Speech: The Supreme Court and Judicial Review* (Englewood Cliffs, NJ: Prentice Hall, 1966).
8. The rules and practices of the Constitutional Council lend a particular and no doubt unintentional spice to the comments of B. Poullain, its former Secretary-General. He writes: 'The procedure is simple. There is nothing mysterious about it. Clearly defined authorities can submit the law to controls, at a particular moment. The effect of the decision is clear: if the law conforms to constitutionality it is promulgated. If it does not, it never sees the light of day ('Remarques sur le modèle français de contrôle de constitutionnalité des lois', *Pouvoirs*, 13 (1986), 179–94).
9. L. Cohen-Tanugi, 'Qui a peur du Cour constitutionnel?', *Le Débat*, 43 (1987), 58.
10. Cited in P. Avril and A. Gicquel, 'Chronique constitutionnelle française (juillet–septembre 1986)', 'Des Fonctionnaires Politisées?', *Pouvoirs*, 40 (1987), 166.
11. K. Schlaich, 'Procédures et techniques de protection des Droits fondamentaux', in L. Favoreu (ed.), *Les Cours Constitutionelles européennes et les droits fondamentaux* (Paris: Economica, Presses Universitaires d'Aix-Marseille, 1982), 138.
12. Reference is often made to the delays (around two to two and a half years) accumulated by the Italian Court. What is seldom mentioned, however, is the fact that the Court, in its capacity as a High Court, had to hear the cases of the Ministers involved in the Lockheed affair, and this halted all its constitutional work for a period of eighteen months. The smooth processing of applications has never recovered.

13. The irresponsibility of the administration in the nineteenth century was also a simple solution . . . except for the wronged citizens.

14. B. Poullain, 'Remarques sur le modèle français de contrôle de constitutionnalité des lois'.

15. L. Favoreu, *Les Cours Constitutionnelles*, Coll. Que sais-je? (Paris: PUF, 1986), 127.

16. Ibid.

17. L. Favoreu, 'L'Apport du Conseil Constitutionnel au droit public', *Pouvoirs*, NS 13 (1986), 17–31.

18. M. Cappelletti, 'Necessité et légitimité de la justice constitutionelle', in Favoreu (ed.), *Actes du colloque 'Cours constitutionnelles et Droits fondamentaux'*, 499.

19. e.g. the German Court is an electoral tribunal and also a High Court of Justice. The Italian Court also passes judgement on political matters. The French Constitutional Council rules on national electoral operations and also acts in a consultative capacity—which is why it is called a 'Council' (in accordance with Article 16, and the decisions taken in connection with it).

20. See C. Grewe-Leymarie, *Le Fédéralisme coopératif en République Fédérale d'Allemagne* (Paris: Economica, 1981).

21. E.g. President Lidio Paladin (President since 1985) is one of the most eminent specialists in regional law.

22. See, in particular, L. Favoreu, 'Constitution et décentralisation', *RDP*, 5 (1982), 1259–87.

23. M. Troper, 'La Signature des ordonnances: Fonctions d'une controverse', 'Le Président', *Pouvoirs*, 41 (1987), 75–91.

24. G. Carcassonne, 'A propos du droit d'amendement: Les errements du Conseil constitutionnel', *Pouvoirs*, no. 41, PUF, Paris, 1987, 163.

25. Cohen-Tanugi, 'Qui a peur du Cour constitutionnel?', 63.

26. J. M. Ely, *Democracy and Distrust: A Theory of Judicial Review* (Cambridge, Mass.: Harvard University Press, 1980).

27. The main exception is the French Senate, whose members are elected for nine years, i.e. for the same duration as the judges of the Constitutional Council.

Bibliography

Introduction

ALMOND, G. A., and POWELL, B. G., *Comparative Politics: A Developmental Approach* (Boston: Little, Brown, and Co., 1966).

DAHL, R., *A Preface to Democratic Theory* (New Haven, Conn.: Yale University Press, 1956).

EISENSTADT, S., and ROKKAN, S., *Building States and Nations* (Beverley Hills, Calif.: Sage, 1977), i.

FLORA, P., and HEIDENHEIMER, A. (eds.), *The Development of the Welfare State in Europe and America* (New Brunswick: Transaction Books, 1981).

GRAWITZ, M., and LECA, J. (eds.), *Traité de science politique*, 4 vols. (Paris: Presses Universitaires de France, 1985).

GREENSTEIN, F. I., and POLSBY, N. W. (eds.), *Handbook of Political Science*, 8 vols. (Reading, Mass.: Addison-Wesley, 1975).

LIJPHART, A., *Democracies: Patterns of Majoritarian and Consensus Government in 21 Countries* (New Haven, Conn.: Yale University Press, 1984).

—— *Democracy in Plural Societies: A Comparative Exploration* (New Haven, Conn.: Yale University Press, 1977).

—— *The Politics of Accommodation: Pluralism and Democracy in the Netherlands* (repr. 1975; Berkeley, Calif.: University of California Press. 1968).

SARTORI, G., *The Theory of Democracy Revisited*, 2 vols. (Chatham, NJ: Chatham House, 1987).

Chapter 1. Politics and Society: Cleavages

ALMOND, G. A., and VERBA, S., *The Civic Culture: Political Attitudes and Democracy in Five Nations* (Princeton, NJ: Princeton University Press, 1963).

—— —— *The Civic Culture Revisited* (Boston, Mass.: Little, Brown, 1980).

BARNES, S. H., and KAASE, M. (eds.), *Political Action: Mass Participation in Four Western Democracies* (Beverly Hills, Calif.: Sage, 1979).

BERGER, S., *Religion in West European Politics* (London: Frank Cass, 1982).

CROUCH, C., and PIZZORNO, A. (eds.), *The Resurgence of Class Conflict in Western Europe*, 2 vols. (London: Macmillan, 1978).

EASMAN, M. J. (ed.), *Ethnic Conflict in the Western World* (Ithaca, NY: Cornell University Press, 1977).

INGLEHART, R., *The Silent Revolution* (Princeton, NJ: Princeton University Press, 1977).

LIJPHART, A., *Democracy in Plural Societies: A Comparative Exploration* (New Haven, Conn.: Yale University Press, 1977).

LIPSET, M. S., *Political Man: The Social Basis of Politics*, 2nd edn. (Baltimore, Md.: Johns Hopkins University Press, 1981).

ROKKAN, S., *Citizens, Elections, Parties* (Oslo: Universiteit Forlaget, 1970).

——and URWIN, D. W. (eds.), *The Politics of Territorial Identity: Studies in European Regionalism* (London: Sage, 1982).

TILLY, C. (eds.), *The Formation of National States in Western Europe* (Princeton, NJ: Princeton University Press, 1975).

Chapter 2. Political Parties

BARTOLINI, S., and MAIR, P. (eds.), *Party Politics in Contemporary Western Europe* (London: Frank Cass, 1984).

BLACKMER, D. L. M., and TARROW, S. (eds.), *Communism in Italy and France* (Princeton, NJ: Princeton University Press, 1975).

BLAKE, R., *The Conservative Party from Peel to Thatcher* (London: Fontana, 1985).

BOGDANOR, V. (ed.), *Liberal Party Politics* (Oxford: Clarendon Press, 1983).

BRAUNTHAL, J., *The West German Social Democrats, 1969–1982* (Boulder, Ohio: Westview Press, 1982).

BUDGE, I., and FARLIE, D., *Voting and Party Competition* (London: Wiley, 1977).

CASTLES, F. G. (ed.), *The Impact of Parties: Politics and Policies in Democratic Capitalist States* (London: Sage, 1982).

DAALDER, H., and MAIR, P. (eds.), *Western European Party Systems: Continuity and Change* (London: Sage, 1983).

DI PALMA, G., *Surviving without Governing: The Italian Parties in Parliament* (Berkeley, Calif.: University of California Press, 1977).

DUVERGER, M., *Les Partis politiques* (Paris: Colin, 1951).

IRVING, R. E. M., *The Christian Democratic Parties of Western Europe* (London: Allen and Unwin, 1979).

LAWSON, K., *The Comparative Study of Political Parties* (New York: St Martin's Press, 1976).

MERKL, P. H. (ed.), *Western European Party Systems: Trends and Prospects* (New York: Free Press, 1980).

PRIDHAM, G., *Christian Democracy in Western Germany* (London: Croom Helm, 1977).

ROKKAN, S., and URWIN, D. W. (eds.), *The Politics of Territorial Identity: Studies in European Regionalism* (London: Sage, 1982).

ROSE, R., *Do Parties Make a Difference?* (London: Macmillan, 1980).

SARTORI, G., *Parties and Party Systems: A Framework for Analysis* (Cambridge: Cambridge University Press, 1976).

SMITH, G., *Democracy in Western Germany: Parties and Politics in the Federal Republic*, 2nd edn. (London: Heinemann, 1979).

VON BEYME, K., *Political Parties in Western Democracies* (Aldershot: Gower, 1985).

Chapter 3. Interest Groups

BENTLEY, A. F., *The Process of Government* (Evanston, Ill.: Principia Press, 1949).

BERGER, S. (ed.), *Organizing Interests in Western Europe: Pluralism, Corporatism and the Transformation of Politics* (Cambridge: Cambridge University Press, 1981).

CASTLES, F. G., *Pressure Groups and Political Cultures* (London: Routledge & Kegan Paul, 1967).

DAHL, R., *Who Governs? Democracy and Power in an American City* (New Haven, Conn.: Yale University Press, 1963).

HARRISON, R., *Pluralism and Corporatism: The Political Evolution of Modern Democracy* (London: Allen and Unwin, 1980).

HIRSCHMAN, A. O., *Shifting Involvements: Private Interest and Public Action* (Princeton, NJ: Princeton University Press, 1982).

LEHMBRUCH, G., and SCHMITTER, P., *Patterns in Corporatist Intermediation* (London: Sage, 1982).

OLSON, M., *The Logic of Collective Action* (Cambridge, Mass.: Harvard University Press, 1965).

——*The Rise and Decline of Nations* (New Haven, Conn.: Yale University Press, 1982).

SCHMITTER, P., *Patterns of Corporatist Policy-Making* (Beverley Hills, Calif.: Sage, 1982).

TRUMAN, D., *The Governmental Process: Political Interests and Public Opinion* (New York: Knopf, 1951).

Chapter 4. Voters, the Elections, and the Elected

BOGDANOR, V., and BUTLER, D. (eds.), *Democracy and Elections: Electoral Systems and Their Political Consequences* (Cambridge: Cambridge University Press, 1983).

BUTLER, D., PENNIMAN, H., and RANNEY, A., *Democracy at the Polls: A Comparative Study of Competitive National Elections* (Washington, DC: American Enterprise Institute, 1981).

DI PALMA, G., *Apathy and Participation* (New York: Free Press, 1970).

HUNTINGTON, S., and NELSON, J., *No Easy Choice: Political Participation in Developing Countries* (Cambridge, Mass.: Harvard University Press, 1976).

ROKKAN, S., *Citizens, Elections, Parties* (Oslo: Universiteit Forlaget, 1970).
ROSE, R., *Electoral Participation: A Comparative Analysis* (Beverly Hills, Calif.: Sage, 1980).
—— (ed.), *Electoral Behaviour: A Comparative Handbook* (New York: Free Press, 1974).
VERBA, S., NIE, N. H., and KIM, J., *Participation and Political Equality: A Seven-Nation Comparison* (Cambridge: Cambridge University Press, 1978).

Chapter 5. Parliaments

BLONDEL, J., *Comparative Legislatures* (Englewood Cliffs, NJ: Prentice Hall, 1973).
BOGDANOR, V. (ed.), *Representatives of the People? Parliamentarians and Constituents in Western Democracies* (Aldershot: Gower, 1985).
COLLIARD, J. C., *Les Régimes parlementaires contemporains* (Paris: FNSP, 1978).
DALE, S. W., *Legislative Drafting: A Comparative Study of Methods in France, Germany, Sweden and the United Kingdom* (London: Butterworths, 1977).
ELDRIDGE, A., *Legislatures in Plural Societies* (Durham, NC: Duke University Press, 1977).
HIRSCH, H., and HANCOCK, M. D., *Comparative Legislative Systems* (New York: Free Press, 1979).
MEZEY, M. L., *Comparative Legislatures* (Durham, NC: Duke University Press, 1979).
OLSON, D. M., *The Legislative Process: A Comparative Approach* (New York: Harper and Row, 1980).
SULEIMAN, E. (ed.), *Parliaments and Parliamentarians in Democratic Politics* (New York: Holmes and Meier, 1986).

Chapter 6. Presidents and Governments

ALLUM, P. A., *Italy, Republic without Government?* (London: Weidenfeld and Nicolson, 1973).
BLONDEL, J., *Government Ministers in the Contemporary World* (London: Sage, 1985).
—— *The Organisation of Governments* (London: Sage, 1982).
—— *World Leaders* (London: Sage, 1980).
BOGDANOR, V. (ed.), *Coalition Governments in Western Europe* (London: Heinemann, 1983).
BUTLER, D., *Governing without a Majority* (London: Macmillan, 1983).
DI PALMA, G., *Surviving without Governing: The Italian Parties in Parliament* (Berkeley, Calif.: University of California Press, 1977).
JOHNSON, N., *State and Government in the Federal Republic of Germany: The Executive at Work*, 2nd edn. (Oxford: Pergamon Press, 1982).

KING, A., *The British Prime Minister*, 2nd edn. (Basingstoke: Macmillan, 1985).

LIJPHART, A., *Democracies: Patterns of Majoritarian and Consensus Government in 21 Countries* (New Haven, Conn.: Yale University Press, 1984).

RICHARDSON, J., *Policy Style in Western Europe* (London: Allen and Unwin, 1982).

ROSE, R., *The Postmodern President: The White House Meets the World* (London: Chatham House, 1988).

——and SULEIMAN, E. (eds.), *Presidents and Prime Ministers* (Washington, DC: American Enterprise Institute, 1980).

VON BEYME, K., *The Political System of the Federal Republic of Germany* (Farnborough, Hants: Gower, 1985).

VON BEYME, K., and SCHMIDT, M. G., *Policy and Politics in the Federal Republic of Germany* (Aldershot: Gower, 1985).

Chapter 7. *Local and Central Bureaucracies*

ABERBACH, J. D. et al., *Bureaucrats and Politicians in Western Democracies* (Cambridge, Mass.: Harvard University Press, 1981).

ARMSTRONG, J., *The European Administrative Elite* (Princeton, NJ: Princeton University Press, 1973).

ASHFORD, D. L., *British Dogmatism and French Pragmatism: Central–Local Policymaking in the Welfare State* (London: Allen and Unwin, 1982).

DOGAN, M. (ed.), *The Mandarins of Western Europe: The Political Role of Top Civil Servants* (New York: Sage, 1975).

DUPUY, F., and THOENIG, J. C., *Sociologie de l'administration* (Paris: Colin, 1983).

DYSON, K. H. F., *Party, State and Bureaucracy in Western Germany* (Beverly Hills, Calif.: Sage, 1977).

FLORA, P., and HEIDENHEIMER, A., *The Development of the Welfare State in Europe and America* (New Brunswick: Transaction Books, 1981).

HANF, K., and SCHARPF, F. W., *Interorganizational Policy-Making* (Beverly Hills, Calif.: Sage, 1978).

JONES, C. (ed.), *New Approaches to the Study of Central–Local Relationships* (Farnborough, Hants: Gower, 1980).

——and THOMAS, R., *Public Policy-Making in a Federal System* (Beverly Hills, Calif.: Sage, 1976).

LAGROYE, J., and WRIGHT, V. (eds.), *Local Government in Britain and France*. (London: Allen and Unwin, 1979).

MACHIN, H., *The Prefect in French Public Administration* (London: Croom Helm, 1977).

MAYNTZ, R., and SCHARPF, F. W., *Policy-Making in the German Federal Bureaucracy* (Amsterdam: Elsevier, 1975).

MÉNY, Y., and WRIGHT, V. (eds.), *Centre–Periphery Relations in Western Europe* (London: Allen and Unwin, 1985).

PAGE, E. C., *Political Authority and Bureaucratic Power: A Comparative Analysis* (Brighton: Harvester Press, 1985).

RHODES, R. A., *Control and Power in Central–Local Government Relations* (Farnborough, Hants: Gower, 1981).

RIDLEY, F. F. (ed.), *Government and Administration in Western Europe* (Oxford: Robertson, 1979).

ROSE, R., *Public Employment in Western Nations* (Cambridge: Cambridge University Press, 1985).

—— *Understanding Big Government* (London: Sage, 1984).

—— *Understanding the United Kingdom: The Territorial Dimension in Government* (London: Longman, 1982).

SHARPE, L. J., and NEWTON, K., *Does Politics Matter? The Determinants of Public Policy* (Oxford: Oxford University Press, 1984).

SULEIMAN, E. (ed.), *Bureaucrats and Policy Making* (London: Holmes and Meier, 1984).

TARROW, S., *Between Center and Periphery: Grassroots Politicians in Italy and France* (New Haven, Conn.: Yale University Press, 1977).

Chapter 8. Constitutional Courts

BLAIR, P. M., *Federalism and Judicial Review in West Germany* (Oxford: Oxford University Press, 1981).

CAPPELLETTI, M., and COHEN, W., *Comparative Constitutional Law: Cases and Materials* (New York: Bobbs-Merrill, 1979).

COHEN-TANUGI, L., *Le Droit sans l'État* (Paris: PUF, 1985).

FAVOREU, L. (ed.), *Les Cours Constitutionnelles et les droits fondamentaux* (Paris: Economica, 1982), 540.

GRIFFITH, J. A. G., *The Politics of the Judiciary*, 2nd edn. (London: Fontana, 1981).

KOMMERS, D. P., *Judicial Politics in West Germany: A Study of the Federal Constitutional Court* (Beverly Hills, Calif.: Sage, 1976).

ZAGREBELSKI, G., *La Giustizia Costituzionale* (Bologna: II Mulino, 1977).

Index